BEST
CONTEMPORARY
JEWISH
WRITING

BEST
CONTEMPORARY
JEWISH
WRITING

MICHAEL LERNER

EDITOR

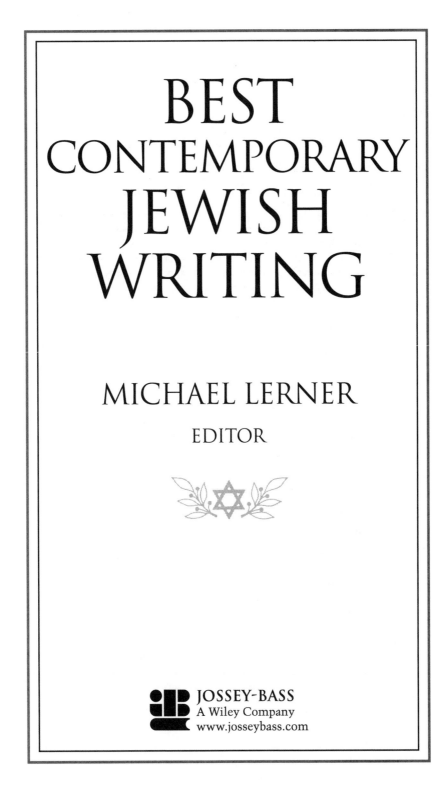

JOSSEY-BASS
A Wiley Company
www.josseybass.com

Published by

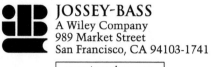

JOSSEY-BASS
A Wiley Company
989 Market Street
San Francisco, CA 94103-1741

www.josseybass.com

Jossey-Bass books and products are available through most bookstores. To
contact Jossey-Bass directly, call (888) 378–2537, fax to (800) 605–2665,
or visit our website at www.josseybass.com.

Substantial discounts on bulk quantities of Jossey-Bass books are available
to corporations, professional associations, and other organizations. For
details and discount information, contact the special sales department at
Jossey-Bass.

We at Jossey-Bass strive to use the most environmentally sensitive paper stocks available to us. Our publications are printed on acid-free recycled stock whenever possible, and our paper always meets or exceeds minimum GPO and EPA requirements.

Library of Congress Cataloging-in-Publication Data

Best contemporary Jewish writing / [selected by] Michael Lerner.—1st ed.
  p. cm.
Includes bibliographical references (p.).
ISBN 0-7879-5972-3 (alk. paper)
ISBN 0-7879-5936-7 (alk. paper) (paperback)
  1. American literature—Jewish authors. 2. American literature—20th century.
3. Judaism—Literary collections. 4. Jews—Literary collections.
I. Lerner, Michael, 1943– II. Title.
PS508.J4 B47 2001
810.9'8924—dc21   2001003013

FIRST EDITION
HB Printing 10 9 8 7 6 5 4 3 2 1
PB Printing 10 9 8 7 6 5 4 3 2 1

CONTENTS

RECLAIMING THE SPIRIT IN JUDAISM

REREADING SACRED TEXTS OF OUR TRADITION

LIVING IN THE SHADOWS OF THE HOLOCAUST

ISRAEL IN CONFLICT

For Sarah Polster
1953–2001

May Her Memory Be a Blessing

INTRODUCTION

JEWISH WRITING AND HEALING THE WORLD

Michael Lerner

MANY JEWS FIND IT HARD to keep up with the burgeoning essays, fiction, and poetry that they might otherwise seek for relaxation, pleasure, and a sense of continuity and identity. And that is one of many reasons why I've decided to produce an annual of the "best Jewish writing." This first volume, *Best Contemporary Jewish Writing,* basically covers the years 1994–2000 (with an occasional exception for something slightly older or slightly newer), and next year I'll be assembling *Best Contemporary Jewish Writing 2002,* presenting material from 2000 and 2001.

The quantity of such material is vast. I've avoided beating the ethnic drum and vaunting writing simply because it is by Jews. Instead, I have sought out writing that connects to or reflects the fundamental Jewish project of healing and transformation, both personal transformation (*tikkun atzmi*) and healing of the world (*tikkun olam*)—understanding that this healing involves not only psychological or social change but also a search for ways to bring holiness into our personal lives and social institutions. I've selected writing which embodies a self-reflective attitude (critical, satirical, appreciative, whatever) toward a tradition that remains alive in the author. Yet I've also sought out writing that was significant in its impact, sometimes selecting a piece that would not win prizes for its style but nevertheless says something of such great importance that it stirs the imagination or challenges accepted assumptions or "the accepted wisdom" about what Jews are supposedly thinking or doing. Though I'm a rabbi, I'm very respectful of the rich secular tradition in Jewish writing and culture. Many of our most gifted writers are bored by or hostile to traditional religious concerns. Yet I've also sought to include religious and spiritual voices that are too often ignored when considering Jewish writing.

A Lesson from History

The Jewish people emerged into history some 3,200 years ago with a startling message: the social, political, and economic order of society needs to be changed and can be changed. The reason it can be changed is that there is a force in the universe, YHVH (God), who makes possible the transformation from what is to what ought to be. We know that this is true because we ourselves were once slaves and are now a free and self-determining people. The most popular Jewish practice in contemporary American Jewish life is the Seder—and its theme that we were slaves but now we are free is understood by the tradition to raise the issue of our own responsibility. We are not victims or powerless any more, and we've learned that human beings need not be slaves to a set of external 'gods' or human tyrants and oppressors. Because we are free and self-determining, we are responsible for our actions, our morality, and the morality of the society in which we live. All the ideologies that tell us that nothing can be fundamentally altered in the universe are necessarily distorted—we personally experienced that the world could be changed.

Our national literature tells this story and its consequences. Our sacred book, the compilation of Torah, Prophets, and Holy Writings (Tanach, or Bible), is the story of what happened to our people as we attempted to live this radical understanding. And that story is of a people who in some way got the message that the world could and should be transformed and yet kept reverting to the very patterns of behavior that our tradition told us could and should be transcended. The getting of this message has traditionally been referred to as "Sinai"—whether, as in the biblical account, it was an actual moment when our people clustered around the mountain and received the word of God and Moses' Torah or whether it was a consciousness that slowly emerged over the course of many centuries and became explicit only with the compiling of the Torah some 2,400 years ago.

Healing and Transformation

The message that the world could be healed and transformed was revolutionary when first articulated by Jewish writers of the past, and it remains radical even today. The Jewish people emerged into a world that was already stratified by class, with some people holding huge amounts of wealth and power and most people living either as slaves or as subsistence farmers who were required to give a significant amount of their produce to the ruling elite.

Through much of history, class societies have maintained their power by force and violence, by convincing people that the existing distribution of wealth and power is the only possible reality and that nothing significant in the way we construct societies can be changed. The powerful convinced the powerless that whatever pain they experienced in their lives was not really a product of the existing social order but rather was caused by some demeaned "other" but for whose existence things would be much better.

The Jewish message posed a dramatic challenge to this notion that nothing could be significantly different. Here was a group of people whose literature told a story that challenged the inevitability of domination and insisted that the most powerful Force in the universe favored freedom and equality, sought a world based on justice and love, and recognized all human beings as fundamentally valuable (in religious language, created in the image of God). And this freedom could be manifested in our daily lives, because we saw ourselves as capable of control from the inside, not doomed to control from the outside—whether it be by capricious pagan nature gods or political tyrants. No wonder, then, that ruling elites, not wanting to have their own people hear this radical story, made the Jews the primary "demeaned other" throughout most of the history of Western civilization.

I don't want to romanticize our history by claiming that the Jewish people did in fact consistently live up to its own message or that our holy texts did not sometimes contain contradictory or opposite messages as well. In my book *Jewish Renewal* I show that there are really two voices speaking in Torah: one the voice of love and compassion, the other the voice of the accumulated pain and cruelty that has been passed from generation to generation. Both voices are attributed to God. The "settler Judaism" of Joshua and the brutal conquest of Canaan were manifestations of the tendency to pass on to others the pain and cruelty of what was done to us when we were oppressed. Yet the Torah's innovation is that cruelty is not destiny. One of the most frequently repeated injunctions of the Torah are various formulations of: "When you come into your own land, do not oppress the stranger. Remember that you were strangers in the land of Egypt." The message is that the compulsion to repeat the past can be broken, that the pain that has been passed on can be transcended. And the reason is that there is a power in the universe, YHVH, God, that makes for the possibility of a radical freedom. Every human being was created in the image of that God and can be partners with that God in the healing and transformation of the world. It was that revolutionary message which both attracted and terrified us as a people—and led many Jews into conflict with existing systems of oppression.

The dangers of seriously embodying a revolutionary message led us into conflict with Hellenistic culture and Roman power. By the time Biblical books like Ecclesiastes (*Kohelet*) and Proverbs (*Mishley*) were being incorporated into the Jewish canon there was already considerable Jewish sentiment to "flow" with rather than confront a world of cruelty and domination. The desire to accommodate rather than challenge became a dominant motif after Jews, having unsuccessfully rebelled against Rome, were exiled from our homeland and began a two-thousand-year experience of relative powerlessness and political marginality. Talmudic and medieval Jewish codifiers, commentators, philosophers, and community leaders warned of trying to challenge established power.

Yet the consciousness that we ought to be agents of transformation persisted and found expression in the Jewish mystical tradition. The Zohar, one of the foundational works of Kabbalah, retells the Creation story in ways that recredit the task of transformation and healing (*tikkun*). According to this telling, God contracted to create space for the universe to come into existence and filled that space with Divine Light. But the vessels built to contain the Light were overwhelmed and shattered, and the world is now filled with fragments of Divine Light, shards of holiness that are broken and need repair. Our human task is to raise and reunite those shards, releasing divine sparks, and through *tikkun,* bring God's presence (the Holy Shekhina) back into the world. The mystical tradition thus preserved the transformative mission even though it depoliticized the hoped-for transformation and envisioned it in terms of more inward spirituality. The view of the world as in need of repair and in need of our own action as part of that process was nourished by our holy texts and has been central to Jewish literature.

Secular Repair

That tradition persisted over the past two centuries when Jews were emancipated from ghetto life and given the opportunity to become part of secular Western society. It is sometimes argued that Jewish oppression is sufficient to explain the disproportionate involvement of Jews in the major movements for social, political, economic, and cultural change in the past several hundred years. But that would not explain why other groups facing just as intense oppression were not equally represented in these movements.

Rather, we should look to the persistence of a distinctly Jewish sensibility nurtured by the literature and spiritual sensibilities of Judaism that made Jews particularly predisposed to seeing the ways in which the world needed to be healed. Latent in these initial formulations of Judaism, I believe, were the seeds of later attempts to change the world in progressive ways.

This sensibility was manifested in much of the important Jewish writing of the twentieth century. Writing in Hebrew, Yiddish, or English, Jews have produced a prodigious literature addressing the psychological, spiritual, political, and economic deformities of the contemporary age and how they might be repaired. True, there have been some formidable Jewish writers like Shalom Aleichem or Isaac Bashevis Singer who have seemed less interested in transforming than in preserving the memory of Jewish experience. Yet the overwhelming majority of Jews who have picked up the pen or turned to the computer have done so with a more transformative agenda in mind.

In doing so, they have created the kind of fiction that energized the Zionist movement—through the works of writers like S. Y. Agnon and Y. L. Peretz. Indeed, the Zionist movement is the most powerful example of this transformative tradition reemerging in Jewish life and challenging the political passivity that had become a feature of many religious communities. But Jews have also kept this transformative tradition alive when they wrote about other issues not specifically related to Jewish themes, and we can see this in the essays of Karl Marx, Sigmund Freud, and Leon Trotsky, of Betty Friedan, Erich Fromm, and Herbert Marcuse, of Hannah Arendt and Emmanuel Levinas. They have done so through the poetry of Allen Ginsberg, Marge Piercy, and Adrienne Rich. Jews have had a disproportionate presence in the movements for economic justice and redistribution of wealth, women's equality, ecological sanity, and an end to discrimination against gays, lesbians, and the disabled but also in movements aimed at personal transformation, from psychoanalysis to the contemporary upsurge in spiritual writing.

Many individuals involved in this kind of writing have views very different from my own. A neoconservative writer like Norman Podhoretz or William Safire or Dennis Prager fits in just as much as any liberal or progressive thinker—such writers' particular vision of the kind of transformation our world needs may be different from that of other writers in this collection, but they are just as certainly involved in the discourse of *tikkun* as those who disagree with them.

They are very different from another strain of writer not represented here: those who have joined the dominant discourse of cynicism and celebration of materialism. There are Jewish writers whose primary energies go into counseling that we become "realistic" and go along with the flow of contemporary political life, the globalization of capital, or the current distribution of power and wealth (I think of many who write for the *New York Times,* for example). There are others who, while open to social change, are more interested in projecting what they take to be their own superior intelligence and a cynical disdain for anyone who openly commits to idealistic visions. I think, for example, of many writers for *The*

New Republic magazine who find it comical to believe in love, caring, spiritual sensitivity, or a search for meaning in life. Some of those writers may be people who share my own political critiques of George W. Bush or Bill Clinton, or may be personally religiously observant or involved in Jewish causes—but their sensibility seems more attuned to *Who Wants to Be a Millionaire?* and *Survivor* than to Y. L. Peretz, S. Agnon, F. Kafka, B. Spinoza, M. Maimonides, Rabbi Akiba, or prophets like Isaiah.

The Limits of Jewish Liberalism

For many decades, Jews were at the center of liberal and progressive social change movements, and Jewish writing reflected that commitment. Liberalism itself became a dominant aspect of Yiddishkeit (Jewishness), an ersatz religion for many Jews who could no longer believe in the kind of God they had been taught about in synagogue and Hebrew school. In the early decades of the twentieth century, that liberalism became a full-blown commitment to the labor movement, to socialism or communism. But after communism transformed into Stalinist dictatorship, betraying many of its Jewish adherents, and socialism transformed into a spineless bureaucratic welfare state, many Jews became equally passionate advocates of an American-style liberalism, whose insistence on tolerance, separation of church and state, and rectification of the worst political manifestations of racism and poverty substituted for any more coherent worldview.

By the beginning of the new secular millennium, faith in this form of liberalism had worn thin. To be sure, American Jews still voted overwhelmingly for Democrats. But as their own Jewish commitments faded, many younger Jews found themselves pulled in two opposite directions. On one hand, the appeal of "making it" in America grew stronger as Jews felt less rooted in the radical, transformative messages of the Jewish tradition. To justify that focus toward money and power, many Jews began to repeat the dominant culture's mantra: everyone is selfish and merely interested in "looking out for number one."

Along these lines, we begin to hear the recurrent voices of a distinctively Jewish selfishness, one that sees Jewish interests as paramount and concerns about others as having no specifically Jewish content (a repudiation of the kind of Jewish liberalism that, according to conservatives, once led liberal Jews to "care about everyone but Jews"). This Jewish selfishness was sometimes tied to Holocaust resentment: "No one else took care of us when we were powerless, so why should we care for anyone else now?" In other cases, it was tied to resentment at black anti-Semitism:

"We did so much for them, yet look at the way they tolerate Farrakhan and other anti-Semitic voices. That's proof that it doesn't pay to be so caring for others; they just resent the caring and see it as patronizing." This new conservatism helped many Jews justify immersion in the growing celebration of American materialist success.

If this sensibility dominated the Jewish institutions within which most Jews over twenty grew up, this and future volumes of *Best Contemporary Jewish Writing* will highlight a new sensibility that is beginning to find expression in Jewish writing. A growing number of Jews have begun to see the old Jewish liberalism as stuck in a set of narrow materialist assumptions that do not adequately credit the realm of Spirit. In the twentieth century, many Jews were obsessed (often for good reason) with a desire to protect themselves from the possible introduction of Christian values into the public sphere, so they fought vigorously for a wide application of the First Amendment principle of separation of church and state. But as market-oriented corporate values became increasingly dominant in the latter part of the twentieth century, increasing concerns about individualism and materialism emptying public life of any commitment to higher values caused a growing reevaluation of radical separationist ideas. When an Orthodox Jewish senator, Joseph I. Lieberman, was nominated as the Democratic party's candidate for vice president, some Jews reacted negatively to his attempts to articulate a role for ethical or spiritual values in politics.

Others have begun to question this aspect of the liberal faith and to articulate what I call a "politics of meaning," an approach to public life that insists that ethical and spiritual values should be central to our public lives together. Increasing numbers of Jewish scholars, social activists, and religious leaders have begun to insist on the limitations of classical Jewish liberalism and to forge new directions in bringing a spiritual dimension into their own thinking. Bringing concerns about ethics and meaning into our thinking about social life has now become a major focus of contemporary Jewish writing. In this volume you will hear not only Joseph Lieberman but also writers like Joseph Telushkin, Arthur Waskow, Naomi Wolf, and many others who reflect this growing concern with our inner lives and simultaneously insist on challenging social injustice and all forms of oppression.

When Jewish Writing Becomes Jewish Healing

I've avoided a narrowly programmatic focus for this book. In this volume, you won't find any calls for a political program or party or for creating a new denomination of Judaism or a new social movement. The writers of

fiction, poetry, and essays assembled here are not part of a single movement in even the broadest sense. But I have tilted toward writers who might
contribute to the healing and transformation that our planet and our community so badly need.

The Holocaust

For example, when turning to the Holocaust, I did not seek to include articles that would show the newest research on how bad the Nazis were
toward the Jews. Rather, I asked myself, "What in relationship to the Holocaust most needs to be fixed?" In the 1960s, it would have been denial
and repression of the fact of the Holocaust. But in 2001 there is a thriving Holocaust industry replete with university professorships endowed by
Holocaust survivors, Holocaust museums, and centers competing with each
other for clientele; foundations funding the important work of retaining
the memories and records of those who perished; and movies, plays, and
commemorations to keep the Holocaust present in the consciousness of the
contemporary age. So instead I've chosen material that is more concerned
with individual and collective recovery from the Holocaust–generated
scars and distorted perceptions of reality that still leave many Jews psy-
chically wounded and in pain. In this volume, Thane Rosenbaum's remarkable fiction and Zygmunt Bauman's analysis of the way Holocaust scars
play a role in shaping contemporary Israeli policies tell the story. Peter
Gabel's interpretation of the meaning of the Holocaust for contemporary
politics demonstrates how much there is to learn, while Jonathan Rosen
and Martin Jay teach us how not to draw the wrong lessons.

Women

Judaism has been patriarchal both in its understanding of the world and
in its religious practices. We have the good fortune to be alive at a moment
when the Jewish community has embraced a new openness with regard
to women and a willingness to challenge patriarchal assumptions—and
you'll find some of these voices in this collection.

Some of the most creative thinking and writing happening in the Jewish
world today is being done by women who are opening new paths to our
understanding of God and of Jewish ritual practice. This new sensibility
is represented in this collection not only in critiques of sexist assumptions
in traditional Jewish texts (for example, Susan Schnur's powerful critique
of the Purim Haggadah in her essay "Our [Meaning Women's] Book-of-

Esther Problem") or in traditional romanticization of the Jewish family (explored in Yona Wallach's "When You Come to Sleep with Me, Come Like My Father") but also in the new attempt to retell traditional stories with a deeper understanding of the experience of women (for example, in Rachel Adler's account of two Creation stories or in the Biblical story of Rachel and Leah retold in Anita Diamant's *The Red Tent*).

Israel

Israel has been at the forefront of Jewish consciousness for the past several years. As I write this introduction in the Spring of 2001, Israeli helicopters are bombing Palestinian cities; the Palestinian populations of several West Bank cities are faced with sieges that have caused critical shortages in food, water, and medical care; and many Palestinians live in constant fear of the Israeli Defense Forces. Since the start of the Al-Aqsa Intifada in September 2000, thousands of Palestinians have been killed, maimed, or wounded. Palestinian terrorists have planted bombs in Israel, killing and wounding Israeli civilians. Palestinian teenagers continue to throw rocks at the IDF troops they consider occupiers. Mortars land shells over the Green Line (the pre-1967 borders of Israel), and Palestinians with rifles shoot and sometimes wound or kill Israeli settlers. As the cycle of violence escalates, each side seems determined to show that it will not be intimidated or silenced by the other—and the result has been a growing despair, demonization of the other side, and a triumph of extremist elements and extremist rhetoric on both sides.

Each side has a convincing story to tell. Israel reminds the world of the time when Jews were escaping the Holocaust, and Palestinians did all they could to prevent them from returning to our ancient homeland. Palestinians turned down a partition agreement in 1947, and surrounding Arab states invaded the newly created State of Israel in 1948. The Occupation of the West Bank and Gaza in 1967 was precipitated by Arab threats to annihilate Israel. Many Jews fled Arab countries—their families were refugees too! In the traditional account, Jews have been reasonable and generous, the Palestinians irrational and self-defeating. Taking that one step further, Daniel Pipes in this volume argues that the peace process was misguided from the start and that the United States should be happy that it failed and unequivocally support the current government of Israel.

Palestinians point to the forced expulsions of hundreds of thousands of Palestinians in 1947–49, Israel's refusal to allow civilian refugees to return to their homes in violation of international law, and Israel's cruel Occupation of the West Bank and Gaza for the past 34 years. Citing the documented history of torture, home demolitions, expansion of Israeli settlements on land taken from Palestinians, settler violence, and a wide array of human rights violations, critics of Israeli policies claim that Israel never lived up to its Oslo Accord to end the occupation by 1998 and that Israel is acting with all the brutality and racism of traditional settler states toward a native population. Benny Morris, the dean of new Israeli historians, summarizes in "The New Historiography" what has now become part of the Israeli high school curriculum (though largely unknown in the United States): a powerful historical record of Israel forcefully throwing Palestinians from their homes in 1948. Jerome Slater, in an article written for this volume, shows that Palestinian outrage at Jewish settlements and their claim to a "right to return" cannot be reduced to anti-Semitic prejudices but must be understood as the logical outgrowth of a history of repression and dispossession imposed by what has become an Israel far more militarily powerful and morally arrogant than most Jews are willing to acknowledge. As long as the Occupation continues, settlements remain, Israeli roads crisscross the West Bank and Gaza, Palestinians are forced to endure humiliating searches at endless military check-points, and millions languish in poverty in Palestinian refugee camps, the struggle will continue.

The problem for many Jews is that both sides are right. Two peoples have claims to the same land, and both claims are legitimate. Both sides can point to acts of violence and violations of agreements by the other.

I cannot claim neutrality. I feel an intense loyalty to Israel and a deep commitment to its future survival. My son served in the Israeli army (in the tzanchanim, or paratroopers), and my family has a fierce loyalty to Israel. It is precisely for this reason that I think it important for Jews to become aware of the needs of our neighbors; Israel cannot hope to survive for long unless we can find a way to create a better relationship with the hundreds of millions of Moslems that surround the Jewish state. To create that better relationship, Jews need to open our hearts to the stories of those around us. I don't mean that we should do that without keeping a strong army—the IDF is the most powerful military force in the region, and Israel should keep it that way. But the ultimate survival of Israel cannot depend entirely on military strength. Israel's greatest strength will come from its ability to embody the highest values of the Jewish tradition— particularly its insistence on love (the Torah states categorically "You shall love the stranger" and does not make that conditional on the stranger's "good behavior"), social justice, and an awareness of the fundamental unity of all human beings and our mutual interdependence.

But today Israel and those who support it tend to dismiss as "naïve" or "idealistic" discussions about social justice, love, and the unity of all being. Nationalist passions lead many in the Jewish establishment and its wholly owned and controlled Jewish media to dismiss as "self-hating Jews" or even as anti-Semites those who question Israeli policy under Ariel Sharon. The very same challenges and critiques that are seen as part of the normal reality of Israeli political life are labeled acts of disloyalty when they are raised by Jews in the Diaspora. Those who talk about Palestinian human rights or the pain that they face under the Occupation are often dismissed as traitors to the Jewish people—after all, we are told, no one has suffered the way the Jews have suffered, and therefore normal moral standards cannot be applied to us. Jewish deaths are (rightly) portrayed as tragedies, Palestinian deaths as "the natural consequence of their violence toward us."

The unfortunate consequence is that many younger Jews have felt the need to separate from the Jewish world in order to remain true to their own ethical intuitions. For most, the process is largely unconscious, they just don't want to hear about Israel and don't feel any connection to it. For others, there is a deep feeling of moral distaste for what the Jewish establishment uncritically celebrates as "the Jewish state" and a sense that this kind of Jewishness could not possibly address their highest spiritual and moral inclinations, so they turn to Buddhism or some other spiritual tradition, or they in some other way try to distance themselves from their Jewish identity. This is ironic, because the very ethical and spiritual intuitions that make them feel so uncomfortable with the cheerleaders for Israeli policies are often the unconscious legacy of the Jewish tradition. At least some of these critics are actually contemporary embodiments of a prophetic tradition that is at the core of Judaism.

Consequently, I have selected for this collection some voices on Israel that are not often given serious consideration in the organized Jewish community. The new historians like Benny Morris are talked about, but rarely have they been allowed to speak for themselves in American Jewish media. Israeli literary critic Sidra Ezrahi provides us with an analysis of the journey that led the Jewish people back to Israel in ways that provide us with cultural tools to begin the process of reconciliation with the Palestinian people. The poetry of Yehuda Amichai sharply confronts the romanticization of Jerusalem that has made ownership of those rocks appear to be an irresolvable dilemma. And I've also included Daniel Pipes who presents the position of those who believe reconciliation with Palestinians has now been shown to be impossible after the failure of Ehud Barak and Yassir Arafat to come to terms.

For me, the most salient reality is not so much the ins and outs of policy debates but the tremendous sadness I feel as a Jew. Sadness first and foremost for my own family—the Jewish people; sadness about the violence we've had to endure in order to survive. Second, a sadness for the Palestinian victims and victimizers and how living under Occupation has hurt and at times deformed their lives. But also a sadness at the distortions that the violence done against us Jews has engendered in our own consciousness. The history of torture, occupation, destruction of Palestinian homes, and systematic lying to ourselves and others about what Israel has actually done demonstrates the frightening possibility that Jews could be just as savage and violent and beastly as any of our enemies.

At times I feel overwhelmed with sadness at how difficult it is for us as Jews to move beyond a chauvinist nationalism so that we can embrace the God within all human beings. This was supposed to be our message to the world—and yet at the current moment so many of us have forgotten what we were supposed to be and what we were supposed to teach. As long as we allow the current leadership of the organized Jewish community to speak in our names, and to justify oppression and moral insensitivity, we, the Jewish people, have momentarily lost our path and abandoned our sacred mandate to be witnesses to the possibility of a world based on love and caring. Yet I do not share the triumphalist "gotcha" consciousness of those who say "you Jews are hypocrites because you fail to practice what you preach." Rather, I acknowledge that Jews are just human—with the same (but not worse) flaws as everyone else. So I approach these issues with a deep compassion for Jews and for all others who have been deeply wounded by a world of pain and oppression. It is that compassion which will shape my choices for this and the future editions of *Best Contemporary Jewish Writing*.

Jewish Spiritual Life

Perhaps the most significant development at the beginning of the secular twenty-first century has been the reemergence in the Jewish world of a powerful new interest in spirituality. For several generations, Jewish life has been more focused on defense against anti-Semitism, raising money for Jewish institutions, political support for Israel, and various (unsuccessful) schemes to prevent intermarriage. Few children growing up in the Jewish world in the second half of the twentieth century ever heard their parents talking about going to synagogue as a way of encountering God or of exploring the spiritual dimension of life.

Though many religious services in Judaism's synagogues and temples produce almost instant spiritual brain death, an increasing number of synagogues have been seeking to reconnect with the wisdom of Jewish spirituality or to forge new directions (sometimes by borrowing techniques from other traditions, just as Jews traditionally borrowed music, food, and customs from surrounding communities). I am myself a rabbi of such a synagogue, which has affiliated with the newest movement in Judaism, the Jewish Renewal movement, with about fifty communities in the United States and Israel. We call our services "neo-Hasidic" because they embody the energy, music, and dancing of early Hasidism but are proudly egalitarian in every respect. The Jewish Renewal movement, with its focus on spiritual life, is not owned by any particular denomination; it is spreading quickly and powerfully in the Orthodox world, in Conservative and Reconstructionist synagogues, and in many Reform temples as well.

I've selected some of the writers who are forging this Jewish spiritual renewal. Arthur Green's "A Kabbalah for the Environmental Age," Mordecai Gafni's rethinking of the erotic element in spirituality, and Zalman M. Schachter-Shalomi's powerful new paradigm for Jewish thought give a taste of this thinking. Marge Piercy's poem "Nishmat," already introduced into many worship services, Nancy Flam's reflections on Jewish healing, and Arthur Waskow's reflections on ecology give us a taste of how these ideas get translated into actual spiritual practice.

Many people dismiss this new spirituality as a passing fad. That seems unlikely. Though some observers have critiqued a certain narcissistic tendency in the rise of American spirituality and noted elements of flakiness in some New Age communities, the Jewish spiritual revival is often deeply rooted in Jewish texts and in the wisdom of Kabbalah. While some people have sought to mass-market this new spirituality and make it yet another commodity for public consumption, many other people have brought a sense of spiritual discipline, immersion in traditional texts, and a willingness to think carefully and systematically about some of the most difficult and challenging issues facing the human race.

To demonstrate the powerful, new textual interpretive writing that is shaping contemporary Jewish thought, I've selected some of the writings of Rachel Adler, Ilana Pardes, Sarah Polster, and Susan Schnur.

Not All Good Writing Is Healing

So far I've highlighted issues where the Jewish world is struggling to rethink and reexperience its Jewishness. But as I promised you from the start, I have also included in this book essays, poems, and short pieces of fiction that don't have any connection to the potential healing or transformation of the world. Rather, they in some way capture or imaginatively suggest some aspect of our contemporary Jewish situation.

Jews have been involved in trying to understand themselves and their relationship to the larger world ever since the ghetto walls began to tumble two centuries ago. Who is a Jew, what it means to be a Jew, and how

Jewish identity connects with larger identities might have been a particularly Jewish conceit a few decades ago. But with the emergence of a multicultural society in the West, the issues that Jews face in formulating our identity have increasingly shaped the way other groups have begun to grapple with the same issues. The globalization of culture and consciousness presents some important challenges for Jewish life. Jewish ways of grounding ourselves in the face of a globalized multicultural world can provide a wellspring of insights and cultural creativity that can be adapted and transformed by other ethnic groups (just as we have drawn from them). Hence this collection begins with a section on the many identities of a Jew. David Biale's reflections on multiculturalist impulses in Jewish life and Kenneth Koch's poem "To Jewishness," and the selection from Phillip Roth's *The Human Stain* give a taste of how Jewish writers are thinking about these issues. Ruth Knafo Setton's "Ten Ways to Recognize a Sephardic 'Jew-ess,'" Steve Greenberg's "Gay and Orthodox," and Daniel Boyarin's "Justify My Love," deal with the multilayers of Jewish identity.

In another section of this collection, I've highlighted what I call the Joys of Jewish Culture. The pleasure of good writing remains one of the treasured joys of contemporary Jewish life. So I've included here a selection from the writing of Nomi Eve, Rebecca Goldstein, and from the poetry of C. K. Williams, the Israeli poet Yona Wallach, and the powerful story "The Twenty-seventh Man" by Nathan Englander. I've also included analyses and new insights on Jewish writing by Norman Podhoretz (on Roth and Bellow), Rodger Kamanetz on Spiritual Writing, Tsvi Blanchard on Jewish stories, and Morris Dickstein's introduction to new directions in Jewish fiction. But throughout this book, I've placed other examples of the craft of Jewish writing, including the poetry of Yehuda Amichai (masterfully translated by Chana Bloch and Chana Kronfeld) and America's former poet laureate Robert Pinsky, the stories of Rachel Naomi Remen, and the powerful fiction of Thane Rosenbaum.

As noted earlier, I plan to make this an annual collection and over the course of time introduce you to many writers whose works deserved to be in this first volume but were excluded for various reasons. Many incredibly important writers have been left out. For example, I have intentionally chosen less famous writers that I think you might appreciate being introduced to over certain gifted writers whose works have been anthologized elsewhere or whose names already generate much respect and excitement.

I don't agree with many of the writers and perspectives articulated here—and some of them I find downright offensive. But that, in my view, is what a Jewish community should be—a place where it's safe to have many divergent views and no one authoritative voice. So if you are interested in my views on some of these questions, I invite you to read *Tikkun* magazine, my book *Jewish Renewal: A Path to Healing and Transformation,* or visit my website at www.tikkun.org. As often as not, the nuances in my own views on issues addressed here are not represented in this collection.

There are simply too many talented and exciting Jewish writers to feature in a single anthology of this length. I have already asked myself at least a hundred times, "How can you print this collection without including Writer X or Y or Z?" I'm sure you have your own list, and you're probably right! Limitations of space have ensured that the range of views is far more restricted than I would have wished and that many longer pieces of fiction were excluded. I do intend in future volumes to include many other perspectives on all the issues addressed in this book. And I'll be happy to hear from you about your suggestions for writings published in 2000 and 2001 for inclusion in the next collection (*Best Jewish Writing 2002,* which will be published in September of 2002). But even so, what appears here is a treasure trove. Enjoy!

Berkeley, California　　　　　　　　　　RABBI MICHAEL LERNER
2001/5761
RabbiLerner@tikkun.org

DISCUSSION GROUPS ON *BEST CONTEMPORARY JEWISH WRITING*

If you wish to assist us in creating a local monthly discussion group focused on the writings in this and future volumes in the Best Jewish Writing series, or wish to be a part of such a group, send us your address, phone number, and a short note.

To: AshReyNU@aol.com

The Many
Identities
of a Jew

TO JEWISHNESS

Kenneth Koch

As you were contained in
Or embodied by
Louise Schlossman
When she was a sophomore
at Walnut Hills
High School
In Cincinnati, Ohio,
I salute you
And thank you
For the fact
That she received
My kisses with tolerance
On New Year's Eve
And was not taken aback
As she well might have been
Had she not had you
And had I not, too.
Ah, you!
Dark, complicated you!
Jewishness, you are the tray—
On it painted
Moses, David and the Ten

Commandments, the handwriting
On the Wall, Daniel
In the lions' den—
On which my childhood
Was served
By a mother
And father
Who took you
To Michigan—
Oh the soft smell
Of the pine
Trees of Michigan
And the gentle roar
Of the Lake! Michigan
Or sent you
To Wisconsin—
I went to camp there—
On vacation, with me
Every year!
My counselors had you
My fellow campers
Had you and "Doc
Ehrenreich" who
Ran the camp had you
We got up in the
Mornings you were there
You were in the canoes
And on the baseball
Diamond, everywhere around.
At home, growing
Taller, you
Thrived, too. Louise had you
And Charles had you
And Jean had you
And her sister Mary
Had you
We all had you
And your Bible
Full of stories
That didn't apply
Or didn't seem to apply

In the soft spring air
Or dancing, or sitting in the cars
To anything we did.
In "religious school"
At the Isaac M. Wise
Synagogue (called "temple")
We studied not you
But Judaism, the one who goes with you
And is your guide, supposedly,
Oddly separated
From you, though there
In the same building, you
In us children, and it
On the blackboards
And in the books—Bibles
And books simplified
From the Bible. How
Like a Bible with shoulders
Rabbi Seligmann is!
You kept my parents and me
Out of the hotels near Crystal Lake
In Michigan and you resulted, for me,
In insults,
At which I felt
Chagrined but
Was energized by you.
You went with me
Into the army, where
One night in a foxhole
On Leyte a fellow soldier
Said Where are the fuckin Jews?
Back in the PX. I'd like to
See one of those bastards
Out here. I'd kill him!
I decided to conceal
You, my you, anyway, for a while.
Forgive me for that.
At Harvard you
Landed me in a room
In Kirkland House
With two other students

Who had you. You
Kept me out of the Harvard clubs
And by this time (I
Was twenty-one) I found
I preferred
Kissing girls who didn't
Have you. Blonde
Hair, blue eyes,
And Christianity (oddly enough) had an
Aphrodisiac effect on me.
And everything that opened
Up to me, of poetry, of painting, of music,
Of architecture in old cities
Didn't have you—
I was
Distressed
Though I knew
Those who had you
Had hardly had the chance
To build cathedrals
Write secular epics
(Like *Orlando Furioso*)
Or paint Annunciations—"Well
I had David
In the wings." David
Was a Jew, even a Hebrew.
He wasn't Jewish.
You're quite
Something else. "I had Mahler,
Einstein, and Freud." I didn't
Want those three (then). I wanted
Shelley, Byron, Keats, Shakespeare,
Mozart, Monet. I wanted
Botticelli and Fra Angelico.
"There you've
Chosen some hard ones
For me to connect to. But
why not admit that I
Gave you the life
Of the mind as a thing
To aspire to? And

Where did you go
To find your 'freedom'? to
New York, which was
Full of me." I do know
Your good qualities, at last
Good things you did
For me—when I was ten
Years old, how you brought
Judaism in, to give ceremony
To everyday things, surprise and
Symbolism and things beyond
Understanding in the
Synagogue then I
Was excited by you, a rescuer
Of me from the flatness of my life.
But then the flatness got you
And I let it keep you
And, perhaps, of all things known,
That was most ignorant. "You
Sound like Yeats, but
You're not. Well, happy
Voyage home, Kenneth, to
The parking lot
Of understood experience. I'll be
Here if you need me and here
After you don't
Need anything else. HERE is a quality
I have, and have had
For you, and for a lot of others,
Just by being it, since you were born."

THE MELTING POT AND BEYOND

JEWS AND THE POLITICS OF AMERICAN IDENTITY

David Biale

AS THE RECENT DEBATE over "national standards" for the teaching of American history attests, the multicultural debate frequently revolves over the struggle between two narratives: America as the site for the realization of freedom and America as the site for oppression, persecution, and even genocide. These stories divide substantially along racial lines, in which "white" ethnicities tend to privilege the narrative of freedom, while "colored" ethnicities focus on narratives of oppression.

In this essay, I wish to take up the curious position that Jews occupy along this narrative divide, a position which has caused them much angst as they confront multiculturalism. Jews came to America, in large measure from Eastern Europe, with a kind of double consciousness. On the one hand, millennia of exile had accustomed them to view themselves as a perennial minority, always vulnerable to the whims of an often hostile majority. Jewish life was, by definition, "abnormal" compared to that of the Jews' hosts, a perception reinforced by Jewish theologies of chosenness and Christian theologies of supersession. During the century or so before the mass immigration to America, movements for Jewish emancipation and integration had proceeded by fits and starts in the various European countries. The process was already well under way in Western and Central Europe, but had only begun in Eastern Europe.

Yet, even in those countries, like France, in which emancipation was well established, Jews often remained a self-conscious minority, indeed, the quintessential minority against whom the status of minority rights was usually defined. Jews came to America with this consciousness of difference firmly engrained, either as a product of their medieval exclusion or as a result of their newer status as the paradigmatic European minority.

On the other hand, if they came to America with this minority mentality, they also viewed America in quasi-messianic terms as a land where they might escape their historic destiny and become part of the majority. The *goldene medina* was not only a state whose streets were paved with gold in the obvious economic sense, but also a state which seemed to promise political "gold": liberation and equality. Although the mass Jewish immigration to America is often contrasted with the much more ideological Zionist settlement in Palestine in the same decades, both were driven by equally strong material and idealistic motives. In their own imaginations, the Jews came to America not as they had wandered from country to country through the centuries of exile, but as if they were coming to their messianic home.

In this regard, they were not that different from other immigrants, from Europe or elsewhere in the world, all of whom saw in America both an economic and political haven. What made the Jews different was the persistence of the first mentality, that of a minority. Most other immigrant groups were themselves from majority populations, although some, like the Irish and the Poles, were also subjugated by other nations. Yet, even these latter groups had much more recent historical memories of majority status, while, for the Jews, living as a minority had been an endemic condition for thousands of years. Thus, while Jews almost universally constructed a narrative of liberation to describe their immigration to America, they did so while retaining a strong memory and consciousness of themselves as a minority.

This double consciousness played an important role earlier in this century in prompting different Jewish thinkers to develop new theories of America that might accommodate the Jews. These thinkers continued to view the Jews as the archetypal minority and they attempted to envision an America in which the Jews might be both integrated and still retain their distinctiveness. I should like to take two paradigmatic examples, both from the first two decades of the twentieth century. The first is Israel Zangwill, an English Jew whose views on both assimilation and America were undoubtedly shaped by the context of Edwardian England. Yet, his play *The Melting Pot*, first produced in Washington, D.C., in 1908 and lauded by Theodore Roosevelt, who later agreed to have a revised edition dedicated to him in 1914, became a pivotal moment in the American debate about the mass immigration of the early part of the century.

Zangwill did not invent the term "melting pot," but he was instrumental in popularizing its use in American political discourse, thus setting in motion the debate which has raged for most of this century. An examination of the play, though, reveals something surprising. Despite its title and the image of America as a "crucible" that would forge a new person, divorced from his or her earlier identity, *The Melting Plot* actually treats the Jews as the model towards which this new American would correspond. Its assimilationist message contains an undercurrent of Jewish ethnic pride, suggesting that Jews would continue to have a distinct identity.

The second thinker, who gave voice to Zangwill's undercurrent, is Horace Kallen, who published a series of articles in 1915 in *The Nation* entitled "Democracy Versus the Melting Pot." Kallen argued that the melting pot could only be achieved by the violation of democratic principles, that is, by coercing the immigrants to accept Americanization and by forbidding expression of their original cultures. Kallen advocated instead what he called "cultural pluralism." His primary example of an ethnic group with a strong cultural heritage was the Jews. Kallen's theory of immigration, based largely on his observation of the Jews, argued that after an initial period of attempting to assimilate, the immigrant group discovers its "permanent group distinctions" and is "thrown back upon . . . [its] ancestry." At this stage, "ethnic and national differences change in status from disadvantages to distinctions." It is American democracy which allows this flourishing of ethnic cultures. Cultural pluralism, in Kallen's account, was based on the involuntary influence of ethnicity. As he wrote in a much quoted passage: "Men may change their clothes, their politics, their wives, their religions, their philosophies, to a greater or less extent; they cannot change their grandfathers."

The examples of Zangwill and Kallen demonstrate how much of the discourse around America as a "melting pot" or as a pluralistic nation of cultural minorities was originated by Jews to address the particular situation of Jewish immigrants. Jews therefore not only adapted to America, but also played central roles in shaping the definitions of their adopted country.

Given the central role that Jews played earlier in the century in defining the terms of debate, the way contemporary multiculturalists have absorbed this discourse and changed its terms has created profound anxiety among Jews, who often still see themselves, despite their increasingly successful integration, as the archetypal minority. The question for Jews today is whether they still have something to contribute to the definition of identity in America, as they did earlier in the century.

I believe that it is possible to imagine a Jewish identity that, if not paradigmatic, can at least help to bridge over what seems now an unbridgeable chasm between racialized majorities and minorities. In one place in the epilogue to the 1914 version of his play, Zangwill makes an interesting argument about the identity of the Britons. Rather than constituting a monolithic ethnicity, he claims that their identity was formed out of a long historical crucible in which virtually every racial type made its way to the British Isles. If the British turn out to be a hybrid people, then perhaps no national identity is actually monolithic or stable. All nations are formed out of melting pots. Thus, despite the racial language of the afterword and the ambiguities of the text itself, Zangwill pointed vaguely in the direction of what might be called a postethnic definition of identity.

Only recently emerging as a theoretical construct, postethnic or multiracial theory criticizes multiculturalism's politics of identity, not from the conservative position of monoculturalism, but rather as insufficiently radical. The problem with identity politics is that it sees categories like race and ethnicity as static and essential: we are nothing more than who our grandparents were, as Kallen's most extreme formulation had it. Postethnic theory argues that race is not a natural category, but rather one that is socially constructed and imposed on groups. Instead of basing identity on these constructs, a new construct would posit that identity can be individually chosen. Identity in such a theory is fluid and often multiple. David Hollinger, for example, poses what he calls "Alex Haley's dilemma." The author of *Roots*, it turns out, was also part Irish American. His "dilemma" is the question: Can Alex Haley choose to march in the St. Patrick's Day parade? To do so would directly challenge the so-called "one drop rule," according to which anyone with one drop of Black blood is defined as one hundred percent Black. The "one drop rule," promulgated by anti-Black racists over the last century or more, has often been implicitly adopted in a positive sense by multiculturalists in their assumption that identity politics follows racial ancestry. The postethnic theorists wish to overturn this racial discourse by unsettling the very category of monolithic race.

In so doing, they are responding to a social reality that is increasingly evident in America: there are no longer pure races or ethnicities (if there ever were), but, instead, multiracial and multiethnic identities. Intermarriage—an inevitability in any open society—has created individuals whose very being subvert any politics of monolithic identity. After nearly a century of counterarguments, Zangwill's melting pot continues to simmer.

Moreover, as Zangwill himself held, the result of this melting process is not conformity to a preexistent American identity, but the creation of something new to which each of the constituent parts makes its contribution.

Yet, postethnic theory suggests something different as well: instead of simply asserting a new amalgam identity, it is possible for a multiracial or multiethnic person to identify at one and the same time as both Irish and Italian, or both Black and White, or, even, Jew and Christian. That is, in place of a new, monolithic identity to take the place of the ethnic or racial identities that make it up, one could imagine multiple identities that are held simultaneously and that are chosen as much as they are inherited. To put it in Horace Kallen's terms, we may not be able to choose our grandparents, but we can choose the extent to which we affirm our connection to this or that grandparent. Freed of its early essentialism, Kallen's cultural pluralism can be resurrected by communities of choice. Identity itself is not a fixed and autonomous essence, but rather an aspect of culture and therefore similarly malleable. Descent may be said to be just as much a matter of cultural construction as other aspects of culture.

Postethnic theory is obviously utopian to a great degree since America continues to be divided along racial [lines]: even if race is a figment of our imaginations, it is a figment that has real consequences. While white ethnicities or sexual preferences can be disguised and therefore more easily "chosen," skin color cannot, and as long as prejudice exists, individuals will not have the freedom to choose this or that identity marked by what is called race. In addition, the intermarriage argument, relevant for groups like Asian and Hispanic Americans, is far less relevant for African Americans, who are intermarrying with other groups at a far lesser rate (although still at a higher rate than a few decades ago). Despite all these caveats, the virtue of postethnic theory is to attempt to change consciousness about categories assumed to be fixed, static, and, above all, "natural." And, even if theory cannot totally alter the way Americans think about race, the inexorable forces of the melting pot may ultimately erode these seemingly rock-solid formations of American identity.

How do the Jews fit into this perhaps utopian vision of a postethnic, postracial America? Because they are now seen as "white" and therefore capable of passing like other whites, I would suggest that Jews at the end of the twentieth century are rapidly becoming a good example of just such a community of choice. American Jews constitute a kind of intermediary ethnic group, one of the most quickly and thoroughly acculturated yet, among European immigrant ethnicities, equally one of the most resistant to complete assimilation. Anti-Semites may have conceived of the Jews as a race, but with historical origins in Europe and the Middle East and with an intermarriage rate now over fifty percent, American Jews defy racializing stereotypes even more now than ever. Jews are at once an ethnic group, but also not an ethnic group traditionally conceived.

Neither are they characterized by uniform religious practice or belief. The instability and multiplicity of Jewish identity, which has a long history going back to the Bible itself, has become even more true today. In a free society, all Jews—and not only converts, for whom the term was coined—are Jews by choice.

The indeterminacy of contemporary Jewish identity is often the cause of much communal handwringing. But instead of bemoaning these multiple identities, Jews need to begin to analyze what it means to negotiate them and, by so doing, perhaps even learn to embrace them. Reconceiving of Jewish identity along postethnic lines would undoubtedly require a sea change in Jewish self-consciousness, since Jews often continue to define themselves according to the old fixed and essentialized categories. In particular, the issue of intermarriage, which got Zangwill in so much trouble in *The Melting Pot,* requires radical reevaluation. Far from siphoning off the Jewish gene pool, perhaps it needs to be seen instead as creating new forms of identity, including multiple identities, that will reshape what it means to be Jewish in ways we can only begin to imagine. For the first time in Jewish history, there are children of mixed marriages who violate the "law of excluded middle" by asserting that they are simultaneously Jewish and Christian or Jewish and Italian.

Whether these new forms of identity spell the end of the Jewish people or its continuation in some new guise cannot be easily predicted, since there is no true historical precedent for this development: it might be compared to the great sea change that took place with the destruction of the Temple by the Romans in the first century of the Common Era. Such moments of revolutionary transformation are always fraught with peril, but whatever one's view of it, the task for those concerned with the place of Jews in America is not to condemn or condone, but rather to respond creatively to what is now an inevitable social process.

Beyond intermarriage, all Jews in the modern period have learned to live with multiple identities: Jew and German, Jew and American, Jew and Israeli. At one time it was fashionable to describe these identities as hyphenated or hybrid, as our discussion of Zangwill and Kallen makes clear. But it is becoming increasingly apparent that multiplicity in the precise sense of the word is more apt a description than hybridity. As opposed to the melting pot, in which a new identity emerges, or the cultural pluralism model, in which only one ethnic identity remains primary, this is the sort of identity in which one might retain at least two different cultural legacies at once. The Jewish Enlightenment slogan "Be a human being on the street and a Jew at home" now comes to fruition in a new guise: one can hold several identities both in the street and at home.

In order to begin this rethinking, Jews will undoubtedly have to give up their sense of themselves as the paradigmatic minority, a sociological version, as we have seen, with the older theology of the chosen people. In a postethnic America, Jews will no longer be such a minority because the very categories of majority and minorities will come into question. Yet, perhaps in this respect, the Jewish experience does remain relevant, precisely as a subversion of the old polarities. In a sense, both Zangwill and Kallen were right about the Jews, for they have simultaneously fulfilled both the vision of the melting pot and that of cultural pluralism. At once part of the American majority, yet also a self-chosen minority, their very belonging to both of these categories undermines the categories themselves. Between the monoculturalists who wish to erase difference and the multiculturalists who see only difference, the Jews may still have a role to play in the definition of American future.

POEMS

Adrienne Rich

Reversion

This woman/ the heart of the matter.
This woman flung into solitary by the prayers of her tribe.
This woman waking/ reaching for scissors/ starting to cut her hair
Hair long shaven/ growing out.
To snip to snip to snip/ creak of sharpness meeting itself against
   the roughness of her hair.

This woman whose voices drive her into exile.
(Exile, exile.)
Drive her toward the other side.
By train and foot and ship, to the other side.
Other side. Of a narrow sea.

This woman/ the heart of the matter.
Heart of the law/ heart of the prophets.
Their voices buzzing like raspsaws in her brain.
Taking ship without a passport.
How does she do it. Even the ships have eyes.
Are painted like birds.
This woman has no address book.

This woman perhaps has a toothbrush.
Somewhere dealing for red/blue dyes to crest her rough-clipped
    hair.

On the other side: stranger to women and to children.
Setting her bare footsole in the print of the stranger's bare foot in
    the sand.
Feeding the stranger's dog from the sack of her exhaustion.

What Kind of Times Are These

There's a place between two stands of trees where the grass grows
    uphill
and the old revolutionary road breaks off into shadows
near a meeting-house abandoned by the persecuted
who disappeared into these shadows.

I've walked there picking mushrooms at the edge of dread, but
    don't be fooled,
this isn't a Russian poem, this is not somewhere else but here,
our country moving closer to its own truth and dread,
its own ways of making people disappear.

I won't tell you where the place is, the dark mesh of the woods
meeting the unmarked strip of light—
ghost-ridden crossroads, leafmold paradise:
I know already who wants to buy it, sell it, make it disappear.

And I won't tell you where it is, so why do I tell you
anything? Because you still listen, because in times like these
to have you listen at all, it's necessary
to talk about trees.

JUSTIFY MY LOVE

Daniel Boyarin

AS I REFLECT on my coming of age in New Jersey, I realize that I had always been in some sense more of a "girl" than a "boy." A sissy who did not like sports, whose mother used to urge me, stop reading and go out and play, in fifth grade I went out for—ballet. (Of course I explained to the guys that it was a kind of sophisticated bodybuilding.) This in itself is rather a familiar story, a story of inexplicable gender dysphoria, but one that had for me, even then, a rather happy ending. I didn't think of myself so much as girlish but rather as Jewish.

I start with what I think is a widespread sensibility that being Jewish in our culture renders a boy effeminate. Rather than producing in me a desire to "pass" and to become a "man," this sensibility resulted in my desire to remain a Jew, where being a sissy was all right. To be sure this meant being marginal, and it has left me with a persistent sense of being on the outside of something, with my nose pressed to the glass looking in, but the cultural and communal place that a sissy occupied in my social world was not one that enforced rage and self-contempt. In a quite similar account another male American Jew of my generation, Harry Brod, writes: "I found the feminist critique of mainstream masculinity personally empowering rather than threatening. As a child and adolescent, I did not fit the mainstream male image. I was an outsider, not an athlete but an intellectual, fat, shy and with a stutter for many years. The feminist critique of mainstream masculinity allowed me to convert my envy of those who fit the approved model to contempt. It converted males previously my superiors on the traditional scale to males below me on the new scale, for I had obviously shown premature insight and sensitivity in rejecting the old male mode. I could pretend that others' rejection of me had really been my rejection of them. Of course, I could not have admitted this at the time. To do so would have seemed effeminate, and confirming of my fears of others' worst judgments of me." Brod moves on to a critique of this sensibility, referring to it as a "shield against other men." While I share his concern about the self-serving (and triumphant) countenance of the "use of my Jewishness to avoid being categorized as a 'real' man, 'real' understood as a term of critique rather than praise,"[1] I want to use the sissy, the Jewish male femme as a location and a critical practice.

I am interested right now in investigating what critical force might still be left in a culture and a cultural memory within which "real men" were sissies. The vector of my theoretical-political work, accordingly, is not to deny as antisemitic fantasy but to reclaim the nineteenth-century notion of the feminized Jewish male, to argue for his reality as one Jewish ideal going back to the Babylonian Talmud. I desire also to find a model for a gentle, nurturing masculinity in the traditional Jewish male ideal—without making claims as to how often realized this ideal was—a male who could be so comfortable with his little, fleshy penis that he would not have to grow it into "The Phallus," a sort of Velvet John. He whom a past dominant culture (as well as those Jews who internalized its values) considers contemptible, the feminized Jewish (colonized) male, may be useful today, for "he" may help us precisely today in our attempts to construct an alternative masculine subjectivity, one that will not have to rediscover such cultural archetypes as Iron Johns, knights, hairy men, and warriors within.

I am increasingly called upon to clarify something that I have never quite been able to explain until now, namely, the grounds for, and possibility of, a dual commitment to radical reclamation of traditional Jewish cultural life/practice/study and to radical reconstruction of the organization of gendered and sexual practices within our society (including necessarily the Jewish subculture). The first commitment is generated out of a sense of cultural/religious continuity as a value in itself and of Judaism as a rich, sustaining, and fulfilling way of life; the second derives from a deeply held conviction (and the affective stance) that Jewish practices have been oppressive to people in ways that I cannot stomach.

I have learned these dual commitments through living experience. Growing up in a way typical of most American Jews of my generation (the 1960s), I experienced Judaism as a vaguely attractive, sometimes silly, sometimes obnoxious set of occasional intrusions in my life, called Rosh Hashana, Yom Kippur, and Pesach. On the positive side, it represented for me a compelling passion for social justice which led me in high school to (almost) join the Communist Party of America. I finally turned, again like many American Jews of my time, to Far Eastern mysticism as a mode of escape from the arid, nonspiritual microclimate that the synagogue had become and the equally arid possibilities and promises of a life without spirit at all.

Chance encounters—with a lulav-wielding Lubavitcher, with a therapist who gave me an English translation of the Zohar, with a young disciple of Zalman Schachter—began to hint that there might be more to Judaism than I had been misled to believe by American liberal Judaism. One night, in my second year in college, I dreamed that I was in Israel, and so came to spend my third year of college in Israel thinking that I was destined for a life as a kabbalist. I wasn't.

The Talmud tempted me away from kabbala. Most American Jews don't have an inkling even of what the Talmud is. I certainly didn't. Sometimes I think I imagined it as a sort of commentary on the Torah (confusing it, I suppose, with midrash); sometimes as something like Euclid's geometry applied to precisely what I couldn't imagine, since my image of Jewish "Law" was that it was something unambiguous and found in a book called the *Shulkhan Arukh*. I had never seen even the outside binding of the Talmud, let alone the *Shulkhan Arukh*.

My friend, the aforementioned disciple of Shachter, had said to me, "Before you can understand Zohar, you have to know Talmud," so at the Hebrew University I signed up for the preparatory course in reading the Talmud and was charmed—in the full antique sense of the word—from almost the first sentence we read. Here was a world so strange and rich, so colorful and exciting, with myths and legends, challenges to the intellect, and, most of all, personalities rendered so vital that they seemed living men, men, moreover, who devoted their lives to the elaboration of what it means to live correctly, as a Jew. And this was all "mine." I became Orthodox for love of the Talmud. I admit freely, ruefully, that it was so absorbing that I hardly noticed they *were* all men, or that the text was primarily addressed to me just because I was a Jewish *man*—I didn't recognize the exclusions and oppressions that those facts encode and mystify.

I believe there is no textual product of human culture that is quite like the jumbled, carnivalesque, raucous, bawdy, vital, exciting Talmud, nor is there anything quite like the practices of study that characterize it and the whole way of life that it subtends.[2] These are not, of course, the adjectives that have been traditionally used, either from within or from without, to describe the talmudic life. I make it sound, and indeed I experience it, as if it were almost Rabelaisian. When after a year and a half of study I came upon a text that described the death of Rav, I underwent an emotional experience akin to hearing of the death of a beloved teacher. It had become almost unimaginable to me that Rav was not alive, because he was so alive in the text—alive I would add because not idealized, because the Talmud was as open to the flawed humanity of its heroes as the Bible had been to its. I have discovered that I am not alone: there are many people, including many women and lesbigay people, who are just as entranced by the Talmud as I have been and just as passionate about devoting their lives to it.

I deeply love and feel connected to rabbinic texts and culture, and even more to the Rabbis themselves, but there is much within them that I find deeply disturbing as well, and much of that has to do with the oppression of women.

This awareness also came to me from significant encounters. In the late 1980s I attended the School of Criticism and Theory at Dartmouth College, and for reasons that I cannot now quite remember or reconstruct, I joined a feminist reading group, as one of two men in the group among approximately twenty women. This little community provided me with my first direct experience of feminism as theory and the experiences that had produced it as practice. Although very different from the affect that had compelled me to devote a life to the study and practice of Talmud, this experience was no less compelling. At the end of the summer I could no longer describe myself only as an Orthodox Jew; I now had to say (for a long time only to myself) that being a male feminist was constitutive and definitive of my experience of self. The contradictions seemed so ungappable that I just endeavored to live with them for a number of years until I could no longer do so. Unable, however, to let go or even diminish either one of these fundamental components of my self, I discovered that I had to find ways to theorize a rapprochement (or at least to make the contradictions creative).

My endeavor is to justify my love, that is, both to explain it and to make it just. I explain my devotion in part by showing that Judaism provides exempla for another kind of masculinity, one in which men do not manifest "a deeply rooted concern about the possible meanings of dependence on other males,"[3] and thus one within which "feminization" is not experienced as a threat or a danger. I cannot, however, paper over, ignore, explain away, or apologize for the oppressions of women and lesbigay people that this culture has practiced, and therefore I endeavor as well to render it just by presenting a way of reading the tradition that may help it surmount or expunge—in time—that which I and many others can no longer live with.

In this dual aspect of resistance to pressure from without and critique from within, my project is homologous to other political, cultural acts of resistance in the face of colonialisms. For some three hundred years now, Jews have been the target of the civilizing mission in Europe. In her recent dissertation, Laura Levitt makes palpably clear the homologies between the "liberal" colonizing impulse directed toward those Others within Europe and toward the colonized outside of Europe insofar as for both it is constituted by a demand that their sexual practices be "reformed" to conform to the liberal bourgeois regime.[4] One of the most common of liberal justifications for the extension of colonial control over a given people and for the maintenance of the civilizing mission is the imputed barbarity of the treatment of women within the culture under attack.[5] The civilizing mission, and its Jewish agents among "the Enlighteners," considered the fact that Jewish women behaved in ways interpreted as masculine by European bourgeois society to be simply monstrous.[6] Modern Jewish culture, liberal and bourgeois in its aspirations and its preferred patterns of gendered life, has been the result of this civilizing mission. As Paula Hyman has recently demonstrated, the very Jewish religiosity of the modern bourgeois Jewish family is an assimilating mimicry of Protestant middle-class piety, not least in its portrayal of proper womanhood.[7] The richness of Jewish life and difference has been largely lost, and the gains for Jewish women were largely illusory.[8] This having been said, however, the Jewish anticolonial project—like any other—cannot refrain from a trenchant, unflinching, and unapologetic internal critique of the harsh oppressions within the very traditional culture that it seeks to protect from destruction from without, namely, the structure of systematic exclusion of women from the practices that the culture most highly regards and especially the study of Torah. This exclusion has been a breeding ground of contempt—sometimes quite extreme—for women and a perpetrator of second-class status within Jewish law.

I repeat that I deeply love and feel connected to rabbinic texts and culture, but there is much within them that I find deeply disturbing as well. If Jewish culture has been a place of safety for a sissy, it has hardly—to understate the case—provided such felicitous conditions for Jewish women. This is a feminist project, at least to the extent that it owes its life to feminism and the work of feminist critics. Male self-fashioning has consequences for women. I feel an inner mandate to see to it that a project of reclamation of Judaic culture from the depredations of the civilizing, colonializing onslaught to which it has been subject does not interfere with (even perhaps, contributes something to) the ongoing project of feminist critique of that same traditional culture from within—to see to it, as best I can, that is, that my practice, whether or not it is part of the solution, is not part of the problem. I thus try to meet the challenge implicit in Tania Modleski's observation that male critique of masculinity is feminist when "it analyzes male power, male hegemony, with a concern for the effects of this power on *the female subject* and with an awareness of how frequently male subjectivity works to appropriate 'femininity' while oppressing women."[9] The dual movement of the political project, to resist the delegitimization of Judaic culture from without, while supporting the feminist critique from within, dictates the structure of my work.

Thinking about the sissy body of the "Jewish man," I think simultaneously about another discourse and practice—possibly but not necessarily liberatory—that constructs the male body in a very different way. The "gay male gym body" is an example of another male body constructed as an alternative to the heterosexual male body. David Halperin (following in part D. A. Miller) has recently given us a brilliant and moving rejoinder to "straight, liberal" attacks on gay male bodybuilding by arguing for an absolute, total differentiation between the "macho straight male body" and "the gay male gym body": "What distinguishes the gay male gym body, then, in addition to its spectacular beauty, is the way it advertises itself as an object of desire. Gay muscles do not signify power." He further makes the impeccable point that the (ideal) gay male body does not look at all like the straight macho body:

> They [gay male bodies] are explicitly designed to be an erotic turn-on, and in their very solicitation of desire they deliberately flaunt the visual norms of straight masculinity, which impose discretion on masculine self-display and require that straight male beauty exhibit itself only casually or inadvertently, that it refuse to acknowledge its own strategies. If, as Foucault hypothesized in *Discipline and Punish,* those whom modern disciplinary society would destroy first it makes visible, then gay male body-builders, in visibly inscribing their erotic desires on the surfaces of their bodies, have not only exposed themselves to considerable social risks in the course of pursuing their ethical projects but have also performed a valuable political service on behalf of everyone, insofar as they have issued a challenge of defiance to the very mechanisms of modern discipline.[10]

This is inarguable—and I am hardly insensible to the attraction of that "spectacular beauty"—but it nevertheless remains the case that the very standard for male beauty that is being prescribed is one of a certain form of muscular development that emphasizes the dimorphism of the gendered body and thus participates, to this extent, in the general cultural standard of masculinity rather than resisting it.[11] The pale, limp, and semiotically unaggressive "nelly" or sissy male body is not seen within this construct as beautiful or erotic at all, but this exclusion as well can be shown to be culturally specific and limited.

Lori Lefkovitz makes the point that Joseph in the midrash is described as having a body that is explicitly designed to be an erotic turn-on, but it is not at all the body of a Muscle-Jew. He penciled his eyes, curled his hair, and lifted his heels, and, moreover, his was a beauty like that of his mother Rachel—and it was *this* beauty that so attracted Potiphar's wife and indeed all the noblewomen of Egypt![12] Thus, on one hand I think that Halperin clearly is right that "the hypermasculine look of gay clones is deceiving. What the new styles of gay virility represent, paradoxically, is a strategy for valorizing various practices of devirilization under the sign of masculinity, thereby forging a new association between masculinity and sexual receptivity or penetrability, while detaching male homosexuality from its phobic association with 'femininity' (conceived in phallic terms as 'passivity' or as an absence of phallic aggressivity)."[13] On the other hand, I fear that this strategy backfires insofar as it continues to register only one kind of male body as desirable, thus "clonedom" (and I do not claim, of course, that this is true for all gay male culture). Thus, in addition to the dislodging of sexual receptivity from "femininity"—conceived of as lack, castration, and the negatively encoded "passivity"—that the gay male gym body enacts, there also has to be a parallel dislodging of the penetrating penis—gay or straight—from masculinity, conceived as "phallic aggressivity," as well as from the ways that, as Foucault has pointed out, such "topness" is still valorized over receptivity in nearly all sectors of our sexual culture.[14]

One place to find the eroticized sissy is at a reading of the rabbinic textual tradition. On one hand, this tradition clearly privileges—to understate again—sexual connections between men and women[15] and also clearly prescribes social domination of men over women; at the same time, it does not privilege "masculinity" over "femininity"—"tops" over "bottoms"— nor stigmatize "femininity" in anything like the ways that hegemonic European culture has come to do particularly since the nineteenth century. In part, Jewish culture demystifies European gender ideologies by reversing their terms, which is not, I hasten to emphasize, a liberatory process in itself but can be mobilized—strategically—for liberation. In any case, the modern Jewish abandonment of our sissy heritage has been a noxious force in modern Jewish culture, an ill wind that has brought no one good. As Paul Breines has written, "[T]he cult of the tough Jew as an alternative to Jewish timidity and gentleness rests on ideals of 'masculine beauty,' health, and normalcy that are conceived *as if their validity were obvious and natural*. They [Muscle-Jews] have, in other words, internalized unquestioningly the physical and psychological ideals of their respective dominating cultures. In doing so they forget that, far from being self-evident cultural universals, those ideals are predicated on a series of exclusions and erasures—of effeminate men, pacifism, Arabs, gentleness, women, homosexuals, and far from least, Jews."[16] For a member of several of these intersecting categories, the politics of this recovery work has, then, a sharp urgency.

The politics of my project to reclaim the eroticized Jewish male sissy has, however, two faces. The traditional valorization of "effeminism" for Jewish men hardly secured good news for Jewish women. There is no question that women were disenfranchised in many ways in traditional Jewish culture. The culture authorized, even if it did not mandate, efflorescences of misogyny. If the ideal Jewish male femme has some critical force vis-à-vis general European models of manliness, at the same time a critique must be mounted against "him" for his oppression of Jewish women—and indeed, frequently enough, for his class-based oppression of other Jewish men as well, namely, the ignorant who were sometimes characterized as being "like women."[17] Any attempt at a feminist rereading of Jewish tradition must come to terms with this material fact and the legacies of pain that it has left behind. My goal is not to preserve rabbinic Judaism "as we know it," but to reconstruct a rabbinic Judaism that will be quite different in some ways from the one we know and yet be and feel credibly grounded in the tradition of the Rabbis. My work is one of changing ethos and culture and I hope it joins with a stream of feminist work on rabbinic Judaism that includes the research of Judith Baskin, Judith Hauptman, Miriam Peskowitz, Laura Levitt, Susan Shapiro, and others.

As significant as the different gendering of Jewish men was, so was there a significant difference in the gendering of Jewish women. While their men were sitting indoors and studying Torah, speaking only a Jewish language, and withdrawn from the world, women of the same class were speaking, reading, and writing the vernacular, maintaining businesses large and small, and dealing with the wide world of tax collectors and irate customers. In short, they were engaging in what must have seemed to many in the larger culture as masculine activities, and if the men were read as sissies, the women were read often enough as phallic monsters. In certain apologies for Judaism, the fact of women's economic activity in traditional Jewish culture has been used as an alibi for the entire system of oppression of women. This economic power, however real, was a double-edged sword. Iris Parush has captured something of this paradoxical double charge of gender politics in early modern European Jewry: "Over the years, the lifestyle which crystallized in Jewish society caused the men to cluster under the sacred tent of Torah study, and the women to stand at the front line of the daily confrontation with the outside world. . . . An interesting combination of weakness and power—of inferiority in terms of the traditional Jewish perspective, and superiority in terms of the trends of Europeanization—opened the 'door of opportunity,' so to speak, for certain circles of the female population."[18]

The "fact" then that Jewish women (of certain classes) had opportunities in the secular world and access to education and economic power and autonomy beyond that of their husbands must not be permitted to erase the fact that, nevertheless, within Jewish culture these roles were genuinely less valued than those of men. The time for the apologetic strategy of pointing to "positive" structures or ideals and allowing them to excuse whole systems of repression has passed, and I have no desire to return to it, for it is a fundamentally reactionary strategy. My desire is not to discount, excuse, or pretend that there was no powerful oppression of women but rather to displace that oppression by arguing that such abuse is a product of a particular reading of the past and its canonical texts. This reading, while not "inauthentic" or "invalid," is nevertheless not the only one possible, nor even a uniquely compelling reading of the tradition. I hope, then, to be making a very different discursive move here, one that maintains the passion of critique of what has been and yet seeks to mobilize that same past for a different future by reinterpreting it.

What I want is to produce a discursive catachresis, not a quick fix by a halakhic committee but a new thing in the world, the horizon of possibility for a militant, feminist, nonhomophobic, traditionalist—Orthodox—Judaism. The reasons for Jewish conservatism are not essential but accidental. The force of my writing is to avow not that traditional Judaism does not need radical change but rather that it can accommodate radical change and still remain viable if the terms of the change themselves can be seen as rooted in the documents, traditions, texts of the Rabbis. The only reason—other than divine mandate—for seeking this accommodation is that such practice brings to many men and women an extraordinary richness of experience and a powerful sense of being rooted somewhere in the world, in a world of memory, intimacy, and connectedness, a pleasure that I call *Jewissance*. Note that I am *not* arguing for a continuation of Judaism on the grounds that it makes people better, although in some sense my justification for indulging in the extreme pleasures of Jewishness is the assumption that it does have something to contribute to the world as well. I treasure in principle and with deep emotion cultural difference per se—not

only my own—and for me the disappearance of a cultural form is attended
with a pathos and pain not unlike that experienced by many people when
a species of bird goes out of the world. The demand for cultural sameness,
universalism, has done much harm and violence in the world, but cultural
difference as well has to work hard to do no harm; to participate in this
work is the calling of the scholar.

My role model for this kind of scholarship is Bertha Pappenheim, co-
hort of such giants of Jewish scholarship as Shmuel Krauss and, among
her many accomplishments, teacher in Rosenzweig and Buber's *Lehrhaus*.
I want to claim Bertha Pappenheim here as a model for an alternative to
the pseudo-objectivity of *Wissenschaft*. Although I can barely stake out
my claim here, I would suggest that it was her first-wave feminism that
fueled her achievements in Judaic scholarship, just as it is second-wave
feminism that has empowered engaged, politically frank scholarship and
critique in our generation. Let her become the foremother of another genealogy for Jewish cultural studies, one that enacts passionate love for the
culture and devotion to its continued creative and vital existence without
losing sight for a moment of the necessity for equally passionate critique.

NOTES

1. Harry Brod, *A Mensch Among Men* (Freedom, California, Crossing,
   1988), 7, 8.

2. Astonishingly to me, I know not why, Eve Kosofsky Sedgwick has captured
   perfectly my sensibility when she writes of "Talmudic desires, to reproduce
   or unfold the text and to giggle" (*Epistemology*, 240). I am grateful for that
   sentence, as for much else in her work. In contrast to this, I wonder at
   Christine Delphy's repeated use of "talmudic" as a pejorative for the discourse of false feminists. This remains a stumbling block for me in my
   appreciation of her otherwise quite wonderful work.

3. Lee Edelman, "Redeeming the Phallus," in *Engendering Men,* ed. Joseph A.
   Boone and Michael Cadden (New York, Routledge, 1990), 50.

4. Laura Sharon Levitt, *Reconfiguring Home: Jewish Feminist Identity/ies,*
   152–73 Ph.D. Diss. Emory U 1993 Microfilm.

5. Judith Butler, "Gender Trouble," in *Thinking Gender* (London, Routledge,
   1990).

6. In an earlier version I had written: "its Jewish agents, the 'Enlighteners,'"
   but as Naomi Seidman has correctly admonished me, this was not entirely
   fair, since there was a genuine feminist impulse animating a not insignificant
   component of the Jewish Enlightenment as well. Nor am I prepared, of
   course, to entirely disavow the Enlightenment project as part of who I am.
   Nevertheless, the insistence of the Jewish Enlightenment that only an eradi-

cation of the "talmudic spirit" could fit the Jews for civilization is an un-remittingly colonialist project. As my student Abe Socher has pointed out: "Jewish Enlighteners (*Maskilim*) even identified the mortifying 'jargon' of Yiddish with the Aramaic of the Talmud. Just as Yiddish was a corruption of the pure language of German and, as such, an impossible vehicle for any-thing but *unbildung,* so too was Aramaic a corruption of the pure Hebrew of the Bible. This equation between the two pure languages of biblical He-brew and eighteenth-century German was epitomized in Mendelssohn's *Biur,* a Hebrew Bible with a running translation into High German, ren-dered in Hebrew letters. Almost a century later, the great nineteenth-cen-tury historian Heinrich Graetz summed up the *Maskilic* attitude when he wrote of the eastern European Talmudists' love of 'twisting, distorting, in-genious quibbling,' which has 'reduced the language of German Jews to a repulsive stammer'" (Socher, "Magus")—QED. See also Aschheim, *Broth-ers,* 14–15.

7. Paula Hyman, *Gender and Assimilation in Modern Jewish History* (The Samuel & Althea Stroum Lectures in Jewish Studies, Seattle, University of Washington Press, 1995), 26–27.

8. Shulamit S. Magnes, "Pauline Wengeroff and the Voice of Jewish Moder-nity" in *Gender and Judaism: The Transformation of Tradition,* ed. T. M. Rudavsky (New York, New York UP, 1995), 181–90.

9. Tania Modleski, *Feminism Without Women: Culture and Criticism in a "Post-Feminist" Age* (New York, Routledge, 1991), 7.

10. David M. Halperin, *Saint Foucault: Towards a Gay Hagiography* (Oxford, Oxford UP, 1995), 117.

11. Put another way, and granting once more the plausibility of Halperin's con-struction, is there not at least the possible danger of misreading—not only by "straight, male liberals"—this "devirilizing" performance as being com-plicit with an earlier, peculiarly Teutonic reading of the homosexual male body as the quintessence of virility? For the latter, see Sedgwick, *Epistemol-ogy,* 134, and, especially now, Mosse, *Image,* 32.

12. Lori Lefkowitz, "Coats and Tales: Joseph Stories and Myths of Jewish Masculinity" in Harry Brod, op. cit.

13. Halperin, op. cit., p. 90.

14. Lawrence D. Kritzman, *Michel Foucault: Politics, Philosophy, Culture, 1977–1984* (New York, Routledge, 1998), 300.

15. D. Boyarin, "Are There Any Jews in the 'History of Sexuality'?" *Journal of the History of Sexuality* 503 (1995), 333–55.

16. Paul Breines, *Tough Jews* (New York, Basic, 1970), 167.

17. Chava Weissler, "For Women and for Men Who Are Like Women," *Journal of Feminist Studies in Religion* 5 (1989) 7–24.

18. Parush, "Women." Pappenheim makes this point herself in quite similar terms: "Particularly the indifference with which everything women and girls

learned was treated (at the time of early marriages 'girlhood' as we understand it hardly existed) compared to what men and boys were to learn and
know, introduced a continuous current into the women's world. . . . Particularly among the Jewish women a thirst for education clearly marked by
German culture grew that made new cultural elements accessible to the
bilingual, often trilingual (if French was added) women of the higher
classes" (Pappenheim, "Jewish Woman").

TEN WAYS TO RECOGNIZE
A SEPHARDIC 'JEW-ESS'

Ruth Knafo Setton

One: *Name*

Often unpronounceable, unmanageable, redolent of incense and cumin. A name that twists letters into spirals the way a djinn emerges from a lamp. Abitbol. Afriat. Bahboul. Buzaglo. Aflalo. Dweck. Ohayon. Ben'Attar. Bensussan. Couraqui. The Spanish echoes too, of arches and Alhambra, dusty streets and brown hoods: Cabessa, Corcos, Mendes, Pinto. But the true names are weirdly resonant, heavy, harsh, satisfying; a name you can sink your teeth into, one that emerges from dirt and mud and roots: Knafo. A certain brilliantly colored cloak, *knaf* also refers to a honey-drenched, shredded phyllo dough Middle Eastern sweet, the kind set a thousand on a large tray in Jaffa or Casablanca that you eat with your fingers, swirling the flaking pastry and syrup and nut mixture on your tongue with burning Moroccan mint tea—perfumed with a drop of orange blossom water. *Knafo.* Say this name aloud, every which way you can imagine. Try being called Knaf-Knuf. Knasoo—a singularly ugly aberration, Konfoo, Kanfa, Knee, or in a stroke of malevolent genius: Kohenfo. The mysterious letter "k." To pronounce or not? Arabs whisper it like a "h." Hanafo. It's a breath, a wing. Knaf in Hebrew is a wing. Legend has it that Knafo means "under God's wing," even to be protected by God because we are literally under His wing. This was especially evident for Maklouf Knafo and his family on a Thursday morning in July 1790, in the Berber village of Oufran hidden in the Anti-Atlas Mountains of Morocco.

Two: *Food*

Feed this child. Wide-eyed and yearning. This child has never tasted a bagel! Her mother distrusts anything served in a gel. Gefilte fish? She whisks her child away from it quickly. Kugel? The dough is too heavy, sinks into the stomach. Lox and cream cheese? Mom clicks her tongue against the roof of her mouth. They don't know how to be subtle, she murmurs, wielding her knife and beginning to chop. Behind her henna'd hair—beautiful auburn waves flowing down her back—I see my American backyard. A swing set on which my little sister soars, lost in her recurring daydream of rescuing stray cats and dogs and bringing them to her doll hospital. A sandbox in which my tiny naked brother sits and throws handfuls of sand back and forth. Mom chops, cuts, slices. I lean on my elbow and watch everyone at once. Even my dad far away at work sorting produce at the A&P, struggling to make sense of English syllables—coiled and Germanic—as opposed to fluid French, guttural Arabic.

I think about my own rescue fantasy. Every night in bed I return to our little backyard. The alley behind is flooded. Help! Help! someone screams. It's *I Love Lucy!* I race from my yard to save her, bring my trusty canoe through the gate, and paddle up the hill. I pull her into the boat. Her red hair gleams in the dark. She thanks me, and I set her safely in my backyard, and return to save Desi and little Ricky. It's a dangerous world, something I can't remember ever learning and yet something I must have always known. To open the front door is to enter danger. I prefer leaving from the back, where I can ease my way into the outside world, through the yard and the gate, down the alley and around the corner past Old Man Minnich's store and his display of comic books and penny candy in the window.

See, Mom says, and gestures towards the salads: oranges and black olives, the colors alone nearly sending me on another voyage; purple beets and celery; cooked peppers red, yellow and green, drizzled with olive oil and seasoned with preserved lemon, chili peppers, and cumin. Flavors shouldn't be obvious, Mom says; mix the unexpected: chicken with sweet tomato jam and dark honey, fish with almond paste and confectioners' sugar, preserves made from baby eggplants and walnuts, *tagines* simmered with *smen,* saffron and *za'atar.* And *ma fille,* remember the importance of cinnamon.

Three: *The Knafo Wheel*

My cousin handed it to me one night at a lecture in New York. A huge sheet of paper to revolve, separated into sections: a round graph. I look at the center: Maklouf Knafo. The one who burned to death along with the other forty-nine *nisrafim* (burnt ones) in Oufran. And the branches spread out from him. Knafos, Knafos, as far as the finger extends. Knafos in Mogador of course, because that's where his wife walked with her baby. I close my eyes and imagine her voyage. A young woman, her eight-day-old infant son (just circumcised by Maklouf that morning), walking down the mountain paths—rocky and steep. But the danger is not in the rocks and winding roads; it is in the robbers and brigands who populate these mountains. A young woman and her baby. I scan the Knafo wheel, turn it around and around, try to read between the black lines and words and letters, but find no name for this young woman. A nameless woman making her way down the mountains to save her son. Nameless—except for her husband's name, Knafo. Is she under God's wing as she stumbles down the road? Sun burns on her head. The baby is hot, hungry, crying. How does she maintain her supply of milk? Everything she owns is on her back. The baby cradled in a blanket against her breasts. Her husband left behind. Her husband, Maklouf Knafo. She walks fast, head down, afraid to breathe, to smell smoke.

Four: *Purple Palestinians*

Now this goes back years: we all lived in a shabby apartment building on Valencia in the Mission in San Francisco—above a bar, across from a bar, next door to a bar. Stumbling over drunks and homeless—only back then we didn't call them homeless, we called them bums. And winos. And I was alone for the first time in my life, scared to death, but—here's the great mixture I can't get a handle on—high on hippie life, memories of my strange isolated family haunting me, trying with my gut to be as American as you, and to that end, sitting in my third-floor apartment in the Mission, looking down at the barmaid, at least eighty, with enormous pale tits and iridescent blue eye-shadow, walking to the bar on the corner to start her shift, and I set pen to paper and begin the American novel—as interpreted by a Moroccan Jewish immigrant girl. But I've been burned already, even though I'm barely twenty-one. The first story I send out returns with a rejection note: *You write well. Next time try writing about the* real *Jews.*

I am frozen to my soul. Too afraid to inquire more deeply into what the editor means. So ashamed I tear the note into a thousand slivers, shred them with my fingers, and throw them down the toilet. There. It's gone.

"And the pain?" as my father would say. He's known for that final aside, the joke after the punch line that sends it spinning into another dimension. He is known for that, the ironic aside that makes people realize that no joke has an end. No story truly finishes.

And so I write about an old Polish Jewish man as I stare outside and ignore Hassan from down the hall, banging on my door and screaming: I'm going to rape you the way you raped Palestine! And Amar, his room-mate, the head cabdriver (the one who gives them all purple Hafiz Cab tee-shirts when they arrive in the city, and the one who cooks for me and gets high with me, and we listen to Procol Harum and wonder over *A White Shade of Pale* together, and stare at each other, attracted though trying not to be). Amar, sweet Amar, with the desert eyes and the tightest purple tee-shirt of all, tells his friend: leave her alone. She's a girl, she can't rape anyone. . . .

Five: *Exotic*

Erotique. I line my eyes with black *kohl* and wear large gold hoops and long gypsy skirts and low-cut hand-embroidered Romanian blouses. Paint my toenails red and wear sandals that tie around my ankles. But my legs are always cold so I begin to wear leggings beneath my skirts—and don't realize it's the way Arab women dress until my mother tells me. I play up the exotic, pronounce words with a faint French accent, *le bagel, qu'est-ce que c'est?* Boys like me; you and your crazy name, one murmurs as he bites my ear. They see me and think of *Casablanca* and Ingrid Bergman and play it again Sam. My first real boyfriend is black. He tells me: I am from Afrikaaa. I tell him: so am I. He tells me: I am black first, a man second. I tell him: in Paris they call me *pieds noirs*, black feet. He tells me: here, they call me nigger. I tell him: they called me *dhimmi*, or the lowest of the low. We outblack each other, and even in bed, scratch and lash and attack, until we lie back, exhausted and content. We're an odd couple: he listens to Jimi and (in secret) Sweet Baby James. I listen to James Brown and John Lee Hooker. I dance better than he does. Later, the best dancer I will ever see, a Moroccan soul-sex machine come to life, whom I watched move to James Brown for hours at a time in a Natanya club called Azazel (or Hell), died at twenty-one in the Yom Kippur War.

Six: *Memory*

The years in the sunless *mellahs* and *juderías* and *quartiers juifs* have bleached our skin until it's fashionably Mediterranean, only a shade or two darker than yours. Our nomadic history has given us a variety of lan-guages, none of which is ours, but all of which we have learned to speak—with a bite. You can recognize us by the rage we carry in us, the rage of the colonized, those who are still not permitted to meet the master class eye to eye. The bitter eyes that now refuse to stay lowered, the angry tongue that can no longer be silenced, the poet's heart that in spite of everything continues to dream and hope, the soul that cannot forget. There is no wind and the smell of burning flesh remains in the square, incapable of moving elsewhere and freeing us.

Seven: *Invisible*

Even within postcolonial, third world, border-crossing, multicultural ethnic feminist identities, I am nowhere to be found. I dare you. Look for me. Born in Morocco, raised in America, in a small town—a Jew from Africa who probably scared my Pennsylvania-Dutch neighbors as much as they scared me—a minority within a minority. Be invisible, my father told me. I tried—but my black feet peeked out from every disguise. And now when I take off my veil and let you see the scratched lines of henna crisscrossing my face, the embroidered scrolls and curlicues that lace my palms, you avert your eyes. By multicultural, I didn't mean you. Latina is hot now. Lesbian Latina even better. Caribbean, mon? Remote Indian provinces, hot as curry. Even Arab American, hotter than you. Who you anyway? Afrikaan? Arab Jew? Oriental Jew? Tied in with Israel. Israel not hot.

Eight: *Nomad*

I believe she traveled north to Taroudant in the Grand Atlas, then wound her way down the rocky hills and ravines to the east and the breezes of the Atlantic Ocean, and north once more, following the coastline past Cap Guir and Tamanar to Mogador. Mountain air is thin and clear, but in the Anti-Atlas Mountains it is pale gray, tainted with smoke. Take a deep breath. The smoke doesn't escape. Locked in the square, over a hundred years later, it smells of death, the end of the oldest Jewish community in Morocco, with a hiss and crack.

Nine: *The Choice: Life or Death?*

Take a deep breath and decide if it's going to be life or death, says Bou Halassa, the sheik who owns the Jews of Oufran. Think carefully, he says. The choice is simple: Die as Jews, or live as Muslims—under my protection. All you have to do is say the words: *There is no God but Allah, and Mohammed is His Prophet.*

The sun is shining. It is a July morning in 1790 in the Anti-Atlas Mountains. Bou Halassa is on horseback, surrounded by his men who are already at work building the funeral pyre. The fifty Jews, merchants all, are wearing black (the only color permitted them); they are barefoot (no shoes allowed for Jews); and they are standing on the ground because they are not permitted to ride a horse. The horse is considered too noble an animal to carry a lowly Jew. Bou has interrupted the *souk el'khemiss,* the Thursday morning market. Merchants selling carpets and leather, artisans with brass trays and iron kettles. Cattle, mules, donkeys, chickens.

The leader of the Jews, Rabbi Naphtali Afriat, tells them: We have no choice. To say the words and live a lie is another form of death. To die for God is to live forever as Jews. It's the only way to carry on our faith so that our children can be Jews. So that everything doesn't die this morning.

A young man on the edge of the group is torn. Only this morning, with his own hands, he circumcised his first son. Die—for what? For Bou Halassa's whim? Bou is a tyrant, a sadist, notorious in the mountains for his hatred of Jews. Even though Bou's men have swords and are now circling the Jews, we are fifty in number—maybe we can fight back? And if they overpower us, then what? If we walk into the flames, will he then turn on our women and children?

Afriat, his gold earring glinting in the sun, announces in his quavering voice: We have decided. We choose death—in the name of God. You do not frighten us, Bou Halassa. You will answer for your brutality to God, not to us.

The young man bolts—without a thought, without hesitation—slips from the crowd of Jews and Arabs, and runs to his small cottage. Then he does—what? I'd love to see this scene: how he convinces her to take the baby and leave without him. I can almost hear her: you've already come this far! They don't know you're gone! Come with us. You'll do more good to us alive than dead. Why should you die for this sadist? Come with us!

He walks his wife and baby to the town wall, the stone wall that enclosed Oufran. She is unwieldy: the blanket that supports her baby forces her to lean forward, while the bag Maklouf stuffed with bread and dates loads down her back. He helps push her up the wall, and for a moment is caught there, in the cobblestones, between death and life—his wife's hand pulling him up, the hand of "God" pulling him back. Beneath his feet, red and purple flowers sprout in crevices between the rocks.

Ten: *The Question of Home*

The sun shines through Amar's window. The Moody Blues sing about nights in white satin. I lean over Amar's shoulder he fries a mixture of eggs, potatoes, and meat on the stove. The violent Hassan has left San Francisco. Crazy, Amar tells us, tapping his temple and handing me a fat joint.

I breathe in the harsh smoke and the pungent spices that smell like my mother's food. You have to create your own home wherever you go, he says. This sounds wise, heavy. But first you have to know what a home is, I say, and hand back the joint. With a deep sigh that echoes through me, I move to the window, sit on the edge and lean out. The sun licks my cheeks with burning tongue. The old barmaid walks down the street. I yell to her. She squints up, sees me, and waves, smiles an orange and yellow smile. Her blue-veined, speckled tits jiggle like blobs of cream cheese, like gefilte fish squashed in satin.

REDEMPTION ON EAST TREMONT

THE KINDNESS OF CHRISTIANS AND A SEDER'S
MATZAH HELPS THE DAUGHTER OF MENDEL BEILIS
FIX THE OLD FEARS

Jonathan Mark

OTHER THAN THE OCCASIONAL MURDER, few newspaper stories, if any, originate from the desolation of East Tremont Avenue; certainly no stories in Jewish newspapers, now that all the Jews have long ago scattered from these Bronx streets. There's nothing left on East Tremont, is there? But let it be written, in the words of the biblical Jacob: "Surely, God is in this place—and I, I did not know."

Oh, a murder did happen on March 20, when a Jew was arrested for the killing of a Christian boy. But first, a question for the youngest child to ask on Passover: Does Elijah still walk the streets of East Tremont on seder nights? It used to be the most Jewish of neighborhoods. In 1929, when Gertrude Berg brought her famous show, *The Goldbergs,* to radio, she situated her fictional Jewish family at 1030 East Tremont. She'd call through the window, "Yooo-hooo, Mrs. Bloooom!" The streets of East Tremont were filled with Goldbergs and Blooms.

Years later, the night wind howls. A solitary tire rolls down the sidewalk. A peddler outside La Antillana Supermarket Carniceria hawks green plantains, yellow brooms, plastic hangers. From a boom-box, Latin dance music punches the air. A poster in a storefront window offers real estate options: "Houses in Ghana . . . Electricity. Water. Tarred roads." Why live on East Tremont when you can live in Ghana?

There are no signs or Stars of David to tip you off, but the one-story building at 236 East Tremont used to be a shul. It is now a senior citizen center. Inside, a black woman plays a gospel piano, sweet and stately: "How Great Thou Art," and "Waiting on the Everlasting Lord." Old black women sing along, jabbing plastic forks and spoons at meatloaf and canned fruit cocktail. There are nearly 20 black and Hispanic seniors here; nearly a dozen old Jews eat at a table across the room.

Welcome to the East Tremont Lunch Club, a glatt kosher kitchen run by JASA, the Jewish Association for Services to the Aged. Thousands of Jews may have moved away, but JASA stays on for the few and the brave. Seniors thumb through house copies of *El Diario, Jet,* and the New York dailies. They are poor, and even the price of a newspaper gives pause. At the Lunch Club, JASA sells a hot meal for 60 cents, but pay what you can. On this particular afternoon, 32 hot meat meals are served; JASA collects $18.60.

Cartons of milk are kept in crates outside the dining room. Danny, the black porter, explains, "It's a glatt kosher lunch, you know. Got to keep the milk away."

A black woman, Mae, director of this senior center, looks to her husband Danny and smiles: "He's the mashgiach."

There'll be a seder here on Passover. The Graenum Berger Bronx Jewish Federation Service Center is providing a rabbi and the food. "We'll probably have chicken," says Danny, "kugel, derma, soup, and macaroons." Mae insists, "My whole concern is that the center remain open as long as we have even one or two Jewish people here, so they can rest assured they can have a glatt kosher meal. There's not even a place around here where they can shop."

"Hey," says one of the Lunch Club Jews after some post-meal story telling. "You want a good story? Talk to Rae."

Rae Beilis, 90 years old, looks up, finishing her lunch. Let's call her Raya, the name her Russian parents would coo to her in a far and distant time.

Yes, about that murder. Raya asks, "You know what happened to me, don't you? You don't? Are you kidding? I thought that's why you wanted to talk to me. My father was Mendel Beilis. It was like yesterday." They found a dead body in Kiev, March 20, 1911—88 years ago yesterday: A 12-year-old Christian boy was stabbed 37 times, his bloody body dumped in a cave. The district attorney pinned it on Beilis, who supposedly needed Christian blood to make matzah.

Beilis, 37, managed a brick factory, overseeing hundreds of non-Jewish workers. "They loved him," says Raya. Sure they did. "I was 2 years old," recalls Raya. "There was a knock on the door. They took father away so fast, he was just in his underwear." The shock of the "blood libel" shot through Poland and Russian Jewry, an international sensation inspiring rallies and campaigns to free Beilis, even in America. After three Passovers in jail, he was acquitted. He left jail a Jewish celebrity, a Czarist-era Sharansky.

As the song says, every generation throws a hero up the pop charts: in 1913 it was Beilis. Sholom Aleichem wrote him letters: "My dear Mendel Beilis. You're going to get offers from all over the world, 'Come here. Go there.' Take time to think things over."

The Beilises—Raya is the youngest and last of five siblings—moved to Palestine. "We had terrible, miserable luck," she says. Mendel Beilis was famous, sure, but how, exactly, did running a brick factory and being tortured in jail qualify him for anything? "He never found steady work," says Raya. He barely learned Hebrew, and after moving to New York he barely learned English. "To be honest with you," says Raya, "he didn't do anything. He was sick." One of his sons committed suicide. "Jewish organizations said, 'Mendel Beilis, come to the United States and we will take care of you.' In New York, they put us up in the Trotsky Hotel. My father entered the dining room, people would stand and applaud." Every Jewish hotel in New York, it seemed, invited the Beilis family—to do what? "To do nothing," says Raya, "just sit. And the guests would say, 'You know who's here? Mendel Beilis!' I don't have to tell you about the Jews, how they carried on."

Jewish landlords let Mendel Beilis live rent-free. The Hunts Point apartment "was full of visitors," says Raya. "When I saw the crowds I'd run out; I didn't want to hear about [the blood libel] every minute. After a while my father would say, 'My dear Jewish people, you put such a big monument on top of me, I'll never get out of my grave!'" Raya simply wanted her father. She remembers touching his clean cheeks, circling around his mustache. She shares his down-turned mouth.

A Jewish banker paid him just to sit in the bank. Businessmen recruited him to sell insurance to other Jews. Wise guys took advantage, says Raya. Jews would yell at him: "Vat, you dink dat you're Mendel Beilis, you can overcharge?" Beilis backed down. He dropped dead in a Saratoga hotel on the Fourth of July, 1934.

Even in death, he was sought after. Raya remembers a millionaire paying for the funeral so the philanthropist could someday share a Queens cemetery with the great Mendel Beilis.

Raya lived alone in the Bronx, never to marry. When March turns to April, the matzah stirs memory of her private Egypt, the years of childhood seders while her father was in jail for a matzah he never made. She'll have seders this year in the lunch club on East Tremont.

"I don't know what I'd do if I didn't have such a seder. Really, to just sit alone in a room and eat matzah?"

They say the neighborhood has changed, and it has: It exemplifies redemption. With no incentive other than a mitzvah, a Jewish group subsidizes her daily meals and makes arrangements for a rabbi to lead the East Tremont seder. Raya once feared "goyim" but now they, too, sustain her: A black man brings glatt kosher chickens and matzah to her seder. A black woman keeps the lunch club going. The police in America stop by to make sure all is well. The non-Jewish Guardian Angels group will send a squad to walk her home in peace.

On seder night, when she opens the doors of 236 East Tremont, is not Elijah there as surely as in Jerusalem?

As Father Jacob said when he awoke from a dream: "Surely, God was in this place—and I, I did not know. . . . This is none other than the house of God and this is the gate of Heaven."

NEWS ABOUT JEWS

William Safire

JEWISHNESS IN AMERICA is not a growth industry.

Fifty years ago, there were about five million Jews in the U.S. Today there are a half million more, about a 10 percent increase—while the total U.S. population has doubled, from the postwar 130 million to today's 260 million. That means the percentage of Jews in America has declined from nearly 4 percent to 2.3 percent.

The phenomenon is not local. Despite the world population explosion, the number of Jews in the world since the end of the Holocaust has remained fairly constant at 13 million. In New York City, not just the proportion but the actual number of Jews has declined by a third; the same in Britain.

The near-halving of the Jewish percentage means that this minority is steadily becoming more of a minority. What's causing it? Should Jews worry about the trend? If so, what can be done to stop the drop?

These questions are triggered by Jonathan Rabinovitz's fine story in the *New York Times* about the decision of an editor of a Jewish weekly newspaper in West Hartford, Conn., not to print announcements of interfaith marriages.

The editor of *The Jewish Ledger* wants to express his concern about Jews marrying outside the faith, a practice that has gone from one in ten marriages 50 years ago to one in two today. His refusal to treat such marriages as a cause for celebration was met with pained and irate reactions from many happily intermarried couples in that community.

The controversy goes to the heart of the matter of Jewish dwindling. A low birth rate is a factor; so is the welcome lowering of anti-Semitic barriers and the sense that Israel is less in danger. But a primary cause of the percentage decline is the inclination of half the nubile generation to marry non-Jews. Because only 1 in 20 of these partners becomes Jewish, and (estimates get fuzzy here) less than half of their offspring are raised to be Jews, the Jewish presence in the population drops.

Not every Jew worries about this. "We are not in competition with the Chinese," says Prof. Jacob Neusner, the most prolific and provocative Judaic scholar. This iconoclastic rabbi sees the quality of Jewish family life as central, and measures the survivability of the people less in ethnicity than in the distinctiveness that comes from the embrace of holiness in individual homes. I see how it works for Jack: his children find joy in their Jewishness, good guidance in the religion, and will marry and bring up observant Jews.

And a case can be made that "reverse ethnic assimilation" is taking place. Yiddishisms enliven the English language (a State Department official on pins and needles reports that "this place is on *spilkes*") and in the American cuisine, the consumption of bagels has now passed that of doughnuts, as ethnic distinctiveness melts into the American pot.

Still, the numbers are troubling; a vibrant community should at least be holding its own.

The answer, I've begun to think, is not in editors making those who intermarry feel like outcasts, or in rabbis setting unenforceable conditions about children's upbringing before performing weddings. That negative strategy just does not work.

Instead, a positive way to preserve Jewish identity is to emphasize religious study, with greater understanding of its symbols and ritual. That's why the Reform movement is becoming more traditional, and why the Orthodox minority is gaining strength.

Religion differentiates people. Sometimes that's destructive (Bosnia, Ireland, the Middle East), but religion actively practiced by non-fanatics (1) provides a sense of tribal belonging that diversifies and transcends nationalism, (2) satisfies an inescapable spiritual longing, and (3) binds the family.

If the weakened family is the source of many of America's ills, the rise of religiosity among all faiths offers hope. Judaism is transmitted not by the nation or the tribe or the congregation but by the family.

Jewishness ain't chicken soup or Israeli politics or affection for guilt. Jewish identity is rooted in a distinctive old religion that builds individual character and group loyalty through close family life. That is how the Jewish people have survived through five millennia and is the light the Jews—whatever our number—must continue to offer the world.

GAY AND ORTHODOX

Steve Greenberg

I AM AN ORTHODOX RABBI AND I AM GAY. For a long while I denied, rejected, railed against this truth. The life story that I had wanted—wife, kids, and a family, a home of Torah and *hesed*—turned out to be an impossible fantasy. I have begun to shape a new life story. This essay is part of that life story, and thus remains unfinished, part of a stream of consciousness rather than a systematic treatise.

It is hard to say how or when I came to know myself as a gay man. In the beginning, it was just an array of bodily sensations. Sweaty palms, warm face, and that excited sort of nervousness in your chest that you get when in the company of certain people occurred without understanding. The arrival of the hormonal hurricane left me completely dumbfounded. Just when my body should have fulfilled social expectations, it began to transgress them. I had no physical response to girls. But I was physically pulled, eyes and body, toward guys. I remember my head turning sharply once in the locker room for an athletic boy whom I admired. At the time, I must have noticed my body's involuntary movement, but it meant nothing to me. I understood nothing. How could I? I had no idea what it meant to be homosexual. "Faggot" or "homo" were words reserved for the boys hounded for being passive, or unathletic. None of this said anything about sexual attraction. There are no categories for this experience, no way to explain the strange muscle spasms, the warm sensation on my face, or the flutter in my chest. Not until years later, after countless repetitions of such events, did it slowly, terrifyingly, breathe through to my consciousness.

When other boys were becoming enraptured by girls, I found my rapture in learning Torah. I was thrilled by the sprawling rabbinic arguments, the imaginative plays on words, and the demand for meaning everywhere. *Negiah,* the prohibition to embrace, kiss, or even touch girls until marriage was my saving grace. The premarital sexual restraint of the Halacha was a perfect mask not only to the world but to myself.

My years in yeshiva were spectacular, in some measure because they were so intensely fueled by a totally denied sexuality. There were many *bachurim* (students) in the yeshiva whose intense and passionate learning was energized with repressed sexual energy. For me, the environment deflected sexual energy and generated it as well. The male spirit and energy I felt in yeshiva was both nourishing and frustrating. I do not know if I was alone among my companions or not. From those early years, I remember no signs by which I could have clearly read my gayness or anyone else's. I only know that I was plagued with stomach aches almost every morning.

Later, on one desperate occasion, beset with an increased awareness of my attraction to a fellow yeshiva student, I visited a sage, Rav Eliashuv, who lives in one of the most secluded right-wing Orthodox communities in Jerusalem. He was old and in failing health, but still taking visitors who daily waited in an anteroom for hours for the privilege of speaking with him for a few minutes. Speaking in Hebrew, I told him what, at the time, I felt was the truth. "Master, I am attracted to both men and women. What shall I do?" He responded, "My dear one, then you have twice the power of love. Use it carefully." I was stunned. I sat in silence for a moment, waiting for more. "Is that all?" I asked. He smiled and said, "That is all. There is nothing more to say."

Rav Eliashuv's words calmed me, permitting me to forget temporarily the awful tensions that would eventually overtake me. His trust and support buoyed me above my fears. I thought that as a bisexual I could have a wider and richer emotional life and perhaps even a deeper spiritual life than is common—and still marry and have a family.

For a long while I felt a self-acceptance that carried me confidently into rabbinical school. I began rabbinical training with great excitement and a sense of promise. At the center of my motivations were those powerful rabbinic traditions that had bowled me over in my early adolescence. I wanted more than anything else to learn and to teach Torah in its full depth and breadth. I finished rabbinical school, still dating and carefully avoiding any physical expression and took my first jobs as a rabbi. There were many failed relationships with wonderful women who could not understand why things just didn't work out. Only after knocking my shins countless times into the hard wood of this truth was I able fully to acknowledge that I am gay.

It has taken a number of years to sift through the wreckage of "my life as I wanted it" to discover "my life as it is." It has taken more time to exorcise the self-hatred that feeds on shattered hopes and ugly stereotypes. I am still engaged in that struggle. I have yet to receive the new tablets, the whole ones, that will take their place in the Ark beside the broken ones. Rav Nachman of Bratzlav teaches that there is nothing so whole as a broken heart. It is in his spirit that I continue to try to make sense of my life.

Although much has changed in the past few years as I have accepted my gayness, much remains the same. I am still a rabbi, and I am still deeply committed to God, Torah, and Israel. My religious life had always been directed by the desire to be a servant of the Lord. None of that has changed. The question is an old one, merely posed anew as I strive to integrate being gay into my life. Given that I am gay, what is it that the God of Israel wants of me?

Of course, many will hear this as an illegitimate question—fallacious in thinking that the God of Israel can somehow accept and move beyond my gayness. Leviticus 18:23 instructs: "Do not lie with a male as one lies with a woman, it is an abhorrence." I do not propose to reject this or any text. For the present, I have no plausible halachic method of interpreting this text in a manner that permits homosexual sex.

As a traditionalist, I hesitate to overturn cultural norms in a flurry of revolutionary zeal. I am committed to a slower and more cautious process of change, which must always begin internally. Halacha, the translation of sacred text into norm, as an activity, is not designed to effect social revolution. It is a society-building enterprise that maintains internal balance by reorganizing itself in response to changing social realities. When social conditions shift, we experience the halachic reapplication as the proper commitment to the Torah's original purposes. That shift in social consciousness in regard to homosexuality is a long way off.

If I have any argument, it is not to press for a resolution, but for a deeper understanding of homosexuality. Within the living Halacha are voices in tension, divergent strands in an imaginative legal tradition that are brought to bear on the real lives of Jews. In order to know how to shape a halachic response to any living question, what is most demanded of us is a deep understanding of the Torah and an attentive ear to the people who struggle with the living question. Confronting new questions can often tease out of the tradition a *hiddush*, a new balancing of the voices and values that have always been there. There is no conclusive *psak halacha* (legal ruling) without the hearing of personal testimonies, and so far, gay people have not been asked to testify to their experience. How can halachists possibly rule responsibly on a matter so complex and so deeply foreign, without a sustained effort at understanding? Whatever the halachic argument will be, we will need to know much more about homosexuality to ensure that people are treated not merely as alien objects of a system but as persons within it. Halachists will need to include in their deliberations the testimony of gay people who wish to remain faithful to the Torah. Unimagined strategies, I believe, will appear under different conditions. We cannot know in advance the outcome of such an investigation. Still, one wonders what the impact might be if Orthodox rabbis had to face the questions posed by traditional Jews, persons they respect and to whom they feel responsible, who are gay.

There is one quasi-halachic issue I must address—that of choice. One of the mitigating factors in halachic discourse is the presence of free will in matters of law. A command is only meaningful in the context of our freedom to obey or disobey. Thus the degree of choice involved in homosexuality is central to the shaping of a halachic response. There is indeed a certain percentage of gay people who claim to exercise some volition in their sexual choices. But for the vast majority of gay people, there is no "choice" in the ordinary sense of the word. Gay feelings are hardwired into our bodies, minds, and hearts. The strangeness and mystery of sexuality is universal. What we share, gay or straight, is the surprising "queerness" of all sexual desire. The experience of heterosexuals may seem less outlandish for its being more common, but all sexual feeling is deeply mysterious, beyond explanation or a simple notion of choice.

The Halacha addresses activities, however, not sexual identities; thus, in halachic Judaism there is no such thing as a gay identity—there are only sexual impulses to control. The tradition describes all sexual desire as *yetzer ha'ra* (evil impulse), rife with chaotic and destructive possibilities. Heterosexual desire is redeemed and integrated back into the system through a series of prescriptions and prohibitions that channel sexuality and limit its range of expression. Confined within marriage, giving and receiving sexual pleasure, even in non-procreative ways, is raised to the level of mitzvah.

Homosexual desire, in contrast, is not seen as redeemable and thus remains in implacable *yetzer ha'ra* that needs to be defeated rather than channeled. In this argument, gay people are treated as people with a dangerous and destructive sexual desire which must be repressed. The spiritual task of a gay person is to overcome that *yetzer ha'ra* which prods one to have erotic relations with members of the same sex.

The unfairness of this argument begins with the recasting of homosexuals as heterosexuals with perverse desires. The Torah is employed to support the idea that there is only one sexuality, heterosexuality. God confirms heterosexual desire, giving heterosexuals the opportunity to enjoy love and companionship. With the impossibility of another sexuality comes the implicit assumption that gay people can "become" straight and marry and indeed should do so.

This has in fact been the ordinary state of affairs of many, if not most, gay men and women throughout history. I know a number of gay (or bisexual) men who have married and sustain relationships with their wives. Of course, most have had an affair at some point which did not end their marriage. Two gay rabbis I know were married and are now divorced, and a third remains happily married, surviving recurrent bouts of depression and emotional exhaustion. What disturbs me most in this sometimes heroic attempt at approximating the traditional ideal is the cost to the heterosexual spouse. While in my first rabbinical post, I decided to come out to an older rabbi and seek his advice. He counseled me to find a woman and marry. I asked him if I was duty-bound to tell her about my attractions to men and my general sexual disinterest in women. He said no. I was shocked to hear that it was all right to deceive a woman who could very easily be damaged by such a marriage. It made no sense to me. Surely some heterosexual women might be willing to marry a gay friend who could provide children and be a wonderful father. There have been rare instances of gay women and men who have worked out marriages where the "disinterest" was mutual. I struggled for a number of years to find such a woman, gay or straight, with whom to begin a family. Sometimes I still torment myself to think that this is all possible—when it is not. I still feel ripped apart by these feelings—wanting a woman at the Shabbat table and a man in my bed. If I am judged for some failure, perhaps it will be that I could not choose the Shabbat table over the bed, either for myself, or for the forlorn woman, who, after dinner wants the comfort of a man who wants her back.

Having rejected this option, the standard Orthodox position is to require celibacy. Many recent articles and responses regard gay sex as indistinguishable from adultery, incest, or bestiality. The heterosexual is asked to limit sexuality to the marital bed, to non-relatives, to human beings; the homosexual is asked to live a loveless life. I have lived portions of my adult life as a celibate clergyman. While it can have spiritual potency for a Moses or a Ben Azzai, who abandoned sexual life for God or Torah, it is not a Jewish way to live. Always sleeping alone, in a cold bed, without touch, without the daily physical interplay of lives morning and night— this celibate scenario is life-denying and, for me, has always led to a shrinking of spirit. What sort of Torah, what voice of God would demand celibacy from all gay people? Such a reading of divine intent is nothing short of cruel.

Many gay people now and in the past have been forced to purchase social acceptance and God's love through a denial of affection and comfort, and, worse, a denial of self. Today many simply leave Judaism behind in order to salvage a sense of dignity and to build a life. This understanding of homosexuality provides no legitimized wholesome context for sexuality; no *kedusha* and no *kedushin*.

I have come to understand my gayness as akin to my Jewishness: It is integral to my sense of self. Others may misunderstand and even wish me harm, but from myself I cannot hide. I did not choose it, and yet now that it is mine, I do. It is neither a mental illness nor a moral failing, but a contour of my soul. To deny it would be self-defeating. There is nothing left to do but celebrate it. Whether in or out of the given halachic rubric, I affirm my desire for a full life, and for sexual expression. Given that I am gay, and cannot be otherwise, and given that I do not believe that God would demand that I remain loveless and celibate, I have chosen to seek a committed love, a man with whom to share my life.

But so little of life is carried on in the bedroom. When I indeed find a partner, what sort of life do we build together? What is it that the God of Israel wants of me in regard to family and community? Struggling with God and with Torah as a gay person was just the beginning. To be Jewish is to be grounded in the continuity of the Jewish people as a witness—a holy people, a light amongst the nations—a blessing to all the families of the earth. How does a gay person help to shape the continuity of the Jewish people? The carrying forth of the Jewish people is accomplished by marriage and procreation. It is both a tool of the Abrahamic covenant and its most profound meaning statement.

We are a people on the side of life—new life, more life, fuller life. The creation story invited the rabbis to read God's blessing of "be fruitful and multiply" as a command to have two children, a male and a female. Every Jewish child makes the possibility of the Torah's promise of a perfected world more real, more attainable. Abraham and Sarah transmit the vision by having children. Often the portrayal of blessing includes being surrounded with many children. Childlessness is a punishment and curse in the tradition, barrenness a calamity.

Gay life does not prevent the possibility of producing or raising Jewish children, but it makes those options very complicated. Being gay means that the ordinary relationship between making love and having children is severed. There is a deep challenge to the structure of Judaism, since its very transmission is dependent on both relationship and reproduction.

For Jews who feel bound by mitzvot, bound by the duty to ensure that life conquers death, the infertility of our loving is at the core of our struggle to understand ourselves in the light of the Torah.

This problem, among others, lies at the root of much of the Jewish community's discomfort with gay people. To a people that was nearly destroyed fifty years ago, gay love seems irresponsible. Jews see the work of their lives in light of the shaping of a world for their children. By contrast, gay people appear narcissistic and self-indulgent. Gay people's sexuality is thus a diversion from the tasks of Jewish family and the survival that it symbolizes, and is perceived as marginal to the Jewish community because we are shirkers of this most central and sacred of communal tasks.

This challenge also has a moral chord which strikes deep into the problems of gay subculture. The tradition understood parenting as one of the major moral crucibles for human development. No judge could serve without first being a parent for fear that without the experience of parenting one could grasp neither human vulnerability nor responsibility. Being heterosexual carries one down a path that demands years of selfless loving in the rearing of children. While not all straight couples have children, and some gay couples become surrogate or adoptive parents, the norm is shaped less by choice and more by biology. Given that gay people do not fall into childbearing as an ordinary outcome of coupling, how do we find our place in the covenant? And what of the moral training that caring for children provides, how do we make up for that? Is there another job to be done that requires our service to God and to the Jewish people? Of all the problems entailed in gay sexuality, this one looms for me, both spiritually and emotionally.

Although there is no obvious biblical resource for this dilemma, there are biblical writers who struggled to address God's will in very new sexual circumstances. Isaiah was one such writer who bridged the worlds before and after the Exile. Some familiar passages have become charged for me with new meaning. In these verses, Isaiah is speaking to his ancient Israelite community and trying to convince them that God's covenantal plan for Israel is larger than they think. The covenant begins with Abraham and Sarah but has become much more than a family affair. He speaks to two obvious outsider groups in chapter 56, the *b'nai ha'nechar,* the foreigners of non-Israelite birth, and the *sarssim,* the eunuchs:

> Let not the foreigner say,
> Who has attached himself to the Lord,
> "The Lord will keep me separate from His people";

And let not the eunuch say,
"I am a withered tree."

In the Talmud, a eunuch is not necessarily a castrated male, but a male who is not going to reproduce for various reasons. Why does Isaiah turn his attention here to the foreigners and the eunuchs? In the chain of the covenantal family, the foreigner has no past and the eunuch no future. They both seem excluded from the covenantal frame of reference. It is this "exclusion" that the prophet addresses:

For thus said the Lord:
"As for the eunuchs who keep my sabbaths,
Who have chosen what I desire
And hold fast to My covenant—
I will give them, in My House
And within my walls,
A monument and a name
Better than sons or daughters.
I will give them an everlasting name
Which shall not perish."

The prophet comforts the pain of eunuchs with the claim that there are other ways in which to observe, fulfill, and sustain the covenant. There is something more permanent than the continuity of children. In God's House, the achievement of each individual soul has account. A name in the Bible is the path toward the essence, the heart of being. It is passed on to progeny. But there is another sort of a name, a name better than the one sons or daughters carry. The covenant is carried forward by those who live it out, in the present. Loyalty to the covenant is measured in God's House in such a way that even if one's name is not passed on through children, an eternal name will nonetheless be etched into the walls. Isaiah offers a place to the placeless, an alternative service to the person who cannot be part of the family in other ways:

As for foreigners
Who attach themselves to the Lord,
to be His servants—
All who keep the sabbath and do not profane it,
And who hold fast to my covenant—
I will bring them to my sacred mount

And let them rejoice in my house of prayer.
Their burnt offerings and sacrifices
Shall be welcome on My altar;
For My House shall be called
A House of prayer for all peoples.
Thus declares the Lord God, Who gathers the dispersed of Israel
I will gather still more to those already gathered.

So inclusive is God's plan for Israel in the world that any foreigner can join. The notion of conversion, so obvious to us now, was a striking innovation for the generation of Isaiah. Conversion is about rewriting the past. Like adoption, conversion redefines the meaning of parents and family. Birth and lineage are not discarded. The central metaphor for Israel is still family. But Isaiah and later tradition open up another avenue into the covenant. Those with no future are promised a future in the House of the Lord; those with no past are nevertheless included in Israel's destiny.

God can only require the doable. A foreigner cannot choose a different birth, or the eunuch a different procreative possibility. Gay people cannot be asked to be straight, but they can be asked to "hold fast to the covenant." God will work the story out and link the loose ends as long as we hold fast to the covenant.

Holding fast to the covenant demands that I fulfill the *mitzvot* that are in my power to fulfill. I cannot marry and bear children, but there are other ways to build a family. Surrogacy and adoption are options. I have a number of friends, gay and lesbian, who have found ways to build wonderfully loving families. If these prove infeasible, the tradition considers a teacher similar to a parent in life-giving and thus frames a way that the *mitzvah* of procreation can be symbolically fulfilled.

A special obligation may fall upon those who do not have children to attend charitably to the needs and the protection of children in distress. However, childlessness offers more than a call to activism and philanthropy in the defense of children. It can be received as way to live with unusually open doors. I have always felt that the open tent of Sarah and Abraham was loving and generous in the extreme because they were for the bulk of their lives, childless. With no children upon whom to focus their affection, the parents par excellence of the covenant spent lifetimes parenting other people's grown children.

Holding fast to the covenant demands that I seek a path towards sanctity in gay sexual life. The Torah has much to say about the way people create *kedusha* in their sexual relationships. The values of marriage, monogamy, modesty, and faithfulness which are central to the tradition's view of holiness need to be applied in ways that shape choices and life styles.

Holding fast to the covenant means that being gay does not free one from the fulfillment of mitzvot. The complexities generated by a verse in Leviticus need not unravel my commitment to the whole of the Torah. There are myriad Jewish concerns, moral, social, intellectual, and spiritual, that I cannot abandon. Being gay need not overwhelm the rest of Jewish life. Single-issue communities are political rather than religious. Religious communities tend to be comprehensive of the human condition. The richness of Jewish living derives in part from its diversity of attention, its fullness.

For gay Orthodox Jews, this imagination of engagement between ourselves and the tradition is both terribly exciting and depressing. Regretfully, the communities that embrace us, both gay and Jewish, also reject us. The Jewish community wishes that we remain invisible. The gay community is largely unsympathetic and often hostile to Judaism. There are some in the gay community who portray Judaism as the original cultural source of homophobia. More often, the lack of sympathy toward Jewish observance derives from the single-mindedness of gay activism. Liberation communities rarely have room for competing loyalties.

Gay synagogues have filled a void for many, providing a place of dignity in a Jewish community. This work is part of a movement toward a fuller integration in the larger Jewish community for which most gay Jews long. Gay-friendly synagogues may well point the way, modeling a community of families and singles, young and old, straight and gay that is in spirit much closer to my hopeful future imagination than anything yet.

Gay Jews who wish to be part of an Orthodox community will find very few synagogues in which there is some level of understanding and tolerance. Some gay Jews attend Orthodox services and remain closeted in their communities. It is crucial that Orthodox rabbis express a loving acceptance for known gays in their synagogues even if public legitimation is not now impossible. Attacks on homosexuality from the pulpit are particularly painful to those who have remained connected to the traditional synagogue, despite the hardships.

For the present, in regard to sexual behavior, I personally have chosen to accept a certain risk and violate the Halacha as it is presently articulated, in the hope of a subsequent, more accepting halachic expression. I realize that this is "civil disobedience." It is not the system itself which I challenge but its application to an issue that has particular meaning for me and for those like me. There is always the possibility that I am wrong. Ultimately, the halachic risks that I take are rooted in my personal relationship with

God, Who I will face in the end. It is this faith that makes me both confident and suspicious of myself.

I have, admittedly, a rather privatized form of community. I am closeted and have chosen to write this essay in anonymity to preserve what is still most precious to me: the teaching of Torah and caring for my community of Jews. What concerns me most is neither rejection by the Orthodox community, nor the loss of my particular pulpit. Were I to come out, I suspect that the controversy would collapse my life, my commitments, my identity as a teacher of Torah, into my gayness. Still, the secrecy and the shadowy existence of the closet are morally repugnant and emotionally draining. I cannot remain forever in darkness. I thank God that for the time being, the Torah still sheds ample light.

I have a small circle of friends, gay and straight, men and women with whom I share a sense of community. We are looking for other tradition-centered Jews who can help build a place that embraces both the Torah and gay people. Not a synagogue, not a building, but a place for all the dispersed who are in search of community with Israel and communion with God. In this place, this House of the Lord, now somewhat hypothetical and private, and soon, I pray, to be concrete and public, those of us who have withered in the darkness, or in the light of day have been banished, will discover our names etched upon the walls.

Postscript

I wrote "Gayness and God" only four years ago, and while it may appear insignificant to those who live in more open societies, much has changed in the Orthodox world in that short span of time. Four years ago the closet was darker and the door shut tighter for most traditional Jews. Social attitudes in the Orthodox community toward homosexuality have moved in two opposing directions due to the greater social acceptance in the larger society. The most important change is that in the past four years the topic has been raised repeatedly in articles, conferences, and newsletters. In short, as homosexuality, as an issue, has come out of the closet, things are worse and better.

Anti-homosexual rhetoric in the Orthodox community has become more shrill over the last few years, with various leaders and writers using gay liberation as a symbol of social and familial disintegration and expressing shock and horror at Reform Judaism for its acceptance of gay commitment ceremonies and gay rabbis. But the effect of the rhetoric has often been to the advantage of those pressing for gay inclusion. A gay and lesbian student organization established by a few graduate students in a professional school associated with Yeshiva University drew public outrage from religious authorities, university students, and community members. The president of the university, Norman Lamm, chose to put the issue to bed by claiming that public funds necessary for the university depended upon a liberal policy in regard to student associations. The public debate has invited Orthodox rabbis to speak from the pulpit on the issue, mostly in unaccepting ways, and be confronted later by parents of gay children and by gay Jews themselves who take the opportunity to come out to their rabbis.

Gay traditional Jews have not come out en masse, but they have begun in larger numbers to make themselves present to each other. Today there is a Gay and Lesbian Yeshiva Day School Alumni group that meets monthly in New York City, has a membership of nearly a hundred people, and even has a web site. Until recently, it was impossible to speak about AIDS prevention in the Orthodox community for fear that any talk was an incitement to promiscuous gay sex. Now there is an AIDS Hotline for Orthodox Jews which especially targets the Haredi neighborhoods of Brooklyn and Queens. Until recently it was common for Jewish hospital groups in religious communities to actively avoid visiting Jewish AIDS patients. Today there are Orthodox synagogues in Manhattan and Queens that have special *Bikkur Holim* groups that deliver meals and visit Jewish AIDS patients.

Fifteen years ago the boundary issue was feminism. Orthodoxy surely constructed its difference in a number of ways, but anti-feminism was a difference that proved evocative both theoretically and pragmatically for its constituents. Until the line was drawn openly, it could not be contested. Once the conversations about women's roles were engaged, everyone was led into consideration and dialogue. This past February one thousand people gathered for a conference on Orthodoxy and Feminism. It used to be an oxymoron to say that one is an Orthodox feminist. It no longer is. Today the line in the sand for many, the boundary case that distinguishes the halachic Jew from the rest, is homosexuality. While the issues are potentially more explosive and the concerned parties much less numerically significant, still engagement begins a conversation. Public formulation actually works to problematize the issues and raise to consciousness the human concerns that expand the possibilities.

After I wrote "Gayness and God" in *Tikkun* magazine I received many letters, mostly from Orthodox or once Orthodox gay men and lesbians grateful for the attempt to make sense of their experience. I met Jews who had been self-accepting homosexuals in their college years and in their thirties were turning toward observance and Torah study as much deeper resources of humanity and identity than those which they had found elsewhere. I received letters from a number of Orthodox rabbis, all but one sincerely engaging if not supportive. I was showered with support from family and friends.

Recently, one Orthodox rabbi was asked by a group of young leaders about his stance on homosexuality. In the public forum he said that only a few years before he knew exactly what he thought about homosexuality and would easily articulate his halachic position. He now admits that he is humble before a profound human dilemma and prefers less rhetoric and more understanding. He doesn't know what he thinks, nor is he quite sure what to say, and that is how he responds when asked.

It takes great faith to stand at the threshold of another human being and really listen. It takes great courage to do so before a person whose inner life is terribly alien, whose experience touches dark fears, or whose commitments seem to shape a threatening ideological frame to thousands of years of tradition. It is much easier, safer, to have the procrustean bed already made. It is true that in most settings those beds are ready made with all the proper arrangements for stretching our legs or cutting off our feet. Most Orthodox rabbis are not like my rabbi friends or the rabbi mentioned above.

Often over the past twenty years I have wanted to storm the heavens, to demand of God an explanation, a reconciliation, a response. In the language of Judith Plaskow, I am standing again at Sinai, insisting to be heard and to hear anew. One of my dearest colleagues is an Orthodox rabbi schooled in black hat yeshivot and a psychologist. A few years ago he accosted me as we walked in New York City to a kosher diner. He told me that he'd had enough of my self-doubt and that he didn't even see how I could make do with mere self-acceptance. "You have no choice," he said, "but to celebrate your gayness." I began to cry on Thirty-seventh Street not knowing what had burst in me. Later I understood my response as surprise. For years my Orthodox compatriots, friends, and family had accompanied me to this Sinai not by the force of a rational argument or a textual proof but by having come to share my demand for sense, my longing for wholeness. I had just not thought to look behind me.

SLIPPING THE PUNCH

Philip Roth

HE STOPPED FIGHTING because of Steena. However mistaken he was about the ominous meaning hidden in her poem, he remained convinced that the mysterious forces that made their sexual ardor inexhaustible— that transformed them into lovers so unbridled that Steena, in a neophyte's distillation of self-marveling self-mockery, midwesternly labeled them "two mental cases"—would one day work to dissolve his story of himself right before her eyes. How this would happen he did not know, and how he could forestall it he did not know. But the boxing wasn't going to help. Once she found out about Silky Silk, questions would be raised that would inevitably lead her to stumble on the truth. She knew that he had a mother in East Orange who was a registered nurse and a regular churchgoer, that he had an older brother who'd begun teaching seventh and eighth grades in Asbury Park and a sister finishing up for her teaching certificate from Montclair State, and that once each month the Sunday in his Sullivan Street bed had to be cut short because Coleman was expected in East Orange for dinner. She knew that his father had been an optician—just that, an optician—and even that he'd come originally from Georgia. Coleman was scrupulous in seeing that she had no reason to doubt the truth of whatever she was told by him, and once he'd given up the boxing for good, he didn't even have to lie about that. He didn't lie to Steena about anything. All he did was to follow the instructions that Doc Chizner had given him the day they were driving up to West Point (and that already had gotten him through the navy): if nothing comes up, you don't bring it up.

His decision to invite her to East Orange for Sunday dinner, like all his other decisions now—even the decision at St. Nick's to silently say fuck you to Solly Tabak by taking out the other guy in the first round—was based on nobody's thinking but his own. It was close to two years since they'd met, Steena was twenty and he was twenty-four, and he could no longer envision himself walking down Eighth Street, let alone proceeding through life, without her. Her undriven, conventional daily demeanor in combination with the intensity of her weekend abandon—all of it subsumed by a physical incandescence, a girlish American flashbulb radiance that was practically voodooish in its power—had achieved a startling supremacy over a will as ruthlessly independent as Coleman's: she had not only severed him from boxing and the combative filial defiance encapsulated in being Silky Silk the undefeated welterweight pro, but had freed him from the desire for anyone else.

Yet he couldn't tell her he was colored. The words he heard himself having to speak were going to make everything sound worse than it was—make *him* sound worse than *he* was. And if he then left it to her to imagine his family, she was going to picture people wholly unlike what they were. Because she knew no Negroes, she would imagine the kind of Negroes she saw in the movies or knew from the radio or heard about in jokes. He realized by now that she was not prejudiced and that if only she were to meet Ernestine and Walt and his mother, she would recognize right off how conventional they were and how much they happened to have in common with the tiresome respectability she had herself been all too glad to leave behind in Fergus Falls. "Don't get me wrong—it's a lovely city," she hastened to tell him, "it's a beautiful city. It's unusual, Fergus Falls, because it has the Otter Tail Lake just to the east, and not far from our house it has the Otter Tail River. And it's, I suppose, a little more sophisticated than other towns out there that size, because it's just south and to the east of Fargo-Moorhead, which is the college town in that section of the country." Her father owned a hardware supply store and a small lumberyard. "An irrepressible, gigantic, amazing person, my father. Huge. Like a slab of ham. He drinks in one night an entire container of whatever alcohol you have around. I could never believe it. I still can't. He just keeps going. He gets a big gash in his calf muscle wrestling with a piece of machinery—he just leaves it there, he doesn't wash it. They tend to be like this, the Icelanders. Bulldozer types. What's interesting is his personality. Most astonishing person. My father in a conversation takes over the whole room. And he's not the only one. My Palsson grandparents, too. His father is that way. His *mother* is that way." "Icelanders.

I didn't even know you call them Icelanders. I didn't even know they were here. I don't know anything about Icelanders at all. When," Coleman asked, "did they come to Minnesota?" She shrugged and laughed. "Good question. I'm going to say after the dinosaurs. That's what it seems like." "And it's him you're escaping?" "I guess. Hard to be the daughter of that sort of feistiness. He kind of submerges you." "And your mother? He submerges her?" "That's the Danish side of the family. That's the Rasmussens. No, she's unsubmergeable. My mother's too practical to be submerged. The characteristics of her family—and I don't think it's peculiar to that family, I think Danes are this way, and they're not too different from Norwegians in this way either—they're interested in objects. *Objects.* Tablecloths. Dishes. Vases. They talk endlessly about how much each object costs. My mother's father is like this too, my grandfather Rasmussen. Her whole family. They don't have any dreams in them. They don't have any unreality. Everything is made up of objects and what they cost and how much you can get them for. She goes into people's houses and examines all the objects and knows where they got half of them and tells them where they could have got them for less. And clothing. Each object of clothing. Same thing. Practicality. A bare-boned practicality about the whole bunch of them. Thrifty. Extremely thrifty. Clean. Extremely clean. She'll notice, when I come home from school, if I have one bit of ink under one fingernail from filling a fountain pen. When she's having guests on a Saturday evening, she sets the table Friday night at about five o'clock. It's there, every glass, every piece of silver. And then she throws a light gossamer thing over it so it won't get dust specks on it. Everything organized perfectly. And a fantastically good cook if you don't like any spices or salt or pepper. Or taste of any kind. So that's my parents. I can't get to the bottom with her particularly. On anything. It's all surface. She's organizing everything and my father's disorganizing everything, and so I got to be eighteen and graduated high school and came here. Since if I'd gone up to Moorhead or North Dakota State, I'd still have to be living at home, I said the heck with college and came to New York. And so here I am. Steena."

That's how she explained who she was and where she came from and why she'd left. For him it was not going to be so simple. *Afterward,* he told himself. Afterward—that's when he could make his explanations and ask her to understand how he could not allow his prospects to be unjustly limited by so arbitrary a designation as race. If she was calm enough to hear him out, he was sure he could make her see why he had chosen to take the future into his own hands rather than to leave it to an unenlightened society to determine his fate—a society in which, more than eighty years after the Emancipation Proclamation, bigots happened to play too large a role to suit him. He would get her to see that far from there being anything wrong with his decision to identify himself as white, it was the most natural thing for someone with his outlook and temperament and skin color to have done. All he'd ever wanted, from earliest childhood on, was to be free: not black, not even white—just on his own and free. He meant to insult no one by his choice, nor was he trying to imitate anyone whom he took to be his superior, nor was he staging some sort of protest against his race or hers. He recognized that to conventional people for whom everything was ready-made and rigidly unalterable what he was doing would never look correct. But to dare to be nothing more than correct had never been his aim. The objective was for his fate to be determined not by the ignorant, hate-filled intentions of a hostile world but, to whatever degree humanly possible, by his own resolve. Why accept a life on any other terms?

This is what he would tell her. And wouldn't it all strike her as nonsense, like one big sales pitch of a pretentious lie? Unless she had first met his family—confronted head-on the fact that he was as much a Negro as they were, and that they were as unlike what she might imagine Negroes to be as he was—these words or any others would seem to her only another form of concealment. Until she sat down to dinner with Ernestine, Walt, and his mother, and they all took a turn over the course of a day at swapping reassuring banalities, whatever explanation he presented to her would sound like so much preening, self-glorifying, self-justifying baloney, high-flown, highfalutin talk whose falseness would shame him in her eyes no less than in his own. No, he couldn't speak this shit either. It was beneath him. If he wanted this girl for good, then it was boldness that was required now and not an elocutionary snow job, à la Clarence Silk.

In the week before the visit, though he didn't prepare anyone else, he readied himself in the same concentrated way he used to prepare mentally for a fight, and when they stepped off the train at the Brick Church Station that Sunday, he even summoned up the phrases that he always chanted semi-mystically in the seconds before the bell sounded: "The task, nothing but the task. At one with the task. Nothing else allowed in." Only then, at the bell, breaking from his corner—or here, starting up the porch stairs to the front door—did he add the ordinary Joe's call to arms: "Go to work."

The Silks had been in their one-family house since 1925, the year before Coleman was born. When they got there, the rest of the street was white, and the small frame house was sold to them by a couple who were mad at the people next door and so were determined to sell it to colored to spite them. But no one in the private houses ran because they'd moved in, and even if the Silks never socialized with their neighbors, everyone was agreeable on that stretch of street leading up toward the Episcopal rectory and church. Agreeable even though the rector, when he arrived some years earlier, had looked around, seen a fair number of Bajians and Barbadians, who were Church of England—many of them domestics working for East Orange's white rich, many of them island people who knew their place and sat at the back and thought they were accepted—leaned on his pulpit, and, before beginning the sermon on his first Sunday, said, "I see we have some colored families here. We'll have to do something about that." After consulting with the seminary in New York, he had seen to it that various services and Sunday schools for the colored were conducted, outside basic church law, in the colored families' houses. Later, the swimming pool at the high school was shut down by the school superintendent so that the white kids wouldn't have to swim with the colored kids. A big swimming pool, used for swimming classes and a swimming team, a part of the physical education program for years, but since there were objections from some of the white kids' parents who were employers of the black kids' parents—the ones working as maids and housemen and chauffeurs and gardeners and yardmen—the pool was drained and covered over.

Within the four square miles of this residential flyspeck of a Jersey town of not quite seventy thousand people, as throughout the country during Coleman's youth, there existed these rigid distinctions between classes and races sanctified by the church and legitimized by the schools. Yet on the Silks' own modest tree-lined side street ordinary people needed not to be quite so responsible to God and the state as those whose vocation it was to maintain a human community, swimming pool and all, untainted by the impurities, and so the neighbors were on the whole friendly with the ultra-respectable, light-skinned Silks—Negroes, to be sure, but, in the words of one tolerant mother of a kindergarten playmate of Coleman's, "people of a very pleasing shade, rather like eggnog"—even to the point of borrowing a tool or a ladder or helping to figure out what was wrong with the car when it wouldn't start. The big apartment house at the corner remained all white until after the war. Then, in late 1945, when colored people began coming in at the Orange end of the street—the families of professional men mainly, of teachers, doctors, and dentists—there was a moving van outside the apartment building every day, and half the white tenants disappeared within months. But things soon settled down, and, though the landlord of the apartment building began renting to colored just in order to keep the place going, the whites who remained in the immediate neighborhood stayed around until they had a reason other than Negrophobia to leave.

Go to work. And he rang the doorbell and pushed open the front door and called, "We're here."

Walt had been unable to make it up that day from Asbury Park but there, coming out of the kitchen and into the hallway, were his mother and Ernestine. And here, in their house, was his girl. She may or may not have been what they were expecting. Coleman's mother hadn't asked. Since he'd unilaterally made his decision to join the navy as a white man, she hardly dared ask him anything, for fear of what she might hear. She was prone now, outside the hospital—where she had at last become the first colored head floor nurse of a Newark hospital, and without help from Dr. Fensterman—to let Walt take charge of her life and of the family altogether. No, she hadn't asked anything about the girl, politely declined to know, and encouraged Ernestine not to inquire. Coleman, in turn, hadn't told anyone anything, and so, fair-complexioned as fair could be, and—with her matching blue handbag and pumps, in her cotton floral shirtwaist dress and her little white gloves and pillbox hat—as immaculately trim and correct as any girl alive and young in 1950, here was Steena Palsson, Iceland and Denmark's American progeny, of the bloodline going back to King Canute and beyond.

He had done it, got it his own way, and no one so much as flinched. Talk about the ability of the species to adapt. Nobody groped for words, nobody went silent, nor did anyone begin jabbering a mile a minute. Commonplaces, yes, cornballisms, you bet—generalities, truisms, clichés aplenty. Steena hadn't been raised along the banks of the Otter Tail River for nothing: if it was hackneyed, she knew how to say it. Chances were that if Coleman had gotten to blindfold the three women before introducing them and to keep them blindfolded throughout the day, their conversation would have no weightier a meaning than it had while they smilingly looked one another right in the eye. Nor would it have embodied an intention other than the standard one: namely, I won't say anything you can possibly take offense with if you won't say anything I can take offense with. Respectability at any cost—that's where the Palssons and the Silks were one.

The point at which all three got addled was, strangely enough, while discussing Steena's height. True, she was five eleven, nearly three full inches taller than Coleman and six inches taller than either his sister or his mother. But Coleman's father had been six one and Walt was an inch and a half taller than that, so tallness in and of itself was nothing new to the family, even if, with Steena and Coleman, it was the woman who happened to be taller than the man. Yet those three inches of Steena's—the distance, say, from her hairline to her eyebrows—caused a careening conversation about physical anomalies to veer precipitously close to disaster for some fifteen minutes before Coleman smelled something acrid and the women—the three of them—rushed for the kitchen to save the biscuits from going up in flames.

After that, throughout dinner and until it was time for the young couple to return to New York, it was all unflagging rectitude, externally a Sunday like every nice family's dream of total Sunday happiness and, consequently, strikingly in contrast with life, which, as experience had already taught even the youngest of these four, could not for half a minute running be purged of its inherent instability, let alone be beaten down into a predictable essence.

Not until the train carrying Coleman and Steena back to New York pulled into Pennsylvania Station early that evening did Steena break down in tears.

As far as he knew, until then she had been fast asleep with her head on his shoulder all the way from Jersey—virtually from the moment they had boarded at Brick Church Station sleeping off the exhaustion of the afternoon's effort at which she had so excelled.

"Steena—what is wrong?"

"I can't do it!" she cried, and, without another word of explanation, gasping, violently weeping, clutching her bag to her chest—and forgetting her hat, which was in his lap, where he'd been holding it while she slept—she raced alone from the train as though from an attacker and did not phone him or try ever to see him again.

It was four years later, in 1954, that they nearly collided outside Grand Central Station and stopped to take each other's hand and to talk just long enough to stir up the original wonder they'd awakened in each other at twenty-two and eighteen and then to walk on, crushed by the certainty that nothing as statistically spectacular as this chance meeting could possibly happen again. He was married by then, an expectant father, in the city for the day from his job as a classics instructor at Adelphi, and she was working in an ad agency down the street on Lexington Avenue, still single, still pretty, but womanly now, very much a smartly dressed New Yorker and clearly someone with whom the trip to East Orange might have ended on a different note if only it had taken place further down the line.

The way it might have ended—the conclusion against which reality had decisively voted—was all he could think about. Stunned by how little he'd gotten over her and she'd gotten over him, he walked away understanding, as outside his reading in classical Greek drama he'd never had to understand before, how easily life can be one thing rather than another and how accidentally a destiny is made . . . on the other hand, how accidental fate may seem when things can never turn out other than they do. That is, he walked away understanding nothing, knowing he could understand nothing, though with the illusion that he *would* have metaphysically understood something of enormous importance about this stubborn determination of his or become his own man if . . . if only such things were understandable.

The charming two-page letter she sent the next week, care of the college, about how incredibly good he'd been at "swooping" their first time together in his Sullivan Street room—"swooping, almost like birds do when they fly over land or sea and spy something moving, something bursting with life, and dive down . . . and seize upon it"—began, "Dear Coleman, I was very happy to see you in New York. Brief as our meeting was, after I saw you I felt an autumnal sadness, perhaps because the six years since we first met make it wrenchingly obvious how many days of my life are 'over.' You look very good, and I'm glad you're happy . . ." and ended in a languid, floating finale of seven little sentences and a wistful closing that after numerous rereadings, he took as the measure of her regret for *her* loss, a veiled admission of remorse as well, poignantly signaling to him a subaudible apology: "Well, that's it. That's enough. I shouldn't even bother you. I promise I won't ever again. Take care. Take care. Take care. Very fondly, Steena."

He never threw the letter away, and when he happened upon it in his files and, in the midst of whatever else he was doing, paused to look it over—having otherwise forgotten it for some five or six years—he thought what he thought out on the street that day after lightly kissing her cheek and saying goodbye to Steena forever: that had she married him—as he'd wanted her to—she would have known everything—as he had wanted her to—and what followed with his family, with hers, with their own children, would have been different from what it was with Iris. What happened with his mother and Walt could as easily never have occurred. Had Steena said fine, he would have lived another life.

I can't do it. There was wisdom in that, an awful lot of wisdom for a young girl, not the kind one ordinarily has at only twenty. But that's why he'd fallen for her—because she had the wisdom that is solid, thinking-for-yourself common sense. If she hadn't . . . but if she hadn't, she wouldn't have been Steena, and he wouldn't have wanted her as a wife.

He thought the same useless thoughts—useless to a man of no great talent like himself, if not to Sophocles: how accidentally a fate is made . . . or how accidental it all may seem when it is inescapable.

As she first portrayed herself and her origins to Coleman, Iris Gittelman had grown up willful, clever, furtively rebellious—secretly plotting, from the second grade on, how to escape her oppressive surroundings—in a Passaic household rumbling with hatred for every form of social oppression, particularly the authority of the rabbis and their impinging lies. Her Yiddish-speaking father, as she characterized him, was such a thoroughgoing hereti-cal anarchist that he hadn't even had Iris's two older brothers circumcised, nor had her parents bothered to acquire a marriage license or to submit to a civil ceremony. They considered themselves husband and wife, claimed to be American, even called themselves Jews, these two uneducated immi-grant atheists who spat on the ground when a rabbi walked by. But they called themselves what they called themselves freely, without asking per-mission or seeking approval from what her father contemptuously de-scribed as the hypocritical enemies of everything that was natural and good—namely, officialdom, those illegitimately holding the power. On the cracking, filth-caked wall over the soda fountain of the family candy store on Myrtle Avenue—a cluttered shop so small, she said, "you couldn't bury the five of us there side by side"—hung two framed pictures, one of Sacco, the other of Vanzetti, photographs torn from the rotogravure section of the newspaper. Every August 22—the anniversary of the day in 1927 when Massachusetts executed the two anarchists for murders Iris and her broth-ers were taught to believe neither man had committed—business was sus-pended and the family retreated upstairs to the tiny, dim apartment whose lunatic disorder exceeded even the store's, so as to observe a day of fast-ing. This was a ritual Iris's father had, like a cult leader, dreamed up all on his own, modeling it wackily on the Jewish Day of Atonement. Her father had no real ideas about what he thought of as ideas—all that ran deep was desperate ignorance and the bitter hopelessness of dispossession, the im-potent revolutionary hatred. Everything was said with a clenched fist, and everything was a harangue. He knew the names Kropotkin and Bakunin, but nothing of their writings, and the anarchist Yiddish weekly *Freie Ar-beiter Stimme,* which he was always carrying around their apartment, he rarely read more than a few words of each night before dropping off to sleep. Her parents, she explained to Coleman—and all this dramatically, scandalously dramatically, in a Bleecker Street café minutes after he had picked her up in Washington Square—her parents were simple people in the grips of a pipe dream that they could not begin to articulate or ratio-nally defend but for which they were zealously willing to sacrifice friends, relatives, business, the good will of neighbors, even their own sanity, even their *children's* sanity. They knew only what they had nothing in common with, which to Iris, the older she got, appeared to be everything. Society as it was constituted—its forces all in constant motion, the intricate un-derwebbing of interests stretched to its limit, the battle for advantage that is ongoing, the subjugation that is ongoing, the factional collisions and col-lusions, the shrewd jargon of morality, the benign despot that is conven-tion, the unstable illusion of stability—society as it was made, always has been and *must* be made, was as foreign to them as was King Arthur's court to the Connecticut Yankee. And yet, this wasn't because they'd been bound by the strongest ties to some other time and place and then forcefully set down in a wholly alien world: they were more like people who'd stepped directly into adulthood from the cradle, having had no intervening education in how human beastliness is run and ruled. Iris could not decide, from the time she was a tot, whether she was being raised by crackpots or visionaries, or whether the passionate loathing she was meant to share was a revelation of the awful truth or utterly ridiculous and possibly insane.

All that afternoon she told Coleman folklorishly enchanting stories that made having survived growing up above the Passaic candy store as the daughter of such vividly benighted individualists as Morris and Ethel Gittelman appear to have been a grim adventure not so much out of Russian literature as out of the Russian funny papers, as though the Gittelmans had been the deranged next-door neighbors in a Sunday comic strip called "The Karamazov Kids." It was a strong, brilliant performance for a girl barely nineteen years old who had fled from Jersey across the Hudson— as who among his Village acquaintances wasn't fleeing, and from places as far away as Amarillo?—without any idea of being anything other than free, a new impoverished exotic on the Eighth Street stage, a theatrically big-featured, vivacious dark girl, emotionally a dynamic force and, in the parlance of the moment, "stacked," a student uptown at the Art Students League who partly earned her scholarship there modeling for the life drawing classes, someone whose style was to hide nothing and who appeared to have no more fear of creating a stir in a public place than a belly dancer. Her head of hair was something, a labyrinthine, billowing wreath of spirals and ringlets, fuzzy as twine and large enough for use as Christmas ornamentation. All the disquiet of her childhood seemed to have passed into the convolutions of her sinuous thicket of hair. Her irreversible hair. You could polish pots with it and no more alter its construction than if it were harvested from the inky depths of the sea, some kind of wiry reef-building organism, a dense living onyx hybrid of coral and shrub, perhaps possessing medicinal properties.

For three hours she held Coleman entranced by her comedy, her outrage, her hair, and by her flair for manufacturing excitement, by a frenzied, untrained adolescent intellect and an actressy ability to enkindle herself and believe her every exaggeration that made Coleman—a cunning self-concoction if ever there was one, a product on which no one but he held a patent—feel by comparison like somebody with no conception of himself at all.

But when he got her back to Sullivan Street that evening, everything changed. It turned out that she had no idea in the world who she was.

Once you'd made your way past the hair, all she was was molten. The antithesis of the arrow aimed at life who was twenty-five-year-old Coleman Silk—a self-freedom fighter too, but the agitated version, the *anarchist* version, of someone wanting to find her way.

It wouldn't have fazed her for five minutes to learn that he had been born and raised in a colored family and identified himself as a Negro nearly all his life, nor would she have been burdened in the slightest by keeping that secret for him if it was what he'd asked her to do. A tolerance for the unusual was not one of Iris Gittelman's deficiencies—unusual to her was what most conformed to the standards of legitimacy. To be two men instead of one? To be two colors instead of one? To walk the streets incognito or in disguise, to be neither this nor that but something in between? To be possessed of a double or a triple or a quadruple personality? To her there was nothing frightening about such seeming deformities. Iris's open-mindedness wasn't even a moral quality of the sort liberals and libertarians pride themselves on; it was more on the order of a mania, the cracked antithesis of bigotry. The expectations indispensable to most people, the assumption of meaning, the confidence in authority, the sanctification of coherence and order, struck her as nothing else in life did—as nonsensical, as totally nuts. Why would things happen as they do and history read as it does if inherent to existence was something called normalcy?

And yet, what he told Iris was that he was Jewish, Silk being an Ellis Island attenuation of Silberzweig, imposed on his father by a charitable customs official. He even bore the biblical mark of circumcision, as not many of his East Orange Negro friends did in that era. His mother, working as a nurse at a hospital staffed predominantly by Jewish doctors, was convinced by burgeoning medical opinion of the significant hygienic benefits of circumcision, and so the Silks had arranged for the rite that was traditional among Jews—and that was beginning, back then, to be elected as a postnatal surgical procedure by an increasing number of Gentile parents—to be performed by a doctor on each of their infant boys in the second week of life.

Coleman had been allowing that he was Jewish for several years now—or letting people think so if they chose to—since coming to realize that at NYU as in his café hangouts, many people he knew seemed to have been assuming he was a Jew all along. What he'd learned in the navy is that all you have to do is give a pretty good and consistent line about yourself and nobody ever inquires, because no one's that interested. His NYU and Village acquaintances could as easily have surmised—as buddies of his had in the service—that he was of Middle Eastern descent, but as this was a moment when Jewish self-infatuation was at a postwar pinnacle among the Washington Square intellectual avant-garde, when the aggrandizing appetite driving their Jewish mental audacity was beginning to look to be uncontrollable and an aura of cultural significance emanated as much from their jokes and their family anecdotes, from their laughter and their clowning and their wisecracks and their arguments—even from their insults— as from *Commentary, Midstream,* and the *Partisan Review,* who was he not to go along for the ride, especially as his high school years assisting Doc Chizner as a boxing instructor of Essex County Jewish kids made claiming a New Jersey Jewish boyhood not so laden with pitfalls as pretending to being a U.S. sailor with Syrian or Lebanese roots. Taking on the ersatz prestige of an aggressively thinking, self-analytic, irreverent American Jew reveling in the ironies of the marginal Manhattan existence turned out to be nothing like so reckless as it might have seemed had he spent years dreaming up and elaborating the disguise on his own, and yet, pleasurably enough, it felt spectacularly reckless—and when he remembered Dr. Fensterman, who'd offered his family three thousand dollars for Coleman to take a dive on his final exams so as to make brilliant Bert the class valedictorian, it struck him as spectacularly comical too, a colossal sui generis score-settling joke. What a great all-encompassing idea the world had had to turn him into this—what sublimely earthly mischief! If ever there was a perfect one-of-a-kind creation—and hadn't singularity been his inmost ego-driven ambition all along?—it was this magical convergence into his father's Fensterman son.

No longer was he playing at something. With Iris—the churned-up, untamed, wholly un-Steena-like, non-Jewish Jewish Iris—as the medium through which to make himself anew, he'd finally got it right. He was no longer trying on and casting off, endlessly practicing and preparing to be. This was it, the solution, the secret to his secret, flavored with just a drop of the ridiculous—the redeeming, reassuring ridiculous, life's little contribution to every human decision.

As a heretofore unknown amalgam of the most unalike of America's historic undesirables, he now made sense.

There was an interlude, however. After Steena and before Iris there was a five-month interlude named Ellie Magee, a petite, shapely colored girl, tawny-skinned, lightly freckled across the nose and cheeks, in appearance not quite over the dividing line between adolescence and womanhood, who worked at the Village Door Shop on Sixth Avenue, excitedly selling shelving units for books and selling doors—doors on legs for desks and doors on legs for beds. The tired old Jewish guy who owned the place said that hiring Ellie had increased his business by fifty percent. "I had nothing going here," he told Coleman. "Eking out a living. But now every guy in the

Village wants a door for a desk. People come in, they don't ask for me—they ask for Ellie. They call on the phone, they want to talk to Ellie. This little gal has changed everything." It was true, nobody could resist her, including Coleman, who was struck, first, by her legs up on high heels and then with all her naturalness. Goes out with white NYU guys who are drawn to her, goes out with colored NYU guys who are drawn to her—a sparkling twenty-three-year-old kid, as yet wounded by nothing, who has moved to the Village from Yonkers, where she grew up, and is living the unconventional life with a small *u*, the Village life as advertised. She is a find, and so Coleman goes in to buy a desk he doesn't need and that night takes her for a drink. After Steena and the shock of losing someone he'd so much wanted, he is having a good time again, he's alive again, and all this from the moment they start flirting in the store. Does she think he's a white guy in the store? He doesn't know. Interesting. Then that evening she laughs and, comically squinting at him, says, "What are you anyway?" Right out she spots something and goes ahead and says it. But now the sweat is not pouring off him as it did when he misread Steena's poem. "What am I? Play it any way you like," Coleman says. "Is that the way *you* play it?" she asks. "Of course that's the way I play it," he says. "So white girls think you're white?" "Whatever they think," he says, "I let them think." "And whatever I think?" Ellie asks. "Same deal," Coleman says. That's the little game they play, and that becomes the excitement for them, playing the ambiguity of it. He's not that close to anybody particularly, but the guys he knows from school think he's taking out a colored girl, and her friends all think she's going around with a white guy. There's some real fun in having other people find them important, and most everywhere they go, people do. It's 1951. Guys ask Coleman, "What's she like?" "Hot," he says, drawing the word out while floppily wiggling one hand the way the Italians did back in East Orange. There's a day-to-day, second-to-second kick in all this, a little movie-star magnitude to his life now: he's always in a scene when he's out with Ellie. Nobody on Eighth Street knows what the hell is going on, and he enjoys that. She's got the legs. She laughs all the time. She's a woman in a natural way—full of ease and a lively innocence that's enchanting to him. Something like Steena, except she's not white, with the result that they don't go rushing off to visit his family and they don't go visiting hers. Why should they? They live in the Village. Taking her to East Orange doesn't even occur to him. Maybe it's because he doesn't want to hear the sigh of relief, to be told, even wordlessly, that he's doing the right thing. He thinks about his motivation for bringing Steena home. To be honest with everyone? And what did that achieve? No, no families—not for now anyway.

Meanwhile, he so enjoys being with her that one night the truth just comes bubbling out. Even about his being a boxer, which he could never tell Steena. It's so easy to tell Ellie. That she's not disapproving gives her another boost up in his estimation. She's not conventional—and yet so sound. He is dealing with someone utterly unnarrow-minded. The splendid girl wants to hear it all. And so he talks, and without restraints he is an extraordinary talker, and Ellie is enthralled. He tells her about the navy. He tells her about his family, which turns out to be a family not much different from hers, except that her father, a pharmacist from a drugstore in Harlem, is living, and though he isn't happy about her having moved to the Village, fortunately for Ellie he can't stop himself from adoring her. Coleman tells her about Howard and how he couldn't stand the place. They talk a lot about Howard because that was where her parents had wanted her to go too. And always, whatever they're talking about, he finds he is effortlessly making her laugh. "I'd never seen so many colored people before, not even in south Jersey at the family reunion. Howard University looked to me like just too many Negroes in one place. Of all persuasions, of every stripe, but I just did not want to be around them like that. Did not at all see what it had to do with me. Everything there was just so concentrated that any sort of pride I ever had was diminished. Completely diminished by a concentrated, false environment." "Like a soda that's too sweet," Ellie said. "Well," he told her, "it's not so much that too much has been put in, it's that everything else has been taken out." Talking openly with Ellie, Coleman finds all his relief. True, he's not a hero anymore, but then he's not in anyway a villain either. Yes, she's a contender this one. Her transcendence into independence, her transformation into a Village girl, the way she handles her folks—she seems to have grown up the way you're supposed to be able to.

One evening she takes him around to a tiny Bleecker Street jewelry shop where the white guy who owns it makes beautiful things out of enamel. Just shopping the street, out looking, but when they leave she tells Coleman that the guy is black. "You're wrong, " Coleman tells her, "he can't be." "Don't tell me that I'm wrong"—she laughs—"*you're* blind." Another night, near midnight, she takes him to a bar on Hudson Street where painters congregate to drink. "See that one? The smoothie?" she says in a soft voice, inclining her head toward a good-looking white guy in his mid-twenties charming all the girls at the bar. "Him," she says. "*No*," says Coleman, who's the laughing one now. "You're in Greenwich Village, Coleman Silk, the four freest square miles in America. There's one on every other block. You're so vain, you thought you'd dreamed it up yourself." And if *she* knows of three—which she does, positively—there are ten, if not more.

"From all over everywhere," she says, "they make straight for Eighth Street. Just like you did from little East Orange." "And," he says, "I don't see it at all." And that too makes them laugh, laugh and laugh and laugh because he is hopeless and cannot see it in others and because Ellie is his guide, pointing them out.

In the beginning, he luxuriates in the solution to his problem. Losing the secret, he feels like a boy again. The boy he'd been before he had the secret. A kind of imp again. He gets from all her naturalness the pleasure and ease of being natural himself. If you're going to be a knight and a hero, you're armored. "You're a lucky man," Ellie's boss tells him. "A lucky man," he repeats, and means it. With Ellie the secret is no longer operative. It's not only that he can tell her everything and that he does, it's that if and when he wants to, he can now go home. He can deal with his brother, and the other way, he knows, he could never have. His mother and he can go on back and resume being as close and easygoing as they always were. And then he meets Iris, and that's it. It's been fun with Ellie, and it continues to be fun, but some dimension is missing. The whole thing lacks the ambition—it fails to feed that conception of himself that's been driving him all his life. Along comes Iris and he's back in the ring. His father had said to him, "Now you can retire undefeated. You're retired." But here he comes roaring out of his corner—he has the secret again. And the *gift* to be secretive again, which is hard to come by. Maybe there *are* a dozen more guys like him hanging around the Village. But not just everybody has that gift. That is, they have it, but in petty ways: they simply lie all the time. They're not secretive in the grand and elaborate way that Coleman is. He's back on the trajectory outward. He's got the elixir of the secret, and it's like being fluent in another language—it's being somewhere that is completely fresh to you. He's lived without it, it was fine, nothing horrible happened, it wasn't objectionable. It was fun. Innocent fun. But insufficiently everything else. Sure, he'd regained his innocence. Ellie gave him that all right. But what use is innocence? Iris gives more. She raises everything to another pitch. Iris gives him back his life on the scale he wants to live it.

THE NIGHT GAME

Robert Pinsky

Some of us believe
We would have conceived romantic
Love out of our own passions
With no precedents,
Without songs and poetry—
Or have invented poetry and music
As a comb of cells for the honey.

Shaped by ignorance,
A succession of new worlds,
Congruities improvised by
Immigrants or children.

I once thought most people were Italian,
Jewish or Colored.
To be white and called
Something like *Ed Ford*
Seemed aristocratic,
A rare distinction.

Possibly I believed only gentiles
And blonds could be left-handed.

Already famous
After one year in the majors,
Whitey Ford was drafted by the Army
To play ball in the flannels
Of the Signal Corps, stationed
In Long Branch, New Jersey.

A night game, the silver potion
Of the lights, his pink skin
Shining like a burn.
Never a player
I liked or hated: a Yankee,
A mere success.

But white the chalked-off lines
In the grass, white and green
The immaculate uniform,
And white the unpigmented
Halo of his hair
When he shifted his cap:

So ordinary and distinct,
So close up, that I felt
As if I could have made him up,
Imagined him as I imagined

The ball, a scintilla
High in the black backdrop
Of the sky. Tight red stitches.
Rawlings. The bleached

Horsehide white: the color
Of nothing. Color of the past
And of the future, of the movie screen
At rest and of blank paper.

"*I could have.*" The mind. The black
Backdrop, the white
Fly picked out by the towering
Lights. A few years later

On a blanket in the grass
By the same river
A girl and I came into
Being together
To the faint muttering
Of unthinkable
Troubadours and radios.

The emerald
Theater, the night.
Another time,
I devised a left-hander
Even more gifted
Than Whitey Ford: a Dodger.
People were amazed by him.
Once, when he was young,
He refused to pitch on Yom Kippur.

FROM THE ROOTS
OF A PUBLIC LIFE

Joseph I. Lieberman

LAST YEAR I ATTENDED the thirty-fifth reunion of my Yale college class. At this advanced age, we are apparently supposed to be thinking of transitions in our lives, so the organizers of the reunion asked Gail Sheehy, the author of *Passages,* a book about life's transitions, to speak to us. In preparation for her remarks, Sheehy interviewed several class members about the paths our lives had followed. During the course of our conversation she surprised me by asking, "How do you *relax?*"

And I surprised myself with my answer: "I observe the Sabbath." I went on to mention other things I like to do to relax. Exercise. Travel. Go to the movies when I can. Read, although I never have time to read as much as I'd like. But before anything else, the Sabbath was what came to my mind because that is when I truly rest and relax. I would probably begin to answer the question of how I got into politics through the same surprising portal of my faith because it has so much to do with the way I navigate through each day, personally and professionally. It has provided a foundation, order and purpose to my life.

I was raised in a religiously observant family, which gave me the clear answers of faith to life's most difficult questions. My parents and my rabbi, Joseph Ehrenkranz, taught me that our lives were a gift from God, the Creator, and with it came a covenantal obligation to serve God with gladness by living as best we could, according to the law and values that God gave Moses on Mount Sinai. The summary of our aspirations was in the

Hebrew phrase *tikkun olam,* which is translated "to improve the world," or, "to repair the world," or, more boldly, "to complete the Creation which God began." In any translation, this concept of *tikkun olam* presumes the inherent but unfulfilled goodness of people and requires action for the benefit of the community. It accepts our imperfections and concludes that we, as individuals and as a society, are constantly in the process of improving and becoming complete. Each of us has the opportunity and responsibility to advance that process both within ourselves and the wider world around us. As Rabbi Tarfon says in the Talmud, "The day is short and there is much work to be done. You are not required to complete the work yourself, but you cannot withdraw from it either." These beliefs were a powerful force in my upbringing, and seem even more profound and true to me today.

My faith was just one of many great gifts my father and mother, Henry and Marcia Lieberman, gave to me. They were extraordinarily supportive parents—and superior role models in living according to the principles of integrity, hard work and community service that they preached. I have a clear memory of my dad sitting behind the counter of his liquor store in Stamford, Connecticut, reading literature and philosophy between customers, as classical music drifted from the radio on the shelf behind him. He didn't go to college—he never had that chance—but he was as civilized, cultured and intellectually curious a man as I have ever known. He read the *New York Times* every day. We watched the news on television every night. Because of him, Edward R. Murrow and Walter Cronkite were presences in our family life, as they were in so many American households in the 1950s. In that sense there was an awareness of current events in our home. But our family—my mother, my father, my two sisters, Rietta and Ellen, and my grandmother, Minnie, whose home we all shared until I was eight—didn't sit around the dinner table each evening discussing and debating the news of the day. Politics came up now and then in our household, but it wasn't a focus.

My grandmother Minnie, who I called by the Yiddish Baba, was a very strong influence on my early life, in ways that still affect me today and that I now realize helped guide me into public life. Baba, my mother's mother, was a heroic figure to me. Born and raised in Central Europe, widowed with five children while she was in her thirties, Baba was a deeply religious woman and very resilient. She was my window to the Old World and my path to appreciating the New World. I could imagine the Old World through the stories she told me. Baba didn't come to America until she was married and a mother. Before that, she spent her life in a European village where Jews were not, to say the least, always treated kindly.

To move from such a place to a small American city where, as she walked to synagogue on a Saturday, her Christian neighbors would pass and say respectfully, "Good Sabbath, Mrs. Manger!" was an endless source of delight and gratitude for her. My grandmother had something with which to compare her life in America. She never took her freedom and opportunity here for granted, and she made sure I didn't either. Baba also set a standard for service in our family, as one of the founders of the Hebrew Ladies Educational League in Stamford, a classic immigrant, self-help, pre-welfare organization which raised money and gave it quietly to those who needed it for food or clothing or birth or burial.

We may not have been a particularly political family, but we were a patriotic one, beginning with my grandmother and continuing with my father, who had served proudly in World War II. I was raised to love my country. I remember my dad saying to me once when I was a teenager that he had no complaint whatsoever about writing the check to pay his taxes to the government because he appreciated the opportunities this country was giving him and his family. I have to say that Dad's attitude shifted a bit toward the end of his life, when he began to feel that some of his tax money was being wasted. But even then, he still wrote his checks to the IRS with gratitude and without complaint.

My first purely political memories are of watching the televised Kefauver committee Senate hearings on organized crime in 1951 and the election night returns of the presidential race between Dwight Eisenhower and Adlai Stevenson in 1952. I remember, as a nine-year-old, being struck by the drama of the Kefauver hearings, the good guys (the senators) against the bad (the underworld), and it was *real*. I was riveted. I was also thrilled watching the broadcast of those 1952 election night returns. I remember sitting beside Baba, both of us rooting for General Eisenhower, who had saved the world from Nazism, and I couldn't understand why my mom and dad were supporting Stevenson.

The community I grew up in, Stamford, Connecticut, of the 1940s and 1950s, was like so many northeastern cities of that time, a melting pot of ethnic groups—Irish, Italian, German, Polish, Jewish and African-American. The suburbs hadn't yet developed to the point where they would draw a significant number of people (and resources) out of such cities. Most of us went to the same high school, the only public high school in Stamford. My family's first house, which sat a block from the railroad tracks in what would generously be called a lower-middle-class neighborhood, was flanked by a six-family walk-up on one side (the father of one of those families, I later learned, was a bookie) and a junkyard on the other. I'm sure there was racism and anti-Semitism in Stamford, as well as cronyism and crookedness among some of the businessmen and politicians, but personally I never saw or experienced any of this. Maybe I was blissfully unaware, or maybe such problems were overshadowed by the fact that we actually lived, worked and played together, that we were real people to one another. We were not concepts, not stereotypes. We were certainly not perfect. But we were neighbors and schoolmates.

My mother would have been the senator in our family if she had been born in my generation. Like my father, she always found time for charitable work. Mom is one of the most naturally outgoing, personable and caring people I've ever known, and has taught me so much about understanding and enjoying people. If you're going to live a public life, I don't think there's any question that you had better be someone who enjoys people. I went out to lunch in New Haven a couple of years ago with a friend. People kept coming up to our table, to say hello, to share their opinion on something, to ask how I felt about this or that. After a while my friend said, "God, this is rough. You don't have any privacy. People don't leave you *alone.*" I responded, "You know, one thing worse than all these people coming over like this would be if no one came over."

Of course, there are times when people are annoying. And sometimes, like anyone else, I just want to be alone. But the fact is that, by definition, if you're going to be a public servant, most of your life is going to be *public.* You are expected to share it. When you go out, you will be noticed. You will be approached. If you can't handle that, let alone enjoy it, if you're not genuinely fed by and fascinated with human interaction, if you don't fundamentally *like* people, then this is probably not the career for you. There are very few loners or misanthropes on Capitol Hill or in America's statehouses or city halls.

When I was a kid, it was probably this enjoyment of people, as well as a still only vaguely understood desire to excel, that helped get me involved in my first "political" experiences in student government. I ran for president of my ninth-grade class in 1956 with a campaign speech featuring the titles of some of that era's hit rock-and-roll songs—"Earth Angel," "See You Later, Alligator," "Rock Around the Clock." After I won, one of my friends told me his social studies teacher said to his class, "I hope you didn't vote for Joe Lieberman just because he used those rock-and-roll songs in his speech."

The teacher's criticism of my "campaign" was on target. My platform was not built around too many issues. How many ninth-grade campaigns are? I wasn't dreaming of the U.S. Senate. I still imagined myself playing center field in the major leagues. But by the time I graduated from high school in the spring of 1960, I was definitely looking at public life as a possible career in an earnest way. The reason had everything to do with role models.

I don't think too many eighteen-year-olds today look at their political leaders the way I and much of my generation saw them in 1960. The succession of dignified, personable mayors who ran Stamford, the statewide leaders like Abe Ribicoff, Prescott Bush and Tom Dodd, the national leaders like Dwight Eisenhower and Adlai Stevenson—these men were, quite simply, figures of respect. That phrase sounds outdated and naive today, which is a shame. From the cop on the beat, whom we considered both a person of authority and our friend, to John F. Kennedy, who was about to become our next president and who symbolized the limitless possibility of our own lives, the world of my adolescence was filled with models to emulate.

Yes, there was much we did not know about some of these people, much we have come to learn. Our society needs, and will always benefit from, the sense of purpose and hope that I and most of my generation felt at the dawn of the 1960s.

Put this all together—my inherited appreciation for what America had provided my family, the ideal of service that was fundamental to my religious faith, the sense of community and connection I felt in the time and the place where I grew up, my belief in and the respect I had for figures of authority, the desire to make my own mark, and the hope and promise of a boundless future that seemed to lie ahead for our nation at the time I finished high school—and it explains why I had become focused on pursuing a public life by the time I began college at Yale in the fall of 1960.

It is impossible to overstate the impact of John Kennedy's election and 1961 inaugural address on our generation's sense of civic duty and public service. We've heard the words so often over the years—"Ask not what your country can do for you; ask what you can do for your country"—that it's easy to become numb to their meaning. Perhaps they no longer resonate the way they did when Kennedy spoke them that wintry January afternoon. But time cannot diminish their meaning and significance. In fact, it has increased them. If we are serious about righting what is wrong with politics and politicians in America today, we could do worse than repeat Kennedy's phrase to ourselves and act on it. Voting, of course, is the very least people can do. Opportunities for community and volunteer service in its myriad forms are there as well. And then there is public service itself, at every level, from local school or park boards, to political committees, to town councils, to regional, state and nationally elected positions.

We are privileged in this country—most of us—to be able to wake up each morning and not worry about survival. We have the luxury of being able to consider the purpose of our lives, to ask ourselves, in secular or spiritual terms, how we might make a difference during this time we are given on earth. We are also a very busy people and work very hard, sometimes at two jobs, often with both husband and wife at work. Yet millions of Americans find the time to volunteer in neighborhood, religious, athletic, social or community service groups, and still more millions could. There is also an abundance of nongovernmental helping professions in our society, from teaching to social work to work in community organizations, where you can make a living while making a difference. That, of course, is the satisfaction of these jobs, which, as the generation coming of age right now seems to realize, can be a reward far more enriching than money or material possessions.

FROM AND WHAT IS
MY LIFESPAN?

Yehuda Amichai

7

I believe with perfect faith that at this very moment
millions of human beings are standing at crossroads
and intersections, in jungles and deserts,
showing each other where to turn, what the right way is,
which direction. They explain exactly where to go,
what is the quickest way to get there, when to stop
and ask again. There, over there. The second
turnoff, not the first, and from there left or right,
near the white house, by the oak tree.
They explain with excited voices, with a wave of the hand
and a nod of the head: There, over there, not *that* there,
    the *other* there,
as in some ancient rite. This too is a new religion.
I believe with perfect faith that at this very moment.

STORIES

Rachel Naomi Remen

Grandmother Eve

When I was small, my grandfather used to tell me stories. Many of these were about women who had lived long ago, heroic women who learned important things through their mistakes. There was Sarah, whose husband's name was Abraham, Rachel, whose husband's name was Jacob, and Esther, who was a queen. It was only after his death that I found out that these stories were Genesis, told by a scholarly, white bearded, orthodox Rabbi to a devoted granddaughter, the child of two young atheistic socialists.

My grandfather's story of Grandmother Eve and the snake is really a story about the importance of the inner life.

In the beginning of the story Grandmother Eve is a little girl and she lives much as I did then, as a child. God is the Father and like all fathers, He provides food and shelter and all the things necessary to life. In return, Eve obeys Him in the same way I was expected to obey my own Daddy.

Life goes on in the garden, much the same from day to day. Very little is asked of Eve. All the animals and plants live there together with Eve, including a tree of great beauty in the center of the Garden called the tree of God's Wisdom. God has offered Eve some very clear guidelines about this tree. She can eat the fruits of all the other trees, but the fruit of this tree is forbidden. In the beginning she accepts this without question, even though the very purpose of life is to grow in wisdom. As time goes by, even though the garden does not change, Eve changes. She begins to grow up, to become a teenager. One day, as she is passing the most beautiful tree, a snake, coiled in its branches, speaks to her. "Eve," he says, "here is one of the apples of this tree. Why not eat it?"

At this point my grandfather would always explain that the snake was not really a snake, but a symbol for the human yearning for wisdom, the seductive power of the unknown and the endless fascination that the mysterious has for human beings. The snake is the first Teacher, and he addresses that part of Eve which is no longer a little girl, but is a Seeker.

Eve thinks back upon what God the Father said. The fruit of the tree is forbidden. But Eve is an adolescent. Like most people her age, she needs to find out for herself. She feels the magnetism of the apple. Drawn towards it, she reaches out for it, takes a bite of it.

The food we eat becomes a part of every one of our cells and is woven into the very fabric of our being. "This apple is no different than any other food," said my Grandfather. When Grandmother Eve eats it, the wisdom of God becomes a part of her inner life, a holy wisdom she carries inside her and not something she speaks to outside of herself. She now carries the voice of God inside every one of her cells like a little compass. As her descendants, so do we.

Eating the apple made possible an enormous change in Grandmother Eve's lifestyle. She no longer needed to live in God's house in the nursery in order to be safe. She was able to leave this protected environment because she carried God with her. She could hear Him if she was willing to listen. When she ate the apple, she became an adult, and gained the freedom of an adult, to go out into a world of complexity, adventure and responsibility and change. To have her own life and make her own choices.

Like most children the literal aspects of the story bothered me. "Why Grandpa," I asked, "did God tell Grandma Eve that she mustn't eat the apple in the first place if it wasn't true?" One of the finest things about my Grandfather was that he did not change his response to a question just because the person asking was very young. He answered me as if I were a fellow Kabbalist. "Neshume-le," he said, "This is a most difficult question, a question worthy of much thought. The Bible is full of the images of God. God as an authoritarian father, God as a lover, God as angry, God as jealous, God as faithful, God as loving. In one place God is walking on the earth and in another His breath blows over the waters. In yet another He is a burning bush. But God is none of these things. These are all images of God in the minds of men. Knowing God may require us to question all of these things."

The God within seemed to require a day-to-day, moment-to-moment sort of inner attention rather than just a simple obedience. I felt sorry for Grandma Eve. It seemed much harder than obedience to me.

The complexity of the real world requires us to struggle to hear the Holy and develop a personal responsibility to live a good life. It demands that we stay awake. Grandfather presented Eve to me as a grownup rather than a sinner. It was years before I heard the official version of the story.

Perhaps there is something for us now in my grandfather's version of the story. We have expected a great deal of our experts and authorities, our doctors, our politicians, our technicians and our educators, even our rabbis, ministers and priests. We have offered them obedience for the hope that they would become responsible for providing us with a good life. It is time to look within.

Consecrating the Ordinary

It is said that the Christian mystic, Theresa D'Avila, found difficulty at first in reconciling the vastness of the life of the spirit with the mundane tasks of her Carmelite Convent; the washing of pots, the sweeping of floors, the folding of laundry. At some point of grace, the mundane became for her a sort of prayer, a way she could experience her ever-present connection to the divine pattern which is the source of life. She began to see the face of God in the folded sheets.

People can most easily recognize mystery when it presents itself in dramatic ways. The person who heals for unknown reasons when all hope is gone, the angelic visitation, the life-altering coincidence. We seem to be able to hear God best when He shouts: even Moses required a burning bush, and Jesus' disciples needed to him to feed multitudes with a single fish. Yet mystery is as common as a trip to the grocery store. In *Guide for the Perplexed*, Schumacher notes that the endless debate about the nature of the world is founded on differences in the sensitivity of the eyes that behold it. "We can see only what we have grown an eye to see." Some of us can only notice miracles. Some of us can only see in times of crisis. Yet we can all learn to see God in the folded sheets.

Soon after I moved to California from New York, I planted a vegetable garden. I had never seen fresh vegetables except in a supermarket, and the first year I found an endless fascination in this tiny garden. I especially loved the lettuce which I had planted tightly in a square whose edges I harvested for dinner every night. One evening, I had gone out to pick the salad as usual and ran a hand lightly over the crisp green square of lettuce leaves marveling at its vitality, almost as if it were bubbling up out of the ground.

Suddenly words from my childhood came back to me, words that I had heard countless times over the dinner tables of aunts and uncles and knew by heart, words that I heard now for the first time:

"Blessed art Thou, O LORD, King of the universe, who bringest forth bread from the earth."

Far from being the usual meaningless mumble, these words suddenly were a potent description of something real, a statement about Grace and the mystery of life itself. Up until then I had taken this blessing as a theory or a hypothesis, someone's idea of how things worked. I had no idea that these familiar words were simply a description of something true. I had never witnessed them happening in the world before.

I had done ritual the way I had done life. Automatically. Life can become habit, something done without thinking. Living life in this way does not awaken us. Yet any of our daily habits can awaken us. All of life can become ritual. When it does, our experience of life changes radically and the ordinary becomes consecrated. Ritual doesn't make mystery happen. It helps us see and experience something which is already real. It does not create the sacred, it only describes what is there and has always been there, deeply hidden in the obvious.

Blessing

On Friday afternoon, when I would arrive at my grandfather's house after school, the tea would be already set on the kitchen table. My grandfather had his own way of serving tea. There were no teacups and saucers or bowls of granulated sugar or honey. Instead he would pour the tea directly from the silver samovar into a drinking glass. There had to be a teaspoon in the glass first; otherwise the glass, being thin, might break. My grandfather did not drink his tea in the same way that the parents of my friends did either. He would put a cube of sugar between his teeth and then drink the hot tea straight from his glass. So would I. I much preferred drinking tea this way to the way I had to drink tea at home. If it was Friday, after we had finished our tea my grandfather would set two candles on the table and light them. Then he would have a word with God in Hebrew. Sometimes he would speak out loud but often he would close his eyes and be quiet. I knew then that he was talking to God in his heart. I would sit and wait patiently because the best part of the week was coming.

When Grandpa finished talking to God, he would turn to me and say "Come, Neshume-le." Then I would stand in front of him and he would rest his hands lightly on the top of my head. He would begin by thanking God for me and for making him my grandpa. He would specifically mention my struggles during that week and tell God something about me that was true. Each week I would wait to find out what that was. If I had made mistakes during the week he would mention my honesty in telling the truth. If I had failed he would appreciate how hard I had tried. If I had slept for even a short nap without my night-light he would celebrate my bravery in sleeping in the dark. Then he would give me his blessing and ask the long-ago women I knew from his many stories—Sarah, Rachel, Rebekah and Leah—to watch over me.

These few moments were the only time in my week that I felt completely safe and at rest. My family of physicians and health professionals were always struggling to learn more and to be more. It seemed there was always more to know. It was never enough. If I brought home a 98 on a test, my father would ask "And what happened to the other two points?" I pursued those two points relentlessly throughout my childhood. But my grandfather did not care about such things. For him, I was already enough. And somehow when I was with him I knew with absolute certainty that this was so.

My grandfather died when I was seven years old. I had never lived in a world without him in it before and it was hard for me. He had looked at me as no one else had and called me by a special name, "Neshume-le," which means "beloved little soul." There was no one left to call me this anymore. At first I was afraid that without him to see me, and tell God who I was, I might disappear. But slowly over time I came to understand that in some mysterious way, I had learned to see myself through his eyes. And that once blessed, we are blessed forever.

Many years later when, in her extreme old age, my mother surprisingly began to light candles and talk to God herself, I told her about these blessings and what they had meant to me. She had smiled at me sadly. "I have blessed you every day of your life, Rachel," she told me. "I just never had the wisdom to do it out loud."

The Reward

My parents, young socialists, had firmly instructed my grandfather, who was a Kabbalist and an Orthodox Rabbi, that he was not to speak to me about God and other such superstitions. They might just as well have told him not to breathe. So the whole of my religious education was covert, which of course made it far more effective than the ordinary Sunday school approach. For many years I thought that it was proper to talk about God only in a whisper.

Concerned that I was too young to fully keep his secret, my grandfather never revealed the source of his wonderful stories nor that most of the people in them were Jewish. This gave the Books of Moses a sort of universal human quality which seems to me to be quite genuine.

Many of Grandfather's stories were family stories, that is, they were about God teaching His children how the world works. As a child myself, this really interested me. What the stories taught me seemed to be a part of all the other things I was learning about how the world worked: cross only on the green, say thank you, the big one is a quarter and the brown one is a penny and the like.

As they tried to figure things out for themselves, the people in Grandfather's stories spoke to God directly and often. I loved when God responded in mysterious ways and my grandfather and I would talk about what He could possibly have meant.

One of the most interesting of these discussions was about Moses and the Promised Land. I was learning about rewards in kindergarten, and had a nice collection of little pieces of paper each with a gold or a silver star pasted on it. I loved these stars and worked very, very hard for them. I knew exactly what I had to do to get a silver star and what further effort would get me a gold. It was all predictable.

But Moses never got to the Promised Land and I just couldn't understand it. Each week, I showed my grandfather my stars and we would count them together. Once, while we were doing this, I asked him why, after all that he had done, God had not given Moses his reward. "Well, Neshume-le," he said, "what makes you think this?" I was puzzled. In the story, he had told me, after all his hard work Moses only got to see the Promised Land and to watch the others go there. Everyone else had been given their dream. It didn't seem fair to me.

When I told this to my grandfather, he smiled. "But Moses did get his dream," he said, "Moses was a leader, Neshume-le, and a leader always has a different dream from the others."

He reminded me of mitzvot, those human actions which help move things in the direction that God is trying to move them. When a person does such an action [he becomes] God's hands in the world. "There are many mitzvot, but the greatest mitzvah of all is said to be the freeing of captives," he told me. "Moses' dream was for his people to be free. And so his reward was that he got to see that happen. Because he was a leader, his dream was different from the dreams of the people, Neshume-le. A real leader has the same dream that God has."

THE LEGACY

A PARABLE ABOUT HISTORY AND BOBE-MAYSES, BARSZCZ, AND BORSCHT AND THE FUTURE OF THE JEWISH PAST

Irena Klepfisz

THIS IS NO *BOBE-MAYSE*.* I never knew my grandmothers, both of whom died in the war, and it's only recently that I've gotten even a glimpse of what my *bobes* might have been like by watching my 81-year-old mother, Mama Lo. Oddly enough, I too, though childless, am experiencing a state of *bobe*-hood. More and more, Mama Lo and I are sharing the aches and pains of getting old and older and bridging our lifelong generation gap. Who would have thought? But then these are peculiar times.

For example, lately Mama Lo has been instructing me about "when the time comes . . ." and showing me the desk drawer with her living will and the jewelry box with Elza's watch, not especially valuable, but the only physical link to my 24-year-old almost-sister who committed suicide over 30 years ago. Occasionally, she walks me through the apartment, pointing to this or that. Sometimes she stares at her well-stocked bookcases of Ringelblum, Levi, Charlotte, Herman Wouk, Howard Fast and Jane Austen

---

*Bobe-mayse: fantasy, fabrication (pejorative); grandmother's story (literal).

and George Eliot, at the framed reproductions of Chagall and Van Gogh, and at the *tshatshkes* of kittens, vases, miniature musicians (many of them presents from me). In a gesture of puzzlement (perhaps despair), she throws up her hands: "What are you going to do with . . . ?" she begins, then stops and changes the subject with a shrug.

Though she has experienced two world wars, poverty and serious illnesses, I suspect Mama Lo is admitting to herself for the first time that she has no choice but to accept her lack of control over her own life and mine. Knowing my forgetfulness and essential anarchism, she cannot feel easy about passing on the pots of sturdy jades and blossoming African violets. Actually, I'm not certain what she feels because I have no idea what it is like to be 81, and also because, with iron-clad tenacity, Mama Lo has kept her inner life a locked vault. It is a vault to which she is not about to bequeath me the key.—History be damned, she is saying.—What is private is private.

So these days we are both silent about what we both know: that at some point, I will take possession of her possessions, dismantle her apartment and, barring catastrophe, continue with my life for possibly two or three decades without her. In other words, my life as a daughter will come to an abrupt end and I will cease being Mama Lo and her generation's future and be transformed into a true *bobe,* the next generation's past.

Theoretically, legacies and inheritances are simple: some things we accept and keep, even if with great sadness; others we discard because they're inconvenient, useless, simply passé. A watch like Elza's—orphan child-survivor, dreaming poet, determined suicide—embodies so much public and private history that I've never been able to claim it for myself. So when the time comes, the watch will be transferred to my desk drawer. But I am determined eventually to bequeath it to someone, someone younger—not a relative, because I have none—but someone to whom its fierce and painful history will be important, and whose arm will display it like an honor, rather than a wound.

Mama Lo's other bequests will be more problematic. Should I, for example, keep a leaky pot—its white enamel worn, its rim dented—but Mama Lo's (and my own) sole physical link to Poland (post-war, of course, but Poland nevertheless)? What historical purpose will it serve standing on a shelf behind my teflon pans, my well-used wok and bamboo steamers? Does such a pot belong in a museum and should I try to donate it? ("It's the very pot in which Mama Lo cooked her borscht—on *both* sides of the Atlantic. Believe me it tells the quintessential 20th-century Jewish story.")

And then there's the album with photographs of people I don't quite re-member: a man and woman standing by the white brick oven in our Lodz apartment or a teenager kneeling by a sandbox in a park—ordinary peo-ple who, because of their imagination, stupidity and/or luck, just hap-pened to survive. Should I ask Mama Lo to name them? I've no family, so what does it matter? Won't such an album inevitably end up in some "collectibles-barn" in Columbia County in upstate New York to be browsed through by eager weekenders trying to furnish their newly built A-frame with an aura of history? On the other hand, the album is part of *my life, my past*—one which my aging brain has increasingly more trouble retain-ing, a past which, I confess, I've already distilled (or thinned—depending on your point of view) as I've tried to "get on" with my life.

The truth is that for most of my adulthood I've been braced against Mama Lo's disapproval, conscious I did not fulfill her wish and emulate her and her one-bedroom apartment in a three-bedroom one of my own fully furnished with a husband and children. Instead, I went off and set-tled into a wall-less, closet-less loft which I share with another woman who has no legal relationship to me, but with whom I also share my life.

Yet, for all my rebelliousness and alternativity, a part of my identity—the *Jewish* part—has been inextricably intertwined with Mama Lo and the life of her generation. My vaulted secret is that I've been a dependent Jew—dependent on Mama Lo's generation to provide me with a sense of *hemshekh*/continuity. They've been the visible *goldene keyt*/the golden chain to which I've wanted to hook the link I've been forging through my life and my work. With them gone, where am I supposed to hang myself?

To put it another way: *Vos iz geshikhte?*/What is history and what is my place in it? And how is time defined with any accuracy by human events? The Middle Ages. The Renaissance. The Age of Reason. How do we know when one age ends and another begins? I wonder with increas-ing urgency as I ready myself to begin the Jewish generation relay race in which I've been entered.

Take borscht, for example. Consider that beets were unknown to us at the time of the destruction of the Temple and were not among the hastily packed foods our *bobes* took into Babylon or later into the northwestern *goles*/exile. Then consider the centrality of borscht in modern Eastern Eu-ropean Jewish culture. By what process did this essential component of Jewish life emerge?

Borscht entered Jewish life many centuries ago—through the kitchen. The first Jewish mention of beets, I believe, occurs in *A bobe, an eydes/A Grand-mother, A Witness,* a recently discovered collection which is bound to rival Glickl's *Memoirs.* Among its many fragmentary stories, *A bobe, an eydes* contains a series of tributes to a certain Gitl *bas* Frume *di frume** who, according to one *bobe-mayse*, lived in the later part of the 13th century in the town of Knin. Knin was far from her ancestors' beloved Ashkenaz, very far east in fact, in a region we nostalgically remember today as *poyln/* Poland—the cradle of *yidishkayt, der yidisher oytser/*the Jewish treasure— but where, in Gitl's time, the buds of *yidishe geshikhte un kultur/*history and culture were barely formed, much less beginning to bloom.

It was some time during that Yiddish dawn that Gitl *bas* Frume *di frume* forged a secret friendship with Grushenka, even though Janek, Grushenka's brother, beat up Yankl, Gitl's brother, on a regular basis. One Sunday morning after sneaking out of church, Grushenka led Gitl (without Frume's knowledge) into her mother's Christian kitchen, where, for the first time, Gitl smelled the sweet, dark aroma of *barszcz*. *"Treyf!" undzer yidishe tokhter/*our young Jewish girl declared that night to her younger sister Chava, thereby conveying her understanding of the nature of the soup's bones and, indeed, its entire culinary context. But then, much to her sister's horror, Gitl added with *emesdike benkshaft/*heartfelt longing: *"Ober es shmekt azoy gut!/*But it smells so good!"

Like other texts whose authors were neither official recorders nor note takers, but ordinary homemakers focused more on an event's ingredients than on its development and denouement, *A bobe, an eydes* gives scant information about the process of Judaization of the Polish *barszcz*. Perhaps once, perhaps more than once, the girl tasted the forbidden friend's forbidden food. In any case, at some point, after numerous visits and sniffs, much finger-pointing at the market place, two or three public tantrums, and repeated posings of the proverbial *"Ober, far vos nisht?/*Why not?"— the impetus behind all creative leaps—Gitl convinced Frume *di frume* to act: (*"Dos meydl makht mir in gantsn meshige. Tog un nakht redt zi bloyz fun* buraki *un* barszcz!/The girl's driving me completely mad. Day and night she talks only of *buraki* and *barszcz!"*) And so the frazzled mother peeled the bleeding vegetables into a pot of boiling water, added some *beyner, tsiker, knobl, un tsibeles/*bones, sugar, garlic and onions and, through trial and error—*tsu gedikht, tsu shiter, tsu zis, tsu zoyer/*too thick, too thin, too sweet, too tart—the soup looked, tasted and smelled exactly like the *barszcz* in Grushenka's mother's kitchen with the added advantage it could pass rabbinic inspection: *s'iz geven kusher/*it was kosher.

The rest *iz poshet/*is simple. By the first decade of the 15th century when Gitl's great-granddaughter, Frume *di freylekhe,** was already a married

---

*Gitl *bas* Frume *di frume*: Gitl daughter of Frume the pious.

baleboste/homemaker, the Slavic rooted *barszcz* had become *borsht,* the Yiddish word for the quintessential Jewish soup.

Given such history it is not surprising that today, near the end of the 20th century, I am preoccupied with leaky pots, with Elza's watch (which, despite being idle for almost 30 years, began ticking the second I wound it), with photo albums and with the survival of borscht itself in Jewish kitchens dominated by woks and bamboo steamers. Nor is it surprising that I am preoccupied with Mama Lo's entire *yerushe,* including everything she lost almost sixty years ago so that when she debarked in *di goldene medine*/the golden land, Mama Lo had nothing but a goose down *koldra* (which a year later caught fire from a faulty heating pad), some crumbling photographs, a pot purchased in Lodz shortly after liberation— and me. That year *poyln* was no longer a blooming garden, but a country-sized wall-less graveyard and Mama Lo's past a *vistenish*/a void, something which history and nature abhor and immediately engulf, thereby allowing the transformation of alien weeds into beloved indigenous flowers and a *treyf barszcz* into the embodiment of a *kushere heym.*

So when the time comes, I will have no choice. Somehow I will find my place on the historical continuum and try to observe and take notes. I will go to Sally and Linda's seder and recline on the Moroccan, Israeli and Native American rugs. Together we will retell the ancient story as it was passed from *bobe* to *bobe* and read from our xeroxed *hagadahs* decorated with images of ancient goddesses and interspersed with the texts of witches' incantations, peace songs between Hagar and Sarah, tributes to midwives, toasts to the liberation of Palestinians, and praisesongs and poems to Hannah Senesh, Yokheved and Gitl *bas* Frume *di frume.* At appropriate moments, my women friends and I will raise our cups of grape juice and greet Miriam the Prophetess, drink the vegetarian chicken soup, dunk the parsley in the bitter waters, chew the symbolic mortar and burn the sweet-scented incense. Each year we will substitute this for that and add that to this and sing and chant recalling the tears and losses and recite (in English, of course) *"hayntiks yor knekht, dos kumendike yor fraye froyen*/this year we are slaves, next year liberated women.*"* And a few years from now, sometime around the year 2000, we will feel familiar, comforted and grounded in our tradition and look back upon the seders of our childhoods as the ancient ceremonies of another century and era—which is exactly what they will have become.

But until then, I am at Mama Lo's service. Whenever she wants to recall more vividly the *poyln fun ire kinderyorn*/Poland of her childhood

---

*Frume *di freylekhe:* Frume the joyous/gay.

and the sweetness of my *bobe* Rokla's *kikh,* a kitchen whose ashes and dust are now indistinguishable from those of the Second Temple—I will take Mama Lo to Second Avenue and Teresa's Polish Café and order borscht, the same *treyf barszcz* Gitl *bas* Frume *di frume* first smelled in Grushenka's mother's kitchen. As Mama Lo and I breathe in its dark, rich aroma, we will begin talking for the first time *bobe tsu bobe* about the miracles of our common past and the mystery of our separate futures.

RECLAIMING THE
SPIRIT IN JUDAISM

NISHMAT

Marge Piercy

When the night slides under with the last dimming star
and the red sky lightens between the trees,
and the heron glides tipping heavy wings in the river,
when crows stir and cry out their harsh joy,
and swift creatures of the night run toward their burrows,
and the deer raises her head and sniffs the freshening air,
and the shadows grow more distinct and then shorten,

then we rise into the day still clean as new snow.
The cat washes its paw and greets the day with gratitude.
Leviathan salutes breaching with a column of steam.
The hawk turning in the sky cries out a prayer like a knife.
We must wonder at the sky now thin as a speckled eggshell,
that now piles up its boulders of storm to crash down,
that now hangs a furry grey belly into the street.

Every day we find a new sky and a new earth
with which we are trusted like a perfect toy.
We are given the salty river of our blood
winding through us, to remember the sea and our
kindred under the waves, the hot pulsing that knocks
in our throats to consider our cousins in the grass
and the trees, all bright scattered rivulets of life.

We are given the wind within us, the breath
to shape into words that steal time, that touch
like hands and pierce like bullets, that waken
truth and deceit, sorrow and pity and joy,
that waste precious air in complaints, in lies,
in floating traps for power on the dirty air.
Yet holy breath still stretches our lungs to sing.

We are given the body, that momentary kibbutz
of elements that have belonged to frog and polar
bear, corn and oak tree, volcano and glacier.
We are lent for a time these minerals in water
and a morning every day, a morning to wake up,
rejoice and praise life in our spines, our throats,
our knees, our genitals, our brains, our tongues.

We are given fire to see against the dark,
to think, to read, to study how we are to live,
to bank in ourselves against defeat and despair
that cool and muddy our resolves, that make us forget
what we saw we must do. We are given passion
to rise like the sun in our minds with the new day
and burn the debris of habit and greed and fear.

We stand in the midst of the burning world
primed to burn with compassionate love and justice,
to turn inward and find holy fire at the core,
to turn outward and see the world that is all
of one flesh with us, see under the trash, through
the smog, the furry bee in the apple blossom,
the trout leaping, the candles our ancestors lit for us.

Fill us as the tide rustles into the reeds in the marsh.
Fill us as the rushing water overflows the pitcher.
Fill us as light fills a room with its dancing.
Let the little quarrels of the bones and the snarling
of the lesser appetites and the whining of the ego cease.
Let silence still us so you may show us your shining
and we can out of that stillness rise and praise.

STARTING ON
MY SPIRITUAL PATH

Naomi Wolf

I WAS RAISED IN A HOME that was comfortable with the idea that there was a mystical dimension to life. But later, as an angry young feminist who wanted to get to the roots of women's oppression, I felt alienated from the patriarchal aspects of Judaism. For instance, once I talked to an important rabbi about the struggle I was going through. I shared some of my thinking about making the liturgy more inclusive, and cited the work of Rabbi Shira Lander, who was using the mikva as a healing and cleansing ritual for survivors of rape. The rabbi told me that if he had to choose between inclusivity and tradition he would choose the tradition. My heart closed down completely.

Of course, the progressive, post-Marxist world of which I was part was profoundly atheistic and hostile to religious and spiritual traditions. Not only was spirituality seen as part of what kept the masses tied to an oppressive social order, it was also seen as "not tough." There was a real macho posturing that made it seem really "wimpy" as well as "bourgeois" to be interested in spirit rather than in, say, guns for the Sandinistas and the redistribution of wealth. Additionally, some of the hostility to religion from feminists I was around at the time derived from their perception that "God language" had been so co-opted by the religious right that to use it was to allow oneself to be co-opted.

So it felt embarrassing, a social liability, to admit an interest in God. It mattered to me that it would feel pathetic and nerdy to tell someone I was interested in spiritual issues in the progressive circles in which I spent my time; to confess *that* would be more uncool than to confess to various forms of vice or addiction.

But then I gave birth two and a half years ago. That was such a miracle that it's hard not to try to figure out how to address it. The manifest miraculousness of having your child wake up in the morning and look at you! It's hard not to speculate about "where did you come from?" The kind of love that being a parent brings out, that donkey-like, repetitive, abject, egoless love, is closer to a spiritual notion of love than any other kind of love I've experienced. Romantic love, perhaps all other kinds of love too, seem more tied up with the ego than does the love of a parent for a child. So having this kind of experience of love made it easier for me to understand some of what the spiritual traditions were addressing.

Around the same time, I went to a consultant for writer's block (from which I was suffering at the time) and this consultant put me into a meditative state. I then had a spiritual experience, an overwhelming and inexplicable mystical encounter that turned my world upside down.

I recently read that 43 percent of Americans have had some sort of mystical experience in the past few years but have not been able to talk about it with people with whom they are otherwise intimate. So many people are having some kind of powerful spiritual encounter, but this experience is outstripping their ability to put it into words. One of the dangers of any spiritual path is that there is a lot of self-delusion. There is a widening industry of books and tapes and gurus aimed at selling or packaging the mystical or spiritual experience, and I think we need to be very wary of that. The struggle for me was to use my critical mind to make sure that I could believe in what I had encountered.

I did a lot of reading about mysticism and spirituality after having had this experience. Great teachers in the past have urged their disciples to be sure that whatever mystical experience they claim to have had be reflected in the way one subsequently lives one's life.

This experience was really different for me from, for example, my accepting various political ideas or ideologies. One difference was that I really didn't want to have this experience, it was upsetting, it shook me, it scared me, it created upheaval in my life, it was painful and unwelcome (as well as joyful and liberating).

Part of what was shocking to me was getting that all the things that the world I knew tended to privilege—things like status, money, beauty, self, fame—were all stripped away. I could see that the only reality is the joy and beauty of service to others and the world. It was painful to realize that the beside-the-pointness of the ego-needs that had previously preoc-cupied so much of my time and energy.

As I've moved into a spiritual path, I've come to realize that every choice matters. Before, if I was having a bad day, I might have snapped at some-one who was taking a long time with an airline ticket, or I might have shaded some aspect of the truth in a conversation because I didn't really want to get too deeply into the truth at the moment, or I might have been lazy or sloppy with my choices because "it doesn't really count" or "no one is really looking" or "on balance I'm a pretty reasonable person so it doesn't really matter what I do in this particular instance." But now, as a result of my spiritual experience, I realize that every single choice matters. To be careful in what I say, for example, because one of my biggest vices was careless speech, gossip, or saying things that were witty that weren't really nice ("hey, it's a cocktail party, so what does it matter?"). Now I'm conscious of how powerful the choice of our words is. I'm conscious that every single thing I put out is going to come back to me, and that every in-tention I have is going to manifest in the world. So I try to live more care-fully now.

One thing that came to me in my mystical experience was that there was no one right way to spiritual truth, that there was no one true religion, that many paths could lead to the Divine. So I started to read voraciously from all religions. I found important truths in Buddhism (particularly its notion that one could be an activist without anger and without demoniz-ing the opposition). I got big truths from reading about Jesus, from Kab-balah, from 20th century Jewish philosophers. But to try to talk to family members about the ways that my heart was being moved, for example, by Jesus' message was very distressing. I found that even to like the guy a little bit was to be seen as being totally disloyal to the tribe. I understand that his message was used in an oppressive way, but what has happened in the name of Christianity has often had so little to do with his original message.

I've had to be very cautious about the spiritual yearning that is at the center of my life now. I think it can be both trivializing and invasive to talk about these issues with people who don't yearn for a spiritual element in their lives. So I'm very wary of being seen as proselytizing. But if I get a sense that there is a hunger there, then I can feel more comfortable about sharing my own thirst for this dimension of reality. I think we have to be a lot more delicate about how we franchise God and how we bring God into the world. Part of that is to be very sensitive about the fact that my experience of God might not be yours.

Yet I also know that part of my reluctance to talk about all this is fear. Particularly as a woman. It's taken me nine years to build up enough credibility in the analytic/linear world that I can now speak and have some expectation of being heard to a certain degree. It's been a long haul, and very much a gendered haul. I've had to lay down brick after brick of linear, traditionally masculine, post-Enlightenment, rational thinking. Now if I say, "And . . . I had a mystical experience," it opens the door wide to the fear that I will lose that base of reasoned discourse that was so hard won. It's traditionally women who light candles and who see angels, so there is a fear of being dismissed as a woman. Humility and service, compassion and love, are traditionally gendered "female." This makes it hard for many men to open themselves to their own mystical or spiritual side, for fear that they will be de-manned by the larger culture.

Moreover, it's embarrassing. To talk about one's spiritual life is to make oneself naked. To acknowledge the role of spirit in the world and to let your relationship to it visibly shine is to make yourself as naked as you can be in the world. You are undefended by cynicism, by ego. To be truly present and truly live from your heart is to make yourself profoundly vulnerable and at risk. That is a leap of faith. If you venture something from your heart in relationship to spirit, it's your absolute truth, so if that gets rejected it's your truth that got rejected, not just some clever thing you said on a television show.

I'm a writer. I've been trained to use very specific and pointed language to identify something real. But in talking about the spiritual realm there are places where our and my language break down. Look at how the language of *The Politics of Meaning* was publicly attacked because it was nonlinear, because it described parts of reality that could not be quantified, even though it described truths that we all know to be true deep down. It's profoundly frightening to me to leave the skill and the defendedness and ego-security I experience as a manipulator of language, and to go into a place where language fails me. If I were to talk about this in public, there I would be, this writer, stammering. It could be mortifying. So it's not easy to come out as spiritual.

The strange thing is that when I do take a leap of faith and talk to an audience and tell this to them and talk about spiritual truths, it often resonates very deeply with people. I haven't been ridiculed—on the contrary, what I'm finding is a hunger that people have to go to this level.

I've also noticed that it's easier to talk about these issues with most of America than it is with the people within the Washington/New York media box. Spiritual truths are more unacceptable in that media/government/ policy corridor than they are anywhere else in America, and that only confirms for me how much those elites are behind the rest of America. The press and government are engaged in ways of behaving that are threatened by a spiritual approach, so they are going to be hostile to it.

I confronted this personally when I was asked to be a trial host on a TV show whose format involved getting people to argue their politics with each other, and the more argument and yelling, the more fireworks, the more we were supposedly succeeding. But after the fourth session I was getting headaches and realizing that this way of interacting was degrading to me and in conflict with why we had been put onto this planet. So I had to quit. There isn't yet room in that context to say, "whoa, let's see if we can find some common ground here and build a different way of talking to each other." So my fears about being "out" as a spiritual person are well-founded, because I can no longer get those perks, because I can't do that kind of communication any longer. That kind of institution and the kind of heart I want to develop are increasingly out of sync with each other. So, I sometimes wonder if I might get to be so evolved that I won't have any job opportunities and won't have an income.

There is another fear: whenever you talk about God, there is always the fear that you will sound or be self-righteous or ego-maniacal. A lot of people use God as a résumé enhancer or to sell their products or themselves. That's why I shut down when I hear people talk about God and seem to be suggesting that they have the highest truth (I want to switch the channel). It's right to be cautious and wary, and to stress, as I want to here, that I'm only a beginner, that I have a spiritual hunger and not the spiritual truth. Even saying, as I did, that I'm more cautious than I used to be about what I say and what I do, could be heard by others as self-righteous and judgmental.

One form that my spiritual life has taken for me is to do Shabbat every week. I don't have many ways in my daily life to ask God to join what I'm doing. So it's very important to me to have a place in which I can do something with other people in which I can ask God to join me. And it's wonderful to me to be able to give this to my daughter Rosa, and to see how naturally children take to it and experience the change of the air as Shabbat comes in and the sacred enters (you can see it in their faces). It balances a week of very worldly activities.

I've moved my place in the progressive world. When I first started moving in this direction, I felt so alone and marginal. But I keep meeting people like Michael Lerner, Jim Wallis, people at the Center for Visionary Leadership, and people at the 1996 Politics of Meaning Summit hosted by the Foundation for Ethics and Meaning and *TIKKUN* magazine— people who are both progressive and share a deep spiritual interest. So I am increasingly drawn to people who are doing politics from a faith center or a vision of common global family or politics that comes out of love. I'm happy to know that they are out there—I really didn't know that they were.

ON RENEWING GOD

Zalman M. Schachter-Shalomi

Paradigm Shift in Consciousness

Right now we find ourselves in the midst of a paradigm shift which is shattering our reality maps. We all have grids of meaning which we express through language. When we say something is "self-evident," we refer to a common reality map, that collusion in which we all play by the same rules of evidence to converse and meet in the same universe of discourse.

Only with great difficulty and subtle discernment can our reality maps become accessible to our explicit inspection. Most of the time we don't even realize that we bring maps of meaning to every situation.

Apologia Pro Vita Sua

When I use the term "paradigm shift" I mean to describe an emerging and radically new way of looking at reality. When the patch jobs on old reality maps, like the Ptolemaic (ca. 100 B.C.E.) worldview (which saw Earth as the center of the Universe), no longer work, and it becomes essential to design a new one, like that of Copernicus (that the Earth revolves around the sun), we have a paradigm shift. A mind-move of such proportions has taken place that it represents not a mere adjustment of the old paradigm, correcting a detail here and another there, but rather a radically changed Weltanschauung.

A religious tradition contains faith-treasures that are independent of the reality maps with which they have become combined. Many religionists confuse the reality maps that arise from their empirical roadmaps with the "magisterium" of their lineage. In this way even though a paradigm no longer works, many people hold on with desperate tenacity to what has become obsolete. For many "true believers" a major shift of their reality-view threatens to unbalance the scaffolding of their value structure. So many of our assumptions and behaviors depend on these value complexes which they cannot separate from the shared and now obsolete reality maps. In the high anxiety about losing their moral moorings, they tend to go into denial about the inadequacies of their maps and declare the new outlook as "heresy." The high anxiety would be allayed if they trusted enough that once we delaminate our faith-treasures from the earlier maps, we can connect these valued treasures of tradition to the new maps.

What I am about to offer is meant as a witnessing to the process of updating religious traditions. All of us who cherish a sacred lineage and are imbedded in it are experiencing serious upheavals. In describing my dealing with my tradition I hope to be of help to others in other traditions dealing with similar problems.

Shift Happens!

Judaism has undergone several such "paradigm shifts": one with Abraham and the Patriarchs, Moses and the First Temple, another after the destruction of the First Temple and an even greater one after the destruction of the Second Temple, when all of our practices and beliefs had to be reframed. There have been some other shifts and adjustments. However, Auschwitz, Hiroshima and the moon walk have instigated yet another and even more dislocating shift. In my *Paradigm Shift* (Jason Aronson, 1993) I offer the journey of my own re-contextualization of Judaism as helped by Jewish mysticism. Having seen the process of regeneration in history, I was part of the application of this transformation in the current Jewish renewal. Jewish renewal differs from Restoration, which seeks to hold on to the last paradigm. People in Jewish renewal do not want to abandon sacred and cherished traditions or to toss them out along with outworn cosmologies. We are now privy to information which floods us with wonder at the view of a wider and ever more complex cosmos, and we don't want to put our minds in pawn as the price of our staying wedded to our tradition. Still, we look to fill our spiritual needs as experienced in the present with a maximum of tradition. To make this happen we have to retrofit our spiritual technology to the demands of our era. We are sensitive to feminism, human potential, ecology and Whole Earth thinking.

Autonomy-Heteronomy

Traditionalists often challenge renewalists: "What right have you got to modify a long-standing and Divinely revealed tradition?" My response is that revelation continues in the present. We are as much at the service of Divine revelation as earlier generations were. We have at this time an additional task, and furthermore, we are aware that we have a task. While there are those who *may be* better equipped than we, they don't perceive this as a need, so it devolves upon us.

In feeling this challenge I did not experience *one* seismic and pivotal moment with its special theophany. The process was gradual. There was a long series of these epiphanies, often unrelated to one another, and the effect was cumulative. And—this is crucial—making sense of these "aha" moments takes, first of all, an introspective attitude as well as some meditative and contemplative training. In this way I kept revising and readjusting my credo. I grew through adolescence during the Holocaust years. In the midst of hopelessness I saw glimpses of the Presence to which I pledged my life. This created a dynamic tension causing me to hold fast to both doubt and faith. The process was amplified by other experiences: by meeting great souls, by deep prayer and by the struggle we call God-wrestling.

I received much help from Jewish mysticism, the Kabbalah. Critics of the Kabbalah, from either rationalistic-scientist circles or fundamentalist ones, criticize those who teach it. Their criteria are largely ideological, intellectual and rationalistic. In those circles, preoccupation with Kabbalah was thought dangerous. Still smarting from the excesses of the followers of pseudo-messiahs, they felt the need to defend themselves from *what they considered* an unstable, reality-denying mysticism.

They Used to Say It Is Getting Worse—but Maybe Not?

Today our situation is different. As one encounters souls in process, one marvels at the amount of inner knowledge and sensitivity they possess. In my own adolescent searches I was blessed to find those who *listened* seriously to my questions and encouraged me to reach for answers that matched my inner learning, my intuition. So I find that those who honor this direct knowing will not place obstacles in the path of the seeker. Because I have a foot in the past and a foot in the future which was my given in life, I, too, was able to listen. I was uniquely placed to comprehend and bridge many worlds, both by historical events and by personal disposition. I held fast to both, often at great personal cost. This put me in a position to understand the complex struggles of the next generation and to teach them from an extraordinary vantage point.

The people I teach are often of much greater soul sophistication than those who have heaps of traditional book learning. The established institutions of Jewish education did not know how to cope with the issues that agitated many of the young of the post-Holocaust generation. They went to look elsewhere for their spiritual nourishment, and found it in a variety of places . . . Zen, Vedanta, psychedelics, etc. Hungry to relate the reality of the experiences to their ancestral tradition, they found very few who could honor their questions and answer them. Most members of the established leadership had not had these experiences and could not relate to them. The exoteric-ideological stance of the establishment repelled the seekers. Traditional esoteric teachers demanded that the seekers relinquish and deny their sacred encounters outside of the tradition and begin basic observances, first acquire Hebrew and study the basic text and only after they were sure of their loyalty to traditional Torah, *Hashkafah*—ideology— would offer them a smidgen of our treasures.

After the Holocaust

This is not the first time Judaism has dealt with paradigm shifts. During the time when there was a Holy Temple in Jerusalem, which was the only venue where we were permitted to make offerings on the altar, we offered animal sacrifices as our way of serving God. But because the Temple, its altars and its priesthood that slaughtered and offered the animals are destroyed, we can no longer make offerings of life that has to be killed for the sacred service. The cause, however, is even deeper than the destruction of a building: Sacrifice was no longer the right sacred technology for serving God. Another sacred technology, utilizing words, had to come to take its place. It has lasted to nearly the present day. Paradigms shift at crisis points: One-third of Jewry was destroyed at Auschwitz, and something fundamental and old in the world was destroyed with Hiroshima and Nagasaki. So we recognize that being Jewish after these events can no longer be a matter of simply following the past.

Being aware that we are going through the birth pangs of a paradigm shift which most traditions have not *yet* found a way to traverse, I am also concerned with the future of the spirituality inherent in those lineages. Treasures in those lineages need to be safeguarded against the breakdown of the old cosmologies with which they were yoked.

From Machine to Organism

There are aids, icons or images, that can allow us to render our maps accessible. The kabbalists called these *partzufim*. In every age and place people have dreamed the *partzufim,* these mythic icons, and from these emerged the legends, stories, meanings, motivations and covenants of the age. The dominant icon of the nineteenth century was the machine, a complex which includes notions of linear causality, of motivation, of causes creating effects. Its message was that in whatever one did, somebody or something was always at one's back, pushing. People call this paradigm "scientism," a way of looking at the universe as mechanical. A new reality map is emerging which is based on an organismic model. It says that Earth is alive; she is Gaia, the living planetary organism. Earth is alive, and every part, every species, every part of the chain of life, the *tz'ror ha-chayyim,* is integral and needed. For example, were it not for the mitochondria inside the cells inside my body, I couldn't live. In the chain of life there is an organismic relationship among things. This is the new *partzuf:* not the machine, but the organism. Naturally, there is a relationship between the dominant reality map and the shape of society.

Hierarchies

Hierarchy means the way the holy rule governs. In the Roman Church there is a hierarchy, topped by the "triple crown": The Pope is (1) the king, the "monarch" of the Vatican, (2) the highest priest of that church, and (3) the supreme legislator, the one who ultimately makes the definitive and final decisions. That is what Papal infallibility really means. It doesn't mean that he is always factually correct; it only means that the people below him in the hierarchy have to follow what he says.

Alas, we have found a problem with hierarchical systems: The ones on the top don't listen to the ones on the bottom. In the case of the Roman Church, for years, people have been saying women should be ordained. For years people have been saying that the priesthood won't work very well if it has to be *only* celibate; you will not get the vocations that you need. You have to pay attention to the needs of the people. You can't tell people to have numberless children when this doesn't work anymore. The world is dealing with overpopulation. Why is it that the ones on top can't listen to voices from below? Because hierarchy is deaf to the words that come from below.

Democracy

As we know, there came a time in history when people said, "We can't go on in the monarchial hierarchical mode." Then there emerged another possibility: *"Liberté, fraternité, égalité."* At that point we flattened everything out. In Scotland there arose the anti-hierarchical Presbyterians and

Congregationalists. There was a notion that everybody has an equal voice. Of course, there is something to be said for idea, expressed exactly in the Bible in Korach's critical words to Moses, the leader: "The entire congregation, they are all holy and God is in their midst. So why are you raising yourself over the congregation of God?" (Numbers 16:5). On the other hand, we also have seen that this flattened-out level, about which there is so much democratic rhetoric, is a lie. In what we call democracies, there are still hierarchies, some people who call the shots and wield power over others, whether in government or in corporations. The question is not so much whether or not there is true egalitarian democracy but rather, "Is laissez-faire democracy the answer?" It leads to so much chaos. There's no plan, no leadership—we are at the mercy of market forces. After all, one reason that there is so much crime today is that there is so much chaos.

We can observe that the mythological scaffolding of the various traditions has collapsed, and new scaffoldings have not arisen. The absence of a vital mythology for a whole and healthy Earth, one shared by all peoples and species, is a cause of great concern. Earth is in dire crisis for survival, and we have as yet no means to re-dream our hoped-for story. We have faced a historic turning point: the millennium. There is a need for visioning the future of human spirituality in harmony with our Gaian understanding. Here, too, most religions are failing us. Established lineages and religions seem to see as their task conserving the treasures of the past, rather than planning the innovations needed in the new era. Most of the theologians drive by looking at the rear-view mirror. Many are still in the thrall of a triumphalist hope that their religion will be ultimately vindicated as the Only True One and thus triumph over all the others. Such people will not be able to help their traditions through the paradigm shift. Advocating a cramped hold on traditions that no longer have transformative power, they cannot understand why they are losing adherents. The skillful means—*upaya*—of the devotional life need to be updated. However, the task of updating the skillful means of all the various traditions and lineages that assist in awakening can only be entrusted to people who come to terms with this paradigm shift.

The Torah of the Future

Torah has many dimensions of meaning for Judaism. When we talk about what the past can teach us, we also confront what the past cannot teach us. Some of the things that the past cannot teach us, we are being taught from the future. I make a simple blessing with the usual formula: "Blessed are you, God." Then I say the next two words, *melekh ha-olam*, literally, "King of the Universe." By that I don't mean an autocratic king with power over us; I mean the governing organismic being, of *ha-olam,* of Earth. The Gaia principle gives this blessing a new, deeper meaning for me.

As Hoyle has stated, once we see a picture of our Earth from outer space, we will have experienced an immense shift of perspective. An even greater mind mutation than any theoretical jump that we have made due to intellectual inquiry is caused by our seeing the image Earth Suspended in Space (from the *Hosha'not* prayer). No religious icon has such compelling force as Earth seen from outer space. There can no longer be a triumphalist attitude by any religion once we have encountered the planet as a living entity. In such an organismic view all traditions are like vital organs of humanity.

When I see a picture of Earth from outer space, I see no national boundaries, but rather an organic wholeness, a completeness. This is part of the Torah of the future. As Earth learns to understand and be aware of herself, she has her *mattan torah,* her gift of Torah. The Earth is waking up to consciousness. In the view of this totality, you and I and all of our little egos melt into a higher state of being conscious cells of that *melech ha-olam,* that vast life being that there is.

The Resurrection of the Dead

Let me give another example of how a tradition such as Judaism spirals in light of a new paradigm: Each day I recite several times the traditional Jewish formula, "Blessed are You who revives the dead." In what way can one affirm this ancient principle of the faith? I do not believe that the crypts will open up in cemeteries and that slimy corpses will crawl out of them. Should I believe that at some time at the end of days the individual cells of my remains will be reconstituted? How many bodies have I already worn out in only one lifetime? We keep on changing. I cannot claim that this body will rise at the time of the resurrection. Which one of my various bodies would it be, from which incarnation, from which time in history? How then can I believe in the resurrection of the dead and mean it? I believe that resurrection occurs when dead matter becomes a conscious living being. This resurrection seems to be happening to the totality of this planet at this very moment. A characteristic of the old machine paradigm is that we thought of matter as dead and unconscious. Today, in this age of nuclear technology, genetic engineering and supercomputers, matter is coming alive to us! We speak of atoms, molecules and cells as strings of information. Biologists have discovered that genetic consciousness is encoded in DNA and RNA. With the advent of the computer we now think of the memory as resident in silicon, a stone chip, in aluminum and now in copper *and traveling through fiber optics.* So what Descartes thought of as a mere machine also contains and holds the information of life. Our thinking about matter and the physical world has undergone a shift from death to life.

It is clear to us what the core of the Universe is saying to us: "As the chief head, this is how I want you to be: harmonious, for this is my purpose. You are integral, you are not an 'oops.' It wasn't a mistake that brought you into the world. You have a right to be here. You are a child of the Universe." I can't imagine anyone saying "No" to that. That integral feeling is the new *mattan torah,* the new revelation. You can't help but say, in Torah's words, *na'aseh v'nishma',* "We will do and we will conform, listen," in response to that, promising to further that aim in the world. I invite our dreaming, mything, midrashing, myth-rushing experiencing and thinking to help shape that next phase of our evolution. This is the blessing that we Jews are given: to serve as the organ of Jewry in the organism of the planet, as an instrument for healing and wholeness and as an agent for holiness. This, too, applies to other people who are "Israel" Godwrestlers, as it applies to all who have experienced an initiation into Gaian membership.

Reconfiguring the *Partzufim*

It is a deep work to reshape the *partzufim,* literally, the faces, masks, the inner templates that govern manifestation on this plane, and it requires our immense concentration and patience. The time for the either/or choices in religion is over. We can no longer consider the other world religions to be idolatry. If an Elijah at Carmel were to appear today demanding us to choose between YHVH, the rider of the clouds, and, let's say, Ba'al, the rider of the clouds, a distinction of name and not function, many of us would tell him to go back to the ultra-orthodox world and not bother us. My commitment to the life of the planet is stronger than my commitment to any philosophy or creed. Many of us have the same commitment. If you have felt commanded by the Divine Imperative to protect Earth from planetary destruction, then you have undergone the first stage of a Gaian initiation.

Gaian Initiation

Such an experience also requires that we, all of us, undergo an identity shift from ethnic to global so that we can begin to live that initiation. In more traditional Jewish language, my theological approach is based on the realization of the pervasiveness of *hashgahah,* Divine Providence, the unfolding of Earthmind. That is, we are deployed from beyond ourselves. Let us have *emunah,* loyal faith, and *bittaḥon,* trust, that the universe is unfolding as it should. Accept that you will be led by Wisdom, *Ḥokhmah,* Sophia, as She arises from the planetary mind. Open up to the possibility of accessing on the "innernet," the inner Internet, what the *melekh ha-olam* requires of us. The Torah that is now coming down vertically will harmonize with what has come down through history longitudinally.

Cleaning Up the Word "God"

I want to take the word "God" and clean it up a little. What happens most of the time when people are faced with a set liturgy in a prayer book? They see words that their head can't take in. This confusion and frustration withdraws energy from the process of prayer. But the words do not belong to the head: They belong to the heart. Taken on the level of the heart, we are not interested in them as information. It is as if my wife says to me, "I love you," and I say, "You told me that yesterday." It's a silly answer because she was not trying to inform me of something I didn't know. It's a feeling she wants to transmit. It's heart to heart. I'm not talking head stuff, I am talking heart stuff. The Siddur, the prayer book, is "heart stuff." There is dualistic language which my head cannot really digest about God, that God is an other, a way, way far off "other." I can't deal with that; I don't see the Santa Claus in the sky. So what am I talking about? I am talking about that Being who is the center of the universe, the volition, the mind center of the universe, the heart and love center of the universe. That's what I want to communicate with. That's the part *speaking in* me that says, "Every moment I energize in your being, and every moment I am prepared to receive your glorification." Now, that nourishes something very deep in the soul that has gotten very hungry among us.

What is it that we have to do in this world? An intuition, an "in-teaching," comes in and says the most risky thing: You have to Love. You have to proceed in the world as if all the chaos and pain, the shadow, were not around. You cannot fight the darkness with the means of darkness; you have to bring in light, and the light has to take risks. Something has to give. Something has to change. The status quo can't be maintained because it has become too expensive for the individual and for the planet.

Out of the Chaos

The blessing in all this is our new understanding of what impermanence is about. The future brings with it a process that undermines the status quo. The old cosmology and its institutions are failing. The pain from the meltdown of the accepted scaffolding is great. It becomes bearable and brings hope when we put our trust in the Source of our lives. There is a providential guidance toward more consciousness, greater cohesion and harmony amidst the burgeoning complexity. Chaos theory has come to open us to the future. The dissipation of known structures points to a higher integration. Growth will likely continue on a higher point of the spiral or, if you like, on the next more containing level of the fractals, the higher holon. After all, we are Theomorphic beings: We can't help but grow toward God.

ETERNITY UTTERS A DAY

David Wolpe

THE MODERN WORLD NEVER WHISPERS. As I drive in my car, the shrill voice of the announcer, punctuated by the even more urgent voice of the commercial, demands attention. On each streetcorner, billboards and signs and promises swirl around me as though I have stepped into an arcade of clanging bells and video games, but the arcade is the city, and there is no exit. I recognize that I am part of this pageant, that I choose to be here, and that the mania is the price of the vibrance and variety.

At home, I can turn on the television and the computer. Each catapults me into another life, another part of the world. I am "linked"—a word all too close to being chained. Still I turn them on, because I do not wish to turn away from my own time. I have taught history, and learned too well that the past is no panacea; neon signs and phone calls at dinner are hardly enough to make me forget the blessings of vaccinations, sanitation and reliable shelter. I live in this world, and yet I cannot help but bang my fists occasionally against the cage, and wonder when the noise will cease, and the bliss promised in every advertisement for every product from automobiles to hand soap, will at last be mine.

Friday night arrives. I know what my task is at this moment: I am to stop affecting the world and to live in harmony with it. Even though I am a tangle of yearnings, on this day everything is to be perfect. I am to be satisfied with the many blessings that I have in my life. For once, I am to be at peace with the universe.

Yet again I remember a little book. It is less than 100 pages, but carries the wisdom of the ages. It was written by A. J. Heschel, and it is called *The Sabbath*. Heschel teaches me the blessing of technology—it obliterates distance. I can turn on my television and be part of life in a country across the globe. The lesson of space is the beginning.

The world changed, wrote the essayist E. B. White, on the day a man walked on the moon. It changed because for the first time millions of people chose to stay inside and watch the moon on a screen in their living rooms rather than step outside and see the thing directly. In other words, we preferred the obliteration of distance, even if it meant seeing the world through a lens. Back in 1950, when he wrote *The Sabbath*, Heschel knew the meaning of that change. For he teaches me that although technology conquers space, we do not live our lives in space alone. We live in time. "This is the task of men: to conquer space and sanctify time."

My friends have no time. Their lives are crowded. They do not see their friends, play with their overscheduled children, put their feet up and stare out the window. They cannot; they must drive somewhere, check their email, return their phone calls—in other words, conquer space.

But even if we correspond at the touch of a button with others around the world, technology does not sanctify time. We do. God's greatest gift is to endow human beings with the capacity to perceive—and to create—holiness.

Jews have not, through their wanderings, had the leisure or the need to build grand cathedrals. Yet we have celebrated the Sabbath, a cathedral in time. It can be celebrated in a ramshackle hut, in a cave, in a barren field. The sanctity of time requires not technology, but devotion of soul.

So on Friday night I stop. Before the candles and the wine we sing, and my wife and I bless our beautiful little girl. She is not yet four years old. She has not yet heard of Heschel, but she understands him.

It takes only three things, wrote this sage, to create a sense of significant being—God, a soul and a moment. And the three, he said, are always present.

A KABBALAH FOR THE ENVIRONMENTAL AGE

Arthur Green

IT IS AN IRONY OF HISTORY that Kabbalah, jettisoned by generations of modern Jews as so much backward nonsense, is now making a comeback. In an age when modernity itself is being questioned, this renewal of interest in mystical aspects of Judaism is both spiritually exciting and potentially dangerous, even explosive. The danger lies in the deep connection to be found between Kabbalah and both the xenophobic and the messianic elements of Jewish tradition. When mystical faith supplants political judgment, or when medieval views of the difference between Jewish and gentile souls are reflected in social policy attitudes of Israeli power-brokers, the entire Jewish people is endangered. But the promise of the mystical tradition and its potential contribution to a Judaism that could appeal to many seekers is so great that this writer, along with many others in our time, is willing to take the risk.

I am certainly not a Kabbalist in the traditional sense, nor do I aspire to be one. The old system, *qua* system, does not work for me. The mythic universe of Kabbalah, for all its beauty, belongs to another age. Whether we look at its hierarchical structure, at the Jewish exclusivism and spiritual racism implied by its doctrine of the soul, or at the passive-subject role assigned to the feminine, I for one do not believe that a return to the mentality of the ancients is the solution to our current woes. Instead, our age is very much in need of *a post-Kabbalistic Jewish mysticism,* one richly nourished, but not dominated, by the old language and structure. That new

Jewish mysticism, Kabbalah in a universalist and pluralist key, has been slowly emerging over the course of the twentieth century, a process that has more recently moved into high gear. This new pace and high degree of interest is part of a much broader world-wide re-examination of the great spiritual traditions, a seeking out of ancient wells of wisdom that might sustain us in a new and unprecedented period in human history.

Humanity is in urgent need of a new sort of piety, a religious attitude fitting to an environmentally concerned future that is already upon us. This new mining of ancient religious truth is being applied to all the traditions. As a Jew who has been studying and teaching Kabbalah and Hasidism for forty years, I believe that our tradition has much to offer, if we combine deep examination of the sources with a willingness to choose carefully among them and update their teachings when necessary. Among the elements I seek is *a Judaism unafraid to proclaim the holiness of the natural world,* one that sees creation, including both world and human self, as a reflection of divinity and a source of religious inspiration. It is in this spirit that I turn to Kabbalah, seeking to learn from, but also to adapt and transform, its vision. The essential truth of mysticism, that all beings are manifestations of the same one, and that the unity of being can be discovered by a disciplined training of the mind toward insight, is one that our age both longs and needs to hear. The understanding that God is the innermost reality of all that is, and that God and universe are related not primarily as Creator and creature, but as deep structure and surface, is key to the Judaism of the future. But the ways in which we develop and act upon that insight will have to be appropriate to our own age.

The magnificent architechtonics of the Kabbalists' vision cannot be articulated here. Their grand picture of the inner universe, in which the One that encompasses all being opens up to reveal itself as ten, is the beginning of the Kabbalistic system. The ten *sefirot* (literally: "numbers") are stations in the flow of energy from the One into the many. The ten-in-one cosmos is a way of responding to the eternal mystical question "How do the many proceed from the One?" The Kabbalists say: "Very slowly and subtly. Let us show you the process." As one gets farther into Kabbalah it turns out that each of the ten *sefirot* contains all the other nine and the whole process of tenfold manifestation repeats itself four times as one journeys through various upper or inner "worlds." There is thus a basic "grid" of four hundred rungs, each discussed with great finesse in the highly refined symbolic language of Kabbalah. Other versions of the Kabbalistic "map" have the ten *sefirot* open themselves further to reveal more decads, becoming hundreds, thousands, and so forth. Later Kabbalists redivide the ten into five configurations of *sefirot* that each exists in six modes or stages, leading to a system of staggering and overwhelming complexity.

For the initiate, the *sefirot* also serve as rungs or marking points of the mystic's inward journey. His goal (it only also can become "hers" in very recent times) is to reverse the journey of God from unity into multiplicity, going back to make the many into one again. The Kabbalist who "ascends" those rungs ideally "uplifts" the lower worlds, taking them along on the journey back to oneness. In this way they, along with the mystic's own soul, may be re-included in the one. This is the Kabbalistic concept of *tikkun,* the restoration of the worlds to their original harmony as carried out in this "uplifting" activity of the mystical life. Each person is a microcosm, also built in that same pattern of the *sefirot,* so that cosmology and psychology, our ways of understanding life's origins and our own innermost selves, are quite identical. God's cosmic journey into multiplicity and your inward journey into unity are mirror images of one another.

This "great chain of being" approach to spirituality can be appreciated more than ever by post-moderns, not only for its beauty but for a certain dimly perceived accuracy as well. Each human being contains the entire universe, claims the ancient myth. All the rungs of descent (and potential ascent) are contained in each soul. But that is true, even in de-mythologized form: all of our ancestors, each stage and mini-step in the evolution of life that brought us to where we are today, are present within us. The DNA that constitutes the life-identity of each of us exists indeed *zekher le-ma'aseh bereshit,* "in memory of the act of Creation," linking us back to our most remote origins.

Part of our work as self-aware, articulate beings is converting that biological "memory" into consciousness and building a holy structure (i.e., a religion or a civilization) that articulates and *sanctifies* those links between past and future. In this way the actual fact of all our past's presence within us is converted into a basis for meaning, for expression of our deep rootedness in all that is and has come before us. The memory of the entire universe lies within each and every one of us. Hopefully the values represented by that ongoing project of civilization-building will lead us forward as well, helping us realize that we must be faithful transmitters to all the many future links in the evolutionary chain, just as we are the grateful recipients of the efforts of all those that have fought the ongoing life-struggle to bring us to this moment. All of the upper and lower "worlds" of the Kabbalist here become manifest in human terms, as generations that lie before and behind us but also as multiple layers of human self-awareness that we seek to peel back in search of our deepest and truest selves.

Creation and Revelation, according to esoteric Judaism, are two different but parallel manifestations of the primordial Torah, or the creative wisdom of God. We might think of this as universal Mind, the wisdom that is manifest both in the ways of nature and in the deepest soul of human beings. At the heart of these twin self-revelations of the One, as understood in Jewish language, lies the barely whispered breath of the four semi-consonants *Yod He Waw He,* the verbal noun that tries to express the divine Self. In the hierarchy of language, this is the supreme word. Too holy to be spoken aloud except by the high priest on the Day of Atonement, it is the word that stands closest to the silence that surpasses all language. This name is an impossible conflation of the verb "to be"; hence the God of Exodus, where the name is introduced, says: "I shall be whatever I shall be," meaning that the elusive Self of the universe will ever escape definition. Those four letters are really a term for being— HaWaYaH—itself. But because they are mere breath (for there is no really consonantal "hard" sound in any of them), they also stand for the birth of language itself, the emergence of the word from the universal silence beyond, from what we Jews call the eternal Torah of God, the wordless truth that "was" before Creation.

God *is* Being: Y-H-W-H, when existence is seen from a fully unitive, harmonic, and all-embracing point of view—a perspective that ever eludes us mere humans, located as we are in particular identities of time and space. The small self and its limitations keep us from seeing the great Self at work both within and around us. But then the letters, like pieces in a puzzle, are mysteriously re-arranged and HaWaYaH, existence itself, reveals itself to be none other than Y-H-W-H, the great name that proclaims so powerful a unity of being that it could be spoken only there, in the innermost holy chamber of the holy Temple.

Kabbalah is a tale of origins, an account of how the many come forth from the One and how we may embark on the return journey to oneness. But our beginning point of understanding has to take us beyond Kabbalah, back to the Biblical tale of origins. The Kabbalists' universe depends entirely on the much older Biblical creation tale, the ingenious opening chapter of Genesis that for nearly twenty-five hundred years served as chief source for the West's understanding of natural, including human, origins. The account of how God in six days spoke each order of existence into being is now of only antiquarian interest as an actual account of how the world came to be, though it remains alive for us as a liturgical text and a source of religious creativity.

But I would like to lift the veil behind Genesis 1 and ask just what it was that this magnificently penned single chapter managed to accomplish. The old Mesopotamian and Canaanite creation myths, now barely recalled, were well-known to the Biblical authors. They include the rising up of the primal forces of chaos, represented chiefly by Yam or Tiamat, gods of the sea, against the order being imposed by the sky-gods. The defeat of that primordial rebellion and its bloody end is well-documented, as scholars have shown, in a number of passages within the Bible: in the prophets, Psalms, Job, and by subtle implication even in the Genesis text itself. That tale of origins was a part of the cultural legacy of ancient Israel. The fact that it is reflected even in post-Biblical Midrashic sources shows that it had a long life, continuing even into the Zohar of the thirteenth century. The original readers/hearers of Genesis 1, in other words, knew of another account of creation, one of conflict, slaughter, and victory, "the survival of the fittest" among the gods. What is striking about this account is precisely the *absence* of those elements of conflict: Genesis 1 offers a purely harmonistic version of the origin of creatures, one where everything has its place as the willed creation of the single Deity and all conflict has mysteriously been forgotten.

Our civilization has been transformed over the past century and a half in no small part by our acceptance of a new tale of origins, one that began with Darwin and is refined daily by the work of life-scientists and physicists, the new Kabbalists of our age who claim even to know the black hole out of which being itself came to be, speculating on the first few seconds of existence as our ancestors once did on the highest triad of the ten *sefirot* or rungs of divine being. The history of living creatures is again depicted as a bloody and violent struggle, the implications of which for human behavior—even for the possibilities of human ethics—have hardly gone unnoticed. We too are urgently in need of a new and powerfully harmonistic vision, one that will allow even the weakest and most threatened of creatures a legitimate place in this world and protection from being wiped out at the careless whim of the creature who stands, at least for now, at the top of the evolutionary mound of corpses. A beautiful attempt at articulating such a vision was made by Brian Swimme and Thomas Berry a few years ago in *The Universe Story*. Such a vision more willing to base itself on the Biblical/Judaic legacy would also be a welcome contribution.

But let us return for a moment to the old creation tale. While I no longer believe it in any literal sense and do not look to it, even through reinterpretation (Each "day" is a geologic era, etc.) as a source of information about geohistory, I claim it still as a *religious* text for me as a Jew and for us as a people. We still read it in the synagogue, and its closing section is the introductory rubric for our most precious and best-beloved sacred form: the observance of the Sabbath. "Heaven and earth were finished, and all their hosts . . ." What then does the text mean to me? What underlies the myth, or to what truth or value am I pointing by so privileging this ancient text?

The text says that before there were many, there was only the one. Before the incredible variety and richness of life as we know it could come to be, there had to exist a simple self, a source from which all the many proceeded. I refer not to some single-celled amoeba that existed in the ocean hundreds of millions of years ago. I read the text on a different level by asserting that *the primacy of the one to the many is not necessarily temporal in meaning.* Sacred myth describes a deep and ineffable reality, one so profound that it is not given to expression except through the veil of narration, through encapsulation in a story. And stories, given the need for a sequential plot, require time. So the precedence of the One over the many, placed into story-form, comes out sounding like: "In the beginning God created . . ." Its meaning, however, is that the One underlies the many then, now, and forever. A dimly perceived but awesome deep structure links all things and ties them to the root out of which they all emerge. Multiplicity is the garbing of the One in the coat-of-many-colors of existence, the transformation of Y-H-W-H, singularity itself, Being, into the infinite varieties of H-W-Y-H, being as we know, encounter, and *are* it.

The Genesis "Creation" story is really a tale of the origins of multiplicity, a Biblical attempt to answer that eternal question of mystics to which the later account of the *sefirot* was also addressed: "How do the many proceed from the One?" This reality is symbolized by the beginning of the Torah with the letter *bet*, long a subject of speculation within Jewish tradition. *Bet* is numerically "two"; its positioning at the beginning of Torah indicates that here is the beginning of *duality*. From now on there is not just "God" but "God and . . ." This meaning is dramatically reinforced by the emergence of Creation in what are repeatedly described as pairs: light and darkness, day and night, heaven and earth, upper and lower waters, sun and moon, male and female, and all the rest. Behind all these twos, however, behind the *bet* of *Bereshit bara'* ["In the beginning God created"], lies the hidden, singular, silent *aleph*. This One, representing the absolute oneness of being, the one after which there is no "two," is to be proclaimed at Sinai in the opening letter of *anokhi*, "I am," the very heart of revelation. So there are two ways in which the One is revealed. One leads through the path of infinite multiplicity and diversity, the one as manifest within the many, God in creation. The other is the invitation to the return journey, revealing to us the aleph that underlies all being, the One to which we all return, both in the ecstatic silence of mystical journey and in the ultimate ego-transcendence of death.

This One, I believe, is the only Being that ever was, is, or will be. It is the One that undergoes the only sacred drama that really matters: the bio-history of the universe. *I believe that it does so as a conscious and willful Self.* From those first seconds of existence, through the emergence of life in its earliest manifestations, and along every step, including the seeming stumblings, missteps, and blind alleys along the way of evolution, it is this single Being that is evolving, entering into each new life-form, ever carrying within itself the memory of all its past. I thus seek to re-vision the evolutionary process, not as the struggle of creature against creature and species against species, but as the emergence of a single life-energy, a single cosmic Mind that *uses* the comparative adaptabilities of all the forms it enters as a means of ongoing striving ever forward into richer and more diverse forms of life. The formless Self searches out endless forms, delighting to rediscover its own identity anew in each of them. That constant movement of the One, expansive in all directions at once, is at the same time directed movement, pointing toward the eventual emergence of a life-form that can fully know and realize the One that lives in all beings. This creature, the one in whom the self-knowledge of Being can be ultimately fulfilled, is thus the *telos* of existence.

In this process, the emergence of humanity with its gifts of intellect, self-awareness, and language, is indeed a major step forward. Judaism has always taught a distinction between humans and other forms of life, a sense in which the human stands beyond the vegetative and animal realms out of which we emerged. Each creature embodies the life-energy and hence the presence of the One, but only humans are called "God's image" in our tradition. This means that we are the first to have the mental capacity to recapitulate the process, to be self-conscious about our roots within the One. The implications of that potential are tremendous if we understand the mystical journey back to oneness as a central value within human existence, the "opposite" that complements our drive toward progress, growth, and forward movement. But surely our being "in the divine image" is not meant to give us license for the rapacious destruction of all so-called "lower" forms. God forbid! That would be the model of the "species eat species" view of evolution. Although we are indeed by design and necessity eaters of the "lower" species, we still seek a life of harmony and balance with them. The Bible provides two models for defining humanity's role in relation to the natural world. One is that of Genesis 1: humans as stewards, the viceroy who is to "rule over the fish of the sea, the birds of the sky, and all the beasts who roam the earth." But if we look into the Psalms, the concluding chapters of Job, and other Scriptural sources, we find another option. I quote from Psalm 148 (using a recent contemporary adaptation by Stephen Mitchell):[1]

> Praise God upon the earth,
>> whales and all creatures of the sea,
> fire, hail, snow, and frost,
>> hurricanes fulfilling his command,
> mountains and barren hills,
>> fruit trees and cedar forests,
> wild animals and tame,
>> reptiles, insects, birds,
> creatures invisible to the eye
>> and tiniest one-celled beings,
> rich and poor, powerful
>> and oppressed, dark-skinned and light-skinned,
> men and women alike,
>> old and young together.

Here the Psalmist envisions us as *part* of the universal chorus of praise, rather than isolating us as the final creation of Friday afternoon, with the message of "stewardship" that accompanies it. A true understanding of the unitive vision being proclaimed here would lead us beyond the demands of "stewardship," the ethic usually derived from the Biblical tale. Life's meaning is to be found in discovering the One, and that means realizing the ultimate unity of all being. It is in *yihud*, discovering and proclaiming the underlying oneness of all existence, that our humanity is fulfilled.

We are of the One; each human mind is a microcosm, a miniature replica of the single Mind that conceives and becomes the universe. To know that oneness and recognize it *in all our fellow-beings* is what life is all about. But that recognition leads us to another level of awareness. The One *delights* in each of the infinite forms in which it is manifest. To play on that lovely English verb, this means that the One sends its *light* into each of these forms. Vegetative forms indeed experience this gift most in sunlight, stretching toward it as they grow. We humans are privileged to experience that same radiating light-energy as delight or love.

The One *loves* the many. The coat-of-many-colors in which Being comes to be garbed is a garment of delight. We, as the self-conscious expression of Being, are called upon to love as well, to partake in and give human expression to the *delightfulness* of existence. This is expressed in Jewish liturgy by the order of our daily prayers. The blessing of God as the source of nature's light is directly followed by a blessing for God's love. The One does nothing different in the interim between these blessings. God does nothing different in giving light to all creatures, plant and animal, and in giving love to human beings and holy communities, assemblies of God-seekers wherever they are. As humans who are creatures of love, we receive the divine life-flow in the form of love, turning toward it and being fulfilled by it just as naturally as plants stretch toward the light. Nature experiences this shining as light; we humans receive it as love. But as recipients of love we are called upon (Dare I say "commanded"?) to love as well.

I am also fully willing to admit that we may be but an early stage in an ongoing evolution of aware beings. Perhaps our period will be looked upon in the distant future, by creatures no more willing to demean themselves by the word "human" than we are comfortable being called "ape," as a primitive life-stage. Surely they will not be wrong, those wise beings of the future, in seeing our age as characterized by nothing so much as pretentiousness and self-glorification on the one hand, and wanton consumption and pillage of earth's resources on the other. Let us hope we leave room for that wise future to emerge.

Discovering the presence of the One within the natural order and therefore the sacred quality of existence itself is exactly what our father Abraham did, according to Philo of Alexandria, the hidden grandfather of all Jewish philosophy. This One manifested itself to him in terms of law: Abraham felt that he was being taught how to live in harmony with the forces of nature. Moses' Torah, according to Philo, is the lawgiver's attempt to legislate for a whole human community the life of harmonic insight with the God of nature that Abraham had already found for himself. I have tried to show elsewhere that certain writings of the Hasidic masters, unaware of the ancient precedent, continue this trend. Rabbi Levi Yizhak of Berdichev, the 18th century Hasidic master, introduces his treatise on hidden miracles, or the miraculous within nature, with precisely this claim: Sinai allows the entire people to apprehend that which wise old Abraham had already long earlier discerned on his own.

The law that teaches us how to live in harmony with the natural world should be one of eternal principles and countless new applications. Its most basic teachings should demand of us that we live ever at the cutting edge of sensitivity toward the suffering we cause God's creatures. We need be aware of the rest and reinvigoration that we give to the soil, the waste of living resources, for each is the embodiment of divine presence. We may not take the endless material gifts with which we are blessed any more casually than we would take God's *name* in vain. We may not take the One's great gift of holy *water* in vain. Or *air,* source of *nishmat kol hai,* the sacred breath of life. To rest on the laurels of forms our ancestors created long ago or boast of their progressivism in the tenth or sixth century B.C.E. is very much not to the point. What is the point of observing *shemitah,* the sabbatical year, but using earth-destroying pesticides? Of insisting on the humanity of *shechitah,* kosher slaughter, but hoisting and shackling and refusing to stun animals to lessen their awareness before they die? Of washing the bugs out of our lettuce while investing that other green stuff in multinational corporations that daily destroy entire forests? How can we *today* create a civilization and a law that will be such a *torat hayyim,* a teaching that enhances life? And what will it demand of us? Surely a return to the reverence for air, water, fire (by limiting the amount that we, including our automobiles, burn!), and soil would be a good place to start.

Another potentially useful rubric within tradition for proclaiming this insight is the parallel between the ten divine utterances (of "let there be . . .") in Creation and the ten "commandments" (the Hebrew might be better rendered as "speech-acts") of Sinai. This is another way of expressing the unity between the revelation that lies within Creation and that which is manifest in Torah. The presence of the One that underlies all being is depicted as pure verbal energy: God is the One who ever, unceasingly, says "*Yehi!*" ["Let there be!"], speaking the world into being. But at Sinai, those ten *yehi*'s are translated into imperatives for us; the inner "law" of God's presence in nature is now manifest in the form of imperatives that can govern human existence, bringing us into harmony with the ten words within ourselves as well as within all creatures. And since the ten "commandments" are the basis of all the six hundred thirteen yeas and nays that comprise Torah, all of it is tied through them to the ten cosmogenerative utterances of the One. This parallel is a great favorite of certain mystical teachers. Creation and revelation are two deeply interrelated manifestations of the same divine Self, one showing us that all existence is fraught with holiness, the other instructing us on how to live in the face of that awareness.

Here the language of Kabbalah may be useful again. These two tens, the utterances and the commandments, are both versions of the ten *sefirot,* those primal numbers that allow us deeper entree into the "secret" of existence. We manifest that secret by turning outward and inward toward the world around us, seeing it in all its awesome beauty and recognizing how deeply we are a part of all that is. We then ask (in good Jewish fashion): "What does this awareness *demand* of us?" Here we have the beginning-point of a new Kabbalah and a new Halakhah ("path" of religious practice) as well. This praxis, one using and adapting the rich forms of Jewish tradition, should be one that leads us to a life of harmony with the natural world and maximum concern for its preservation.

All this talk must seem terribly mythical to readers of a more scientific bent of mind. Perhaps is also seems obscure and irrelevant to some of those most keenly aware of the several immediate threats to global existence. Let me assure you that I share that sense of urgency. Life has so evolved that the fate of the biosphere itself is now determined by human actions. We are masters not only over our own species and over those we consume, as so many others have been. The very existence of our planet as a fit habitat for *any* living thing has now fallen into human hands.

With this increase in human power comes a manifold increase of responsibility. It is the future not only of our own offspring that we threaten each day with a million decisions weighted with political, economic, and competitive baggage. The land itself, the *adamah* from which we humans derive our name, is threatened by us, the earth and all that is upon it. The changes needed in collective human behavior in order to save us from self-destruction are stupendous. Belief in their possibility stretches our credulity as much as it is demanded by our need for hope. Our economic system, including the value we place on constant expansion and growth, will have to change. The standards of consumption, created by our wealthiest economies and now the goal of all others, will have to be diminished. Effective world government, perhaps even at the cost of some of our precious freedoms, will have to triumph over the childish bickerings and threats that currently characterize world affairs.

Hardly believable, indeed. But consider the alternative. If any of this deep-seated change is to come about, religious leaders and thinkers need to take an early lead. A seismic shift in the mythical underpinnings of our consciousness is required; nothing less will do the trick. That shift will have to come about within the framework of the religious languages now spoken by large sections of the human race. Experience tells us that newly created myths do not readily take hold; they usually lack the power to withstand great challenge. But a re-routing of ancient symbols, along channels already half-cleared by the most open-eyed thinkers of earlier centuries, might indeed enable this conversion of the human heart of which we speak.

In the emergence of a new tale of origins, we Jews, who have for so long been bearers of the old tale, have a special interest. The new tale will need to achieve its own harmony, summarized with no less genius than was possessed by the author of Genesis 1. It will need to tell of the unity of all beings and help us to feel that fellow-creaturehood with trees and rivers as well as with animals and humans. As it brings us to awareness of our common source, ever-present in each of us, so must it value the distinctiveness and sacred integrity of each creature on its own, even the animals, or fish, or plants we eat, even the trees we cut down. If we Jews are allowed to have a hand in it, it will also speak of a human dignity that still needs to be shared with most of our species and of a time of rest, periodic liberation from the treadmill of our struggle for existence, in which we can contemplate and enjoy our fellow-feeling with all that is. This sacred time also serves as a model for the world that we believe "with perfect faith" is still to come, a world of which we have never ceased to dream.

NOTE

1. Stephen Mitchell, *A Book of Psalms, Selected and Adapted from the Hebrew* (New York: HarperCollins, 1993), Psalm 148.

IS GOD IN TREES?

Dennis Prager

When people stop believing in God,
they don't believe in nothing, they believe in anything.
—G. K. Chesterton, 1874–1936

IN THE WEST in the twentieth century, the decline of belief in God and God-based religion has led to belief in communism, Fascism, Nazism, national-ism, racism, innumerable cults, the equation of humans and animals, and numerous other foolish ideas, especially among secularized intellectuals.

At the present time, the most powerful belief substituting for God and traditional religion is belief in nature. One expression of this belief can be found in environmentalism. Concern for the environment is vitally impor-tant, and anyone concerned with human survival, let alone with protect-ing the beauty of nature, should be seriously concerned with protecting the environment. But the term environmentalism signals more than love and concern for the environment. When a cause becomes an "ism," it has be-come in most instances a form of religion, and caution is called for. (People who place stickers on their car bumpers that read "Love your Mother"—with a picture of the planet earth ensuring that we know which mother they mean—probably do love the earth as much as they love their mother.)

The second major contemporary expression of nature-worship—one which divides lovers of the environment from worshippers of it—threatens traditional beliefs even more, for it is taking place within, as well as outside, religion. It is pantheism, the equating of God with nature.

Pantheism is not new; indeed, it is as old as recorded history. But it has not played a prominent role in Western thinking until the contemporary era.

Few present day pantheists—whether followers of New Age thinking or active Jews or Christians who have adopted pantheistic thinking—actually label themselves as such. But whatever the terminology, pantheism is returning.

The Hebrew Bible's Preoccupation with Separating God from Nature

The return of pantheism is not surprising. Belief in the God introduced by the Hebrew Bible has never been particularly popular; it denies too many of the gods that people really want to worship.

And the most popular god of humanity—indeed, the most natural one—has always been nature. There is nothing nearly as powerful, as frightening, and as beautiful as nature. It is also the one thing that human beings cannot fully conquer.

Given all of nature's awesome qualities, it is quite understandable that it would be worshipped, and that most of humanity's gods would be gods of nature.

Against all of this came the Hebrew Bible, specifically the Torah (the Five of Books of Moses), to declare that there are no nature-gods, that there is one God who is not contained within nature, but who is infinitely beyond nature—the Creator-God of nature.

- That is why Genesis One is unique among the opening chapters of sacred scriptures of the world's religions. It doesn't mention the founder(s) of the religion, or the religion itself, or the adherents of the religion; it doesn't mention Jews, Judaism, Israel or Abraham. Rather, Genesis One concerns itself solely with God creating nature. The Torah begins with its preoccupation—removing God from nature. The idea that God is not natural is the essence of monotheistic religion. From the Torah's point of view, to compromise with this idea is as serious a departure from belief as atheism (which ought to lead Jews to be at least as concerned with Jews for Nature as they are with "Jews for Jesus").

- That is why no images of God are allowed in the Ten Commandments. Professor Nahum Sarna, in his commentary on the Book of Exodus, explains this with regard to the Commandment against graven images: "The revolutionary Israelite concept of God entails His being wholly separate from the world of His creation and wholly other than what the human mind can conceive or the human imagination depict."

- That is why the plagues against Egypt were in fact plagues against the nature-gods of Egypt—from the first plague of changing the Nile River god to blood, to the ninth plague of blocking out the sun god, the chief god of Egypt. It was essential that the Hebrews leave Egypt understanding that the nature-gods of Egypt were not gods.

There is no mainstream Jewish biblical commentary—Orthodox or non-Orthodox—that does not emphasize the Torah's unique and revolutionary struggle against deifying nature. To cite one other biblical scholar, the late Umberto Cassuto of Italy, who became Professor of Bible at the Hebrew University of Jerusalem:

> Relative to the ideas prevailing among the peoples of the ancient East, we are confronted here [in the Torah] with a basically new conception and a spiritual revolution. . . .
>
> The basically new conception consists in the completely transcendental view of the Godhead. This breaks entirely new ground even vis-à-vis the trend . . . to acknowledge the dominion of one god, namely, the sun-disc, called Aton. But Aton is still a body and force in nature, and the Egyptian king is his incarnation in human form, whereas the God of Israel is outside and above nature, and the whole of nature, the sun, and the moon, and all the hosts of heaven, and the earth beneath, and the sea that is under the earth, and all that is in them—they are all His creatures which He created according to His will.

Why Nature Cannot be Divine

It is quite understandable that people who use feelings more than reason to form their spiritual beliefs would deify nature. What is puzzling is that many people who want to rely more on reason would do so. Is it not obvious that nature is amoral? That it is largely compassionless? That nature has no moral laws, only the law of Survival of the Fittest?

Why would people who venerate compassion and kindness want to venerate nature? The notion of caring for the weak is unique to humanity. In the rest of nature, the weak are to be killed so as to better preserve the species. The individual means nothing to nature; the individual is every-thing to humans. A hospital, for example, is a profoundly unnatural, in-deed anti-natural, creation. To expend precious resources on keeping the most frail alive is simply against nature.

The romanticization of nature involves ignoring so much of what re-ally happens in nature. I wonder if American schoolchildren would have conducted their campaign on behalf of freeing a killer whale (the whale in the film, *Free Willy*) if they had seen films of killer whale behavior that I have seen. These National Geographic videos show, among other things, killer whales tossing a terrified baby seal back and forth to each other be-fore finally eating it.

Perhaps we should start a campaign to have American schoolchildren petition killer whales not to treat baby seals sadistically.

If God Is in Trees, Then God Is in Cancer

I recently heard a Jewish professor/author lecture on the Kabbalah. Like many other non-traditional Jews, he uses the Kabbalah (Jewish mysticism) to sustain his nature-centered views. "God is in the bark of a tree," he told the audience.

Many non-traditional Jews and Christians, not to mention followers of New Age thinking, maintain as this professor does, that "God is in trees" and "Trees are divine."

There are three problems with this view: theological, logical and moral.

- The theological problem is that there are no bases for this view in mainstream Judaism or, to the best of my knowledge, mainstream Christianity. As noted, one of the Bible's greatest battles is against the notion that nature has any divinity. Jews and Christians are, fortunately, free to say anything they want in the name of their respective religions. But intellectual integrity should keep them from labeling pantheistic ideas Jewish or Christian.

- The logical problem is that if trees are divine, so are Anopheles mosquitoes, the carriers of malaria; and so are Alzheimer's Disease and heart attacks and Tay-Sachs Disease. Yet, I have never heard anyone say, "God is in cancer." Those who hold that God is in trees presumably know in which parts of nature God resides and in which He doesn't.

- The moral problem with "God is in nature" should be the most ob-vious: Since nature is amoral, we cannot discern good and evil from it. God cares about the weak, but nature couldn't care less about the weak. God commands us to take care of our neighbor; while nature commands nothing ethical—only take care of yourself.

Nature Exists for Mankind

Mainstream Judaism's view of nature is certainly not Politically Correct. Nature was created as the vehicle by which God created the human being, and in order to give emotional, aesthetic and biological sustenance to mankind. Nature in and of itself has no purpose without the existence of human beings to appreciate it. In the words of the Talmud, every person should look at the world and say, "The world was created for me." (If animals had a purpose independent of man, God would not have destroyed all of them except for the two pair each to replenish the species when He destroyed mankind in the Flood.)

God's directive to the first humans was to conquer nature and subdue it for human good. If this sounds abusive, it is important to recall that the polio vaccine is a direct result of the belief that humans are to conquer nature.

But Nature May Not Be Abused

Does this mean that the biblical view of nature gives man the right to pollute the earth or to abuse animals? Absolutely not. Abusing animals is forbidden in the Torah and by later Judaism in the myriad laws governing the treatment of animals. To cause gratuitous suffering to an animal is not merely a sin, it is a grave sin. Even from a non-religious perspective, people should declare such behavior a grave sin. One of the few clear predictors of later criminal violence is when a child tortures animals (though the converse is not true—kind treatment of animals does not predict kind treatment of humans).

As for polluting the earth, this, too, is religiously prohibited. If the purpose of nature is to ennoble human life, by what understanding of this concept can a religious person defend the polluting of rivers? None. Therefore, environmentally speaking, the difference between a monotheist and a pantheist is not that the former is apathetic to river pollution and the latter opposes it. Both must oppose it. The difference between them is their differing reasons for opposing pollution. The monotheistic opponent of pollution wants to bequeath to the next generation of human beings as beautiful a world as possible and to keep God's beautiful handiwork as beautiful as He made it. The pantheistic opponent of pollution cares about nature first and foremost for nature's own sake—as a great deal of present-day environmentalist rhetoric makes clear.

The monotheist must be as concerned as the pantheist about protecting rivers. But the monotheist must announce clearly, publicly and repeatedly that he shares no ideology with the pantheist. This is easily forgotten because, when faced with a common enemy, it is easy to forget that the enemy of your enemy is not necessarily your friend. To cite one such example, Western liberals and Communists both opposed Hitler (except when the Communists stopped opposing Hitler after Stalin signed a peace pact with Hitler), and many liberals consequently began to regard Communists as ideological allies, not only as fellow opponents of Hitler.

So, too, many erstwhile monotheists have become confused by the pantheists in the environmental movement. They forgot, or never knew, that the only thing they share with pantheists who oppose river pollution is opposition to river pollution. Like too many liberals who forgot that liberals must oppose Communism as well as Hitler, many members of monotheistic faiths have forgotten that monotheists must oppose pantheism as well as pollution.

If God Is Not in Nature, What Is Nature?

If nature is not divine, what is it? Nature is God's handiwork. Next to man, the rest of nature is God's greatest achievement. In addition to sustaining human beings in all the ways mentioned, one reason for nature's existence is to provide man with a source of glory to its Creator—a sort of omnipresent pointer to God. When God finally answers Job's questions concerning God and the existence of evil, God asks Job, "Who is it that taught a mother bear to guide her cubs?" and "Who is it that guides the eagle to make its nest?" In other words, God Himself regards nature as a means for man to see the hand of God at work—and, yes, even to come to faith in God.

A monotheist can certainly go to a beautiful place in nature and feel closer to God. Indeed, in such a place, any monotheist ought to bless God when witnessing nature's marvels; as in the words of the Psalmist, "How great are Thy works, oh God." But it is one thing to see nature as a manifestation of God's greatness, and it is quite another to see it as God. There is divine greatness in a tree, and one might even say that there is a spark of the divine in nature, but God remains the Creator, separate from His creation.

And Where Is God?

And if God is not in nature, where is God? Physically, the answer is simple—nowhere. As God is not physical, He cannot be placed in a physical place. Spiritually, however, God is everywhere, or in the well chosen words of one Hasidic rabbi, "God is wherever we let Him in," i.e., through human acts of kindness and holiness. The movement to identify God with nature is not a good one; and it is certainly not a Jewish one. It reduces God (God is no longer the Creator but a creation), and it reduces God's greatest creation, man (who is now only one more part of nature, created in the image of stardust and bacteria, not in the image of God).

It is time for serious Jews and Christians to do what they should always be doing—identifying the idols of the times in which they live, and struggling with them. That this task will be profoundly resisted makes it all the more obvious that in nature-worship we have a competing religion, not a kindred spirit.

THE EMERGENCE
OF ECO-JUDAISM

Arthur Waskow

DURING THE PAST THIRTY YEARS, there have been three distinct responses of Jewish thought to the ecological challenge.

The first was a defensive and apologetic one, responding to scientists' accusations that the Hebrew Bible and its daughters, Rabbinic Judaism and Christianity, were responsible for creating a rapacious modern human culture that is endangering the planetary web of life. This first set of responses celebrated the aspects of Judaism that affirmed protection of the earth and pooh-poohed the claim that Judaism, especially, had set the stage for eco-destruction.

The second response was a more nuanced examination of the veerings in one direction or another through which particular Jewish teachings (especially Rabbinic and Zionist) have sometimes treated the earth as simply a resource for human use, and sometimes treated it as bearing the independent sacred value of being God's creation.

The third response has been to look beyond the specific rules and symbols of Biblical or Rabbinic Judaism or of Zionism and to ask some broader questions:

- Why does the relationship between the earth and human earthlings now seem to be in such intense crisis?

- Is this a profoundly new and unprecedented situation, or just another version of an old dilemma?

- Why are the tones and teachings of Biblical and Rabbinic Judaism on issues of the earth so different from each other?
- Does the ecological crisis give us any reason to reassess our images of the relationships among God, Torah, and Israel?
- Does the history of Planet Earth have anything to do with God and Torah?
- Do the other crises Judaism faces—in the profoundly changing relationships among women and men and the profoundly changing relationship of Judaism and Jews with other traditions and their practitioners—have anything to do with the ecological crisis?

Let us look more carefully at these three sets of responses. The first set was keyed to a famous challenge from Lynn White that appeared in *Science* magazine.[1] White blamed much of the (even then dangerous) eco-destruction on the Christian ethos that he said underlay Western thought—even secular scientific modernity and the scientific-industrial complex. He traced the Christian outlook on the natural world to Biblical Judaism, summarizing the Creation story as follows: "God planned all this explicitly for man's benefit and rule: no item in the physical creation had any purpose save to serve man's purposes."

White ended by saying, "Since the roots of our trouble are so largely religious, the remedy must also be essentially religious, whether we call it that or not. . . . I propose [Saint] Francis as a patron saint for ecologists."

The initial Jewish responses to this challenge were mostly the quotation of a passage here, a verse there, or a major category of Biblical or Rabbinic thought like the tradition of Shabbat or of "*bal tashchit*" ("Do not destroy"), to show that the "subdual" passage did not mean what it sounded like, and that Biblical and Rabbinic Jewish tradition did indeed care for the earth.

There followed some more subtle readings of the tradition to show, for example, that the *bal tashchit* teaching of the rabbis often came down on the side of using natural resources for human benefit, rather than protecting them—so long as the use was not wasteful.

More recently, however, there have been efforts to look more deeply into the present ecological crisis as itself an index to a changing relationship among God, humans, and other strands of the Web of Life—in which God's place in the relationship shifts along with the places of the other partners.

That effort begins by looking more deeply into the whole gestalt of the Bible for clues to previous such transformational crises, and how such crises may have shaped the very foundations of Jewish peoplehood and spirituality.

The fullest and deepest examination of Biblical Judaism from this perspective is *The Ecology of Eden* by Evan Eisenberg, in part an anthropological-historical analysis of how the onset of agriculture affected the worldview of ancient Israel, and how the resulting tugs between "the Tower" (Babylon, the city) and "the Mountain" (Sinai, the wild) affected not only biblical but more recent understandings of what is sacred in the world.

Eisenberg sets the Eden story in its ecological context as a tale told by West-Semites who mixed small-scale hill farming with nomadic and semi-nomadic herding and hunting-gathering. At one level, he suggests, the story of Eden is "about" the rise of agriculture, in particular grain agriculture. Together with the tale of the Tower of Babel, it forms a part of a larger mythic structure that describes the encroachment into West-Semitic lives of a great agricultural empire, Babylonia. (There are obviously other levels through which this story also enriches our spiritual lives. The different levels are non-exclusive, and may even be complementary.)

From this perspective, Eden was a story about how the victory of agriculture—ultimately, large-scale irrigated agriculture—brought new knowledge into human hands, increased the alienation between adam and adamah, and subordinated women to men.

Let us look further at this model. Babylonia had become powerful precisely because it was one of the places where highly organized agriculture was invented. This invention was a step "forward" in controlling the food supply and multiplying humans, and at the same time it was a step into alienation from and coercion of the earth by human beings. That the same act could have both meanings should be no surprise: In the individual life-cycle, for example, we are used to the idea that birth itself, "the terrible two's," and "adolescence" are all steps in growing up, involving both rejection and rebellion toward Mama/Papa, and striking out on one's own.

So we might say that for the human race as a whole, just as for individuals, this process of self-definition/rebellion comes in stages. The "birth" of the human race is told by the Bible as a tale of earth and breath: A lump of reddish clay (*adamah*) loses the final letter "*hei*" from its name—the sound of a breath—and receives the "*ruaḥ elohim*"—the Breath of God—to become *adam* (Human/Earthling). Perhaps we can see the lost "*hei*" as the unconscious breathing through the placenta that is lost in birthing, and the *ruaḥ* as the conscious, independent breath that comes soon after.

On the species level, the human race tears itself from the womb of earth (perhaps a relationship much more like that of the other primates) and separates itself into a slightly—but only slightly—alienated being. Hunter-gatherer humans were not so different from our primate cousins. They—and even shepherds—had a playful relationship with the earth, moving from place to place to avoid exhausting it, and thus also avoiding exhausting themselves.

But the process of maturation/alienation did not halt there. Agriculture—especially mono-crop imperial agriculture—was another step toward separating ourselves from the earth so as to subdue it. And in subduing earth, we subdued ourselves and each other. More births, more birth-pangs. Women ruled by men. Ownership, and governments to enforce it, with armies to protect it. From the standpoint of small farmers, hunter-gatherers, and shepherds, the agro-revolution was a disastrous, dangerous, oppressive event.

So from this perspective, Eden becomes the story of a tragic mistake built around an act of eating, the results of which are war between earth and human-earthling; role differentiation and pain between women and men and between the generations; and conflict between centralized power and the stubborn local cultures.

And from this perspective, as Eisenberg points out, the ancient midrash that the Tree of Eden was a wheat plant makes good historical-anthropological sense.

Yet this newly alienated being, the farmer-human, is not an alien—but one of the results of the earth's own processes of evolution.

The hill-farmer-shepherd Semites were ultimately drawn into the orbit of imperial agriculture. But—they kept drawing on their own past experience as hill farmers, shepherds, and gatherers to build in such protections of the earth and of their own long-term vision as the Shabbat, the *shmitah* (Sabbatical) Year, and the Jubilee, during which humans become gatherers again one-seventh of the time.

What is crucial here is seeing the emergent Torah as a response to the great traumatic leap forward of the agro-revolution. A response that tried to create new forms of community, so as to bind into livability and decency the radically new forms of controlling other human beings and the earth.

Does this kind of analysis eliminate God from Torah? No; it sees the Torah as the record of many generations of spiritual seekers in search of the Divine, seeking especially in times of profound social crisis and transformation for Divine teachings about how to live a holy life. That Shabbat might become a central teaching for a people trying to renew its I-Thou contact with the earth in the face of I-It agriculture is not a dismissal but a celebration of God.

And now let us turn to how the spiritual seekers and religious activists of our own day might draw upon this way of understanding the Tanakh. We can see that the process continues. We can draw on the experience of a number of revolutions like the agro-revolution.

One of these, the victory of Hellenistic/Roman civilization, shattered Biblical Judaism and called forth a response (analogous to the response of Torah) in the form of Rabbinic Judaism, Christianity, and Islam.

Most recently, the industrial and techno-revolutions are calling forth movements for renewal and transformation of all the faith traditions on the planet, and are also calling forth such new approaches to community as feminism and ecology. (They also, in all the ancient religious communities, call forth retrogressive efforts to vomit out Modernity by restoring their old religious and social forms—putting women back in their place, other communities in theirs, and the earth in its—all, of course, subordinate.)

And so we have learned to see more clearly both the alienating and the maturing aspects of this continuing story. And we can ask ourselves: How does the human race keep growing up?

That means: How do we respond to the great recent leaps in technology, in control of the earth and each other, by creating, renewing, and revitalizing the other aspect of growing-up—adding not only new ability to control and make and produce, but new ability to love, to commune, to be?

In our own generation, what could we do that would be analogous to the West-Semites' insistence on observance of the Sabbath and Sabbatical year as ways of taming the most destructive urges of the agro-revolution, and celebrating the spiritual value of a rhythm in which communing with earth alternates with controlling it?

We should note that the kind of reading we have done here differs both from the classic Traditional ways of reading religious texts and from the Modernist way of reading these ancient documents. In the Traditional way, the text itself was understood to be all-sufficient as the Word of God, and midrash (or other forms of reinterpretation) was almost always justified on the basis of a textual indication or oddity.

From the Modernist standpoint, on the other hand, the text is seen as only a reflection of the social-historical context. It has no independent validity as an ethical or moral teaching, and by many Modernists is analyzed into different documents and in other ways so totally relativized that it is radically diminished or even nullified as ethical, moral, or religious teaching with any meaning for our own era.

Among Jewish renewal circles in the last generation (and of course among some Christian thinkers as well; I am less familiar with their work), there has grown up a different model. It looks at the biblical text (and other traditional texts, like the Talmud) as the records of spiritual seekers who in the context of their own societies are struggling to hear and respond to God.

As process, their struggles and the records of them in these texts are sacred; the specific content and the specific responses they made to what they heard as God's will may or may not be specifically sacred, depending on the arenas in which society has and has not changed.

That means the history and sociology of the Biblical or Talmudic or other sacred literatures must be understood in order to decide what specific content to accept and what to transcend. To take one major case, understanding the relationships of women and men in the societies out of which the speaking and writing of various sacred literatures arose will have a deep impact on spiritual seekers of today, when their own values (and the underlying social reality) about relationships between women and men may be so different.

This approach, which has been so strong among some feminist Jews and Christians—who are ready neither to relativize their Traditions into meaninglessness nor to accept them as fully God's Word—is having an impact on "environmentalist" readers of the Traditions, as well. Faced with a Judaism or a Christianity that has sometimes demeaned non-human aspects of Creation just as it demeaned non-male members of the human race, some readers today are similarly seeking ways to understand the ancient text as a guide through its process, more than its content, to an affirmation of all Creation.

This approach does not counterpose the historical/political to the spiritual, but sees each as an expression of the other.

So far, we have explored this version of our people's spiritual history from the side of human beings seeking God. Can we also look at this process from the side that may include human yearning but is not limited to it? In other words, what might this process look like if we turn our attention to God's side of it?

We might draw both on the Kabbalah of Isaac Luria and the radical Catholic theology of Teilhard de Chardin (without being limited to their formulations).

Luria saw the universe as itself an aspect of God—the enfolded *reshimu* or residue of the Divinity that was left over in the void that emerged from the Infinite's *tzimtzum*, Its inward contraction. The *reshimu* twirled, folded, grew, robed Itself in garments of Itself so as to seem material—and look, a world!

Similarly, Teilhard saw the whole process of evolution, including human cultural evolution, as an expression of God Unfolding, through which

ultimately at the Omega Point the universe, through human self-awareness and the emergence of the Noosphere (an all-encompassing sphere of
consciousness) would come to full Self-awareness.

We have till now looked at the alternating leaps of Control and Love,
Making and Being, as historical surges merely: A surge in Control through
Babylonian agriculture; deeper Loving/Being through Israelite Shabbat. A
surge in Control through Hellenistic civilization; deeper Loving/Being
through Talmud. A surge in Control through Modernity; deeper Loving/
Being through—the next stages in the renewal of Judaism, Christianity,
Buddhism, Islam, feminism, ecology.

What if, following in the direction pointed by Luria and Teilhard, we
were to see this historical process and its undulating spiral of growing
power to control interwoven with growing community as the fits and
starts through which God's Presence becomes more fully manifest in the
world?

A hypothesis, put forward as a way of thinking about the earth-human-
God interaction:

That the *tzimtzum* is the Infinite God's attempt to see Itself mirrored, reflected, through the unfolding God that emerges from the Divine *reshimu*—
that is, through the finite universe that hazily reflects the Infinite. And that
the resulting aspect of God, God-embodied-in-the-universe, grows toward
revealing Itself, toward becoming able to mirror the Infinite Beyond.

This growth then appears to us as a double spiral:

In one spiral, growing self-awareness is used in the service of greater efficiency at controlling the surrounding universe—greater power.

In the other spiral, growing self-awareness is turned toward creating
deeper love, broader connection.

In one spiral, my I eyes what I have just done, to do it more effectively.

In the other spiral, my I eyes the face of an Other and sees within it my
own face, sees within its differentness my own uniqueness, and so can love
my neighbor as deeply as my Self.

These two spirals are rooted in the living universe long before there
emerges what we call life, or humankind. What we call life, and then what
we call humankind, are themselves leaps forward in both spirals—the one
that is more efficient, and the one that is more loving.

The two spirals are not independent of each other. They are intertwined. What Martin Buber called "I-It" intertwined with I-Thou. One
spiral of stronger Doing intertwined with one of deeper Being.

Each of these comes into the world as a step in the journey of the world
to become more and more a Mirror for God, more and more a fully aware
being, ever more fully aware of its own Unity.

What makes each of them a spiral is the other. As each moves forward in what might have been a straight line, it reaches a point of impending self-destruction that calls forth the other into vigor. Each curve forward in the one spiral calls for a curve forward in the other. An increase in efficiency unaccompanied by any increase in a sense of connection threatens that the more efficient being will gobble up its own nurturing environment—and ultimately find itself without nourishment—unless it learns to become part of a larger whole, a deeper, fuller community. Whether the being is a proto-protein hmmming in a sweet and early sea, or an amoeba devouring all the sugar-water in the neighborhood, or a global human civilization using up all the space in which other species can survive, the discipline of learning to love, to connect—or to die—is very strict.

And the creation of a new level of community—a multi-celled creature at one level of this double spiral; at another level, a society that understands it is part of a larger, richer habitat in which grow other species—the achievement of this new level creates the context for another leap forward in efficiency and power.

One of these spirals—the one in which self-awareness gives a being the ability to "look" at its techniques for acquisition, see its shortcomings, imagine a more effective solution, and make it happen—is the "competitive natural selection" aspect of evolution. The mistake of "social Darwinists" is to see this as the only aspect of evolution, ignoring the I-Thou spiral.

The emergence of life was one enormous leap forward in the ability of aspects of the universe to understand and control, and then of these same aspects to pause, reflect, love, and be self-aware.

The emergence of the human race was another such great step. For the universe to continue on this journey toward self-awareness, there needs to be a species capable of self-awareness—made up of individuals who can reflect upon their own selves, and also able as a species to reflect upon itself and to see itself as part of the Unity of the universe—on which it is also capable of reflecting.

That is what it means to live in the Image of God—to reflect upon the Unity, and thus to mirror God's Own Self. Among the species on this planet, the human race so far bears this Image of God—the self-awareness of Unity—most fully. That does not mean other beings have no share in this Image, nor does it mean that the unfolding of the Image stops with us.

And within human history, the pastoral and agricultural revolutions were further leaps forward in accessing the Divine attributes of power. Each meant that human beings were able to hold and use powers that previously had been held only by Divine "outsiders"—gods, spirits, God. Each meant that some aspect of Divine power became more available to human hands. And in response to each, human beings created new forms of connective community, intended to cradle the new energy of doing in new forms of loving.

And so the thin film of God that became the universe revealed Itself more and more fully, as the universe grew toward mirroring the Infinite.

And on each of these occasions, a leap forward in power and control had to be followed by a broadening of love and a deepening of self-aware reflection. Otherwise the new intensity of power would have swallowed up the world. And each growth of broader community gave the context and the impetus for another leap forward in Doing, Making, I-It. Thus the double spiral continued.

The agricultural revolution was one such turn on the Doing, I-It spiral—and it required the emergence of biblical Israel, Buddhism, and the other great ancient traditions on the Being, I-Thou spiral.

The next great turn on the Doing, I-It spiral came when Hellenism brought a more powerful form of economics, science, politics, and war to the Mediterranean basin. This leap shattered Biblical Judaism as well as other traditional cultural and religious forms. The "I-Thou" response was the creation of Rabbinic Judaism, Christianity, and Islam.

In the last several hundred years, we have been living through another such leap forward in the I-It powers of the human race. This leap is what we call Modernity. It is by far the greatest of these leaps, for it brings the human race into the arena in which it is transforming the very web of planetary life from which it sprang.

That we would reach this point was probably inevitable. For to be capable of "self-awaring" life inevitably also means to be capable of creating the technology that can wreck the planet. Human social history is simply incomparably swifter than biological evolution at applying self-awareness to technological improvement—so swift that it reaches the asymptote of possible self-destruction.

That swiftness, to some extent throughout human history but with utter urgency today, gives the human race a mandate unique among all species: to act as if it were a steward for the planet. If we fail in this task, the planet's ruination will take us with it. In that sense, we are strange stewards and the "steward" model is partly useful but not fully adequate—for we remain partially embedded in the earth we steward.

Today, what is the alternative to ruination? It is another curve forward on the spiral of Being, Loving, I-Thou-ing. It is the renewal and transformation of Judaism, Christianity, Islam, Buddhism, Hinduism, the spiritual traditions of all indigenous peoples—a renewal and transformation that can deepen each tradition in its own uniqueness while broadening the circle of love it can encompass. It is the bringing of restfulness and reflectiveness to a deeper level, just as work has been brought by modernity to a higher level. It is extending our love to the whole of the earth of which we are a part, without denying our uniqueness in its web of life.

Now that we live in the era of high-tech industrialism, and are not shepherds or farmers or foresters in the ordinary sense, we must learn to be shepherds, farmers, tree-keepers again in a different sense. For shepherds, farmers, and orchard-keepers knew you must not exhaust the earth you live on. If you're a shepherd and you let the sheep eat all the grass in one year, the sheep may be fatter and the wool thicker this year, but you're finished off. And farmers, vintners, and orchard-keepers learn the same thing.

What does this mean for us who have forgotten it—in the wild rush of making, doing, inventing, producing over the last couple of hundred years? What does it mean for us to renew that shepherds' wisdom, the wisdom which knew that consuming what comes from the earth is a central sacred act, is a way of being in touch with God? What would it mean for us to renew that wisdom?

I want to imagine a new version of the Jewish people—a new way of understanding and shaping ourselves. Imagine that we were to decide to see ourselves as having a mission, a purpose on the earth. A purpose to heal the earth—one that is not brand new but is described in the Torah as one of the great purposes of the Jewish people.

What does it mean that Shabbat is a symbol, a sign between the God of the universe and "His" once whole people? The Shabbat of Sinai comes in two different guises. In Exodus, we hear it as the moment when our restfulness connects us with the cosmic resting that imbues all of creation. In Deuteronomy, Shabbat renews the liberation of human beings and the earth.

And there is also the Shabbat that we often forget—the Shabbat that comes before Sinai. It comes with the manna in the Wilderness, betokening our free and playful reconnection with the earth. This Shabbat betokens the peace agreement ending the primordial war between ourselves and earth which began as we left Eden—which came from a misdeed of eating and brought us painful toil and turmoil in our eating.

What would it mean for us to renew the sense that deep in our very covenant, deep in our covenant-sign Shabbat, is the call to be healers of the earth?

Imagine a people that can renew

- its forms of prayer to celebrate the earth and confront its despoilers;
- its daily practice to become an "eco-kosher" lifepath;
- its forms of Torah-study to intertwine Jewish texts with scientific and socio-political knowledge;

- its relationships with other peoples and spiritual communities to seek allies in the effort to heal our planet.

In short, imagine the Jewish people as a kind of transgenerational, transnational "movement," committed for seven generations, from one generation to the next and beyond, to transmit the wisdom and the practice that can heal the earth.

And imagine this movement/people as one direct expression of God's need at this moment to unfold in the mode of deeper community: deeper Love and deeper Being.

NOTE

1. *Science,* vol. 155, March 10, 1967, pp. 1202–1207.

A THEOLOGY OF ILLNESS
AND HEALING

Nancy Flam

OVER THE PAST TWO AND A HALF YEARS, I have worked with dozens of sick Jews who have turned to the Jewish community and tradition in the hope of finding strength, meaning, comfort, and guidance in the face of illness. My task has been twofold: (1) to teach people what the tradition has to offer and (2) to help them struggle toward authentic articulations of what their illness may mean to them.

My own working theology of illness and healing comes out of the dialogues I have maintained with ill Jews, but perhaps most of all in relation to one woman whom I will call Rebekah.

The Search for Meaning

When Rebekah was diagnosed with breast cancer, she felt ambivalent. On the one hand, she had all the "expected" responses: fear, anger, sadness. On the other hand, she began to feel relief, as if an enormous burden was being lifted from her. Having entered "crisis mode," Rebekah was no longer able to "do" her regular life: working as a high-powered psychiatrist, taking charge of household management, her family's financial planning, and so on. All of those concerns receded as she began to manage the one great task before her: how to seek treatment and recover health.

The shock of serious diagnosis propelled Rebekah to examine her life, determine what was of real value, and restructure the way she was spending her time and energy. Without question, she would have preferred to have been spared life-threatening illness and grown to reorder her life in a gentler fashion. Yet, somehow, she was experiencing her illness as a blessing at the same time as she believed it to be a curse.

Rebekah sought a theological framework with which to understand her illness. She refused to believe that God actually sent her this disease with the intent of helping her reorder her life; she didn't believe that God worked that way. Her illness seemed to her a random event in the universe: unearned, without moral cause. And yet, she was able to find some good, in fact, she was creating some good, out of the painful circumstances.

Meaning Beyond Morality

It was important to Rebekah to resist the urge to attribute divine intent to her illness: either as punishment or as a "blessing in disguise." Such formulations, though emotionally compelling, seemed facile. Searching her deeds, she reckoned that there was nothing she did or failed to do which was commensurate with this affliction. Some part of her wished there were a correlation between "sin" and "punishment," because she might then be able to affect her situation positively through *teshuvah*. But she did not believe that God intervened this way in individual human lives, meting out rewards and punishments.

Likewise, she could not accept her illness as a divinely intended "blessing" sent by God to help her change her ways, what rabbinic theology calls *yisurin shel ahavah* (chastisements of love): afflictions sent by God as prods to do *teshuvah*. Although some good emerged from her suffering, she did not believe that this was the reason for her affliction.

Victor Frankl asserts that humanity's essential drive is to make meaning. Rebekah struggled to find the meaning of her illness. But her experience suggests to me that disease may be devoid of moral meaning; perhaps disease has nothing to do with merit or demerit and is simply a necessary though sometimes agonizingly painful feature of this physical creation. When Elisha ben Abuya watched the obedient young boy climb the ladder to send the mother bird away before collecting its eggs, falling on the way down to a horrifying and untimely death, Elisha ben Abuya denounced God as the arbiter of justice. There was no justice in the boy's death. The boy had simply slipped from a ladder that did not support him; his death expressed the laws of gravity and physics, not a moral law.

Din Is the Divine Imposition of Limits

To Elisha ben Abuya's mind, there was no *din* and no *dayan* (judge) in this picture. But I think the element of *din* is here. By this I do not mean "judgment" or "justice" in the way the rabbis usually mean it. I mean a morally neutral *din: din* as the imposition of limits, the correct determination of things, the *din* Cordovera talks about as inherent in all the things insofar as all things need to remain what they are, to stay within their boundaries (*Pardes Rimonim,* ch. 8).

Midat hadin (the divine attribute of *din*), then, carries within it the necessity of limits and finitude. Disease and death are expressions of *midat hadin.* Physical bodies are limited; they are created with a finite capacity for life and health. They are vulnerable to disease, injury, and decay. We are created and, without exception, pass away. This is part of God's holy design.

It is with this understanding that I am able to accept the instruction to recite *tziduk hadin* upon hearing bad news, specifically upon hearing of a death. The core of the prayer blesses God as *Dayan ha'emet* (the judge of truth). On the level of *pshat, Dayan ha'emet* implies moral judgment, of course, where God knows in God's wisdom who should die, when, and for what reasons.

But the tradition hints of a morally neutral *din* as well. Consider the new year of Tu B'Shvat, what is sometimes referred to as the *yom din* for trees. Certainly it is not the righteous trees that will bear fruit in the new year, but rather those whose structures are fitting, those that can conduct water efficiently from root to branch. So perhaps *Dayan ha'emet* makes better sense on the level of *drash*. Perhaps *Dayan ha'emet* refers to God who sets down the hard and fast laws of physical creation.

To say *Dayan ha'emet* would affirm that God's law and God's truth are expressed when there is illness or death: not moral law, but natural law, the God-given truth of limits and finitude. Blessed is Adonai our God, Ruler of the universe, who sets limits and ordains the physical laws of creation.

Rahamim Is the Expression of Healing

Whereas illness expresses *midat hadin,* healing expresses *midat harahamim* (the divine attribute of mercy). *Rahamim* is classically envisioned as the force which mitigates the severity of the *din*; in cases where *midat hadin* would exact strict punishment, *midat harahamim* comes to commute the sentence, to soften the decree. *Rahamim* makes it possible for us to live within the reality of *din*. Though originally, according to one midrash, God thought to create the world with the attribute of *din* alone, God found that the world would not endure without *rahamim*. The two principles had to work together in the formation and daily re-creation of the world.

To my mind, this is indeed how the world works. Our human acts of mercy, compassion, and empathy make it possible for us to endure, to suffer the sometimes excruciatingly painful limits and losses of creation.

And it seems to me that the Jewish impulse is to add to the principle of *rahamim* so that it might outweigh—indeed ideally, messianically, overcome—the power of *din*. It doesn't seem to be our task to add to the power of *din*. Consider the instruction that we should imitate God's ways. God's ways are various, but the examples given in our sources about "following in God's ways" are all instances of *rahamim*: to clothe the naked, visit the sick, comfort the mourner, bury the dead. We are not told to imitate God in strictness and severity. Perhaps the very nature of *din* as setting the principles of creation precludes human imitation, whereas the nature of *rahamim* invites it. As Abraham Joshua Heschel wrote, "Justice is a standard, mercy an attitude; justice is detachment, mercy attachment; justice is objective, mercy personal" (*The Prophets*).

Softening the Edges of *Din* with *Rahamim*

When it comes to illness, our acts of *rahamim* can affect our experience of *din*. We may not be able to make disease disappear, but we can profoundly affect how we cope with illness, thereby "softening the decree," if you will. In Nedarim 39b, we learn that a visitor can take away part of a sick person's pain, can affect the experience of illness. Enough love, Rav Huna asserts, might entirely eradicate the pain, the *tza'ar*, the subjective burden.

I would go further. Acts of *rahamim* may not only make the limits more bearable but may actually affect the limits themselves. The growing field of mind-body medicine suggests this possibility. For instance, Dr. David Spiegel of Stanford University conducted a classic study in which he found that women with metastatic breast cancer who provided emotional support and care for one another lived twice as long as those who did not receive such care. Although all the women eventually died of the cancer, the realm of *din*, of limits and infinitude, was moved.

Our classic Jewish sources speak of the power of *rahamim* to affect the realm of *din*. Consider Rabbi Akiva's visit to his sick disciple. Upon the cleaning of the sick man's room and tidying up, the man revived; a simple act of care and dignity cured the patient of his ills (Berakhot 39b). Or the various people Rabbi Yohanan ben Zakkai would visit: Upon honest conversation and a show of care, Yohanan ben Zakkai would reach out his hand and the fellow would be cured, not just comforted—as if our very human love, compassion, and empathy, as well as our research, science, and treatment, could move nature to overcome previously known limits; as if our love, our attention, our presence, our bestowal of dignity could heal both spiritually and physically.

This is the messianic vision toward which we strive; to overcome the limits of *din* with the power of *rahamim*. I do not suggest that *din* ought to be or even could be eliminated entirely. The same midrash which says that the world cannot be ruled by pure *din* also says that it would not stand if guided only by *rahamim*. But our desire, our vision, is to move the world toward holding a greater share of *rahamim* than of *din*. Even God is imagined to exclaim in Berakhot 7a, "O that I might forever let my mercy prevail over my justice."

I hope that this rethinking of *din* and *rahamim* may help us fulfill the imperative to recognize God at all times. At moments of blessing, release, relief, healing, beauty, or communion of spirits, it is not hard for us to affirm God's presence. It is decidedly more challenging to affirm God's presence in the midst of loss or limitation. But, as Jews, this is what we are called upon to do. In the Book of Isaiah, God says: "I the Lord do all these things."

Sometimes we recognize God only in what is positive, in blessing, as *hatov ve hametiv,* the One who is good and who brings goodness. But this view mistakes a part for the whole and leaves open the possibility of a dualistic theology. If God is the One who inspires us with strength to cope with difficult circumstances such as illness, who or what is responsible for the fact of illness itself, the limitations of creation which bring us so much suffering? This is God, too, *Dayan ha'emet,* the Maker of limits and finitude.

Let us together construct a theology which affirms the truth of our experience as well as the truth which the Zohar teaches: "There is no place where God is not."

DEATH AND WHAT'S NEXT

Rami Shapiro

"RABBI, DO JEWS BELIEVE in reincarnation?" I am asked this all the time. Americans seem to be obsessed with the idea. They want to come back.

Most Americans get their idea of reincarnation from Hinduism. But the Hindus seem to believe that life basically sucks, and that if we are good enough we will escape the karmic wheel of birth and death. Hindus don't want to come back.

Most Americans, on the other hand, don't want to escape life; they want to consume more of it. In the American version of reincarnation, life is a perpetual Home Shopping Network. We come back to buy more stuff. Of course the assumption most Americans make is that they will return as Americans, or, at worst, as Canadians. No American ever imagines that he or she will take rebirth as a leper in Calcutta.

Does Judaism subscribe to any of these views? Actually, yes. Some kabbalists are close to Hindus in this: you have a separate soul that comes back to learn its lessons, and, if it learns them well, it graduates to heaven where it will study Torah with God. Ever notice how everything good in Judaism ends up being school? You get three chances at graduation. If you fail you come back as a rock. At this point your only hope is that a sage sits on you.

I don't find any of this convincing. I don't believe in separateness, and I already own more stuff than I can use. To me, the self is a temporary manifestation of God, the Source and Substance of all reality. Our relation to God is analogous to that of a wave to the ocean. The wave is an extension of the ocean. We are extensions of God.

If waves were self-conscious, they, like we, would focus on the surface view of things, and insist upon their separateness from each other and from the ocean as a whole. As they watch their fellows crashing upon the shore, they, like we, would worry: "Is there life after beach?"

From an outside observer's point of view the question is ludicrous: the wave is the ocean and the ocean is forever. If the wave would only realize its oceanic essence, the whole furor about birth and death would dissolve of its own accord.

Yet, like these hypothetically self-conscious waves, we, too, look about us and insist upon separateness. We see others die, panic about the end, and invent alternatives to it. But the fact is, we are God, and God is forever. If we would only realize this, all our worry about birth and death would just drop away.

"But what about past lives, Rabbi?" someone always objects. "What about people who remember prior reincarnations?"

Past life memories are real. What is false is the notion that they belong to the person doing the remembering.

Since we are one with all in God, we have the potential for encountering other elements of God's peopling. There are some among us who tap more clearly into this shared wisdom and experience than others. Not knowing what to make of it, however, they fold it into the delusion of separateness and claim it as their personal experience from a past life. It isn't. It is part of the collective experience of Life of which they are a temporary manifestation. If you experience a past life, honor it, but do not lay claim to it.

The problem with my belief is that few people find it comforting. No heaven for me? No hell for you? No second chance at leasing that new Jaguar? What fun is that?

None, I suppose. Yet to the extent that I am open to the oceanic; to the extent that I recognize my interdependence with all things and my unity with God; to that extent life deepens in meaning, fills with compassion, commands justice, and ultimately loosens my grip on self and stuff. And what could be more comforting than that?

EROS AND THE NINTH OF AV

Mordechai Gafni

THE NINTH OF AV—the anniversary of the destruction of the Mikdash, the holy temple—is an intense day of mourning for Jews worldwide. An omnipresent motif in Jewish consciousness, the loss of the temple leads us not only to mourn its destruction but also to yearn for its rebuilding. And yet what is it that we yearn for? Surely another building on the bitterly contested temple mount holds no inherent redemptive promise. Further, it seems likely that mystic philosopher Abraham Kook was right when he said that the animal sacrifices which demarcated the ancient temple would hold little attraction for spiritually evolved moderns.

Three talmudic texts and an ancient esoteric mystical tradition can guide us in our search for understanding what we might yearn for on Tisha B'Av (July 22) this year.

The first text, by its very strangeness, jolts us into the realization that our intuitive impressions of the holy may need fundamental re-orienting. Said R. Isaac, "From the day the temple was destroyed, the taste of sex was taken away, and given to the sinners, i.e., those engaged in illicit sex . . . as the verse says in Proverbs, 'stolen waters are sweet.'" In the context of this passage, illicit sex refers specifically to adultery; the "taste of sex" is an idiom meant to refer to the ultimate sexual experience. According to this eyebrow-raising passage, the difference between temple and post-temple spirituality is that after the destruction, the fullest erotic joy of sex was very difficult to access with our partners. The yearning for the temple is in effect understood as a yearning for Eros of the most intense kind.

Lest you think that this passage is anomalous, let us proceed in our investigation. The second rather shocking text is a description of the innermost sanctum of the temple. In the holy of holies, relates the Talmud, were two angelic cherubs locked in embrace. A careful reading of the Hebrew phrase indicates that they were in fact erotically intertwined. Furthermore, according to the first book of Kings, the walls of the first temple were covered with erotic pictures of these sexually intertwined cherubs. The primary image in the holy of holies—the innermost precinct of holiness in the temple—is a symbol of Eros. To realize how far we have strayed from this conception, one has only to imagine the reaction of today's congregants upon walking into their synagogue and finding the walls covered with pictures of figures in explicit sexual embrace.

To understand, however, what Eros meant in the religiocultural context of the temple, we need to unpack a final source. The Talmud describes a mythic dialogue between the Rabbis and God. The internal reference of the text locates the dialogue historically as taking place in the Second Temple era at the close of the era of prophecy. The Rabbis entreat God to nullify the power of the drive towards idolatry. Immediately, a lion of fire emerges from the holy of holies and is identified by the prophet as the primal urge toward idolatry. The Rabbis realize that it cannot be slain, so they weaken it instead. Feeling that they are privy to a moment of grace, the Rabbis entreat God again. Allow us, they say, to slay the drive for sexuality. God grants their wish and again a lion of fire emerges from the holy of holies. When they attempt to slay this lion, however, the world simply stops. Chickens don't lay eggs, people don't go to work, all productivity and, according to the Hasidic reading of the text, all spiritual work grinds to a standstill. The Rabbis understand that they have gone too far and retract their request. This drive as well is weakened, but not slain.

What is this strange and holy mythic tale trying to teach us? The underlying teaching would seem to be that the seat of Eros and the seat of holiness are one.

The first lion to emerge from the holy of holies personifies the drive for idolatry, the second the sexual drive. Both, however, are but expressions of a common underlying reality—that of Eros. Idolatry at its core is not primitive fetishism. It is, rather, a burning lust for the holy. Under every tree, in every brook, courses primal divinity. The idolater, like the prophet, experiences the world as an erotic manifestation of the God force. The symbolism of the lions emerging from the holy of holies is the text's way of teaching that Eros is holiness.

Eros in this understanding includes but is not limited to sex. Rather, it refers to the primal energy of the universe. Eros is where essence and existence meet. To experience the world erotically is to be plugged into the divine erotic essence of reality. As the tale of the lions indicates, the drive to uncover the divine sensuality of the world is not without its dangers. The erotic may overwhelm us to the point that our ethical sensitivities are swept away and our sacred boundaries overrun. And yet the need to experience the world in all of its divine Eros remains a primal human need—and according to this text, the temple of Jerusalem was organized in response to that need.

The destruction of the temple thus heralded the fall of Eros in two distinct ways. First Eros came to be limited to genital sexuality. When we seek the realization of our full need for Eros in sex, we are bound to be disillusioned. Sex cannot, by itself, sate us in our lust for essence. Sex itself cannot re-enchant our world with the magic of Eros. When we mourn the temple's destruction, we yearn to live erotically in all the facets of our lives once again.

The Talmud relates that at the time of the destruction, fruits lost their taste. Laughter vanished from the life of the polis, and the vitality of sexuality was reserved for those seeking an illicit adulterous thrill. When fruits lose their full erotic taste, when laughter becomes mechanical and only in response to sexual humor, then true Eros, the temple, has been destroyed.

The passionate yearning for rebuilding the temple is the longing to redeem Eros from its distortions. We need to move from the Eros of longing which symbolized the exile to an Eros of fulfillment. We need to experience the full intensity of erotic relationship with our partners. Put succinctly, rebuilding the temple is to touch the passion of illicit sex within the holy and ethical context of my relationship with my partner. This is the deep intent of Akiva, the mystic sage who witnessed the destruction of the temple. All the books are holy, taught Akiva, and the Song of Songs is the holy of holies. In making this statement, Akiva is doing more than extolling the virtue of the God-Israel relationship, which the Song of Songs allegorizes in terms of passion and sensuality. Akiva is teaching us that the essence of the temple, the holy of holies, is the Song of Songs; that is, the experience of passion and sensuality as the guiding force in all of our relationships with the world. It is for this that we yearn on the Ninth of Av.

FROM THE BOOK
OF JEWISH VALUES

Joseph Telushkin

On Hearing a Siren

What is your reaction when you are talking with a friend and your conversation is suddenly interrupted by the piercing wail of an ambulance siren? Is it pure sympathy for the person inside—or about to be picked up by—the ambulance, or do you feel some measure of annoyance? Similarly, how do you react when you are awakened from a deep sleep by a series of clanging fire trucks or the wail of a police car?

I am embarrassed to admit that, along with many others, my initial reaction to such noises is often impatience and annoyance rather than empathy. My friend Rabbi Zalman Schachter-Shalomi, known throughout the Jewish world as "Reb Zalman," suggests that whenever we hear the sound of a passing ambulance we offer a prayer that the ambulance arrive in time. Similarly, whenever our sense of calm is interrupted by fire trucks, we should pray to God that the trucks arrive in time to save the endangered people and home. We should also pray that no firefighter be injured. And when we hear police sirens, we should implore God that the police respond in time to the emergency.

Reb Zalman's suggestion is profound. By accustoming ourselves to uttering a prayer at the very moment we feel unjustly annoyed, we become better, more loving people. The very act of praying motivates us to empathize with those who are suffering and in need of our prayers. Furthermore, imagine how encouraging it would be for those being rushed to a hospital to know that hundreds of people who hear the ambulance sirens are praying for their recovery.

Speaking to a Jewish group once in Baltimore, I shared Reb Zalman's suggestion. After my talk, several people commented on how moved they were by this idea, but one woman seemed particularly emotional when she spoke of this suggestion. When she was ten, she told me, she had been awakened from a deep sleep by passing fire trucks. It was almost one in the morning, and now, twenty-five years later, she still remembered her first response: it was so unfair that her sleep had been ruined.

The next morning she learned that her closest friend, a girl who lived only a few blocks away, had died in the fire. Ever since, she told me, whenever she hears fire trucks go by, she prays that they arrive at their destination in time.

Loving one's neighbor is usually carried out through tangible acts, by giving money or food to those in need, by stepping in and offering assistance to a neighbor who is ill, or by bringing guests into one's home. But sometimes loving is expressed through a prayer that connects us to our neighbor, even when we have no way of knowing just who our neighbor is.

"Let Your Fellow's Money Be as Precious to You as Your Own"

If one is honest in his business dealings and people esteem him,
it is accounted to him as though he had fulfilled the whole Torah.

—Mechilta, *B'Shalach* 1

Most Jews associate being religious with observing Judaism's rituals. Thus, if two people are talking about a third, and the question arises whether he or she is religious, the response invariably will be based on the person's level of ritual observance (for example, "She observes the Sabbath, she is religious," or "He doesn't keep kosher, he is not religious"). From these kinds of comments, common among Jews of all denominations, one could form the impression that, in Judaism, ethics are a fairly unimportant extracurricular activity.

How bracing it is, therefore, to learn that according to Jewish tradition, honesty in one's dealings with others is equaled with observance of the whole Torah. A talmudic source powerfully reinforces this teaching: "In the hour when an individual is brought before the heavenly court for judgment, the person is asked: 'Did you conduct your business affairs honestly?'" (*Shabbat* 31a).

Having discussed this text before dozens of audiences, in synagogues and elsewhere, I know how surprised most people are to learn that the Talmud believes that the *first* question one will be asked by the heavenly court after one dies is not "Did you believe in God?" or "Did you observe the Jewish holidays?" but rather "Did you conduct your business affairs honestly?"

The Bible itself goes so far as to predicate Jewish national survival in Israel on merchants not defrauding their customers: "You must have completely honest weights and completely honest measures. If you do, you will long endure on the land that the Lord your God is giving you" (Deuteronomy 25:15).

Ethics of the Fathers (*Pirkei Avot*) comprises the favorite ethical aphorisms of rabbis, most of whom lived between the period from just before the Common Era until about 200 C.E. One prominent sage, Rabbi Yossi, offers a useful guideline concerning virtually any business situation in which you might find yourself: "Let your fellow's money be as precious to you as your own . . ." (*Ethics of the Fathers* 2:7).

Of course, the principle underlying Rabbi Yossi's comment is the Golden Rule, "Love your neighbor as yourself" (Leviticus 19:18). In the context of business ethics, such a criterion would, for example, forbid taking risks with another person's money that you would not take with your own (unless, of course, the money's owner has instructed you to take such risks).

Instructing people to observe the Golden Rule while trying to earn a living might strike some as utterly unrealistic, even naïve. Of course, that is precisely why many people prefer to assess religiosity on the basis of ritual observance and faith: by and large, it is easier to be punctilious about such matters than to act ethically in a consistent manner, particularly in financial areas.

Still, Jewish tradition insists on the primacy of ethical behavior. Commenting on the verse in Psalms (116:9), "I shall walk before the Lord in the lands of the living," the Rabbis were struck by the odd phrase "the lands of the living." Explained Rabbi Judah, the leading scholar of his age, "that means the marketplaces" (Babylonian Talmud, *Yoma* 71a). Whether or not a person truly worships God can be determined even more by how he acts in the marketplace than in the synagogue. As Rabbi Tzvi Hirsch Koidonover (d. 1712), a scholar as well as a successful businessman, wrote in his ethical treatise *Kav Hayashar* (*An Honest Measure*): "Only he who is reliable in money matters may be considered pious."

The Jewish Ethics of Speech: What Is *Lashon Hara*?

While libel and slander, which involve the transmission of untrue statements, are universally regarded as immoral and generally illegal, most people regard a negative but true statement made about another as morally permissible.

Jewish law opposes this view. The fact that something is true doesn't mean it is anybody else's business. The Hebrew term for forbidden speech about others, *lashon hara* (literally "bad tongue"), refers to any statement that is true, but that lowers the status of the person about whom it is said.* Thus, sharing with your friends the news that so-and-so eats like a pig, is sexually promiscuous, or is regarded by her coworkers as lazy, is forbidden, even if true.

Admittedly, this standard is sometimes difficult to observe: The Talmud itself concedes that virtually everyone will violate the laws of ethical speech at least once a day (*Bava Baikra* 164b–165a). Nonetheless, those who make an effort to practice these regulations will find that they soon start speaking about others in a far fairer manner.

When it comes to gossip, most of us routinely violate the Golden Rule, "Do unto others as you would have others do unto you." For example, if you were about to enter a room and heard the people inside talking about you, what you probably would least like to hear them talking about are your character flaws or the intimate details of your social life. Yet, when we speak of others, these are the things we generally find most interesting to discuss.

There *are* times when it is permitted to relate detrimental information about another but they are relatively rare. While the fact that something negative is true might serve as a defense against a charge of libel or slander in a court of law, it is an invalid defense against the charge that you have violated an important Jewish ethical law.

Don't Pass On Negative Comments

A woman I know, whose father had died, had long planned to have her older brother escort her down the aisle at her wedding. However, a short time before the event, her sister informed her of something she had heard the brother say: "Carol's a very sweet girl, but David is much more accomplished than she is. I'm afraid he's going to get bored with her." Devastated by these words, Carol refused to walk down the aisle with her brother; now, years later, their relationship is almost nonexistent.

Some time later I ran into the sister, and asked her about the incident. She told me that she had been talking with her sister, and the comment

---

*The Hebrew term that encompasses libel and slander is *motzi shem ra* (giving another a bad name), and constitutes the most grievous violation of the Jewish laws of ethical speech.

just "slipped out"; she thought her sister was entitled to know just what her brother thought of her.

The sister's response, a standard justification offered by those who pass on hurtful comments, sounds logical: Shouldn't we know if people who act warmly when they are with us say unkind things when we are not present?

But the brother's one comment did not express his full opinion of his sister. And her sister certainly had never bothered to pass on all the complimentary things he had said about her. While his comment may have been unkind, in truth almost all of us have said insensitive things about people we love. As Blaise Pascal, the great seventeenth-century French philosopher, wrote: "I lay it down as a fact that if all men knew what others say of them, there would not be four friends in the world."

Mark Twain highlighted the pain caused by people who pass on hurtful comments: "It takes your enemy and your friend, working together, to hurt you to the quick: the one to slander you and the other to get the news to you."

The Torah teaches how wrong it is to pass on hurtful comments, and the one who refrains from doing so is God Himself. Genesis 18 tells of three angels who came to Abraham's house to inform him that Sarah, his elderly wife, would give birth to her first child a year later. Standing some distance from the angels, Sarah heard their comment and laughed to herself, saying, "Now that I am withered, am I to have [the] enjoyment [of having a child], with my husband so old?"

A verse later, God appears to Abraham and says to him, "Why did Sarah laugh, saying, 'Shall I in truth bear a child, old as I am?'"

The Rabbis of the Talmud were struck by what God said—and did not say. In transmitting the substance of Sarah's statement, He left out her final words, "with my husband so old." Abraham in fact was old, but God apparently feared that he would resent Sarah saying so, in a manner that he might have regarded as dismissive.

The Talmud concludes from this incident, "Great is peace, seeing that for its sake even God modified the truth" (*Yevamot* 65b).

Of course, there are instances in which it is important to pass on negative comments. Let's say you hear someone accuse a person you know to be honest of acting dishonestly. Not only should you publicly dispute the accusation, but you should also warn the person who is being slandered. But such cases are relatively rare; unless there is a constructive reason to pass on a negative comment, you should not do so.

While Jewish ethics normally forbids lying, you are permitted to be less than fully honest when someone asks you, "What did so-and-so say about me?" When you know the response will provoke hurt or animosity, you are permitted to speak as God spoke to Abraham, relating some details and omitting others. If you are pressed for more information, Jewish ethics teaches that you can answer that the person said nothing critical. In short, when no constructive purpose is served by being truthful, peace is valued more highly than truth.

Tzedaka Is More Than Charity

From Judaism's perspective, one who gives *tzedaka* is acting justly, while one who doesn't is acting unjustly, which is why Jewish law regards withholding *tzedaka* as not only ugly but also illegal. Throughout Jewish history, when Jewish communities were self-governing, Jews were assessed *tzedaka,* as today people are assessed taxes.*

The giving of *tzedaka* was first legislated in the Torah. Deuteronomy (26:12) ordained that Jews give ten percent of their earnings to the poor every third year, and an additional unspecified percentage of their harvest annually (Leviticus 19:9–10). The Torah also tried to encourage a generosity of spirit: "If, however, there is a needy person among you . . . do not harden your heart and shut your hand against your needy kinsman. Rather, you must open your hand . . ." (Deuteronomy 15:7–8). Lest one become tired of the recurring demands made by the poor, the Torah reminds us, "For there will never cease to be needy people in your land which is why I command you: open your hand to the poor and needy" (Deuteronomy 15:11).

After the Temple was destroyed, and the annual ten percent tax Jews were required to pay for the support of the priests and Levites became inoperable, Jewish law eventually decreed ten percent as the minimum percentage of net income it expected Jews to donate to the needy (see Maimonides, *Mishneh Torah,* "Laws Concerning Gifts for the Poor," 7:5).

Why is Jewish law so insistent on requiring one to donate a set percentage of his or her income to charity? Perhaps because it intuits that if no percentage is specified, people will give much less than is needed. In-

---

*Ample historical evidence documents that the idea of *tzedaka* was not only prescribed in Jewish books, but was also widely practiced. To cite one example, in seventeenth-century Rome a Jewish community numbering only several thousand maintained seven charitable societies that provided clothes, shoes, beds, and food for the poor. There was a special organization to aid families struck by sudden death, and another responsible for visiting the sick. One society collected charity for Jews in Israel, and eleven raised money for various Jewish educational and religious activities.

deed, tens of millions of Americans donate less than three percent of their earnings to charity; many give almost nothing at all. And while Jewish law would love people to give charity from their hearts, it understands that waiting for people's hearts to motivate them to give ten percent of their income might require a very long wait. Therefore, as Dennis Prager observes, "Judaism says, 'Give ten percent.' And if your heart catches up, terrific. In the meantime, good has been done."

A suggestion: If you currently donate less than ten percent of your income to charity, perhaps a lot less, try to increase your donations during this coming year by one percent (for example, if you currently contribute four percent of your income, give five). While this may feel like a financial "stretch," you will gain the satisfaction of having done significantly more good.

POEMS

Jacqueline Osherow

Yom Kippur Sonnet, with a Line from Lamentations

Can a person atone for pure bewilderment?
For hyperbole? For being wrong
In a thousand categorical opinions?
For never opening her mouth, except too soon?
For ignoring, all week long, the waning moon
Retreating from its haunt above the local canyons,
Signaling her season to repent,
Then deflecting her repentance with a song?
Because the rest is just too difficult to face—
What we are—I mean—in all its meagerness—
The way we stint on any modicum of kindness—
What we allow ourselves—what we don't learn—
How each lapsed, unchanging year resigns us—
Return us, Lord, to you, and we'll return.

Science Psalm

The heavens are the heavens of God,
and the earth He gave to man.

Psalm 115:16

They will fear You as long as the sun and moon endure.

Psalm 72:5

Scientific evidence is nothing to rabbis—
Bring them some ancient rocks, carbon-dated,
And they'll say *so God created the world old . . .*
(I mean, of course, the ones who still insist
That fifty-seven-hundred years ago the Lord created
Everything in seven days, including rest),
And the rabbis have a point—though I'm not sold—
Since what are a couple of allosaurus vertebras

To a Guy whose single word produces light?
My Hebrew teacher told us about a Yemenite
Who, against the solemn oath of television,
Dismissed the moon landing as a fraud.
The heavens are the heavens of God,
And the earth He gave to man was his position—
He needed a different kind of imagination
Or, at least, a better definition.

Earth means whatever's given to us,
Which now includes the moon and, shortly, Mars.
I'm inclined to welcome the new expanse
Since, otherwise, this is all there is,
And I like picturing myself among the ancients,
This English of mine a language safely dead,
And schoolchildren uncertain whether Xerxes, El Cid,
or Jimmy Carter fought the Trojan Wars,

Giggling, no doubt, at the ridiculous lengths of time
It took our crude machines to get to Saturn . . .
Relativity, if not utterly forsaken,

Evolved into a simple grade-school theorem
(Amazing what such primitives could discern!)
Why should our particular errors last?
And what chance is there, given our record in the past,
That, in anything at all, we're not mistaken?

Is *accuracy* that heaven, only God's?
Don't laugh. It isn't utterly impossible;
Who's to say it doesn't exist somewhere,
A place, by definition, inaccessible,
But pleasant to believe in, nonetheless,
Since, if it existed, God would also be there,
And maybe even—though I'm not laying any odds—
They'll end up finding Jews in outer space,

In some backwater galaxy, studying Torah,
Not a single word diverging from ours;
They'd be up there, oblivious, thinking *theirs*
Is the heaven and earth Moses was talking about
And why not? Maybe ours is a dry run,
It would explain that line about the moon and sun—
Why would God rely on such ephemera?
He *must* be banking on that other planet.

There could be a spare Jerusalem just sitting there—
No suicide bombs, no checkpoints, no soldiers—
Its Holy Temple still intact!
And we could do an airlift of the Lubavitchers;
We'll tell them Rabbi Schneerson will meet them there,
Most of his disciples are already packed.
(He's expected to rise from the dead
Any minute now—real estate has skyrocketed

Around the Queens cemetery where he's buried;
They all want to be first in his entourage.)
We'll send along sufficient stores of kosher meat
(They'd never trust the butchers on another planet)
And stones, in case some women try to pray. . . .
It beats coming to America in steerage,
Not quite as crowded, if a bit more hurried,
And, in terms of going home, no farther away. . . .

But where did this come from, wasn't I writing
A poem about how we can't know anything?
(Not, admittedly, the most original subject
But one, it seems to me, you have to face.)
Still, when there's no sign of an obliging muse,
If you've got to be wrong, you might as well be funny;
And even if a muse showed up now, I suspect
I wouldn't have the heart for the uncanny
Intimacy of what would have to follow—
That is, with any muse who pulled her weight.
I'm not entirely ready to disintegrate
In the face of the encyclopedic darkness
Which is—isn't it?—my subject here:
A nothingness so stringent and so thorough
That it conveys intelligence, however imprecise,
Of just how comprehensively you'll disappear.

Is it possible you don't know what I mean?
So familiar, so regular, it would be comforting
If it didn't bring such undiluted terror—
Which is where this religion stuff comes in;
It has an obsessive way of diverting
Your attention, and, though it's anybody's guess,
The rabbis have put three thousand years into this
And I don't much go in for trial and error.

Besides, imagine actually believing
That the old bearded rebbe to whom my grandma used to point
From her Parkway bench on Shabbos afternoon
(Not that I knew which guy in a black caftan
With a big black hat and long gray beard she meant)
Is going to rise from the dead and take me with him—
I, for one, am quite attached to living;
Don't think I wouldn't be tempted, if he came,

To sit in the women's section for all eternity,
A wig on my head, my knees and elbows covered. . . .
On second thought, some fates are worse than death.
Sorry. Enough jokes. I take that back.
I believe—despite my weakness for a wisecrack—
That something or other has to be revered,

And the truth is I envy those people's faith
Even if I do think they're all *meshugene*

And, worse, true enemies of peace;
But I'm not talking politics in all this darkness.
I'm just looking for a little light,
And please don't point me to those fly-by-night
Creations: the stars and moon and sun—
As far as I'm concerned, their deadline's passed.
God, was there nothing tougher you could give to man?
I'd so like something that will last.

REREADING SACRED TEXTS OF OUR TRADITION

FROM AND PEACE
AND JUSTICE SHALL KISS

Rachel Adler

The Creation of Humanity: Two Accounts[1]

If we needed to prove that scripture can affect the real world, Genesis 1 and 2 would be chief among the prooftexts. Creation stories would seem to invite speculations about theological anthropology: What are we? What is our place in the scheme of things? What links us to our creator and to the rest of creation? Of all the human capacities that can be inferred from these stories, the one that has riveted the attention of traditional commentators is power. There is hardly a detail of these two accounts that has not been a prooftext for man's power over woman, over the earth and its creatures, in favor of or against some system of human government.[2] One imagines the two chapters buckling under the slagheap of human and geophysical suffering piled upon them by interpreters.

This mass of interpretation also weighs us down as readers, for it overdetermines our experience of the texts. How can we fail to be affected by their lengthy history as prooftexts for the subjugation of women and ecological dominance? What we are about to read has been used by past generations of interpreters to legislate circumscribed definitions of humanness, maleness, and femaleness and to justify privilege on the basis of gender.

More recently, these creation texts have become battlegrounds for feminist countercommentary.[3] Counterreadings employing literary, philosophical, and historical methods have been used by feminist scholars to expose and critique ideologies of sexuality and power. One influential version of this critique argues that opposition and subjugation particularly characterize patriarchal modes of making categories and making sense, and that, consequently, in patriarchal cultures, the structure of thought itself predisposes us to split and separate rather than to perceive interconnections and interdependencies.[4] At the heart of this universe carved into dualisms is a definition of normative humanity as maleness and irreducible otherness as femaleness. According to this account, woman is the first stranger.

The critique goes on to argue that from patriarchal man's alienation from woman proceeds an infinite series of dualisms. In each, the superior term is associated with patriarchal man, while the inferior and opposed term is associated with woman. Heaven and earth, light and darkness, spirit and body, cleanliness and filth, good and evil, freedom and slavery all are made to mirror the estrangement of patriarchal man from the woman he has cast out. These dichotomies then justify the subordination and exclusion of all those consigned to the feminized category of the other, for the ramifications of patriarchal dualism are political as well as psychological.

Feminist process theologian Catherine Keller traces these themes of hostility to the other throughout the history of Western theology and philosophy.[5] In Keller's account, patriarchal man, pained by the fragmentation of self and world that he has engineered, longs for unity. He conceives of it, however, not as the reunion of all he has driven apart, but as the conquest and incorporation of the realms of the other. As in the later philosophical works through which Keller traces this theme, selfhood is attained aggressively, by opposing and subjugating the other. The resulting separative masculine self is complemented by a soluble feminine self, the object of opposition and subjugation whose feeble boundaries collapse into his.[6] Like Jessica Benjamin, whose feminist object-relations theory also describes a pathological complementarity of dominator and dominated, Keller proposes the dissolution of gender polarity and its ensuing structures of domination. Keller's solution is to regard selves and world as related processes rather than separate stable entities.

The exemplary texts of patriarchal domination, according to Keller, are the Genesis creation stories.[7] Genesis 1, Keller argues, incorporates but abstracts the violent fragmentation of the body of the mother by which the world is created in the Mesopotamian creation myth upon which the Genesis creation is modeled. Behind the demythologized deity of monotheism, she contends, the antimatriarchal warrior gods and heroes of polytheism still lurk. The monotheistic deity of the creation accounts is a projection of the dualizing, autonomy-worshipping, patriarchal consciousness. This god-projection serves both as a model and as a justification for all patriarchy's tyrannies and exclusions, as well as for its militarism. YHWH's ethicized battles, His concern for social justice, is a mere façade, masking the objectifying violence beneath.[8]

This critique raises serious questions for Judaism and for other monotheistic traditions. Does worshipping God as One inevitably entail sexism and separatism? Dos it require characterizing all relations between self and other in terms of dominance and submission? Is the primordial category making and establishment of boundaries that the creation stories depict understandable only as a normalization of patriarchal fragmentation and opposition?

If the answer to all these questions were yes, how could one avoid concluding that Judaism is an evil and destructive belief system? This is not to say that there is no truth in the critiques and that patriarchal oppositions cannot be found in our sacred texts and in our traditions. But Keller's argument is reductive. She writes as if the Bible were a unitary text that represents God or men or women in a single consistent way and as if the Bible alone defined Judaism. But after the Bible, Judaism continued to develop other sacred texts and exegetical traditions which it does not share with Christianity and whose importance is sometimes discounted by scholars who are primarily interested in Judaism's impact on Christianity. Because the influential rereadings of texts or shifts of emphasis that have shaped later versions of Judaism are not noted in Keller's analysis, her presentation of Judaism is both static and one dimensional.

It is not necessary to discard Judaism or its texts to make a world of meaning in which women and men are equal subjects. Instead, our task is theological: to read these texts as believing Jewish women and men today without evading or denying their patriarchal past and to seek in them redemptive meanings to propel us toward a more just and loving future.

Progressive theologians read Scripture both as human constructions framed by time and as sacred text whose interpretive possibilities transcend any single historical time. We begin by learning what we can about our texts as historical entities. Historical critics assign the authorship of Genesis 1 and 2 to different documentary sources, Genesis 1 to P, the priestly document, and Genesis 2 to J, the Yahwist source. They explain differences in the chapters by pointing to the particular interests and emphases of these two authorial groups. This information helps us to separate the two stories and to account for their discrepancies. But although source criticism is necessary, it is theologically insufficient. Without obliterating their differences, we must illuminate both stories as Torah, as sacred text, to hear what they can teach us about what we are and what we ought to become and yet bring to them our own insights about where we have been and what we hope to be. To do such a reading, we must keep returning to the questions of boundary making and power distribution and how they affect our understandings of sexuality and gender.

Genesis 1: The Beginning of Boundaries

In the beginning, we are told, there was *tohu va-vohu*, a formless void. Creation both fills the void and gives it shape. Shaping is accomplished by means of boundaries, which differentiate the primeval wholeness into a multitude of entities, defining their contours and extent, what is inside and what is out. Boundaries maintain the integrity of entities, preserving them from inundation and restraining them from dribbling out into everything else. Without a boundary there can be no I and no other. Setting one's own boundaries, setting the boundaries of other entities, and placing them in categories are ways for societies and individuals to draw relationships among the components of a vast and various world. But while bounding and categorizing are acts of relation, they are also acts of power.[9] Power determines who draws the boundary and how and who makes the categories and for what reasons. Both boundary making and the exercise of power are basic human activities. They have no intrinsic moral valence. Boundaries are not intrinsically divisive any more than power is intrinsically oppressive. Indeed, as we shall see in our Genesis and Leviticus readings, both are indispensable for the creation of just societies and just relations between the self and the other. But acts of distinction and acts of power are morally charged. They carry implications for how members of categories are to behave and how others are to behave toward them. Hence, acts of definition are vulnerable to abuse.

Some boundaries are purely barricades—chainlink fences patrolled by Dobermans, borders scoured by searchlights, trenches, bastions, stockades, outposts of the Hobbesian war of all against all. Other boundaries are not primarily barriers but loci of interaction. A cell membrane, for instance, is part of the living substance of the cell. It is the perimeter at which the cell conducts its interchanges with other cells, the contacts, the flowings in and out that maintain its life within its environment. Human beings begin life with flexible, rather than rigid, boundaries. Born tiny and helpless, we are from the start profoundly interdependent. Only through perceiving our impact upon others and their impact upon us do we become distinct and particular beings. Intimacy with others is a survival need for our species. Even if they are fed and cleaned, babies who lack a caring other die in alarming numbers from a syndrome known simply as "failure to thrive." We affect and are affected by nonhuman others as well. From birth to death, we inhabit a great network of living things whose existence is interwoven with our own and to whom we are therefore responsible.

Physically, emotionally, ethically, we are best served by boundaries that acknowledge the integrity of both self and other yet are flexible enough to allow for creativity and communion. These are the boundaries advocated by feminist object-relations theorists. Benjamin, relying upon Winnicott, traces the origins of these flexible boundaries to the development of a holding environment between mother and infant in which the child reaches out to play and explore unhindered and yet unabandoned by the other.[10]

> Winnicott often quoted a line of poetry from Tagore to express the quality of the holding environment and the child's transitional area: "on the seashore of endless worlds children play." The image suggests a place that forms a boundary and yet opens up into unbounded possibility; it evokes a particular kind of holding, a feeling of safety without confinement.[11]

According to Benjamin, the mature version of this combination of mutual attunement and freedom to know one's own desires is enacted in the erotic space two people create who recognize one another as subjects. In such a union, she observes, "receptivity and self-expression, the sense of losing the self in the other and the sense of being truly known for oneself all coalesce."[12]

This boundary fluidity, these delicate calibrations of closeness and distance, interpenetration and distinctness characterize relations in Genesis 1 between God and humanity, between humanity and world, and between man and woman. As we shall see in Genesis 2 and 3, however, boundaries undergo a terrible transformation. In the world of these texts, closeness can only be imagined as fusion and distance as estrangement. Rather than creating distinctions, boundaries set up oppositions.

In contrast, both distinctions and similarities constitute the harmonious world of Genesis 1. Although the sequence of creation exactly parallels the Mesopotamian creation story, there is a crucial difference. In Genesis 1, creation is not the aftermath of war. The primeval watery chaos (*tehom*) is not imaged as an enemy of God, nor is it annihilated by the creation. Instead, God distinguishes various elements of the watery chaos and establishes their boundaries by naming them. Juxtaposed verses underline the parallels among these created elements. Stretched over the kindred waters above and below are kindred solid expanses, sky and earth.[13] The earth is sown with trees and grasses. The sky is sown with lights. The sea and air bring forth their many kinds of creatures. The earth brings forth its many beasts. The creation of humankind continues the themes of both the uniqueness of created things and their similitude with some differing other.

The Creation of Adam and the Boundary of Sexuality

> God said, "Let us make *adam* in our image, after our likeness. They shall rule the fish of the sea, the birds of the sky, the cattle, the whole earth, and all the creeping things that creep upon the earth." God created *adam* in his own image; in the image of God he created him [it]; male and female he created them. God blessed them and God said to them, "Be fertile and increase, fill the earth and master it; and rule the fish of the sea, the birds of the sky, and all the living things that creep upon the earth" (Gen. 1:26–27).[14]

Adam is the Bible's first name for humankind. It is derived from the Hebrew root 'DM, the root associated with redness.[15] Red is the color of the clayey earth (*adamah*), of blood (*dam*), of raw flesh. *Adam* is the red-earth creature, a continent of flesh reticulated by rivers of blood. *Adam* is God's conundrum: an earthy, fleshy, bloody being resembling (*domeh*) God.[16] The text dwells insistently upon the linkage. In the space of two verses, the likeness between God and *adam* is reiterated four times. Two terms, image, *tzelem,* and likeness, *d'mut,* describe the relation of *adam* to God. *Tzelem,* in its primary sense, means a physical representation, often a statue or an idol.[17] *D'mut,* from the root *DMH,* to resemble, is a more generalized word for similitude. Both terms are used in verse 26: "God said, 'Let us make *adam* in our image [*tzelem*], after our likeness [*d'mut*],' leaving the nature of *adam's* likeness to God delicately poised between the substantial and the insubstantial. But in verse 27, the more abstract term *d'mut* is dropped; likeness to God is realized in the flesh: "God created *adam* in his own image [*tzelem*], in the image [*tzelem*] of God he created him [it], male and female he created them" (Gen. 1:27).[18] *The one piece of new information in this verse is adam's embodiment as male and female.*

Human sexuality is presented as unique, Phyllis Trible notes. None of the animals have been specifically designated as male and female.[19] But what does it mean to link this unique sexuality with the divine image, as the text does? The metaphor of the divine image conferred upon male and female, Trible argues, preserves not only likeness to God but also the dissimilarity between a God who transcends sexuality and creatures endowed with it.[20] Both males and females bear in common a likeness to God, but their maleness and femaleness are not signifiers of this likeness but of unlikeness.

Yet by its placement of the creation of sexual difference, the text suggests precisely the contrary. Had the text set the creation of maleness and femaleness off by itself in a separate verse, or had it linked them to verse 28 in which God bestows the blessings of fertility and dominion, that would suggest that these characteristics mark a dissimilarity to God. Instead, the creation of sexual difference climaxes verses wholly devoted to establishing human similarity to God. Genesis 5:1–3 reiterates the link between likeness to God and gendered humanity: "This is the record of *adam's* line. When God created *adam,* he made him [it] in the likeness of God; male and female he created them (*bar'am*). And when they were created, he blessed them and called them *adam.*"

I want to turn Trible's argument upside down and argue that in Genesis 1 human sexuality is itself a metaphor for some element of the divine nature.[21] Something in God seeks to restate itself in flesh and blood. Perhaps it is God's creativity, or delight, or the ingrained yearning for communion with the other that serves as impetus for creation and for covenant.[22] But something in God, in seeking its human mirror, reveals itself as both infinitely varied and utterly whole. That something is, as it were, God's sexuality, which our own sexuality was created to reflect.

Genesis 1 refers to God both in the singular and in the plural and, like Genesis 5, attributes both singularity and plurality to *adam. Adam's* plurality is its sexual diversity. We are incalculably various, and the most basic of our variations are sexual. We are capable of unity, and our desire for sexual union adumbrates this gift. Sexuality, the most primary way in which humankind is at once many and one, is a metaphor for the infinitude and unity of God.

Our sexuality marks us both as boundaried and boundary-transcending. It is at once personal and transpersonal, private and public. Within ourselves, all by ourselves, is the capacity for eroticism. It is in our skin, our muscles, forested with twining nerves, our blood gusting through us like rising and falling winds our genitals raining their fluids, our senses all alive to joy. Yet sexuality also turns us toward the other. Overriding the physical and emotional boundaries that keep human beings distinct from one another, it urges us to open our portals, to extend ourselves, to create places of co/habitation where we and the other are interlinked. They are "the seashore of endless worlds" upon which we play, rapt in our desire, ever aware of the desire and the presence of the other. These places of communion we establish with our bodies, dissolving the boundaries of inside-outside, yours-mine, giver-getter, haver-holder, bespeak our likeness to the God the rabbis called *Ha-Makom,* the Place. The capacity to create intersubjective space, which we and God share, is what makes covenant possible.

Humanity and the Conferral of Power

The other Godlike characteristic bestowed upon the different forms of *adam* in Genesis 1:28 is power, specifically the capacity for power over the earth and its creatures. In Judaism's exegetical history, this verse has been used as a justification for the interconnected subordinations of woman and nature (although it was not easy making the verse cooperate). Extracting a proof for male supremacy from a verse enjoining humanity in plural imperatives to "be fertile and increase and fill the earth and master it" is a difficult proposition. Rabbinic tradition accomplished it by seizing upon a variant spelling in the Masoretic text as an exegetical hint of women's exclusion from mastery. The word *kibshuha,* "master it [lit. her]," lacks the vav of the plural form, making it possible to read the word as a command in the masculine singular "master it [her]."[23]

This missing vav is perhaps the most influential spelling error in the history of theology. In a legal dispute in the talmudic tractate Yebamot, it provides ammunition for the majority opinion that only men have the obligation to procreate.[24] Talmudic and midrashic[25] explanations of the missing vav are welded together by the eleventh-century exegete Rashi into a comprehensive justification for the subjugation of women: "The missing vav is to teach you that the male masters the female, so that she should not be a gadabout and it also teaches you that man whose disposition (*derekh*) is to master is commanded concerning procreation and not woman."[26]

Some feminist critics have charged that Genesis 1:28 endorses the pillage of the environment and the alienation of humanity from the rest of the natural world.[27] Interpreting mastery as a license for destruction, however, ignores the limitation on its use established in verse 29, where humans are assigned only the seed-bearing grasses and the fruit-bearing trees for food. Since humanity is implicitly forbidden to prey upon the fishes, birds, and cattle over which they have mastery, mastery in Genesis 1 cannot mean the right to tyrannize over other creatures.[28] Permission to eat flesh is not given until after the Flood, and its price is estrangement from other creatures: "The fear and the dread of you shall be upon all the beasts of the earth and upon all of the birds of the sky" (Gen. 9:2).

For the text's ancient readers, the promise of mastery was probably understood as a promise of survival in a perilous and unpredictable world.[29]

Droughts, famines, epidemics, cattle plagues, earthquakes, floods, and incursions of wild animals haunt their stories, their psalms, and their supplications. Mastery is, at best, a temporary blessing, for human beings share the same needs and terrors as other living creatures.

> All of them look to You
> to give them their food when it is due.
> Give it to them, they gather it up;
> Open Your hand, they are well satisfied;
> hide Your face, they are terrified:
> take away their breath, they perish
> and turn again into dust.
>
> —Ps. 104:27–29

For many Americans, power has become disreputable. In comparison with its atrocities and its deceits, its good deeds seem weak and unmemorable. In the news, on the talk shows, in discussions of political and social policy, power is too often confused with abuse, and victimization is valorized as if it were a moral position. Actually, victimization cannot be a moral stance, because a victim is a person under constraint, a person who has been robbed of choice. Choices require some degree of power. But instead of determining what power we do have or could acquire together with others, instead of organizing to maximize our power and share it more broadly, we vie with one another in a kind of moral poor-mouthing, as if denying our power relieved us of the obligation of sharing it and exercising it responsibly. Confronted with evidence of our destructive impact on the earth and our fellow creatures, we confess ourselves overwhelmed and go right on polluting, wasting, and destroying. It is significant that, in Genesis 1, where humanity is created and empowered coequally, power is conferred as a blessing. As we shall see, in Genesis 2 and 3, power is part of a curse. The injunction to master the earth, then, carries with it the potential for sin, the possibility of abusing power.

Two other forboding terms are the words that distinguish male and female, *zakhar* and *nekeva*. In Genesis 1, and in its reiteration in Genesis 5, *adam* is an inclusive term for a sexually diverse humankind. *Zakhar* and *nekeva* merely specify *adam's* sexual variations. But the roots of these words, laden with the connotations of doer and done-to, foreshadow situations in which *zakhar* and *nekeva* are not equally called *adam*.

The Hebrew word *zakhar* means the creature with the male member.[30] Female is *nekeva*, the pierced one. In these two terms the entire history of patriarchy is distilled. It is probably more than the coincidence of homophony that the *zakhar* is also the *zokher* and the *zakhur,* the rememberer and the remembered. The only memory in patriarchies is male memory because the only members are male members. They are the rememberers and the remembered because they are the recipients and transmitters of tradition, law, ritual, and story, the authorized interpreters of experience.

Zakhar names as his Other *nekeva,* the pierced one, the one whose boundaries are penetrated. He sets her up as his antithesis. His name for her declares that she and only she is permeable; despite all evidence to the contrary, he sees himself as impenetrably sealed. He is the invader and the conqueror. She is the invaded, the subjugated. He is the remembered. She is the forgotten. What she called herself, what tales she told, what wisdom she imparted, have fallen into silence. In drawing the boundary between himself and her, *zakhar* did not concern himself with what she was; only with what she was not. Through his memories she may be glimpsed dim and distant behind the rigid boundary of gender polarity. Genesis 2 and 3 hints at the earliest of these memories.

Genesis 2: The Closing of the Borders Between Woman and Man

> When YHWH God (*elohim*) made earth and heaven—when no shrub
> of the field was yet on earth and no grasses of the field had yet sprouted,
> because YHWH God had not sent rain upon the earth and there was
> no *adam* to till the soil . . . . YHWH God formed *adam* from clods of
> earth.[31] He blew into his nostrils the breath of life, and *adam* became
> a living being. YHWH God planted a garden in Eden, in the east, and
> placed there the *adam* whom he had formed. (Gen. 2:4–8)

In Genesis 2, the creation of humanity is depicted as a process of opposition and segregation. *Adam* is no conundrum here. Rather than being akin to his creator, he is an artifact molded (*yatzar*) out of earth as God later forms the animals and birds (2:19). Nor is the meaning of his creation mysterious. In contrast to Genesis 1, where *adam* has no instrumental purpose, in Genesis 2, as in Mesopotamian myth, *adam* is designed for labor. His purpose is to serve the earth (*adama*) out of which he has been shaped. I say "he" because the *Adam* of this narrative is both generic human and gendered male. His maleness represents the original human condition, rather than one variety of it. Hence there is no mention of the creation of maleness, as there is in Genesis 1.

Competent and adult from the moment of his creation, endowed with language and engaged in labor, he bears a curious resemblance to the motherless asocial resident of the state of nature in liberal political theory. The creation of woman, like the creation of the social contract, is planned as an improvement on the inconveniences of the original human condition.

> YHWH God said, "It is not good for the *adam* to be alone; I will make a fitting helper for him." And YHWH formed out of the earth all the wild beasts and all the birds of the sky and brought them to the *adam* to see what he would call them . . . but for the *adam* no fitting helper was found. So YHWH God cast a deep sleep upon the *adam;* and while he slept, he took one of his ribs and closed up the flesh at that spot. And YHWH fashioned the rib that he had taken from the *adam* into a woman; and he brought her to the *adam.* (Gen. 2:18–22)

Although human sociality is recognized as a necessity, the remedy for man's isolation is the creation of an oppositional other: "I will make him a helper *k'negdo.*" The word *neged* means both "against" and "corresponding"; hence the term *k'negdo,* translated by the JPS Tanakh as "fitting," actually carries dual senses of polarity and likeness: "a helper who is his counter/part." Instead of the tension of like and other sustained in intersubjective relations, an equal complementarity is established in which man is the subject and woman, his helper and reflection, is both counter to him and part of him.

Woman is brought into being in a manner unlike that of all other creatures. She is not created (BRH) like *adam* in Genesis 1 nor formed (YTzR) like Adam and the animals in Genesis 2; instead she is constructed (BNH). "YHWH God built the rib into a woman and brought her to the *adam.*" Adam greets her with joy. She does not seem to him to be an other at all. "This one at last/is bone of my bones/and flesh of my flesh./This one shall be called Woman (*ishah*),/For from man (*ish*) was she taken./Hence a man leaves his father and mother and clings to his woman (*isha*), so that they become one flesh."[32]

Unlike the P texts, Genesis 1 and 5, Genesis 2 never recognizes the woman as *adam,* only as *isha,* a creature derived from *adam,* contrasted to him and possessed by him, a construction designed to meet his specifications. In contrast, only in the wordplay that establishes woman as derivative is Adam identified by his gender. "This one shall be called Woman (*isha*) for from man (*ish*) was she taken" (Gen. 2:23). Together they will be *ha-adam v'ishto,* "the human and his woman" (Gen. 2:25).

Whereas in Genesis 1, God declares the various features of creation intrinsically good, Genesis 2 presents earth and its living things as a collection of resources valuable insofar as man can use them. The trees of Eden are "a delight to the eye and good for eating." The rivers that branch out from Eden point to the location of gold and precious stones or mark off the territory of nations. The birds and animals are noted because *adam* names them. Woman's importance lies in the function she fulfills for man. Unlike the beasts and birds, she will serve as a suitable mate. In this world where everything is viewed extractively, the tree of the knowledge of good and evil is an anomaly, a resource whose consumption is mysteriously forbidden.

Genesis 2, then, is a description not of the creation of the universe, but of the creation of the patriarchal perspective, in which the self relates to what is external to it by subjugating or devouring. Its account of the construction of woman to alleviate man's loneliness, of the process of splitting off and opposing femininity to masculinity, and of the resulting sense of mutilation in patriarchal man resembles the theoretical account offered by feminist object-relations psychology. As I summarized in Chapter 2, these theorists view the primal severing of identification with mother as the precipitating event in the construction of oppositional masculine identity. Because the man did not differentiate by learning to regard woman as another independent subject with whom interrelation is possible, he both craves and fears the infantile merger that would heal his estrangement by obliterating his autonomy. He seeks to resolve his dilemma by annexing and reincorporating the other, obliterating her independent selfhood. In both the object-relations story and Genesis, these attempts end badly. Disaster is inevitable in an Eden founded upon fantasies of obliteration. These fantasies carry the seed of death, the ultimate loss of all autonomy and recognition from the other. They are the bridge from the patriarchal Eden to the patriarchal world beyond its boundaries.

In the world brought about in Genesis 3, domination constrains the human couple, fettering humanity to a treadmill of compulsive and futile activity. Woman's sexual desire dooms her to be subjugated by man and to painful childbirths. Man's desire is not even mentioned. His energies are to be exhausted by the unabating struggle to pull food from the dust by which he himself will be devoured. The goodness of creation and mastery conferred in Genesis 1 are complicated by pain, alienation, and defeat.

The redemptive truth offered by this grim depiction is that patriarchal social relations construct a world that cries out to be mended. Yet mending is contingent upon the healing of gender relations. Gender polarity creates a world where power is a burden both for those who wield it and for those under its foot. Compulsive toil and unrelenting watchfulness replace freedom and trust, while hierarchy and caste obstruct fellowship and communion. Boundaries become fearful places where the reciprocal enmity between the serpent and the children of woman lurks. The underling strikes at the heel of his superior, who, in turn, bruises his subordinate's head. At the top of the ladder, privileged man, facing his unrewarding labors, most doubly watch his back, first against the hostility of the serpent on the bottom and then against his nearest other, his competitor for subjectivity.

However unhappy the world of patriarchy may be, it is unnecessary to conclude that it is God's will that we continue to inhabit it.[33] Judaism provides ample precedent for reading Genesis 2 and 3 as an etiological tale about the hardships of human life rather than as a normative statement. The rabbinic tradition does not use the story as a source of legal prooftexts, nor is there any prohibition on alleviating its conditions.[34] Some antitechnological Christian sects have understood the curses following the eating of the fruit as literal prescriptions, but no Orthodox kibbutz harvests with sickles because of the verse "by the sweat of your brow shall you get bread to eat" or refrains from hydroponic gardening because "Thorns and thistles shall it sprout for you. But your food shall be the grasses of the field." When childbirth anesthesia was invented, some Victorian clergymen saw it as a rebellion against the decree "In pain shall you bear children,"[35] but Jewish law never forbade the alleviation of childbirth pain. A consistent reading of the passage would not allow singling out "Your desire shall be for your husband and he shall rule over you" and endowing it alone with prescriptive force.

Passive acceptance of conditions is not an option in the post-Edenic world of Genesis 3. Humanity must act upon its environment simply to survive. This does not necessitate making adversaries of the earth or of one another. Just as we can invent technologies that ease our farming without damaging the earth or decimating its species and techniques that ease our birthing without seizing control from birthing mothers, we can invent ways of coexisting without dominating one another.

The urge to oppose and conquer the other may ultimately be more deadly to our kind than any of its earlier hardships. Dorothy Sayers once asked, "If women are the opposite sex, then what is the neighboring sex?"[36] When woman is defined as derivative *isha* or invaded *nekeva*, a shared reality is denied. We all live deeply within one another's boundaries. The question is whether we can do so in justice.

NOTES

1. This section incorporates much of my article "A Question of Boundaries: Towards a Jewish Feminist Theology of Self and Other," in *Tikkun Anthology*, ed. Michael Lerner (Oakland, CA: Tikkun Books, 1992), 465–471.

2. A separate book would be needed to catalogue and analyze traditional patriarchalist interpretations such as 1 Timothy 2:11–14 or B. Berakhot, 61, as well as their reuse in later, more systematized theologies. For summaries of male supremacist translation and commentary, see Carol Meyers, *Discovering Eve* (New York: Oxford University Press, 1988); Phyllis Trible, *God and the Rhetoric of Sexuality* (Philadelphia: Fortress, 1978), 73; Merlin Stone, *When God Was a Woman* (New York: Dial Press, 1976), 5–8, 198–233; and Elaine Pagels, "The Politics of Paradise," *New York Review of Books* (May 12, 1988), 28–37.

3. For a summary of six representative views, see Ilana Pardes, *Countertraditions in the Bible: A Feminist Approach* (Cambridge, MA: Harvard University Press, 1992), 13–38; Catherine Keller, *From a Broken Web: Separation, Sexism and the Self* (Boston: Beacon, 1986), 33–36, 78–92, *Lethal Love: Feminist Readings of Biblical Love Stories* (Bloomington: Indiana University Press, 1987), 104–130.

4. Rosemary Radford Ruether, "Motherearth and the Megamachine," in *Womanspirit Rising*, ed. Carol P. Christ and Judith Plaskow (San Francisco: Harper and Row, 1979), 43–52; Rosemary Radford Roether, *New Woman/New Earth: Sexist Ideologies and Human Liberation* (New York: Seabury Press, 1975); Carol P. Christ, *Diving Deep and Surfacing: Women Writers on Spiritual Quest* (Boston: Beacon, 1980), 120, 130; Susan Griffin, *Pornography and Silence: Culture's Revenge Against Nature* (New York: Harper and Row, 1981), 156–199; Judith Plaskow, *Standing Again at Sinai* (San Francisco: Harper and Row, 1979), 121–169, 192–194. In her later writing, Ruether gives a more nuanced account that recognizes that all dualisms are not alike either conceptually or in their effects upon women's lives. For example, in *Sexism and God-Talk* (Boston: Beacon, 1983), 72–82, she points out that Greek thought represents a more radical mind/body, male/female dualism than Hebrew thought. A consequence of Gnosticism's dualistic cosmology was a kind of egalitarianism. It invited women along with men to renounce body and sexuality and to become pure spirit.

5. Catherine Keller, *From a Broken Web: Separation, Sexism, and Self* (Boston: Beacon, 1998), 7–46.

6. Ibid, 11–15.

7. Ibid, 33–38.

8. Ibid, 78–92.

9. Mary Douglas, *Purity and Danger* (London: Routledge and Kegan Paul, 1966). Howard Eilberg-Schwartz, *The Savage in Judaism* (Bloomington: Indiana University Press, 1990).

10. Jessica Benjamin, *The Bonds of Love: Separation, Sexism, and Self* (Pantheon Books, 1988), 126–127.

11. Ibid, 127.

12. Ibid, 126.

13. This first dividing of the waters is paralleled by the splitting of Tiamat "like a shellfish" in the Enuma Elis. "Akkadian Myths and Epics: The Creation Epic," trans. E. A. Speiser, in *The Ancient Near East: An Anthology of Texts and Pictures*, vol. 1, ed. James B. Pritchard (Princeton, NJ: Princeton University Press, 1958), 35.

14. These translations of Genesis 1 and 2 are adaptations of JPS Tanakh. I have left *adam* and YHWH untranslated, because by translating *adam* as "man" and YHWH as "Lord," the JPS attributes gender and hierarchical status that these Hebrew terms do not imply. Another problem for translators is that Hebrew has no neuter gender. Every noun is either masculine or feminine, although grammatical gender assignment may be arbitrary. Thus, in one quotation from Genesis 1, I have bracketed "it" next to the literal translation "him." I have also chosen not to capitalize masculine pronouns referring to God as JPS does. The capitals predispose readers to regard masculinity as a divine attribute even where a particular text may not image God as masculine. There are *no* capitals in the original.

15. Ludwig Kohler and Walter Baumgartner, *Hebraisches und Aramaisches Lexikon Zum Alten Testament,* 3rd ed., with contributions from B. Hartman and E.Y. Kutscher (Letden: E.J. Brill, 1967), s.v., ADM, 13; DM, 215. Kohler-Baumgartner's lexicon, incorporating the latest philological research, maintains that *adam* and *adamah*, "soil," are derivatives from this primary root meaning concerning redness, and that *dam,* "blood," is a related root. These conclusions differ from the conjectural derivation proposed by the older lexicon of Brown, Driver, and Briggs that the primary root of ADM, "humankind," is "make or produce," cognate to an Assyrian root, whereas ADM, "red," is separately derived from an Arabic root meaning "tawny." See I. ADM and II. ADM.

16. There is a complex constellation of wordplays in Genesis 1 and 2 involving the words *adam, adamah* (earth), *dam* (blood), and *domeh* and *d'mut* from the root DMH, "to resemble." Genesis 1 emphasizes kinship with God with puns on *adam* and *domeh*, whereas Genesis 2 emphasizes earthiness with the pun on *adamah* (2:7). *Tardemah,* from RDM, the deep sleep during which *adam* has a rib extracted in Genesis 2, may also participate in this wordplay.

17. Although some indisputably metaphorical meanings for *tzelem* can be documented, they are rare. See, for example, Psalm 39:7: "Man walks about as a mere shadow (*tzelem*)," where contextually it is indisputable that *tzelem* means a semblance without substance.

18. Hebrew has no neuter gender. Whether the grammatical masculine gender of God or *adam* also confers actual masculinity is a matter of debate among translators and commentators. I am going to argue that, in Genesis 1, there is insufficient evidence to prove that God and *adam* are narratively portrayed as masculine, whereas they are clearly masculine in Genesis 2.

19. Phyllis Trible, *God and the Rhetoric of Sexuality* (Philadelphia: Fortress, 1978), 13–21.

20. Ibid, 21.

21. This is also a gnostic argument, although with strikingly different corollaries than mine. Elaine H. Pagels, *The Gnostic Gospels* (New York: Random House, 1979).

22. The theme of God's need for the other is found in the midrashic tradition, in classical mysticism, and in hasidism. Modern theologians who utilize the idea include Abraham Joshua Heschel and Martin Buber.

23. Because its Masoretic voweling is plural, the rabbis do not contest the word's plurality as scripture. Its missing yay functions for them merely as *remez,* an exegetical hint that the word could also be read as *kibshah,* "[you, masc.sing.] master her/it."

24. B. Yehamot 65b. It can be inferred that the rabbis are not satisfied with this proof because another prooftext is proposed that restates the commandment in the singular (Gen. 35:11). However, that it is not the first statement of the obligation weakens this second proof. Ultimately, argument, rather than prooftext, is conclusive in establishing the law. A probably unintended side effect of this ruling is that it provides a strong argument for women's freedom to use birth control, leaving men to fulfill their obligations on their own. Centuries of legal controversy focus upon this dangerous loophole. David M. Feldman, *Marital Relations, Birth Control, and Abortion in Jewish Law* (New York: Schocken, 1974), 53–56, 123–131, 169–248.

25. Bereshit Rabbah 8:12.

26. Rashi on Genesis 1:28.

27. This issue is addressed in ecofeminist theologies. A classic example is Rosemary Radford Reuther, *New Woman/New Earth.* A more current collection is *Ecofeminism and the Sacred,* ed. Carol J. Adams (New York: Continuum, 1993).

28. Permission to eat flesh is not given until after the Flood, when the disharmony between humanity and the other creatures is intensified (Gen. 9:1–5).

29. Carol Meyers, *Discovering Eve: Ancient Israelite Women in Context* (New York: Oxford University Press, 1991), 47–71.

30. Ludwig Kohler and Walter Baumgartner, *Hebraisches und Aramaisches Lexikon, s.v.* ZKhR. The noun meaning "male member" and the verb "to remember" are listed separately. Their etymologies do not preclude the possibility of a single root, although this is not proposed by the lexicon. It therefore seems plausible to suggest that the two terms *zakhar/zakhor* reflect a social fact confirmed by the Hebrew Bible's patrilineal genealogies and inheritances, its predominantly male subject matter, and its assignment of authorship almost exclusively to males. I am indebted to Professor Bruce Zuckerman for access to this lexicon and for his assistance in interpreting its entries.

31. I have followed Speiser's translation here, Genesis, vol. 1 of The *Anchor Bible,* trans. and with introduction and commentary by E. A. Speiser (Garden City, NY: Doubleday, 1964), 16n.

32. I have changed one word in the JPS translation. JPS has "clings to his wife," where I have put "clings to his woman." The word *ishah* was introduced in the previous verse, where it clearly means woman and not wife. Clearly, he clings to her not because of the social rules pertaining to marriage, but because these rules enact the reincorporation of a derivative part of man. The translation is problematic because *ishah* means both woman, generally, and wife. In Chapter 5 I discuss the implications of Hebrew's lack of a specific term for wife.

33. That the text itself does not express normativity is a central point of Carol Meyers's *Discovering Eve*.

34. One arguable exception is B. Berakhot 61a, an aggadic passage from which the rabbis derive rules forbidding men from walking behind a woman from man's original antecedence of woman. It is debatable, however, whether these rules have the force of law.

35. See Adrienne Rich, *Of Woman Born* (New York: W.W. Norton, 1976), 162–165.

36. Dorothy Sayers, "The Human-Not-Quite-Human," in *Are Women Human?* (Grand Rapids, MI: William B. Eerdmans Publishing, 1971), 17–47.

FROM IMAGINING THE BIRTH
OF A NATION

Ilana Pardes

The Question of National Identity

The figuration of Israel's birth is a forceful unifying strategy, but the metaphor does not provide what Benedict Anderson calls "unisonance." Nations may try to fashion a coherent conception of identity, or origin, or seek unity at points of clear disjunction, but they are bound to fail. The intertwined biographies of Moses and Israel poignantly disclose the problematic of defining national identity both for the individual and for the community. Moses' birth story differs from that of his heroic counterparts at another point as well. He is transferred back and forth between his Hebrew and Egyptian mothers. Yocheved places him in a basket at the Nile; he is found by Pharaoh's daughter who then hands him back to Yocheved (believing her to be a wet nurse). Later Moses is brought back to the palace, where the princess adopts him and endows him with a name. He is raised in the palace but ultimately returns to his family and people.

The very fact that there are two sets of parents in the myth of the birth of the hero already intimates the difficulties involved in fashioning an identity. The myth addresses primary questions: Who am I? Who are my parents? Where do I come from? But the questions of origin become all the more complex when the two sets of parents pertain to two different nations. Moses' split national identity at birth will follow him for the rest of his life. When his first son is born in Midian he chooses to name him Gershom, saying, "I have been a stranger in a strange land" (Exod. 2:22). His naming speech relies on a pun that links the name "Gershom" with the word *stranger* (*ger*). But in what sense is Moses a stranger at this point—in relation to Midian (Jethro's daughters regard him as an Egyptian), or Egypt (his words echo the oracular announcement of Israel's troubling future as "a stranger [*ger*] in a land that is not theirs" in Gen. 15:13)?[1] Moses will devote most of his life to constructing the concept of Canaan as homeland and will lead his people persistently toward the land of "milk and honey," but ultimately he will die in the wilderness, between Egypt and the Promised Land.

And the nation? Israel's lineage is far more complicated than Moses' family tree, but here too the multiple parental figures point to diverse national origins. The conflict between God and Pharaoh is but one expression of the issue. The nebulous national identity of the two midwives is another case in point. Are the two midwives who deliver the Hebrew babies Egyptian or Hebrew? The problem stems from the indefinite use of "Hebrew" (*'ivriyot*) in Exodus 1:16. If it is to be read as an adjective, then Shiphrah and Puah are Hebrew midwives. But then there is another possibility. The verse may mean that these are Egyptian midwives who specialize in delivering Hebrew women. Numerous commentators have tried to solve the problem. Thus Josephus suggests that the king chose Egyptian midwives, assuming that they "were not likely to transgress his will." Similarly, Abarbanel claims that "they were not Hebrews but Egyptians, for how could he trust Hebrew women to put their own children to death." The midrash, however, perceived them as Hebrews and identified the two midwives with Yocheved and Miriam.[2] What these commentaries neglect to take into account is the significance of the indeterminate origin of the midwives, the extent to which the nation's story repeats the confusion about identity embedded in Moses' biography.

The children of Israel are torn between the two lands, between their deep ties to Egypt and their desire to seek another land. They were not raised in the Egyptian court, as Moses was, but nonetheless Egypt is not only the site of traumas for them: it served, however partially, as a nurturing motherland of sorts, especially the luscious land of Goshen. The birth of Israel entails a painful process of individuation from Egypt that is never fully resolved.[3] Just before the parting of the Red Sea, God promises the children of Israel that they shall see the Egyptians no more (Exod. 14:13). But the drowning of the Egyptians does not lead to the effacement of Israel's strong longings for the land of Egypt. National identity is thus poised on the bank of a "loss of identity."[4]

The Emergence of the National Voice:
Internal Antinatal Forces

The nation's first words are delivered on the way out of Egypt, marking the rise of what Homi K. Bhabha calls "counter-narratives of the nation."[5] On seeing the Egyptian chariots pursuing them, the children of Israel cry out unto the Lord:

> And they said unto Moses, Because there were no graves in Egypt, hast thou taken us away to die in the wilderness? wherefore hast thou dealt thus with us, to carry us forth out of Egypt? Is not this the word that we did tell thee in Egypt, saying, Let us alone, that we may serve the Egyptians? For it had been better for us to serve the Egyptians, than that we should die in the wilderness? (Exod. 14:11–12)

National birth means gaining consciousness and the power of verbal expression. During their bondage in Egypt, the Israelites could only moan and groan. They were in a preverbal and preconscious state, unaware of God's providence. Or else their discourse was silenced (as they now claim), not deemed worthy of attention. Something changes with the Exodus. They acquire the capacity to verbalize their needs and cry out to the Lord through Moses. And yet the emergence of the voice of the nation is accompanied by antinatal cravings. They use their new power of expression to convey their discontent, their desire to return to Egypt, to undo the birth of the nation. In a fascinating way they question the official biography. God here turns out to be not the Deliverer of the nation but rather the bearer of death, an abusive Father who seeks to kill His children in the wilderness. God now seems to be just as bad as, or even worse than, Pharaoh.

The children of Israel are masters of complaint. This is just their first complaint, but it initiates a long series of murmurings in the desert. It has the characteristic rhetorical questions, much anguish, and anger. Nehama Leibowitz points to the obsessive evocation of the land they left behind in their grumbling. "'Egypt' is an eternal refrain in their mouths, recurring five times. They yearned for 'Egypt' as a babe for its mother's breasts."[6] Egypt seems to have far more to offer than the desert—even its graves (and Egypt does indeed excel in its death culture) are more attractive than those available in the wilderness. The primary national biography is far from linear. Birth does not necessarily move the children of Israel unambiguously forward. Another forceful desire compels them to look back toward Egypt.

Pharaoh, then, is not alone in wishing to stop the birth of the nation. Antinatal forces erupt from within as well. "The problem," as Bhabha claims, "is not simply the 'selfhood' of the nation as opposed to the otherness of other nations. We are confronted with the national split within itself, articulating the heterogeneity of the population."[7] Bhabha attributes such fractures to the disruptive power of minorities. The story of Israel is somewhat different. In this case, it is the *majority*—the vox populi—that questions the national presuppositions of the leading minority: Moses, his limited supporters—and God. The split is thus even more radical than in Bhabha's account of the modern nation, given its centrality. It stems from the conflicting desires of the bulk of the nation.

In a famous passage in "What Is a Nation?" Ernest Renan claims that "a nation's existence is, if you will pardon the metaphor, a daily plebiscite, just as an individual's existence is a perpetual affirmation of life."[8] For Renan, the nation is a spiritual principle, represented in the will to nationhood. It is this will that unifies a people, endowing them with a past, a future, and the lust for life. Renan, much like the biblical writers, cannot but rely on a personification of the nation in his exploration of nationhood. What the Bible adds to the picture, however, is an understanding of the complexity of national imagination; it reveals the extent to which the national affirmation of life may be accompanied by counterforces that do not see the formation of the nation as an urgent or essential project. A "daily plebiscite" in ancient Israel would have been a disaster. The children of Israel oscillate between a euphoric celebration of their deliverance—as is the case after the parting of the Red Sea—and a continual questioning of the official consecration of national birth.

Before the Israelites actually leave Egypt, Moses already turns the Exodus into a ritual to be cherished now and in days to come. He demands that they commemorate the event and pass the story on from one generation to another.

> And Moses said unto the people, Remember this day, in which ye came out from Egypt, out of the house of bondage; for by strength of hand the Lord brought you out from this place: there shall no leavened bread be eaten, . . . And thou shalt shew thy son in that day saying, This is done because of that which the Lord did unto me when I came forth out of Egypt. (Exod. 13:3–8)

Yerushalmi offers a fascinating analysis of the biblical injunction to remember the Exodus and the consequent ritualization of the event. What Yerushalmi overlooks is the extent to which the children of Israel cherish other memories as well. Against the recurrent command to remember the Exodus, they set up a countermemory: Egypt. Relentless, they persist in recalling life by the Nile, where they took pleasure in fleshpots and other Egyptian delights. Individuation from Egypt does not seem to be the only route. Memory can be shaped in a variety of ways.

Such counternarratives would seem to deflate national pride. Israel's heroism does not follow traditional perceptions of male courage. There is a good deal of fear of life in the nation's nascent voice and an acute horror of what lies ahead. God Himself often regrets having delivered the nation. The children of Israel do not succeed in fulfilling His expectations, and He never hesitates to express His disappointment in them. "You neglected the Rock that begot you, Forgot the God who brought you forth" (Deut. 32:18), claims Moses in God's name.[9] The people are blamed for being ungrateful, for forgetting even the unforgettable—the God who miraculously begot them. Of the numerous unflattering national designations God provides, the most resonant one is His definition of Israel as "a stiffnecked people" (Exod. 32:9). The nation withholds its body from God and in doing so reveals a sinful lack of faith and an unwillingness to open up to the divine Word.

But then Israel's challenge to the national plans of Moses and God is not merely a sign of weakness. There is something about the stiff neck of the nation and the refusal to take national imaginings for granted that reveals an unmistakable force. The nation's very name "Israel" means to struggle with God, and in a sense this is the nation's raison d'être. In this respect the biography of the eponymous father is also relevant to the understanding of national birth. Already in the womb Jacob struggles forcefully, trying to gain priority over his elder brother, Esau. Rebekah, who asks the Lord to explain the significance of the turmoil in her womb, is told, "Two nations are in thy womb, and two manners of people shall be separated from thy bowels; and the one people shall be stronger than the other people; and the elder shall serve the younger" (Gen. 25:23). We have seen the significance of the reversal of the primogeniture law on the national level, but what this primal scene equally emphasizes is the importance of the struggle for national formation. Not only the struggle with the other (Esau or Edom in this case) but also a struggle from within, a struggle with the Ultimate Precursor: God.[10] The uterine struggle between Jacob and Esau prefigures the momentous struggle with the angel. It is through wrestling in the night with a divine being that Jacob acquires the nation's name. "Thy name shall be called no more Jacob, but Israel," says the divine opponent, "for as a prince hast thou power with God and with men, and hast prevailed" (Gen. 32:28). Jacob does not become angelic as a result of this nocturnal encounter, but the struggle reveals a certain kind of intimacy with God that is unparalleled.

The nation, not unlike the eponymous father, is both the chosen son and the rebel son, and accordingly its relationship with the Father is at once intimate and strained. From the moment of Israel's birth, mutual adoration and disappointment mark the bond of the nation and God, and this is true of later stages in the nation's life as well. The tension between Israel and God only increases as the nation becomes a restless adolescent in the wilderness. In its rendition of the ambivalence that characterizes the father-son relationship, the primary biography of ancient Israel offers a penetrating representation of national ambivalence, making clear from the outset that the story of the nation is not a story without fissures and lapses.

The national biography of Israel surely relies on certain heroic motifs, but it does not omit unflattering moments in the nation's history. The representation of national birth in Exodus is not an idealized narrative about a flawless birth but rather a text that takes into account the darker aspects of national formation as it explores the baffling emergence of a new people. What makes nations come into being is one of the greatest enigmas that national biographies attempt to tackle. Exodus, I believe, can contribute much to our understanding of the imagining of such formative moments in its examination of how one nation jumped into the water despite itself and wondered why.

NOTES

1. Nahum N. Sarna, *Exploring Exodus,* (New York: Schocken Books, 1986) provides an extensive consideration of the etymology of the name " Gershom."

2. Nehama Leibowitz, *Studies in Shemot,* (Jerusalem: Ahva Press, 1981:31–38) offers an insightful analysis of the various traditions regarding the two midwives.

3. For more on the question of Israel's distinctiveness, see Peter Machinist "Distinctiveness in Ancient Israel," from Studies in *Assyrian History and Ancient Near East Historiography,* eds. Mordechai Cogn and Israel Eph'al, vol. 33 (Jerusalem Press, 1991).

4. Julia Kristeva, "Women's Time," in the *Kristeva Reader,* ed. Toril Moi, (New York: Columbia University Press, 1986).

5. Homi K. Bhabha, *The Location of Culture* (London: Routledge, 1994), 194.

6. Leibowitz op. cit. 1981: 245.

7. Bhabha op. cit. 1994: 148.

8. Ernest Renan "What Is a Nation?" In *Nation and Narration,* ed. Homi K. Bhabba, 8–22, 1992: 19.

9. New Jewish Publication Society translation.

10. Esau is the eponymous father of Edom. "Edom," in fact, is another name for Esau attributed to him (according to Gen. 25:30) for gulping down the red (*'adom*) stew Jacob prepared for him. The pun, as Alter (1996: 129) suggests, "forever associates crude impatient appetite with Israel's perennial enemy."

FROM THE RED TENT

Anita Diamant

Prologue

We have been lost to each other for so long.

My name means nothing to you. My memory is dust.

This is not your fault, or mine. The chain connecting mother to daughter was broken and the word passed to the keeping of men, who had no way of knowing. That is why I became a footnote, my story a brief detour between the well-known history of my father, Jacob, and the celebrated chronicle of Joseph, my brother. On those rare occasions when I was remembered, it was as a victim. Near the beginning of your holy book, there is a passage that seems to say I was raped and continues with the bloody tale of how my honor was avenged.

It's a wonder that any mother ever called a daughter Dinah again. But some did. Maybe you guessed that there was more to me than the voiceless cipher in the text. Maybe you heard it in the music of my name: the first vowel high and clear, as when a mother calls to her child at dusk; the second sound soft, for whispering secrets on pillows. Dee-nah.

No one recalled my skill as a midwife, or the songs I sang, or the bread I baked for my insatiable brothers. Nothing remained except a few mangled details about those weeks in Shechem.

There was far more to tell. Had I been asked to speak of it, I would have begun with the story of the generation that raised me, which is the only place to begin. If you want to understand any woman you must first ask about her mother and then listen carefully. Stories about food show a strong connection. Wistful silences demonstrate unfinished business. The more a daughter knows the details of her mother's life—without flinching or whining—the stronger the daughter.

Of course, this is more complicated for me because I had four mothers, each of them scolding, teaching, and cherishing something different about me, giving me different gifts, cursing me with different fears. Leah gave me birth and her splendid arrogance. Rachel showed me where to place the midwife's bricks and how to fix my hair. Zilpah made me think. Bilhah listened. No two of my mothers seasoned her stew the same way. No two of them spoke to my father in the same tone of voice—nor he to them. And you should know that my mothers were sisters as well, Laban's daughters by different wives, though my grandfather never acknowledged Zilpah and Bilhah; that would have cost him two more dowries, and he was a stingy pig.

Like any sisters who live together and share a husband, my mother and aunties spun a sticky web of loyalties and grudges. They traded secrets like bracelets, and these were handed down to me, the only surviving girl. They told me things I was too young to hear. They held my face between their hands and made me swear to remember.

My mothers were proud to give my father so many sons. Sons were a woman's pride and her measure. But the birth of one boy after another was not an unalloyed source of joy in the women's tents. My father boasted about his noisy tribe, and the women loved my brothers, but they longed for daughters, too, and complained among themselves about the maleness of Jacob's seed.

Daughters eased their mothers' burdens—helping with the spinning, the grinding of grain, and the endless task of looking after baby boys, who were forever peeing into the corners of the tents, no matter what you told them.

But the other reason women wanted daughters was to keep their memories alive. Sons did not hear their mothers' stories after weaning. So I was the one. My mother and my mother-aunties told me endless stories about themselves. No matter what their hands were doing—holding babies, cooking, spinning, weaving—they filled my ears.

In the ruddy shade of the red tent, the menstrual tent, they ran their fingers through my curls, repeating the escapades of their youths, the sagas of their childbirths. Their stories were like offerings of hope and strength poured out before the Queen of Heaven, only these gifts were not for any god or goddess—but for me.

I can still feel how my mothers loved me. I have cherished their love always. It sustained me. It kept me alive. Even after I left them, and even now, so long after their deaths, I am comforted by their memory.

I carried my mothers' tales into the next generation, but the stories of my life were forbidden to me, and that silence nearly killed the heart in me. I did not die but lived long enough for other stories to fill up my days and nights. I watched babies open their eyes upon a new world. I found cause for laughter and gratitude. I was loved.

And now you come to me—women with hands and feet as soft as a queen's, with more cooking pots than you need, so safe in child-bed and so free with your tongues. You come hungry for the story that was lost. You crave words to fill the great silence that swallowed me, and my mothers, and my grandmothers before them.

I wish I had more to tell of my grandmothers. It is terrible how much has been forgotten, which is why, I suppose, remembering seems a holy thing.

I am so grateful that you have come. I will pour out everything inside me so you may leave this table satisfied and fortified. Blessings on your eyes. Blessings on your children. Blessings on the ground beneath you. My heart is a ladle of sweet water, brimming over.

Selah.

Chapter Eight

I was the first they knew of it. My own mother saw me and shrieked at the sight of my bloodied body. She fell to the ground, keening over her murdered child, and the tents emptied to learn the cause of Leah's grief. But Bilhah unbound me and helped me to stand, while Leah stared—first horrified, then relieved, and finally thunderstruck. She reached out her hands toward me but her face stopped her.

I turned, intending to walk back to Shechem. But my mothers lifted me off my feet, and I was too weak to resist. They stripped off my blankets and robes, black and stiff with the blood of Shalem. They washed me and anointed me with oil and brushed my hair. They put food to my lips, but I would not eat. They laid me down on a blanket, but I did not sleep. For the rest of that day, no one dared speak to me, and I had nothing to say.

When night fell again, I listened to my brothers' return and heard the sound of their booty: weeping women, wailing children, bleating animals, carts creaking under the weight of stolen goods. Simon and Levi shouted hoarse orders. Jacob's voice was nowhere to be heard.

I should have been defeated by grief. I should have been exhausted past seeing. But hatred had stiffened my spine. The journey up the mountain, bound like a sacrifice, had jolted me into a rage that fed upon itself as I lay on the blanket, rigid and alert. The sound of my brothers' voices lifted me off of my bed and I walked out to face them.

Fire shot from my eyes. I might have burned them all to a cinder with a word, a breath, a glance. "Jacob," I cried with the voice of a wounded animal. "Jacob," I howled, summoning him by name, as though I were the father and he the wayward child.

Jacob emerged from his tent, trembling. Later he claimed that he had no knowledge of what had been done in his name. He blamed Simon and Levi and turned his back on them. But I saw full understanding in his clouded eyes as he stood before me. I saw his guilt before he had time to deny it.

"Jacob, your sons have done murder," I said, in a voice I did not recognize as my own. "You have lied and connived, and your sons have murdered righteous men, striking them down in weakness of your own invention. You have despoiled the bodies of the dead and plundered their burying places, so their shadows will haunt you forever. You and your sons have raised up a generation of widows and orphans who will never forgive you.

"Jacob," I said, in a voice that echoed like thunder, "Jacob," I hissed, in the voice of the serpent who sheds life and still lives, "Jacob," I howled, and the moon vanished.

"Jacob shall never know peace again. He will lose what he treasures and repudiate those he should embrace. He will never again find rest, and his prayers will not find the favor of his father's god.

"Jacob knows my words are true. Look at me, for I wear the blood of the righteous men of Shechem. Their blood stains your hands and your head, and you will never be clean again.

"You are unclean and you are cursed," I said, spitting into the face of the man who had been my father. Then I turned my back upon him, and he was dead to me.

I cursed them all. With the smell of my husband's blood still in my nostrils, I named them each and called forth the power of every god and every goddess, every demon and every torment, to destroy and devour them: the sons of my mother Leah, and the son of my mother Rachel, and the sons of my mother Zilpah, and the son of my mother Bilhah. The blood of Shalem was embedded beneath my fingernails, and there was no pity in my heart for any of them.

"The sons of Jacob are vipers," I said to my cowering brothers. "They are putrid as the worms that feed on carrion. The sons of Jacob will each suffer in his turn, and turn the suffering upon their father."

The silence was absolute and solid as a wall when I turned away from them. Barefoot, wearing nothing but a shift, I walked away from my brothers and my father and everything that had been home. I walked away from love as well, never again to see my reflection in my mothers' eyes. But I could not live among them.

I walked into a moonless night, bloodying my feet and battering my knees on the path to the valley, but never stopped until I arrived at the gates of Shechem. I kept a vision before me.

I would bury my husband and be buried with him. I would find his body and wrap him in linen, take the knife that had stolen his life and open my wrists with it so we could sleep together in the dust. We would pass eternity in the quiet, sad, gray world of the dead, eating dust, looking through eyes made of dust upon the false world of men.

I had no other thought. I was alone and empty. I was a grave looking to be filled with the peace of death. I walked until I found myself before the great gate of Shechem, on my knees, unable to move.

If Reuben had found me and carried me back, my life would have ended. I might have walked and wept for many years more, half mad, finishing my days in the doorway of a lesser brother's third wife. But my life would have been finished.

If Reuben had found me, Simon and Levi would surely have killed my baby, leaving it out in the night for the jackals to tear apart. They might have sold me into slavery along with Joseph, ripping my tongue out first, to stop me from cursing their eyes, skin, bones, scrotums. I would never be appeased by their pain and suffering, no matter how ghastly.

Nor would I have been mollified when Jacob cowered and took a new name, Isra'El, so that the people would not remember him as the butcher of Shechem. He fled from the name Jacob, which became another word for "liar," so that "You serve the god of Jacob" was one of the worst insults one man could hurl at another in that land for many generations. Had I been there to see it, I might have smiled when his gift with animals deserted him and even his dogs ran from his side. He deserved no less than the agony of learning that Joseph had been torn by wild beasts.

Had Reuben found me at the gates of Shechem, I would have been there to give Rachel the burial she deserved. Rachel died on the highway, where Jacob had gone to flee the wrath of the valley, which set out to avenge the destruction of Hamor and the peace of Shechem. Rachel perished in agony, giving birth to Jacob's last son. "Son of woe," she named the little boy who cost her a river of black blood. But the name Rachel chose for her son was too much of an accusation, so Jacob defied the wish of his dying wife and pretended that Ben-Oni was Benjamin.

Jacob's fear chased him away from Rachel's poor drained body, which he buried hastily and without ceremony at the side of the road, with nothing but a few pebbles to remember the great love of his life. Perhaps I would have stayed there at Rachel's grave with Inna, who planted herself in that spot and gathered beautiful stones to make an altar to the memory of her only daughter. Inna taught the women of the valley to speak the name of Rachel and tie red cords around her pillar, promising that, in return, their wombs would bear only living fruit, and ensuring that my aunt's name would always live in the mouths of women.

If Reuben had found me, I would have watched my curse wrap itself around his neck, unleashing a lifetime of unspent passion and unspoken declarations of love for Bilhah and of hers for him. When that dam broke, they went breathlessly into each other's arms, embracing in the fields, under the stars, and even inside Bilhah's own tent. They were the truest lovers, the very image of the Queen of the Sea and her Lord-Brother, made for each other yet doomed for it.

When Jacob came upon them, he disinherited the most deserving of his sons and sent him to a distant pasture, where he could not protect Joseph. Jacob struck Bilhah across the face, breaking her teeth. After that, she began to disappear. The sweet one, the little mother, became smaller and thinner, more silent, more watchful. She did not cook anymore but only spun, and her string was finer than any woman had ever spun, as fine as a spider's web.

Then one day, she was gone. Her clothes lay upon her blanket and her few rings were found where her hands might have lain. No footprints led into the distance. She vanished, and Jacob never spoke her name again.

Zilpah died of fever the night that Jacob smashed the last of Rachel's household gods under a sacred tree. He had come across the little frog goddess—the one that had unlocked the wombs of generations of women—and he took an ax to the ancient idol. He urinated on the crushed stone, cursing it as the cause of all his misfortune. Seeing this, Zilpah ripped at her hair and screamed into the sky. She begged for death and spit upon the memory of the mother who left her. She lay on the ground and put handfuls of dirt into her mouth. Three men were needed to tie her down to keep her from doing herself harm. It was an awful death, and as they prepared her for the grave, her body broke into pieces like a brittle old clay lamp.

I am glad I did not see that. I am grateful I was not there as Leah lost the use of her hands and then her arms, nor to see her on the morning she awoke in her own filth, unable to stand. She would have begged me, as she begged her unfeeling daughters-in-law, to give her poison, and I would have done it. I would have taken pity and cooked the deadly drink and killed her and buried her. Better that than to die mortified.

Had Reuben carried me back to the tents of the men who had turned me into the instrument of Shalem's death, I would have done murder in my heart every day. I would have tasted bile and bitterness in my dreams. I would have been a blot upon the earth.

But the gods had other plans for me. Reuben came too late. The sun shone above the walls of the city when he arrived at the eastern gate, and by then other arms had carried me away.

FROM THE BIBLE AND YOU, THE BIBLE AND YOU AND OTHER MIDRASHIM

Yehuda Amichai

15

I don't imagine that on the night of the exodus from Egypt,
between midnight and dawn, any couple could lie together
in love. (We could have.) In haste,
blood dripping from lintels and doorposts,
silver and gold dishes clanging in the dark, between the firstborn's
stifled death cry and the shrieking of mothers' wombs
emptying like wineskins. And standing over them, legs wide apart,
the Angel of Death, crotch gaping male and female
like a bloody sun in the thick of frizzled black death.
Sandaled feet slapping against the soft dough of matza
and the flesh of belly and thigh, hard belts
cinched tight at the waist, buckles
scraping against skin, tangled in one another.
To roll like that, locked in eternal love,
with all the rabble from the house of slavery
into the Promised Desert.

AARON'S GOD—AND OURS

A YOM KIPPUR REFLECTION

Sarah Polster

LAST FALL, I WAS ASKED to share my thoughts on the Torah portion for Yom Kippur at my synagogue's High Holy Day services. I said yes without quite remembering what the parsha was about, and when I opened my Chumash to refresh myself on Leviticus 16, it momentarily knocked the wind out of me.

No scholar of Torah, I am the most typical of contemporary Jews—raised in a secular environment by parents who retained a strong cultural attachment to Judaism while thoroughly rejecting its religious teachings. Though I had been indoctrinated into Judaism through compulsory attendance at Sunday School as a child, when I joined Beyt Tikkun I had not spent serious time in a synagogue since I was thirteen and my parents offered me my freedom (sans bat mitzvah) from even this token Jewish commitment.

Like many of us set free as children from religious strictures our parents (legitimately) found confining, I have spent much of my life trying to reinvent a spiritual framework spacious enough and subtle enough to lend context and meaning to my life's joys and sorrows. Not until well into my adulthood did it even occur to me to look for it in Judaism. And like many liberal secular Jews raised to read religious texts literally and suspiciously, I have found that the most daunting stumbling block in my return to

Judaism has been the Torah itself and specifically the image of a harsh, judgmental, petty, abusive, and quixotic God that springs from many of its pages. I read with anger and incomprehension as the God of Torah time and time again seems to engage in senseless acts of murder and cruelty. My visceral response is "this is not the God I know."

The Torah portion we read on Yom Kippur—Leviticus 16—is one of those passages. This parsha must be read in the context of an earlier portion, Leviticus 10, which tells us that God killed two of Aaron's sons right before Aaron's eyes, because in their offering of incense during an elaborate ritual involving animal sacrifices, they somehow "offered before the Lord alien fire, which He had not enjoined upon them." Though commentators have offered numerous explanations of what "alien" or "strange fire" might actually have been, and how it could have caused these deaths, these explanations are oddly lacking in conviction—the commentators themselves appear baffled by these deaths. In Leviticus 11 through 15, God not only makes no comment upon Aaron's loss, but lectures Moses and Aaron on the dietary laws and laws of purification. And Aaron— except for refusing to eat the meat of the animal slaughtered when his sons died—has also been silent. Then in Leviticus 16, God invites Aaron to return to God's presence to atone for his sins and the sins of his household, and gives elaborate instructions about how to bathe and dress for the occasion, what animals to sacrifice, and how exactly the sacrifices should be offered.

In this parsha is just about everything that I find repugnant in Torah, and yet it is the reading we are called to attend to on the holiest day of the year.

I have learned not to gloss over the kinds of discomfort that texts like this engender in us, but to use that discomfort to reengage the texts with fresh eyes. In particular, I have taken to heart Rabbi Michael Lerner's advice (in *Jewish Renewal: A Path to Healing and Transformation*) that we find in Torah both the true voice of God speaking profoundly and timelessly through the human beings who wrote the Torah and also the distortions of God's voice that these human writers introduced—distortions that are inevitable products of the times and cultures in which these writers lived and the personal pain and limitations they were subject to.

So how do we tease out the true voice of God in this parsha? If we know a loving and compassionate God who invites us into partnership with Him in the ongoing, unending task of creation, where is God's voice in these instructions to Aaron, his grieving priest, about how safely to approach Him in the wake of a searing and inexplicable loss for which

Aaron holds Him responsible? And what are the sins of Aaron and his household—and let us remember that *we* are Aaron's household—for which Aaron and all of us are called to atone on Yom Kippur?

If your experience of the ten days between Rosh Hashanah and Yom Kippur is anything like mine, as you identify all the ways in which you have fallen short this year, and the ways in which you have caused pain, you have been struggling between the competing tugs of grief and blame. You surface something you have said or done that you regret, that you are ashamed of, and it makes you wince. You mourn for the person you could have been, but are not. Then in the same breath, you blame it on somebody. Not my fault, you think. And for a moment you actually feel not so bad—you're still regretful, but you're not so ashamed. And if you can muster up a good head of anger at whomever you've just blamed for your shortcoming, you feel even better still. And if you believe this somebody to be very much more powerful than you are, you feel almost totally absolved, perhaps even righteous. But somewhere the sense of powerlessness this leaves us—powerless to be the people we were put here to be—lingers underneath as a source of profound, if unconsidered, grief. So here we are on this holy day, with this mixed bag of regrets and blame and grief, hoping to approach God and through that encounter to recover our sense of possibility and to find the strength and the wisdom to begin the new year afresh.

So who is this God we're hoping to approach on this day? Is it literally true that God is the killer of Aaron's sons, an all-powerful unrepentant murderer who is here strong-arming Aaron and all of us to account for *our* sins? Or did a grieving people, trying to find an explanation for the inexplicable simply blame God for the death of these young men and then cower in fear to approach this cruel and all-powerful deity, which they themselves had constructed? Was this the sin for which Aaron was called to atone? Perhaps God's instructions to Aaron regarding bathing and dressing and the enactment of ritual are the invitation of a compassionate God who knows our grief and fear, who knows we want to blame him for our losses and shortcomings, who also knows the power of His presence and how overwhelming it can seem, and who nonetheless wishes to see contact restored. If this is our understanding of God, then in this passage we can see him seeking to heal the rift, to provide a safe way for frightened, angry people to reenter his presence and come to know him again.

Reading this text with a loving and compassionate God in mind, I was reminded of a story a friend told me about her recovery from a time of grief. Stephanie suffered a devastating miscarriage during her first pregnancy and in its wake spent an hour on the phone with her best friend Kay lamenting the loss of her baby while Kay listened patiently. Kay had just emerged from a sabbatical year of silent prayer and meditation, part of her own growth as a Christian minister. Stephanie, who is a minister herself, was particularly lamenting her inability to pray since her miscarriage, and her sadness over her loss of contact with God. A few days later, a small brown paper package arrived in the mail, in which Stephanie found a simple beige linen jumper, soft and long and roomy. It came with a note from Kay, which said: "I have prayed in this dress every day for a year. You don't have to pray. Just wear this dress. It is full of prayers." And Stephanie wore that dress, and wept in it, and let the prayers in that dress pray for her when her mouth and her heart could not. She said of both the dress and the prayers: "they were spacious enough to gather up my fear and grief and anger."

Consider God's instructions to Aaron about preparing to enter the Shrine: "He shall be dressed in a sacral linen tunic, with linen breeches next to his flesh, and be girt with a linen sash, and he shall wear a linen turban. They are sacral vestments; he shall bathe his body in water and then put them on." Let us imagine these garments gathering up his fear and grief and anger, and allowing him to feel clothed—which is to say, safe—before God, rather than raw and naked in his loss.

Dressed in God's compassion, but still angry and fearful, Aaron enters God's dwelling place, where he reenacts the same ritual of animal sacrifice during which, the last time it was performed, he watched his sons die. But the ritual of slaughter is familiar to Aaron, and God is careful explicitly to ensure that this encounter will be safe for Aaron, twice spelling out ways in which Aaron can protect himself from getting closer to God than a human can handle. Aaron performs this ritual with practiced hands but a new mindfulness.

What strikes me about this passage is its unrelenting physicality. Put yourself in Aaron's shoes.

Still blaming God for the death of your sons, you are to bathe, dress, and enter God's dwelling place, alone. You are to perform a ritual in which you get so much blood on your hands that it drips from your fingers, and then splash the curtains and the altar and the Ark with it. You are to burn so much incense that you can barely see for the sweet-smelling smoke. It probably makes you cough; it probably makes your eyes water and your throat burn. Standing amid the blood and dung and carcasses of the bull and the goat you've slaughtered, you are to confess your sins while resting your hands on the head of a live goat. You are to send this goat—a witness to the entire ritual—running into the wilderness with all your sins heaped on his head. And then you are to emerge from the Shrine, strip off your bloody clothes, bathe again, put on full priestly regalia, and rejoin your people.

What happens here that restores Aaron's and Aaron's household's right relationship with God? What happens is that God reminds Aaron who God really is. To understand this, we must put aside our knee-jerk repugnance for ritual sacrifice, which had a very different meaning for Aaron than it does for us today. The equivalent for us, I think, would be to take a week's paycheck and set it on fire. It is about giving up to God some basic element of our sustenance, without which we could not live. But even as we are repelled by the image of animal sacrifice, I think we can nonetheless appreciate the power in such a ritual, a ritual that was Aaron's familiar way to approach God. In performing this ritual, Aaron finds himself once again intensely in the presence of the true God—a God who guides him into doing what will release him, and makes the process safe.

Then, there is the innovation for Aaron in this ritual: his confession of sin—never before today has this been part of the ceremony. And the final way in which God reminds Aaron who he is: God makes no comment upon his confession. He simply invites Aaron to speak his sins aloud and then offers him a way to let them go. It is Aaron's letting go of sin, not God's judgment of sin, that sets Aaron free and returns him and his people to joyful participation in a covenantal relationship—which is to say, a two-way relationship—with God.

This is the sort of relationship into which God is inviting us on this holy day—not one in which we are judged, but one in which we are released. Yom Kippur offers us the opportunity to let go of the attitudes and behaviors that create estrangements of all kinds—including estrangement from God—and enter into renewed contact and renewed possibility.

OUR (MEANING WOMEN'S)
BOOK-OF-ESTHER PROBLEM

Susan Schnur

And the King sent letters to all the provinces, saying,
"Every man shall rule in his own home."
—Esther 1:22

WHEN IS THE LAST TIME you read the first two chapters of the Book of Esther? I mean really *read* them? They are so patently a polemic against women that it's painful to think of Jews (especially young ones) at synagogues all over the world on Purim enjoying this dangerous induction into woman-hating.

See chapter 1:16–22, in which one of the King's officers responds to the fact that Vashti has refused to appear nude before a palace full of drunken males:

> It is not only the King whom Vashti the Queen has wronged, but also all the officials and all the people in all the provinces of King Ahasuerus. For this deed of the Queen will come to the attention of all women, making their husbands contemptible in their eyes, by saying: "King Ahasuerus commanded Vashti the Queen to be brought before him but she did not come!"

And this day the princesses of Persia and Media who have heard of the Queen's deed will cite it to all the King's officials, and there will be much contempt and wrath.

If it pleases the King, let there go forth a royal edict from him, and let it be written into the laws of the Persians and the Medes, that it be not revoked, that Vashti never again appear before King Ahasuerus; and let the King confer her royal estate upon another who is better than she. Then, when the King's decree which he shall proclaim shall be resounded throughout all his kingdom—great though it be—all the wives will show respect to their husbands, great and small alike.

This proposal pleased the King and the officials, and the King did according to the word of Memuchan [his officer]; and he sent letters into all the King's provinces, to each province in its own script, and to each people in its own language, to the effect that every man should rule in his own home.

Sitting in the synagogue, its standard-issue annotated prayer book in my lap (the ArtScroll Family *Megillah,* edited by Rabbi Meir Zlotowitz), I scan the midrashic commentaries in the margins, which only add insight to injury. For example: *"Vashti refused [to appear nude before the men], not because of modesty. The reason for her refusal was that God caused leprosy to break out on her, and paved the way for her downfall."* Whew. My teenage son leans over and whispers, "How about gang rape? Do you think something was wrong with Vashti because she didn't like gang rape?"

When I saunter, newborn each year, across the pages of Rabbi Zlotowitz's dependable marginalia, it's like meeting up again with an old friend. "Thank you, Reb Z.," I want to tell him, "for your spiritual largesse. For your misogyny and insensitivity, and for the constancy of your commitment to the moral low ground." Sitting on my right is my very Conservadox 80-year-old mother who is also—not oxymoronically—a longtime board member of a women's domestic violence shelter. "What?" I say to her, sensing that she's getting hot under her collar. "Your *Megillah* is missing the commentary that talks about the terrifying threat of violence that accompanies male substance abuse?? Let me see that copy you're using! *What?* It doesn't mention the sexual sadism and degradation implicit in the King's pimping??" She shooshes me.

My 10-year-old daughter elbows my husband and points to a midrashic note that explains that the King wanted Vashti to come to his party naked except for the "royal crown." "Gross," she synopsizes brilliantly. A moment later she adds, "That's like what they did at that fraternity at Colgate. Vashti's harem girls need to get together and do a 'Take Back the Night' like we do at camp. Hey, I've got an idea! Why don't we do a 'Take Back the Night' right here in the middle of the *Megillah* reading?"

I whisper back, "Actually, that's a clever idea."

Soon we're on to a section of the *Megillah* which describes the captivity rites in the girls' harem, "*six months of anointing with oil of myrrh, and six months with perfumes and feminine cosmetics,*" after which each girl goes to the King "in the evening" and "the next morning she would return to the second harem." I look over at my pre-pubescent daughter and see that she's again reading the helpful commentary: "*Having consorted with the King, it would not be proper for them to marry other men. They were required to return to the harem and remain there for the rest of their lives as concubines.*" Again I thank Rabbi Z. for the exquisite sharing of his knowledge of ancient Persian sex etiquette as well as his pornographic fantasies, and for causing me to sink into this personal trough of sarcasm and bitterness, which I hate.

What are contemporary Jews *supposed* to make of a religious text that dishes up such disturbing garbage? Most Jewishly committed women I know, even feminists, solve the problem of these offensive narratives (rabbinic and biblical) by fighting valiantly to stay in denial. So, okay, we feel upset for a minute, but then we think, achh, Purim, it only comes once a year, *don't start. Just don't start.* Shoosh yourself.

When, though, I wonder, will women finally create a morally defensible re-write of these chapters? Why aren't we insisting that our synagogue communities cheer and stomp their feet at the mention of Vashti's name? She is a foremother in the best sense of the word—assertive, appropriate, courageous. My educated supposition is that the full moon of Adar—now the date for Purim—used to be a pagan occasion for autonomous women's rites that could not be reined in by men, and that these chapters, therefore, represent one of Purim's many core "reversals"; that is, they represent a male revolt against women. Yeah, I think, looking around the room, but why does it feel like our row in the synagogue is the only one that gets this?

As the children around me flail their *graggers,* I think about how participating in this public reading of the *Megillah* represents our complicity in the degradation of people, and about how I, for one, should figure out how not to sanction this anymore. I think back a decade or so to the year when the Hebrew day school principal gave all the "beautiful Esthers" (that is, every single female child in the costume parade) Barbie dolls. (I tried, but failed, to engage our rabbi in a discussion about this.) And then I remember the year after that, and the year after that, and the year after that. . . .

We women have worked hard to be represented, *as females,* in Judaism: We are cantors, scholars, mothers, *davenners,* teachers, writers, rabbis;

we have created female institutions for study and prayer, egalitarian re-writes of liturgy and texts, feminist reconstructions of Jewish foremoth-ers, et cetera. *But still, at the base of it all, we live with many Jewish texts whose core agonistic purpose was to censure women's rituals,* to decry deities that uplifted females, to erase antecedent women's history, to dero-gate and render invisible women's intimate empowering relationship to the earth's cycles and generativity, and, in general, to set—in concrete and steel beams (over the rubble of feminine experience)—the foundations of patriarchy. It is high time for women and sympathetic men to be chal-lenging this, to be educating ourselves, for example, in the pre-biblical Zeitgeist, so that we can best remediate some morally reprehensible Jew-ish texts (not only, of course, in relation to women).

Doubtless some of us female rabble-rousers have already been called "pagans," "idolaters" and "polytheists" for our attempts to unearth the women-positive rites, attitudes and theology that lie crushed beneath He-brew Scriptures. These accusations are, of course, silly, but they intimidate us nonetheless because we have internalized, after all, our dispossession.

Let me say that Jewish women seeking feminine antecedents don't "be-lieve in the goddesses" whose pentimenti can be seen behind some Jewish texts (like Ishtar, for example, Esther's namesake, who lurks behind the holiday of Purim), nor do we fail to recognize the developmental impor-tance of monotheism. We are saying something different (that has noth-ing to do with "worshipping idols"): that we are no longer willing to throw out the pink-ribboned baby with the bath water. The foremothers of Es-ther, Eve, Sarah and Miriam *were* female deities—Ishtar, Lilith, Meri, the Queen of Heaven and others. There was once a theological language and a set of rites that uplifted women and brought us self-esteem and author-ity. *That's* the pentimento we want to scratch away at, that's the part we are clamoring to uncover and reclaim . . . so that it's good for *us,* too.

In Regina Schwartz's new book, *The Curse of Cain,* she struggles with the two sides of the Bible. On the one hand, she writes, the Bible is a text that has a humane "accountability for the widow, the orphan, the poor." On the other, however, it's a text that models a religious commitment to genocide—for example, "obliterating the Canaanites" (fill in your word of choice here: Hutu, Copt, Cherokee, Muslim, kulak, Croat, Jew). He-brew Scriptures were also fairly committed to the cultural genocide of the feminine—because the latter threatened the nascent, ever-shaky and cas-tratable Israelite patriarchy. The Hebrew God's human male "children," in Scriptures, are fairly consistently defined against inferior others, includ-ing us females.

All of this is just to say that the *Megillah* is a good example of a Jewish text that's deeply interested in this idea of insider vs. outsider. Not only is Haman an outsider, but so are women and women's natal theological families: that is, our sustaining myths, our bodies, our primordial connection to nature, our female initiations. That's all off limits. To this day, text-sanctioned history means that it is "heresy" for women to inquire after "our" side of the family, after "our" side of the past. In some ways, the Hebrew Scriptures is an intimidating, ungenerous book, and its self-interested defenders can be ungenerous and intimidating, too.

So, dear readers, *hazak v'ematz*, be strong and take courage. As Mordechai once said to Esther (chapter 4:14): "If you persist in keeping silent at a time like this . . . you and yours will perish. And who knows whether it was just for such a time as this that you attained your elevated position?"

And Esther looked him straight in the eye and answered, "Gotcha."

LIVING IN THE
SHADOWS OF THE
HOLOCAUST

CATTLE CAR COMPLEX

Thane Rosenbaum

HE PUSHED THE BUTTON marked "Down." He pushed again. The machine ignored the command. Slowly he pivoted his head back, staring up at the stainless-steel eyebrow just over the door. No movement of descending light. The numbers remained frozen, like a row of stalled traffic.

For bodily emphasis, he leaned against the panel—pressing "Down," "Up," "Lobby," "Open," "Close"—trying vainly to breathe some life into the motionless elevator. But there was no pulse. The car remained inert, suspended in the hollow lung of the skyscraper.

"Help!" he yelled. "Get me out of here!" The echo of his own voice returned to him.

Still no transit. The elevator was stuck on 17. A malfunctioning car with a mind for blackjack.

"Remain calm," he reminded himself. "I'll push the emergency alarm."

Then he saw a conspicuous red knob that jutted out more prominently than all the other buttons. Adam reached and pulled. A pulsating ring shook the car and traveled down the shaft, triggering a flood of memories he had buried inside him. He covered his ears; a briefcase dropped to the floor.

"That should reach them," he said, running his hand through his hair, trying to relax.

It was late, well past midnight. Adam Posner had been working on a motion for court the next day. Out his window the lights of the Manhattan skyline glittered with a radiance that belied the stillness of the hour.

A lawyer's life, connected to a punchless carousel of a clock. He hated being among them—being *one* of them—with their upscale suits and shallow predicaments; those conveniently gymnastic ethical values, bending and mutating with the slightest change of financial weather. Gliding by colleagues in the corridors, walking zombies with glazed eyes and mumbling mouths. No time to exchange pleasantries. That deathly anxiety over deadlines—the exhaust of a tireless treadmill, legs moving fleetingly, furiously.

He played the game reluctantly, knowing what it was doing to his spirit, but also painfully aware of his own legacy, and its contribution to the choices he was destined to make. Above all else he wanted to feel safe, and whatever club offered him the privilege of membership, he was duty-bound to join.

And so another night on the late shift. He was working on behalf of a lucrative client, his ticket to a partnership at the firm. He was the last attorney or staff member to leave that night, something he always sought to avoid. Adam didn't like being alone in dark places, and he didn't like elevators—especially when riding alone.

Some of the lights in the interior hallway had been turned off, leaving a trail of soft shadows along the beige, spotless carpet. His Hermès tie, with the new fleur-de-lis pattern, was hanging from his neck in the shape of a noose, and the two top buttons of his shirt stayed clear of their respective eyelets. A warrior of late-night occupations.

There was a car waiting for him downstairs, one of those plush Lincolns that cater to New York's high-salaried slaves. When he entered the elevator, he could think of nothing but returning to his apartment building, commandeering yet another elevator, and rising to his honeycombed domain overlooking the Empire State Building. He lived alone in a voiceless, sanitized shrine—his very own space in the sky. Not even a pet greeted him, just the hum of an empty refrigerator filled with nothing but a half-empty carton of ice cream, a solitary microwave dinner, and a box of baking soda.

Sleep. How desperately he wanted to sleep. But now the night would take longer to end, and sleep was not yet possible.

"Behave rationally," he said, a lawyerly response to a strained situation. "They'll come and get me. At the very least, they'll need to get the elevator back," he reasoned.

Then with a nervous thumb, he stabbed away at the panel in all manner of chaotic selection. At that moment, any floor, any longitude, would do. Defeated by the inertia of the cab, he ran his hands against the board as though he were playing a harp, palms floating over waves of oval buttons and coded Braille, searching for some hidden escape hatch.

The dimensions of the car began to close in on him. The already tight space seemed to be growing smaller, a shrinking enclosure, miniaturizing with each breath.

Adam's parents had been in the camps, transported there by rail, cattle cars, in fact. That was a long time ago, another country, another time, another people. An old, trite subject—unfit for dinnertime discussion, not in front of the children, not the way to win friends among Gentiles. The Holocaust fades like a painting exposed to too much sun. A gradual diminishing of interest—once the rallying cry of the modern Diaspora; now like a freak accident of history, locked away in the attic, a hideous Anne Frank, trotted out only occasionally, as metaphorical mirror, reminding those of what was once done under the black eye of indifference.

Adam himself knew a little something about tight, confining spaces. It was unavoidable. The legacy that flowed through his veins. Parental reminiscences had become the genetic material that was to be passed on by survivors to their children. Some family histories are forever silent, transmitting no echoes of discord into the future. Others are like seashells, those curved volutes of the mind—the steady drone of memory always present. All one needs to do is press an ear to the right place. Adam had often heard the screams of his parents at night. Their own terrible visions from a haunted past became his. He had inherited their perceptions of space, and the knowledge of how much one needs to live, to hide, how to breathe where there is no air.

He carried on their ancient sufferings without protest—feeding on the milk of terror; forever acknowledging—with himself as living proof—the umbilical connection between the unmurdered and the long buried.

All his life he had suffered from bouts of claustrophobia, and also a profound fear of the dark. He refused to find his way into a movie theater when a film was already in progress; not even a sympathetic usher could rid him of this paralyzing impasse. At crowded parties he always kept to the door, stationed at the exit, where there was air, where he knew he could get out.

Condemned to living a sleepless nightmare, he began to pace like an animal. His breath grew stronger and more jagged. He tore his glasses from his face and threw them down on the elevator floor. An unbalanced goose step shattered the frames, scattering the pieces around him. Dangling in the air and trapped in a box, a braided copper cable held him hostage to all his arresting fears.

"Where are they? Isn't there someone at the security desk?" He undid yet another shirt button, slamming a fist against the wall. The car rattled with the sound of a screaming saw. He yanked against the strip of a guardrail. It refused to budge. With clenched fists he punched as many numbers of random floors as his stamina allowed, trying to get through to the other side without opening a door. Ramming his head against the panel, he merely encountered the steely panel of unsympathetic buttons. The tantrum finally ended with the thrust of an angry leg.

Adam's chest tightened. A surge of anxiety possessed him. His mind alternated between control and chaos, trying to mediate the sudden emptiness. His eyes lost focus, as though forced to experience a new way of seeing. He wanted to die, but would that be enough? What had once been a reliably sharp and precise lawyer's mind rapidly became undone, replaced by something from another world, from another time, the imprinting of his legacy. Time lost all sensation; each second now palpable and deafening.

"Hel . . . p! Help!"

The sweat poured down his face in sheaths of salt, and the deepening furrows in his forehead assumed a most peculiar epidermal geometry. In abject surrender, with his back against the wall of the car, he slid down to his ankles and covered his face with his hands. Nerves had overtaken his sanity. He was now totally at the mercy of those demons that would deprive him of any rational thought. And he had no one but himself to blame; the psychic pranks of his deepest monstrous self had been summoned, reducing him to a prisoner within the locked walls of the elevator.

Suddenly a voice could be heard, glib scratches filtering through a metallic strainer built right into the panel.

"Hello, hello, are you all right in der, son?"

The voice of God? Adam wondered. So silent at Auschwitz, but here, shockingly, in the elevator—delivered with a surprisingly lilting pitch. An incomprehensible choosing of divine intervention.

"It's the night guard from the lobby. Can ya hear me?"

Adam looked up to the ceiling. He squinted, trying to make out the shapes and sounds of rescue amidst an evolving fog of subconscious turmoil.

"Can ya hear me?" an urgent male voice persisted in reaching him. The voice carried the melody of an Irishman from an outer borough, but Adam, unaccountably, heard only a strident German.

"Yes, I am here," Adam replied, absently, weakly, almost inaudibly.

"Are ya all right?"

"No."

"We 'ave a situation 'ere," the security guard said calmly. "The motor to the elevator is jam'd. I can't repair it from 'ere; so I've called the maint'nance people. There's a fire in another buildin' downtown; and they're busy wit' dat. They said they'll be here as soon as humanly possible. Will you be okay, son?"

Adam lifted himself to his feet, pressed his mouth against the intercom—a static current startled his face—and then screamed: "What do you mean by 'okay'? How can I be okay? This is not life—being trapped in a box made for animals! Is there no dignity for man?" After another pause, he wailed, "You are barbarians! Get me out!"

The guard's lips pursed with all due bewilderment, and his tone sank. "You 'aven't been inside der long, mister. I know ya want to get out and go home for de night, but let's not make this a bigger ordeal than it already 'tis."

Adam then volunteered the nature of this "ordeal."

"Why should we be forced to resettle? This is our home. We are Germans! We have done nothing wrong! Nazis! Murderers! Nazis!"

The lobby of the building was barren, the only sound the quiet gurgle of water dripping down the side of a Henry Moore fountain. The stark marble walls were spare. The interior lights dimmed for the evening.

The security guard pondered Adam's reply, and then muttered to himself: "It takes all kinds. The elevator gets stuck, and he calls *me* a Nazi. Who told him to labor so long? Goddamn yuppie, asshole." Recovering, he picked up the receiver and said, "I'm sorry, sir. I don't get your meanin'. Say, ya got a German in der wit' ya?"

"We can't breathe in here! And the children, what will they eat? How can we dispose of our waste? We are not animals! We are not cattle! There are no windows in here, and the air is too thin for all of us to share. You have already taken our homes. What more do you want? Please give us some air to breathe."

By now the guard was joined by the driver of the limousine, who had been parked on Third Avenue waiting for Adam to arrive. The driver, a Russian émigré, had grown anxious and bored, staring out onto an endless stream of yellow cabs; honking fireflies passing into the night, heading uptown. By radio he called his dispatcher, trying to find out what had happened to his passenger, this Mr. Posner, this lawyer who needed the comforts of a plush sedan to travel thirty blocks back to his co-op. The dispatcher knew of no cancellation. Adam Posner was still expected downstairs to claim his ride. This was America after all, the driver mused. The elite take their time and leave others waiting.

So the driver left his car to stretch his legs. Electronically activated doors opened as he entered the building and shuffled over a burnished floor to a circular reception pedestal. The security guard was still struggling to communicate with Adam.

"I am looking for a Mr. Posner," the driver said, with Russian conviction. "I should pick him up outside, and to drive him to Twenty-Ninth Street, East Side. Do you know this man?"

With a phone cradled under his chin, and a disturbed expression on his face, the guard said, "All I know is we have an elevator down, and at least one man stuck inside. But who knows who—or what—else he's got in der with 'im. I tink he's actin' out parts in a play. To tell you the truth, he sounds a bit daft to me."

With the aplomb of a police hostage negotiator, the Russian said, "Let me talk to him. I'll find out who he is." The guard shrugged as the phone changed hands. The Russian removed his angular chauffeur's cap and wiped his brow. A determined expression seized his face as he lifted the cradle to his mouth, and said, "Excuse me. Is a Mr. Posner in there?"

"What will become of the women and children?" Adam replied. "Why should we be resettled in Poland?" He did not wait for a reply. A brief interlude of silence was then followed by a chorus of moans and shrieks, as if a ward in a veterans' hospital had become an orchestra of human misery, tuning up for a concert. "I don't believe they are work camps! We won't be happy. We will die there! I can feel it!"

The Russian was himself a Jew and winced with all too much recognition. "Is this Mr. Posner?" he continued. "This is your limo. Don't worry, we will get you out. We will rescue you."

Adam now heard this man from Brighton Beach with his Russian accent, the intoned voice of liberation. Who better to free him from his bondage than a Bolshevik from the east—in this case from Minsk or Lvov—the army that could still defeat the Germans. "Liberate us! We are starving! We are skeletons, walking bones, ghosts! Get us out of this hell!"

"What's 'e sayin'?" the security guard asked.

"I'm not exactly sure, but I think it has something to do with the Holocaust, my friend."

"Ah, de Holycost; a terrible thing, dat."

The Russian nodded—the recognition of evil, a common language between them. "I'll talk to him again," he said, and grabbed the intercom again. "Mr. Posner, don't worry. We will get you out. You are not in camps. You are not in cattle car. You are just inside elevator, in your office building. You are a lawyer; you've worked late. You are tired, and scared. You must calm down."

"Calm down, calm down, so easy for you Russians to say," Adam replied, abruptly. "We have been selected for extermination. We cannot survive. Who will believe what has happened to us? Who will be able to comprehend? Who will say kaddish for me?"

The lobby was crowding up. Two drowsy-looking repairmen, their sleep disturbed by the downtown fire and now this, entered the building and went up to the guard console. "What's the problem here?" one of them asked. "We're with the elevator company."

Fully exasperated, the guard indignantly replied, "Ya want to know what's wrong, do ya? Ya want to know what the *problem* is? I'll tell ya! It's supposed to be de graveyard shift. Piece o' cake, they say, nothin' ever happens, right? Not when I'm on duty. No, sir. When I'm 'ere, graveyard means all the ghosts come out, the mummies, the wackos! We 'ave a loony tune stuck in one o' the elevators!" Jauntily, winking at one of the maintenance men, he added, "I think de guy in de elevator thinks he's in some fuckin' World War Two movie."

"This man in elevator is not crazy," the Russian driver said in defense. "It is world that is crazy; he is only one of its victims. Who knows what made him like this?"

One of the repairmen dashed off to the control room. Moments later he returned, carrying a large mechanical device, an extraction that would bring the night to an end and allow everyone to go home. "I think I fixed the problem," he announced. "It was just a jammed crank."

As he was about to finish explaining the exploits behind the repair, the elevator began its appointment with gravity. The four men moved from the center of the lobby and gathered in front of the arriving elevator car.

"Should we ring an ambulance?" the security guard wondered. "I hope I don't lose me wages over this. I've done all anyone could. You know," he gestured toward the limousine driver, "you were here." The driver refused to take his eyes off the blinking lights, the overhead constellation that signaled the car's gradual descent.

The elevator glided to a safe stop. Like a performer on opening night, the car indulged in a brief hesitation—a momentary hiccup, of sorts—before the doors opened.

As the elevator doors separated like a curtain, the four men, in one tiny choreographed step, edged closer to the threshold, eager to glimpse the man inside. Suddenly there was a collective shudder, and then a retreat.

The unveiling of Adam Posner.

Light filtered into the car. The stench of amassed filth was evident. It had been a long journey. An unfathomable end.

Adam was sitting on the floor, dressed in soiled rags. Silvery flecks of stubble dappled his bearded face. Haltingly, he stared at those who greeted him. Were they liberators or tormentors? He did not yet know. His eyes slowly adjusted to the light, as though his confinement offered nothing but darkness. He presented the men of the transport with an empty stare, a vacancy of inner peace. As he lifted himself to his feet, he reached for a suitcase stuffed with a life's worth of possessions, held together by leather straps fastened like rope. Grabbing his hat and pressing it on his head, Adam emerged, each step the punctuation of an uncertain sentence. His eyes were wide open as he awaited the pronouncement: right or left, in which line was he required to stand?

FORCE FIELDS

Martin Jay

THE TRIP BY BUS northwest from Prague to Terezín—better known to the world by its German name, Theresienstadt—takes about an hour and traverses some of the prettiest countryside in Bohemia. Arriving late at the bus station, the little group with whom I traveled one morning in April of 1994 was forced to stand for the entire trip, a somehow fitting reminder that this was to be anything but a pleasure outing. When we descended at the bus stop next to the town square, the grim and blustery weather further deepened the sense of bleak uneasiness that would accompany any visit to such a place, even under the sunniest of skies. No less forbidding was the virtual emptiness of the square itself, once the passengers disgorged by the bus scattered their separate ways. Only a few children played in the park in its center, a park surrounded by nondescript buildings betraying nothing of their sinister past.

One, a former school and children's home, has been turned, we soon discovered, into a museum of sorts, which is in the process of mounting a permanent exhibition recording the events in Theresienstadt during its most troubled years. Now that the Communist rulers of Czechoslovakia have departed, that story can be told without the anti-Semitic inflection they had imposed on it (an inflection perhaps best expressed by the petty gesture of erasing the names of Holocaust victims painstakingly written on the walls of one of the synagogues in Prague's ghetto as a "protest" against Israeli politics in the mid-1980s). The story it tells is of a showcase concentration camp, planned by Reinhard Heydrich shortly before his assassination, a model ghetto given over from June, 1942, to May, 1945, almost entirely to Jewish detainees, who were supposedly allowed to continue their lives with only minor inconvenience. It was designed especially for those Jews whose prominence abroad might have meant that their disappearance would have been noticed; among the most eminent was Leo Baeck, the chief rabbi of Berlin. Others "lucky" enough to be assigned there were decorated or disabled Jewish veterans of the first world war, and those deemed too old or too young for labor service.

In late 1943, early 1944, a cynical "beautification" of the camp, whose name was changed to a "Jewish Settlement," was carried out with the intention of hoodwinking world opinion. Represented by Danish and Swiss delegates, the Red Cross, to its everlasting shame, was fooled into believing—or deliberately chose not to expose—the Nazis' sham, giving the camp its seal of approval in June, 1944, by which time transports of prisoners were already making their way east to considerably less hospitable conditions in Auschwitz-Birkenau. As part of the Nazi deception, some were forced to send postcards back to their relatives assuring them of their well-being. Of the 140,000 Jews who passed through Theresienstadt, only from 17,000 to 29,000—the estimates in the literature differ—remained alive when the Red Army liberated it in 1945.

The new museum has on its ground floor several rooms filled with the art produced by Theresienstadt's inmates, many of them young children, which was miraculously hidden before the camp was dismantled. Although I had seen examples in Berkeley where a travelling exhibition came a few years before, the cumulative effect of encountering them in the place where they were made was shattering. Daily life in a concentration camp seen through the innocent eyes of a child produces images that are unbearably poignant, especially those that try to preserve the individual faces of the people around them. Upstairs, the exhibition contained a mixture of documents from the camp, including programs for concerts, cabarets and theatrical performances, as well as photographs and other reproduced evidence of the melancholy history endured by Hitler's "protected Jews," the term cynically used in the propaganda film about Theresienstadt made by the Nazis to mask their actual intentions.

It is, of course, a cliché that stories of mass horror move us most when we can identify with one or a few of the victims on an individual basis. In my case, it is most often a young man at the stage of life when he is poised on the threshold of self-definition through the choice of a career and a mate. Somehow, I remember the promise and uncertainty of those years with a heightened sense of their significance and pathos and thus inevitably find their abrupt termination especially disturbing. Among the victims of Theresienstadt fitting this description was a playwright, poet and painter named Petr Kien, whose confident, open face is preserved in one of the individual photographs on display, a photograph that has the air of a graduation picture or publicity still. In an adjoining cabinet is a stunning puppet of a rabbi fashioned by Kien for one of his productions, a marionette in the great tradition of imaginative Czech puppetry. I have no idea of his theatrical talents or whether or not any of his work endures, but so skilled a puppet-maker surely deserved a better chance to realize his promise.

Leaving the museum, our small party walked the fifteen minutes out of the center of town it takes to get to the business end of Theresienstadt, the so-called "Small Fortress." First constructed in the late 18th century at the confluence of the rivers Eger and Elbe as part of the northern defense perimeter of the Habsburg empire—Theresienstadt was, in fact, named by Emperor Joseph II in honor of his mother, Maria Theresa—the complex of barracks and cells that make up the fortress was used during the Holocaust to punish Jews who were having trouble adjusting to the comforts of life in the center of town, as well as to house other victims of Nazi terror. Some 32,000 inmates in all spent part of World War II in the Small Fortress of Theresienstadt. Although most were ultimately deported to their deaths elsewhere, a gallows and a platform for public executions at the end of a large courtyard testify to the fate many suffered there as well.

Before actually passing through the gate of the Small Fortress, inscribed, as were other such gates in other such places, with the infamous words "Arbeit macht frei," we paused for lunch at the only place to eat within sight. The dreary café turned out to be the former canteen for the SS men who were charged with guarding the camp. With only a kind of a gallows humor to protect us against the profound sense of discomfort that accompanied this wretched meal, we soon began a serious discussion of our responses to the visit. Three of us were American Jewish men (the two others both psychoanalysts and experts in continental philosophy, myself a student of European intellectual history), who had been preoccupied by post-Holocaust questions for as long as we could remember. Like that of the "imaginary Jew" sensitively dissected by the French writer Alain Finkielkraut, our Jewish identity was in significant measure a product of identification with the victims rather than a positive embrace of the tenets of Judaism or adherence to the pre-assimilated culture of Yiddishkeit. With Finkielkraut, we could all easily have said, "I was born too close to the Holocaust to be able to keep it from view, and at the same time I was protected by all the horror of this event from a renewal of anti-Semitism, at least in its organized and violent form. In a sense I was *overjoyed:* the war's proximity at once magnified and preserved me; it invited me to identify with the victims while giving the all but certain assurance that I would never be one."[1]

Although there was not much joy, let alone "overjoy," evident on that day, it was nonetheless true that our relation to the Holocaust was clearly different from that of our companions, two women from Ireland, both professors of philosophy, and a man from Denmark, who taught political and social theory. For not only could we more viscerally identify with the victims, but we were also far more intimate with what might be called the many tropes of Holocaust response than they. That is, having been so long immersed in both learned and popular accounts, depictions and reenactments of the Holocaust, having been drawn professionally as well as personally to many of the survivors teaching in America, we had come to Theresienstadt with our expectations of what we were to see and how we were to respond—or at least the range of permissible responses—already firmly in place (in my own case, I had made earlier melancholy pilgrimages to Dachau and the Warsaw Ghetto, so that even being on an actual site of horror was not entirely unprecedented).

We were thus supremely aware of the mediated quality of our reactions in a way that our companions perhaps were not. For to be an American intellectual and particularly a Jewish one the past few years is to be especially alert to the ways in which modes of narration and memorialization give the Holocaust an inevitable inflection, even in cases far less heavy-handed than the Communist white-washing of the Prague synagogue walls. Recent books like James Young's *Writing and Rewriting the Holocaust: Narrative and the Consequences of Interpretation,* Saul Friedlander's collection *Probing the Limits of Representation: Nazism and the "Final Solution,"* Berel Lang's collection *Writing and the Holocaust* and Dominick La Capra's *Representing the Holocaust: History, Theory, Trauma* have made it increasingly difficult to ignore the constructive moment in our reconstruction of the events, no matter how dry and factual the account. The impassioned public response to the Holocaust Memorial Museum in Washington and the Simon Wiesenthal Center for Holocaust Studies and Museum of Tolerance in Los Angeles, the burgeoning field of "Holocaust Studies" in American universities, shadowed by the alarming upsurge of so-called Holocaust "revisionists" who question its very existence, heated polemics over the right-wing Zionist manipulation of the "lessons" of the Holocaust and the German historians' attempt to "normalize" the past, all these have combined to make second- or even third-order reflection on the meaning of it all impossible to avoid. What the German magazine *Der*

Spiegel in a particularly distasteful article of 1993 entitled "Das Shoah-Business" called America's "Holocaust intoxication"[2] has at least meant that no visit by people like me to an actual concentration camp can hope to escape its already scripted quality, its filtration through a myriad of prior reflections and feelings. Even the sound of those maudlin and lachrymose violins playing incessantly in a minor key throughout *Schindler's List* could not be kept from the mind's ear as we plodded through the silent streets of Theresienstadt.

Or rather everything conformed to a certain tropic prefiguration until one remarkable and completely unexpected moment in our trip. In one of the small cells used for holding prisoners in solitary confinement in the Small Fortress, we came upon a pair of iron manacles chained to the far wall, rusted but still formidable in their weighty horror. I don't recall if there was a small sign identifying them or if our guidebook gave us the information, but much to our astonishment they turned out to be the manacles not of a Holocaust victim, but rather of no less a historical figure than Gavrilo Princip, the man—or rather nineteen-year-old boy—whose assassination of the Archduke Franz Ferdinand and his wife Sophie in Sarajevo on June 28, 1914, precipitated the crisis that led to World War I.

As soon after the trip as I was able to get to a library, I tried to find out how he had come to this miserable destination. Princip had taken cyanide after he fired his shots, but somehow survived. Too young to be executed by the law of the Dual Monarchy, he and two other members of the so-called Black Hand, the conspiratorial group of Serbian nationalist fanatics who had plotted and almost bungled the assassination, were imprisoned instead in Theresienstadt, which had housed other celebrated political prisoners in the past, such as the Greek freedom fighter Alexander Ypsilanti, Jr. Already suffering from tuberculosis of the bones, Princip literally rotted away in his solitary confinement, his body covered with sores, his left arm ultimately amputated. He died in agony on April 28, 1918, only a few months before the war he helped unleash finally itself expired. He was buried anonymously by the Austrians, who wanted to avoid creating another Slav martyr by acknowledging his grave. But one of the soldiers in the burial party was an anti-Habsburg Czech who remembered the spot, allowing the Serbs to exhume and bury the body with honors in Sarajevo in 1920. What made the surprising discovery of the manacles of Gavrilo Princip so remarkable was their effect on my experience of Theresienstadt as a site of the Holocaust, or rather on the script that I was following in doing so. Initially, they seemed an annoying intrusion from another, totally different narrative, which somehow had gotten mixed up with the one I was so intensely following. It was as if suddenly in the pages of *Middlemarch,* someone had surreptitiously inserted a chapter, say, from *The Charterhouse of Parma.* What was a Serb nationalist martyr, whose desperate act had precipitated one world war, doing in a concentration camp created in another? Why, I wondered, was my identification with one young man whose premature death had so moved me a short time before suddenly being disrupted by the appearance of a second, and one to boot with whom I had no real ability to empathize? How could I reconcile my admiring reverie for the gifted hands of an innocent young puppeteer with the shock I felt in the "presence" of the manacled hands of an infamous assassin?

No less insistent were thoughts of the ironic undercutting of the heroism attributed to Princip by those who mourned him as a martyr, an undercutting produced not only by the horrible slaughter of the war he helped unleash, but also by events in the Balkans eighty years later. Serb nationalism, after all, has shown a face today far darker than its defenders before World War I would have thought possible. The people who reburied Princip with honors in 1920 seemed not so far removed, I couldn't help from thinking, from the people who were trying to bury Sarajevo and Gorazde in 1994. The imagined sound of Spielberg's violins began to fade as I held Princip's rusted manacles in my hands, and that of the guns bombarding those unhappy cities filled their place.

But perhaps of all the effects produced by the unexpected intrusion, the most profound had to do with the challenge it presented to the self-contained and incommensurable quality of the events that posterity has chosen to call the Holocaust or the Shoah. There has, of course, been a problematic attempt to diminish their importance by comparing the genocidal "war against the Jews," as Lucy Dawidovicz famously called it, with other such campaigns, such as the Soviet extermination of the Kulaks or the Nazis' decimation of the Poles. When such "relativization" of the Holocaust is done with the purpose of minimizing Jewish suffering or playing the treacherous game of victim one-up-manship, it is rightly decried.

But perhaps no less problematic is the utter isolation of the Holocaust from the larger historical context, its elevation into a metahistorical phenomenon so unlike anything before and since that its meaningful relation to any other events in history is severed. Its radical incommensurability can then become an excuse to attribute to it a no less absolute incomprehensibility, which, as my colleague Amos Funkenstein has warned, gives the Nazis the posthumous victory of robbing the victims of whatever narrative meanings their lives may have had.[3]

The rude intrusion of Princip's miserable story into that of Hitler's Potemkin Village is a reminder of the tangled web of violence and its ideological justifications that allowed the Holocaust to happen and that permits new atrocities today. For even though we are wisely told not to attribute great and overdetermined events to the acts of individuals—a warning made as far back as Pascal's famous gloss on the putative effects of Cleopatra's nose—it is nonetheless true that seemingly minor acts can have extraordinary consequences. The war triggered by Princip's fatal bullet was an indispensable precondition of the discontent that spawned a second global war and the opportunity for Theresienstadt to become a reality. The lessons in "ethnic cleansing" taught so well by the Nazis have not been forgotten by the descendents of those who applauded Princip's bold deed.

Only in Hollywood movies can the Holocaust be contained within the boundaries of an aesthetic frame; in real life, it spills out and mingles with the countless other narratives of our century. Its real horror, we might say, is not confined to the actual genocidal acts it has come to signify. Historicizing the Holocaust need not mean reducing it to the level of the "normal" massacres of the innocents that punctuate all of recorded history, but rather remembering those quickly forgotten and implicitly forgiven events with the same intransigent refusal to normalize that is the only justifiable response to the Holocaust itself.

No wonder that when I held the rusting manacles of Gavrilo Princip in my hands, the impulse that overwhelmed me was to shake them as furiously as I could, while impotently hurling at the ghost of the boy who once filled them the earthy epithet that the inmates of Theresienstadt would have understood all too well: "Schmuck!!!"

NOTES

1. Alain Finkielkraut, *The Imaginary Jew,* trans. Kevin O'Neill and David Suchoff (Lincoln: University of Nebraska Press, 1994), p. 12.

2. Henryk M. Broder, "Das Shoah-Business," *Der Spiegel,* 16 (1993), 249.

3. Amos Funkenstein, "The Incomprehensible Catastrophe: Memory and Narrative," in Ruthellen Josselson and Amia Leiblich (eds.), *The Narrative Study of Lives* (Thousand Oaks, Calif.: Sage, 1993). Funkenstein argues that the pictures of the Theresienstadt artists imply their ability to sustain a certain narrative control over their lives, which was denied to other Holocaust victims.

THE SANCTUARY

Alan Shapiro

Somewhere in a book about the camps,
caught in articulate sentences, among
precise descriptions of the causal chains
of small coincidences, the step by step
emergence of the will, the protocols,
the rational mechanisms, is a man
who every morning, till his final morning,
despite how weak he may have been, or sick,
even in winter, in the freezing air,
surrounded by all the other nameless ones,
would strip his clothes off, bend over a sink
that wasn't there and with imagined water
flowing from an imaginary tap
fastidiously scrub his face, his neck,
armpits and genitals.

Here in the room
in which I write these words, one moment it's
the nameless man I see, the next my father,
his palsied hand lifting the fork so shakily
that by the time it finally gets from plate
to mouth the food is mostly gone, and he

is mostly eating air for dinner, though
he keeps on eating till his plate is clean.
Inside the room in which I write this down,
somewhere inside a chapter of the book
I haven't taken from the shelf in years,
on that page, and on this one, his and my father's
bodies in the motion of a dream
of normalcy are held, preserved, protected
within a kind of sanctuary where,
bad as it surely is, it can't get worse.

Over and over, one chews his phantom food,
the other washes with imagined water.
Only subservient to the rules of grammar,
inside the rational structure of the lines,
in soundless sentences and scentless words,
one lifts the dish towel like a serviette,
dabs delicately at his mouth, his chin,
before he gets up shakily and all
the food falls from his lap onto the floor;
the other now meticulously puts
the foul rags on again, as if they were
a suit or uniform, and he were someone
on any normal day with work to do.

THE TRIVIALIZATION
OF TRAGEDY

Jonathan Rosen

THE ONLY HATE MAIL I have ever received has been from survivors of the Holocaust.

"You must be mentally sick and insane," a survivor of Dachau scribbled. "You should be thrown into one of those notorious gas ovens which the Nazis used so successfully."

Another man wrote: "I feel sure that God, in his infinite wisdom, will give you the harsh punishment you deserve."

What had I done to inspire such outrage? I had written an Op-Ed piece in the *New York Times* suggesting that it was a mistake to construct a Holocaust museum on federal land in Washington, D.C. My goal was not to deny Holocaust survivors a real reflection of their tragic experience, but to prevent Americans from seeing that reflection and mistaking it for their own. This had something to do with the museum itself and a great deal to do with contemporary American culture, which has a habit of trivializing tragedy and adapting it for personal use.

The museum, of course, was opened with great fanfare despite my Op-Ed piece. President Clinton stood on its front steps and denounced evil in all its forms. Eli Wiesel spoke and urged President Clinton, in the name of the six million Jewish dead, to bomb Bosnian Serbs. The opening of the museum coincided with a march for gay rights on Washington and many chose to end their rally with a visit to the museum. Writing in the *Times Literary Supplement,* James Bowman reported finding the following messages in the Hall of Remembrance, which invites people to leave notes in honor of the dead. "I am a lesbian. It could have been me. It could happen again, and if it does this time it could be me. Never again."* Another visitor recorded the observation that "AIDS is the holocaust of our era."

It is to take nothing away from the struggle for gay rights, or the horror of AIDS, to say that the Holocaust seems a hyperbolic emblem for the situation of homosexuals in America in the 1990s. But the museum planners were conscious of offering up a historical tragedy for convenient use by American culture. Two years before the museum was completed I spoke to Michael Berenbaum, the project director of the museum, for an article I was writing for the *Forward*. He told me that "the museum is based on the idea that you can take the bereaved memories of a parochial community and make them American life." It was the goal of the planners to graft a European-grown flower of evil onto the prickly body of multicultural America. "We're taking Jewish memories and speaking to the very heart and soul of the nation," Mr. Berenbaum boasted.

The claims of American relevance were no doubt necessary in the bargain the museum planners made for federal land—give us a place on the Mall and we'll give you an American experience. Obsessed with the details of the Nazi destruction—real hair from Auschwitz, a genuine cattle car—the curators' reassemblage of these disparate, though authentic, elements can't help but have an oddly spurious effect when reshaped by American mythic needs. The very placement of the museum in the civic heart of Washington, D.C., puts a symbolic burden on the catastrophe of European Jewry unsuited to the actual event.

Increasingly, Americans feel it is necessary to house history in buildings instead of books, which is unfortunate, since the more that history is embodied in buildings, the more historical events are turned into theatrical or symbolic moments stripped of the larger context that makes history valuable. As the written word itself is devalued, written records, however well researched and secure, are viewed as impermanent. In our new understanding, whoever trusts his history to a mere book is like the little pig content to have a house of straw. The first denier who huffs and puffs will blow the whole thing down. Museums are seen as the brick houses of history, and already battles are shaping up over the fight to create museums of slavery and of the American Indian experience in Washington.

Memory was not always so literally viewed. In her wonderful book *The Art of Memory*, Frances Yates tells a story that illustrates how memory rose out of literal bricks and mortar and into language, the opposite of our present trend. The story she tells is recounted by Cicero in "De Oratore," about the poet Simonides. A praise singer, Simonides was invited to a banquet by Scopas, a nobleman of Thessaly. In honor of the occasion, Simonides composes a lyric to praise his host, but he praises, as well, the gods Castor and Pollux. Scopas, insulted at having to share his honors, only pays half of what he promised to the poet. "Get the rest from Castor and Pollux," he tells Simonides. Midway through the feast, the shortchanged praise singer is told that two men wish to speak to him outside. Simonides gets up from his place at the table and goes outside, where he sees no one, but, before he can go back inside, the roof of the banquet hall caves in, crushing all the guests. The bodies, including the nobleman, Scopas, are so badly mangled they cannot be recognized by the relatives who come to claim them. Simonides, however, remembers where every guest had sat. In his mind, he recreates the order of the banquet and so is able to identify the bodies, which are borne off to the funeral pyre by their grieving kin.

Cicero goes on to say that Simonides became the inventor of the art of memory, pioneering the system, known as a "memory palace," used by the ancient Romans and later by medieval scholars for remembering speeches and manuscripts of tremendous length. In that system, a mansion full of rooms is imagined. In each room the orator deposits an idea. Then, during the speech, he revisits his imaginary palace, going from room to room in a set order and reclaiming the ideas he had planted there, thus delivering a speech, or recalling a manuscript of great length, without notes of any kind.

The home of memory, as Simonides and Cicero understood, is language. Simonides does not decide to rebuild the banquet hall so that passing Romans can sit inside and feel the fate of their fellows. The calamity did not befall them—or him, however close it came—and what separates Simonides from the victims is the story he can tell about it. The memory palace he goes on to devise lives in the imagination; its roof can never fall. The memory that grows inside the imaginary rooms, however, is real. Our own urge to bind history in mortar and brick seems driven by an opposite impulse. Our memory palaces, in this literal age, are real. The quality of our memory is another story.

More and more, museums are striving to re-create the mood of an original catastrophe and to provide an atmosphere that allows visitors to feel they are in the place represented. Some museums go so far as to make visitors feel that they are the people whose fate is on display. The Walt Disney Corporation recently had it in mind to build a historical theme park near the Civil War battlefield of Manassas in northern Virginia. Protesting in an August 1994 Op-Ed piece in the *New York Times,* William Styron quoted with disgust the words of Robert Weis, a proponent of the project: "We want to make you feel what it was like to be a slave, and what it was like to escape through the Underground Railroad."

Styron devoted several years to *The Confessions of Nat Turner,* a novel that, in his words, "was partly intended to make the reader feel what it was like to be a slave," and he was leery of Disney's ability to induce that feeling in the minds of distracted tourists out for a Sunday afternoon. Styron recalled his grandmother, who as a girl owned two slaves and, after their liberation by Union troops, mourned for them the rest of her life. Admitting that his grandmother's grief paled beside the suffering of slaves and those freed from slavery, he nevertheless wondered if a museum could ever capture the subtle intertwining of lives that slavery wrought over its 250 years on American soil.

"The falseness," Styron argued, "is in the assumption that by viewing the artifacts of cruelty and oppression, or whatever the imagineers cook up—the cabins, the chains, the auction block—one will have succumbed in a 'disturbing and agonizing' manner to the catharsis of a completed tragedy."

Partly because of protests like Styron's, Disney canceled its plans. But the spirit that inspired them seems here to stay. On Columbus Day, 1994, Colonial Williamsburg added a slave auction to the candle-dipping and bread-baking that usually go on. A pregnant woman was sold to a new master, separating her from her husband. A freed slave bought his wife. A carpenter and his tools were sold. Three thousand people, mostly white, attended. Many wept. Afterwards they clapped. Here, certainly, was the catharsis of a completed tragedy Styron had feared. For dramatic tragedy offers closure that historical tragedy never possesses.

Not that everyone was pleased. Jack Gravely, political action chairman of the Virginia chapter of the NAACP, said, before the auction, "We don't want the history of people who have come so far and done so much to be trivialized in a carnival atmosphere such as we have here." But later, Mr. Gravely, like Balaam in the Bible, changed his mind. He had come to curse. Afterwards, he praised. "I was wrong," he said. "Suffering had a face. Pain had a body."

But whose face? What body? "Living history" is the oxymoronic name some give this kind of interaction with the past. Certainly it stirs people up. Tourists, the same people Disney believed could feel "what it was like to be a slave," played their own weird part in the dramatization. Members of the audience called out to the actor portraying the slave owner, urging him not to separate a pregnant slave from her husband. The auction was scripted and the sale went through. But after all, to whom was the audience calling? The auction was based on a sale that took place circa 1773.

We would all love to shout down the evils of the past with modern voices of outrage, but we cannot. Tragic history is being treated increasingly like tragic theater, instilling fear, pity, and, ultimately, purgation. The strange ritual is becoming a kind of contemporary rite of atonement. This is not history but something else almost magical in its method and extremely ambiguous in its effect.

At the Holocaust Museum in Washington, each visitor to the museum is issued a kind of invitation to suffering. It is called an "identity" card and it carries the picture of someone who passed through the Holocaust. It might be a twelve-year-old gypsy boy from Romania or an eighteen-year-old Jewish girl from Vilna. You carry the card through the museum and on each floor punch it into a machine that "updates" your victim. The card is a ghostly guide through hell. By the end you learn what happened to your guide. Did he die in Auschwitz? Escape across the border? Allied to the fate of a single person, the theory goes, the museum visitor will care about the fate of a whole people.

The Holocaust Museum believes that identification with the victim is a good thing. To that end the museum itself, though in restrained fashion, echoes the claustrophobia of the ghetto, with narrow hallways channeling viewers uncomfortably together as they file past exhibits. The elevators, which move with excruciating slowness while an audiotape plays the voice of a survivor recalling his calamity, have been built to conjure associations with the interior of a cattle car or gas chamber. The walls are dark with riveted surfaces that suggest incarceration.

Identification and understanding are not the same. In fact, identification often comes at the expense of understanding. The Poles like to call themselves the Jews of Europe. That they should see their own fate in the fate of those they helped exterminate is one of those ironies so vast and subtle it almost defies explanation. It is also common. Jewish history is particularly fraught with such usurpations, and it makes the universalizing impulse behind the museum all the more disconcerting.

A perfect example of identification displacing understanding can be found in that handbook of intolerance, *The Autobiography of Malcolm X*. Malcolm X didn't like Jews, but he knew all about the Holocaust. Indeed, he used it as part of his attack on American culture. In his autobiography, he writes about the German Jews. Their tragedy, Malcolm tells his readers, is that they thought they were German. They believed they had achieved acceptance. "The Jew," Malcolm writes,

> had made greater contributions to Germany than Germans themselves had. Jews had won over half of Germany's Nobel Prizes. Every culture

in Germany was led by the Jew; he published the greatest newspaper. Jews were the greatest artists, the greatest poets, composers, stage directors. But those Jews made a fatal mistake—assimilating.

The Jews of Germany become the basis of his argument against integration. Whites hate blacks, he says, and the more blacks integrate, the more they'll be like the German Jews, disarming themselves against the final assault. Knowing about the Holocaust didn't diminish Malcolm's anti-Semitism, it merely refined his anti-Americanism. The Jews as Jews do not interest Malcolm X. He instead imagines himself into their place and views their fate as his fate. He makes a metaphor of their suffering divorced from the specificity of their time and place. He sees the Holocaust as a parable about America. He does exactly what Michael Berenbaum told me he hoped would happen. Malcolm took the bereaved memory of a parochial community and made it American life. It was because he was appropriating an experience that he hated most those to whom the experience actually belonged.

Unearned identification has become a pattern of our culture. Malcolm Little unmade himself into Malcolm X to eradicate the legacy of slavery. He has in turn been appropriated by hundreds of Americans collapsing the space between themselves and Malcolm X. At the end of Spike Lee's film *Malcolm X,* child after child stands up and proclaims, "I am Malcolm X." Whatever one thinks of Malcolm X, his experience, as hustler, criminal, preacher, was his own. He paid for his life with his life, and it is a cheap moment in the movie, and a sad cheapening of experience, when a chorus of Americans declare, "I am Malcolm X."

Something has changed in our understanding of what history is that makes us wish to conjure the past and have it perform for us. We seem to have lost respect for the sheer pastness of it, the elusiveness of anything gone. Perhaps television and movies have had a larger impact than we know on the way we perceive reality, for of course nothing in a movie or on television is ever lost. The central attractions of the Holocaust Museum are the video screens situated behind "privacy" walls (to prevent children from seeing over), giving them an almost pornographic appeal, where Nazi footage shows the dying endlessly dying.

At work, too, is a peculiar dimension of American spirituality best exemplified by Walt Whitman's haunting and egotistical declaration in "Song of Myself": "I am the man, I was there, I suffered." Harold Bloom examines this American Jesus in his essay on Whitman in *The Western Canon* and quotes a notebook fragment that makes Whitman's identification even more astonishing and telling:

In vain were nails driven through my hands.
I remember my crucifixion and bloody coronation
I remember the mockers and the buffeting insults
The sepulchre and the white linen have yielded me up
I am alive in New York and San Francisco,
Again I tread the streets after two thousand years.
Not all the traditions can put vitality in churches
They are not alive, they are cold mortar and brick,
I can easily build as good, and so can you:—
Books are not men—

For Bloom this is a good illustration of the American religion he examined more closely in his book of that name, which he sees as "post-Christian" but emerging from Christianity. "The American Jesus," he writes, "is no First-Century Palestinian Jew but a 19th and 20th Century American," who feeds off the notion of the resurrected Jesus walking the earth. Without question, the trends Bloom identified have intensified. Just look at the number of near-death experiences, in which people die and come back to earth and then testify to the experience in print. It is nothing less than the personalization of the experience of Jesus: "In vain were nails driven through my hands."

This has a great deal to do with the planning of museums devoted to victims. "Incarnational theology works," Michael Berenbaum told me in my interview with him about the Holocaust Museum, and that is what identity cards, "personalizing" the experience of suffering, facilitate. That is what the Walt Disney Corporation wanted when a spokesman said tourists would "feel what it was like . . . to escape through the Underground Railroad." That is what Spike Lee was enacting when he filmed child after child rising and declaring, "I am Malcolm X," which is another way of saying, "I am the man, I was there, I suffered."

Whitman's poetic conceit, focused on a distant religious moment, has become a way of relating to all tragic occurrences. It may be strange to say, but the Holocaust Museum and other museums like it are the churches of the American religion: "I can easily build as good, and so can you." Walk inside and experience the suffering. Become, for an afternoon, the Jew on the cross. But inhabiting history is the opposite of understanding history.

Steven Spielberg fell prey to this trivializing tendency when he created *Schindler's List,* which, like the Holocaust Museum, fits secular history into a religious framework—an American post-Christian religious framework. The film has been adopted as the representative Holocaust movie, complete with grainy newsreel footage from the war spliced in to give it the feel of a documentary, but the story is not a small representative piece of the past. It is virtually the opposite of the larger history of the Holocaust. It is about a Christian man, a Nazi, who rescues Jews from the jaws of death, even marching into Auschwitz where he literally puts Jews back on a cattle car leaving the death camp. The horrifying image of *Shoah*, Claude Lanzman's epic examination of the Nazi destruction of European Jewish life, in which train after train rolls to the gates of the death camp, is undone in a kind of Indiana Jones moment of pluck and daring. The nails run through but they do not kill. The movie becomes a story not of annihilation, which the Holocaust was, but of salvation, which the Holocaust was not. That a real Schindler once walked the earth does not make him the emblematic man the film enshrines.

At the end of the story, his Jews saved, Schindler himself dresses in the outfit of a prisoner in order to escape. Jews yank gold teeth out of their own mouths and give them to the man still wearing a swastika button, to help him make his getaway. Schindler the savior descends, in a final act of martyrdom, into the despised form of those he has rescued. He is Nazi and Jew, hero and victim. He is the American Jesus, God and man, Jew and Christian, and something more than all of these. The swastika he wears in his lapel comes to seem a kind of cross, a symbol not of death but of life.

Like Spike Lee's *Malcolm X, Schindler's List* presents a coda, filmed in Jerusalem at the grave of the real Schindler. The actors, no longer dressed for their parts, lead the actual survivors they portrayed in the film to Schindler's gravesite. The fictional and the literal join hands, and the actor who played Schindler himself comes and puts a stone on his own grave, standing triumphant like the risen Christ.

It is hard to keep straight at the end of *Schindler's List* who is the savior and who is the saved, who is the soldier and who is the sufferer, who is the Christian and who is the Jew, who is an actor and who is a man, what is fiction and what is real. Spielberg, perhaps unconsciously moved to repair the break between Jews and Christians that the Holocaust so horribly implies, has created a fantasy inspired by history but whose mythic impulse overpowers the historic grounding of the film. Clearly Spielberg's own identification is with Schindler, the only full-blooded character in the film, and he allows himself to have it both ways by dressing Schindler, at the end of the film, like a concentration-camp inmate.

Hollywood, that ultimate homogenizer of history and fantasy, creates a Holocaust perfect for American audiences. Obsessed, like the Holocaust Museum, with real details (the Auschwitz scenes were filmed at Auschwitz), it recasts those details into an American mythic mold. Not only does *Schindler's List* have a happy ending, it is an invitation to identify with a charming hero, handsome and strong, who, however corrupt he may initially seem, becomes a savior. It is a celebration of the American Jesus, and it is fitting that it ends not at a place where Jews died but at Schindler's Jerusalem grave, out of which the movie rises to offer its viewers a soothing vision of redemption.

The Holocaust Museum in Washington follows a similar pattern. The first view visitors have when they enter the museum is from the perspective of liberating American soldiers. The first thing you see is giant photographs of concentration camps taken by American troops. Only then do you get your identity card that allows you to pass from the savior to the sufferer. Entering an American hero, you then inhabit the lowly role of the victim. The visitor, experiencing both, becomes an American Jesus.

That is why the frame of the museum, for all the imported evil within, is American. It is not a museum of Jewish life and culture before the war, for only the death of Jews fits the needs of the American religion. The justification for all the horror contained in the Holocaust Museum, and for the slave drama at Colonial Williamsburg, and for all the other museums of victimization in the works, is that these are teaching tools that eloquently argue the importance of democracy. Were there not some added mythical appeal to museums of suffering, particularly of the Holocaust, were they not constructed as churches of the American religion offering their strange promise of redemption through suffering, it seems unlikely they would be built.

Without understanding the American Christian mythic framework, it would be difficult to understand why so many people are convinced that the Holocaust can be put to practical use. That it is an agent of democracy. That images of hell necessarily frighten people toward heaven.

The arguments put forward are that the Holocaust Museum in Washington is a giant vaccine, a kind of inoculation against the evil contained within. This is American hopefulness neutralizing the dark knowledge of Europe. This is a view of tragedy that doesn't believe the gun in Act I will go off in Act V because it is the nature of guns to go off, of men to kill each other, of people to die. This is a view of tragedy that believes that the gun in Act I doesn't have to go off if gun-control laws are passed in Act III. This is a view of tragedy that believes it leads to redemption, not the dread conclusions of the truly tragic nature, which would challenge the optimism by which America functions.

At the same time there is a powerful and perhaps equally American desire to see and touch the evil of Europe, especially as it relates to the Holocaust, which feeds into American fundamentalist longings for apocalypse, for final confrontations, for Judeo-Christian resolution. I sincerely doubt that people are flocking in record numbers to view images of the extermination of European Jewry because they want to strengthen their ideas of democracy. There is an almost panting intensity to the tourists who come, a piety tinged with prurient titillation that has little to do with history. Would they come, after all, to see a museum of Jewish culture? Of Jewish life before the war?

Tragedy is what draws the tourists. They come to feel that calamitous events are somehow informing their own lives, enriching them, making them better. But that is not the same as learning what happened to particular people, in a particular place and time, and facing the honest consequences of those events. By all means we should, we must, study the Holocaust. But why should we assume that there are positive lessons to be learned from it?

Allow me to make a sinister suggestion. What if some history doesn't have anything to teach us? What if studying radical evil doesn't make us better? What if, walking through the haunted halls of the Holocaust Museum, looking at evidence of the destruction of European Jewry, visitors do not emerge with a greater belief that all men are created equal but with a belief that man is by nature evil? What if an appropriate response to touring the Holocaust Museum is to buy a gun? What if the message of the museum, of the Holocaust itself, is that the Enlightenment was an idle dream, that civilization itself is a cruel hoax? That there is something about Christian culture that feeds on death? That the death drive in all of us is more powerful than the instinct for life?

What if Christians, seeing Jews suffering the fate of the damned—babies burnt, bodies stript, corpses piled high—are secretly confirmed in believing that Jews are meant to be the burnt offerings of the age. After all, images of the suffering Jew were prevalent through 1,000 years of European civilization. Those images did not prevent the Holocaust. They may, indeed, have prepared Europe for it by making Jewish suffering seem a kind of inevitability, perhaps even in keeping with divine wishes.

Planners of the Disney theme park and even of the well-intentioned Holocaust Museum are letting Americans have it both ways, letting them savor irrational ugly evil and feel, at the same time, they are better democrats for it. You can watch men and women on the auction block—a spectacle in slave days, too—and feel good about yourself by yelling at the slave owners.

In my Op-Ed article criticizing the idea of the Holocaust Museum, I recalled a conversation I had with Lucy Dawidowicz, the pioneering Holocaust historian who died in 1990. Did she think the Holocaust should be taught in schools? I'd asked her once. She wasn't opposed to it, she told me, but it wasn't a priority. "I'd feel a lot safer," she said, "if they learned the meaning of the Constitution instead." She did not mean that the history of the Holocaust should not be taught, studied, preserved. She only meant that American decency isn't based on deep knowledge of the irrational indecency of the world but on positive principles of equality. The letters I received from Holocaust survivors—"I am sure that God, in his infinite wisdom, will give you the harsh punishment you deserve"; "You should be thrown into one of those notorious gas ovens which the Nazis used so successfully"—were the understandable expressions of people who hadn't just read about or seen evil but who had experienced it. For real encounters with evil so batter and bruise the soul as to misshape it forever. Who else broods so on the punishment of God? Who else dreams vengefully of putting people into ovens? Those letters were smudged with the ash of suffered tragedy and it was bracing to receive them. Their authors wrote irrationally because that is what happens to people who pass through what the Holocaust Museum, which is only the shadow of a shadow, purports to represent. You do not necessarily emerge a democrat. You do not emerge singing that all men are brothers. More likely you emerge believing that Beethoven's Ninth died at Auschwitz along with the rest of German culture and who knows what else.

None of this is to say that teaching history is wrong or bad or, God forbid, that goodness comes from ignoring evil. It is only to say that the passion plays Americans have taken to putting on for one another in recent years do not necessarily end in redemption, and that the facile identification with victims does not lead to better behavior. Victims don't occupy a higher moral plane. They've just suffered more. Which is only liable to make them, like the survivors who wrote me hate mail, full of rage.

*Re-reading this essay, which was written in 1995, I realize I was wrong to criticize a gay woman for declaring, "it could have been me"—homosexuals were indeed targeted by the Nazis.

HEREDITARY VICTIMHOOD

THE HOLOCAUST'S LIFE AS A GHOST

Zygmunt Bauman

HALF A CENTURY HAS PASSED since the victory of the Allied troops put an abrupt end to Hitler's "final solution of the Jewish question"—but the memory of the Holocaust goes on polluting the world of the living, and the inventory of its insidious poisons seems anything but complete. We are all to some degree possessed by that memory, though the Jews among us, the prime targets of the Holocaust, are perhaps more than most. For Jews especially, living in a world contaminated with the possibility of a holocaust rebounds time and again in fear and horror. To many, the world appears suspect at the core; no worldly event is truly neutral—each event is burdened with sinister undertones, each contains an ominous message for the Jews. As E. M. Cioran, the incisive and bitter French philosopher, put it:

> To be afraid is to think of yourself continually, to be unable to imagine an objective course of events. The sensation of the terrible, the sensation that it is all happening *against* you, supposes a world conceived without *indifferent* dangers. The frightened man—victim of an exaggerated subjectivity—believes himself to be, much more than the rest of his kind, the target of hostile events. . . . [He has attained] the extremity of a self-infatuated consciousness; everything conspires against [him].

Self-defense calls the victim to learn the lesson of history, though in order to learn it, the victim needs to decide first what the lesson is. The precept of staying alive as the sole thing that counts, as the supreme value that dwarfs all other values, is among the most tempting, and the most common, interpretations of the lesson. As the direct experience of the victims recedes and fades, the memory of the Holocaust tapers and congeals into a precept of survival: life is about surviving, to succeed in life is to outlive the others. . . . Whoever survives—wins.

This reading of the Holocaust's lesson has been recently displayed—to worldwide acclaim and huge box-office success—in Spielberg's now well-nigh canonical image of the Holocaust. According to the *Schindler's List* version of the Holocaust experience, the sole goal of that most inhuman among human tragedies was to remain alive—while the humanity of life, and particularly its *dignity and ethical value,* was at best of secondary importance and was never allowed to interfere with the principal goal. The goal of staying alive took care of moral concerns. What counted in the last resort was to outlive the others—even if the escape from death required being put on a separate, unique, and exclusive list of the privileged. When offered by the commandant of Birkenau a replacement for "his Jewesses," Schindler refuses; it was not the saving of lives that counted, but the saving of specific, chosen lives. By definition, survival is selective; it is coveted *because of its* selectiveness.

In Spielberg's film, the value of staying alive is not diminished, but made more salient yet by the fact that others, less fortunate, traveled to the extermination camp; viewers of *Schindler's List* are invited to rejoice in the sight of Schindler's master of works pulled out in the nick of time—he alone—from the train destined for Treblinka. Through a willful travestying of the Talmud's precepts, Spielberg's film translates the issue of humanity's salvation into the decision of who is to live and who is to die. As the late Gillian Rose, a sublime philosopher and Judaic scholar, pointed out in her last public lecture, "The Talmud is ironic—the most ironic holy commentary in world literature: for no human being can save the world." Rose spoke of the "ruthlessness of saving one or one thousand" and comments that while Keneally's original book, *Schindler's Arc,* "makes clear the pitiless immorality of this in the context," Spielberg's film *Schindler's List* "depends on it as congratulation."

That elevation of survival to the rank of the supreme, perhaps the only value, is not Spielberg's invention and not at all a phenomenon confined to artistic representations of the Holocaust's experience.

Soon after the end of the war psychiatrists coined the term "survivor's guilt"—a complex psychical ailment which they ascribed to the habitual way survivors ask themselves why they stayed alive when so many of their near and dear perished. According to these psychiatrists, the joy of escaping death was permanently poisoned for the survivors by their acute moral uncertainty about the propriety of sailing safely out of the sea of perdition; that uncertainty, in turn, had disastrous consequences for the survivors' will to live and to succeed in life after their rescue. Many practicing psychiatrists acquired fame and fortune treating so-construed "survivor's syndrome." Whether the syndrome was rightly spotted and the psychiatric treatment well aimed was and remains a moot question; what is rather obvious, though, is that in the course of time the "guilt" aspect, looming prominently in the beginning, has been progressively exorcised from the model of the "survival complex," leaving the pure and unalloyed, unambiguous and uncontested approval of self-preservation for the sake of self-preservation.

Such a shift brings us dangerously close to the spine-chilling image of the survivor as painted by Elias Canetti—as the man for whom "the most elementary and obvious form of success is to remain alive." For Canetti's survivor, survival—unlike mere self-preservation—is framed in relation to the other, not the self: "They want to survive their contemporaries. They know that many die early and they want a different fate for themselves." At the far end of the survivalist obsession, Canetti's survivor "wants to kill so that he can survive others; he wants to stay alive so as not to have others surviving him." For Canetti, "The survivor's most fantastic triumphs have taken place in our own time, among people who set a great store about the idea of humanity. . . . The survivor is mankind's worst evil, its curse and perhaps its doom."

The wider repercussions of that cult of survival contain dangers of potentially formidable proportions. Time and again the lessons of the Holocaust are reduced for popular consumption to a simple formula: "who strikes first, survives"; or to an even simpler one: "the stronger lives." The awesome two-pronged legacy of the Holocaust is the tendency, on the one hand, to treat survival as the sole, or at any rate the topmost value and purpose of life, and, on the other hand, to posit the issue of survival as that of a competition for a scarce resource, and survival itself as a site of conflict between incompatible interests in which the success of some depends on the non-survival of others.

Sinister, pernicious, and morally destructive as it is in its own right, this is not the only avatar of the Holocaust's ghost and not its only misdeed. Another is the phenomenon dubbed by Alain Finkielkraut *le juif imaginaire*— a Jew manifesting his Jewishness, so to speak, by living on the account and at the expense of a "categorical martyrdom," basking in the fame of his ancestral martyrs without paying the price of the glory. Such "imaginary Jews," in Finkielkraut's caustic description, are the "habitués of unreality," who "have taken up residence in fiction . . . live in borrowed identities . . . have chosen to pass their time in a novelistic space full of sound and fury"— and have become, as a result, "armchair Jews, since, after the Catastrophe, Judaism cannot offer them any content but suffering, and they themselves do not suffer." For this generation, Alain Finkielkraut, the prolific and re- fined French writer born in 1949 and one of that generation's most illustri- ous and famous members, is full of contempt: they are, he says, "cowards in life, martyred in dream"—"they mask their inborn softness with the out- cast's courage."

There is admittedly a specifically French flavor to Finkielkraut's analy- sis. When he writes of this group's "desperate striving . . . to plug into the great revolt of the day," his words may sound outlandish and exotic to the members of that generation scattered in other, particularly English- speaking, parts of the Jewish diaspora. And yet—the acid remarks about the "pastiche" that "was the governing principle of deeds," about the "fran- tic masquerade [that] sought to appease bad conscience," about "exorcis- ing the vapidity of lives . . . through acts of fictive intensity," and altogether looking "at current events the way Emma Bovary read popular fiction: en- raptured by escapism"—may find an echo in many memories and cause the beating of many breasts. Living on a borrowed identity—as martyrs by appointment, *martyrs who never suffered*—"we could only bear to face ourselves unrecognizably disguised"; this spiritual predicament was the fate which the whole generation shared, even if the disguises were locally diversified dresses.

Anne Karpf has recently reported, in a penetrating and sharply ironic survey of the thriving "Holocaust syndrome" literature, her own feelings of relief and spiritual comfort when first hearing of the inherited trauma of the survivors' children. Finding out that she "belonged to a group which might warrant being helped, rather than being purely privileged and morally obliged to help others," she "was relieved and even elated that [her] years of problems weren't necessarily the result of personal pathol- ogy but might have a shared and external source."

Karpf put her finger on an open wound, gaping in many a soul. In this heretic, chameleon-like, deregulated, and unpredictable world of priva- tized loners, one has a lot of problems finding and guarding one's place in life; one is indeed greatly relieved if at least the blame for one's trou- bles can be shifted onto something other than one's own shoulders.

Seventy years ago Sigmund Freud, in his seminal study *Civilization and Its Discontents,* suggested that "civilization" is a trade-off: one cherished value is sacrificed for another, equally close to the heart. He proposed that in the civilized society of his time a lot of personal freedom of expression had been sacrificed in exchange for a good deal of collectively guaranteed security. In my *Postmodernity and Its Discontents* (Polity Press, 1997), I have suggested that were Freud writing his book seventy years later, he would probably need to reverse his diagnosis: our present-day troubles and discontents are, like their predecessors, products of a trade-off, but this time it is security which is daily sacrificed on the altar of an ever-expanding individual freedom. On the way to whatever passes for greater individual liberty of choice and self-expression, we have lost a good deal of that security which modern civilization supplied, and even more of the security it promised to supply. Worse still, we have stopped hearing promises that this supply of security will be resumed, and instead hear more and more often that security is contrary to human dignity, much too treacherous to be sought and much too dependency-breeding, addictive, and altogether quagmire-ish to be desired.

And so there are good enough reasons to be nervous, anxious, and angry. It is not clear, though, where the ambient fear derives, what one is truly afraid of, where the danger lies, and what one can do to mitigate it. Anxiety seeks a peg and while searching for it may easily hang itself on a wrong one, prompting actions glaringly irrelevant to the genuine cause of trouble. When genuine reasons for agitation are difficult to locate and even less easy to control if discovered, we are powerfully tempted to construe and name putative, yet credible, culprits against whom we can wage a sensible defensive (or better still, offensive) action. We may bark up a wrong tree, but at least we are barking and cannot deprecate ourselves or be reproached by others for taking the blows against us hands down.

Throughout the United States, "self-help" groups were formed by the "children of the Holocaust"; these self-invigorating group discussions added an extra dimension of collectively sustained interpretation (and thus the authority of numbers) to the zealous search for a collective Holocaust trauma, which would put the missing sense back into these individuals' present personal troubles. This search was also given the authority of the psychiatric profession; all over the country, psychoanalysts told their patients in no uncertain terms that the roots of their "maladjustments" were buried in the Holocaust. Some therapeutic experts, like Harvey and Carol Barocas (quoted by Karpf and prestigious enough to contribute to the *International Review of Psychoanalysis*), went so far as to suggest that "the children of survivors show symptoms that would be expected if they actually lived through the Holocaust." And so the ghost has been issued an official permission of domicile, recognized as the lawful plenipotentiary of the "real thing," and so (in tune with the spirit of our time) the troublesome and worrying distinction between the "real" and "virtual" reality has been declared null and void.

For those involved, the message hammered home by the psychiatrists, and sunk ever deeper in the course of the self-help sessions, could not but be richly rewarding. In Anne Karpf's words, "There's undoubtedly something satisfying in joining the ranks of unequivocally wronged, those with an irrefutably legitimate claim on our sympathy." To acquire the right to sympathy and benevolence before one earns it through personal exertions is an opportunity few people would willingly forfeit. The side effect of all this is, however, a sort of "competition for victimhood," a "pecking order of pain" reminiscent—we may recall—of the rivalry among the tuberculous residents of Thomas Mann's *The Magic Mountain* who quickly established their own eerie hierarchy of prestige and influence measured by the size of their pulmonary caverns.

There is something else, though, to the status of a "victim by proxy"— one of belonging to a *sui generis* "aristocracy of victimhood" (that is, having a *hereditary* claim to sympathy and to the ethical indulgence owed to those who suffer). That status can be, and often is, brandished as a signed-in-advance and *in blanco* certificate of moral righteousness; whatever the offspring of the victims do must be morally proper (or at least *ethically correct*) as long as it can be shown that it was done in order to stave off the repetition of the lot visited on their ancestors; or as long as it can be shown to be psychologically understandable, nay "normal," in view of the supersusceptibility of the hereditary bearers of victimhood to the threat of a new victimization.

The ancestors are pitied, but also blamed for letting themselves be led, like sheep, to slaughter; how one can blame their descendants for sniffing out a future slaughterhouse in every suspicious-looking street or building and—more importantly still—for taking preventive measures to disempower the potential slaughterers? Those who are to be disempowered may not be kith and kin of the perpetrators of the Holocaust, neither bodily nor spiritually nor in any juridical or ethically sensible way charged with responsibility for their ancestors' perdition; it is, after all, the heredity of the "hereditary victims," and *not* the continuity of their assumed victimizers, which makes the "connection." And yet in a world haunted by the ghost of the Holocaust, such assumed would-be persecutors are guilty in advance, guilty of *being seen* as inclined or able to engage in another genocide. They need commit no crime; standing accused or just *being suspect*, true to the message of Kafka's *The Trial*, is already their crime, the only crime needed to cast them as criminals and to justify harsh preventive/

punitive measures. The ethics of hereditary victimhood reverses the logic of the Law; the accused remain criminals until they have proven their innocence—and since it is their prosecutors who conduct the hearings and decide the validity of the argument, they have slim chance of their arguments being accepted in court and every chance of staying guilty for a long time to come—whatever they do.

Thus the status of hereditary victim may take the moral reprobation off such new victimization—this time perpetrated in the name of erasing the hereditary stigma. We often say that violence breeds more violence; we remind ourselves much too rarely, though, that victimization breeds more victimization. Victims are not guaranteed to be morally superior to their victimizers, and seldom emerge from the victimization morally ennobled. Martyrdom—whether lived in a real or a virtual reality—is not a warrant for saintliness.

Memory of suffering does not assure life-long dedication to the fight against inhumanity, cruelty, and the infliction of pain as such, wherever they happen and whoever are the sufferers. At least an equally probable outcome of martyrdom is the tendency to draw an opposite lesson: that humankind is divided into the victims and the victimizers, and so if you are (or expect to be) a victim, your task is to reverse the tables ("the stronger lives"). It is this lesson that the specter of the Holocaust whispers into many ears. And for this reason we cannot be sure whether the lasting legacy of the Holocaust was not the very opposite of what many had hoped and some anticipated: the moral reawakening or ethical purification of the world as a whole or any of its sections.

The pernicious legacy of the Holocaust is that today's persecutors may inflict new pains and create new generations of victims eagerly awaiting their chance to do the same, while acting under the conviction that they avenge yesterday's pain and ward off the pains of tomorrow—while being convinced, in other words, that ethics is on their side. This is perhaps the most awesome among the Holocaust's curses and the greatest of Hitler's posthumous victories. The crowds which applauded Goldstein's massacre of the Muslim worshippers in Hebron, which flocked to his funeral and go on writing his name on their political and religious banners, are the most terminally afflicted, but not the only bearers of that curse.

The phenomenon of hereditary victimhood ought not to be confused with genetic kinship, or with family tradition preserved through parental influence over the educational setting. Heredity in this case is mainly imagined, acting through the collective production of memory and through individual acts of self-enlisting and self-identification. Thus the status of the "Holocaust children," that is of hereditary victim, is open to every Jew, whatever his or her parents might have been "doing in the war" (in fact, embracing this status has turned for many into their main vehicle of Jewish self-definition). Psychiatrists conducted ample studies of the biological descendants (and/or educational objects) of the inmates of concentration camps and the dwellers of ghettos; but the swelling numbers of the "sons and daughters of the Holocaust" who *are not children of either* still await a comprehensive study. There are many clues, though, of what such a study may reveal. It may well transpire that the complexes of such "imagined children" (and for the same reason "children *manqués*"—flawed, if not fraudulent, children) are more severe and vicious, and burdened with more sinister consequences, than those which the psychiatrists have described thus far.

One may say: this stands to reason (whatever "reason" may mean in the world of the possessed). For the "children *manqués*," the site which they occupy in the world, from which they view the world and in which they want to be viewed by the world, is that of martyrdom; but it so happens that they are not, nor have been, personally, the butt of anybody's wrath and wrongdoing. They do not suffer, or they suffer not enough for the victims-by-birth that they are. The world seems reluctant to harm them and make them suffer, and under the circumstances such a world is too good to be acceptable—since the reality of a harmless world means the irreality of a life which derives its sense from the harm done to it and the harm yet to be done.

Living in a not-hostile and harmless world means the betrayal of that sense-giving parentage. To reach completeness, to fulfill their destiny, to get rid of their present deficiency and to efface their vexing (and in the end humiliating) impairment, to turn from children *manqués* into children pure and simple, they would need to re-forge their own imagined continuity of victimhood into the world's real continuity of victimization. That can be done only by acting *as if* their present site in the world was really and truly a site of the victims; through abiding by a strategy which may gain rationality only in a victimizing world. Children *manqués* cannot be fulfilled unless the world they live in reveals its hostility, conspires against them—and, indeed, contains the possibility of another holocaust.

The awesome truth is that, contrary to what they say and think they wish, children *manqués*—the "flawed children"—are unfit to live, and feel out of place in a world free of that possibility. They would feel more comfortable living in a world more like that other world, populated by the Jew-hating murderers who would not stop short of including them among its victims if given a chance and not having their blood-soaked hands tied. They draw a sense-giving reassurance from every sign of hostility toward them; and they are eager to interpret every move of those around them as overt or latent expression of such hostility. In their lives the ghost of the Holocaust may feel safe; in their deeds it has found a magic counter-spell against other people's exorcisms.

The flawed children of the martyrs do not live in homes; they live in fortresses. And to make their homes into fortresses, they need them besieged and under fire. Where else can one come closer to their dreams than among the famished and destitute, despaired and desperate, cursing and stone-throwing Palestinians. . . . Here, the comfortable and commodious, all-mod-con houses are unlike the houses the children *manqués* have abandoned—those comfortable and commodious, all-mod-houses over there in the stale and dull, too-safe-for-comfort American suburbs, where children would be bound to stay as they are, *manqués*. Here, in Israel, one can tightly wrap the houses with barbed wire, one can build watchtowers in every corner and one can walk from one house to another proudly caressing the gun hanging from one's shoulder. The hostile, Jew-baiting world once forced Jews into ghettos. By making a home in the likeness of the ghetto one can make the world once more hostile and Jew-baiting. In that fully and truly flawed world, the children, at long last, would be no more flawed. The chance of martyrdom missed by the generation would have been repossessed by its chosen representatives, who want to be seen as its spokesmen as well.

Whichever way you look at it, the ghost of the Holocaust appears self-perpetuating and self-reproducing. It made itself indispensable to too many to be easily exorcised. Haunted houses have an added value, and being possessed has turned for many into a valued, meaning-bestowing life formula. In this effect one can spy out the greatest posthumous triumph of the *Endlösung* designers. What the latter failed to accomplish when alive they may yet hope to achieve in death. They did not manage to turn the world against the Jews, but in their graves they can still dream of turning the Jews against the world, and thus—one way or another—to make the Jewish reconciliation with the world, their peaceful cohabitation with the world, all that more difficult, if not downright impossible. The prophecies of the Holocaust are not quite self-fulfilling, but they do fulfill—render plausible—the prospect of a world in which the Holocaust may never stop being prophesied, with all the deleterious and disastrous psychical, cultural and political consequences which such prophesying is bound to bring forth and propagate.

Can one exorcise the ghost of the Holocaust? A big question and a daunting task, no doubt. *And a different one from making the world Holocaust-proof,* although the state of being possessed makes that other task yet more daunting. It is not easy to write out a foolproof recipe for exorcism, and even if a medicine were available, there would be no guarantee that the patient would swallow the prescribed pills.

Being possessed means seeing the world as one-dimensional while being blinkered to all other dimensions, not to mention their interplay. The sole dimension which the ghost of the Holocaust renders visible to the eyes of the possessed (while effacing or removing from sight all other dimensions) is that measured by the degree of Jew-resentment. The world, though, is multi-dimensional.

Jean-Paul Sartre proposed that the Jew is a person whom others define as a Jew. What Sartre must have meant was that the act of such defining is also the act of *reductive selectiveness;* one of the manifold traits of an irretrievably multifaceted person is thereby given prominence, rendering all other traits secondary, derivative, or irrelevant. In the practice of the possessed, the Sartrean procedure is conducted once more, though in the opposite direction. To the possessed, the others, the non-Jews, emerge as one-dimensional as the Jews appear in the vision of their haters. For the possessed, the others are not benign or cruel *patri familiae,* caring or selfish husbands, benevolent or malicious bosses, good or bad citizens, peaceful or pugnacious neighbors, oppressors or oppressed, pained or pain-inflicting, privileged or dispossessed, threatening or threatened; more precisely, they may be any or all of that, but the fact that they are all that and more is but of secondary and minor importance and does not count for much. What truly counts—perhaps the only thing that counts—is their attitude toward the Jews (and let us recall that the possessed take every stance directed toward a person who happens to *also* be a Jew as manifestation and derivative of the attitude taken toward *the Jews as such*).

That is why it is so tremendously important to accept and remember that many declared anti-Semites stoutly refused to cooperate with the perpetrators of the Holocaust, while the ranks of the executors were full of law-abiding citizens and disciplined functionaries who happened to be free of any peculiar grudge against the Jews. To accept and remember that extermination of the Jews was conceived in the framework of a total "cleansing of the world" operation (which included also the mentally deficient, physically handicapped, ideologically deviant, and sexually unorthodox) by a state powerful enough and sufficiently immune to all opposition to afford such total plans and to execute them without fear of effective dissent.

That some of the participants of mass murder did enjoy their part in crime either because of their sadistic inclinations or because of their hatred of the Jews or for both reasons simultaneously is not, of course, Daniel Goldhagen's fantasy (though it is not his discovery either). Taking that fact, however, as the explanation of the Holocaust, as its central point or deepest meaning, says a lot about the ghosts haunting the house, while turning our attention away from what is the most sinister truth of that genocide and what is still the most salutary lesson which our haunted world could learn from the recent history which contains the Holocaust as its major event.

The point is that for every villain of Goldhagen's book, for every German who killed his victims with pleasure and enthusiasm, there were dozens and hundreds of Germans and non-Germans who contributed to the mass murder no less effectively without feeling anything about their victims and about the nature of the actions involved.

And the point is that while we know quite well that prejudice threatens humanity, and we know even how to fight and constrain the ill intentions of people poisoned with prejudice, we know little how to stave off the threat of a murder which masquerades as the routine and unemotional function of an orderly society. As Enzo Traverso put it recently in reference to France, the causes of the Holocaust in general, and that "wall of indifference" which surrounded the mass slaughter of the French Jews, need to be sought not in the "Jewish question," as Jean-Paul Sartre saw fit, nor even in the circumstances of the genocide itself, but in the French pre-Vichy society. A genocide of unwanted strangers cannot take place in just any society, and the presence of a quantity of Jew-haters is not the only, not even the necessary, condition which needs to be met to make that genocide a possibility.

Hannah Arendt pointed out a long time ago that the phenomenon of Holocaust anti-Semitism may explain at most the choice of the victims, but not the nature of the crime. Nothing happened since then to invalidate Arendt's verdict, while the monumental memoirs of Primo Levi, the monumental historical research of Raoul Hilberg, and the monumental documentary of Claude Lanzman, to mention but a few landmarks, did a lot to confirm and reinforce it.

This is not to say that the world we live in differs from the world of the Holocaust to an extent which makes it holocaust-proof and that holocaust fears are therefore illusory. But it does mean that the threat of such holocausts as may yet come is all too often sniffed out today and searched in the wrong places and our sight is diverted from the grounds in which genuine threats are rooted. These are the grave risks of living in a haunted house.

THE MEANING
OF THE HOLOCAUST

SOCIAL ALIENATION AND THE INFLICTION

OF HUMAN SUFFERING

Peter Gabel

CAN THE POLITICS OF MEANING help us to understand the Holocaust? The recent articles in *Tikkun* by Daniel Goldhagen and Zygmunt Bauman demonstrate such a need because both of these articles make assertions about the meaning of the Holocaust that the authors themselves cannot account for. Goldhagen's now famous claim that the German people as a whole were willing executioners wants to locate the meaning of the Holocaust in a relentless, culturally pervasive anti-Semitism. He argues that this anti-Semitism was literally a historical constituent of German consciousness that through cultural conditioning long preceding Nazism came to, in part, define Germanness itself. But even if this were true (and I do not believe that it is), it would only lead us to the question of what this type of nationalism built on dehumanization *means* for those who are taken over by it. Unless we are to assume that newborn children are blank slates upon which any conditioning can simply be imprinted in a way that then "fills up" their consciousness, we are pushed to ask deeper questions about the meaning of that conditioning process itself, about whether it is an expression of some distortion, denial, repression, humiliation that would inherently transcend the formation of German identity as such and point toward a more universal problem.

Bauman's thought-provoking counter-position is that analyses like Gold-hagen's are actually expressions of a "hereditary victimhood" on the part of post-Holocaust Jews—that these Jews want to find meaning in a mar-tyrdom borrowed from a holocaust that they did not themselves experi-ence, leading them to elevate "survival" above all ethical values and to color the world as being comprised of one-dimensional persecutors capable of providing them with the victim-centered meaning that they seek. He shows how Goldhagen's version of the Holocaust as primarily the story of the voluntary actions of Hitler's Jew-hating helpers involves a distortion of the evidence Goldhagen uses to support his own position and a blindness to the very substantial evidence that contradicts it. According to Bauman, Goldhagen distorts his evidence in this way because he, and people like him, are reassured by the sense of meaning gained from their hereditary victimhood and so cannot be fulfilled unless the world continually reveals open hostility, violent conspiracies, and the ever-present possibility of an-other holocaust. Yet in reading Bauman's piece too we are simply pushed to the deeper question of what this paranoid sense of meaning itself means.

If this Jewish survivalism is counter-rational and even potentially dan-gerous to Jewish survival itself (since it is arguably an aspect of Jewish con-sciousness in Israel that makes another war in the Middle East more likely), then the sense of meaning provided by this preoccupation with survival and victimhood must itself be accounted for by some deeper meaning, some immanent distortion and self-deception, that would make it "worth it" for these post-Holocaust Jews to pursue such a contradictory and po-tentially self-destructive course of conduct. Understanding that deeper meaning requires going beyond the particular form of Jewish identity char-acteristic of post-Holocaust Jews toward revealing that universal under-lying meaning of which it is but a particular manifestation.

The politics of meaning aims exactly at understandings of this type. We seek to illuminate distortions of the longing for meaning as manifesta-tions of that very longing, as pathological particular incarnations of a fundamental universal need. That need for meaning itself emerges from a desire that is at the heart of our very social existence—the desire for a mu-tual recognition through which we become fully present to each other as social beings in connection, fully confirmed in the relation Martin Buber called "I and Thou." In the unalienated social existence to which we aspire, meaningfulness is the realization, through a potentially infinite number of particular cultural embodiments, of the I and Thou of mutual recognition. That is why movements for social justice are inherently meaningful—as they "rise up," these movements generate the very experience of becoming-present-to-each-other through a confirming recognition that grounds the call for the correction of injustice, which is always manifested as a denial of this I-Thou relation, in a particular social-historical context. At the same time, it is the emergent awareness of injustice as a denial of the I-Thou relation that exerts an ethical pull on the wider culture and in turn pulls the movement, as realization of the desire for mutual recognition, into existence.

The great problem that we face, and here we begin to reach the question of the meaning of the Holocaust, is that the aspiration toward the affirmation of mutual recognition that exists within all of us remains subordinated to the legacy of alienation that makes the other appear to us as a threat. Rather than ascribe the source of this problem to, say, the distrust fostered by the competitive capitalist market, I think it is more accurate to understand this problem as located in the spiritual evolution of being itself, and in the as yet incomplete struggle of being to know itself as Love that realizes itself through the affirmation of the other, through the I-Thou relation. The achievement of this relation in its full social manifestation—that is, in a manifestation that is able to attain a confidence that can surpass the doubt of alienation and become the foundation of a fully human social history—requires a movement of social development that is at once spiritual, political, and material. We may well be in an ecological race against time to succeed in building such a movement.

But insofar as we have not yet achieved it, the other remains to us a threat to which we must deny our desire for full relation, since the revelation of that desire requires a letting-go of the withdrawn ego that would leave us vulnerable to an unthinkable humiliation. And insofar as we retain the withdrawn ego, we appear to the other as threatening also—as "one of the others" like the other whom we ourselves perceive as threatening us with the humiliation of non-recognition.

The entire process of acculturation that each of us has gone through in the formation of our present social selves has carried the weight—across many generations—of the threatening nature of the other. It has led us to develop a painful social split between the artificial self of the outer persona and the concealed inner self full of the hidden longing for recognition that the outer self, in its very artificiality, denies and renders inaccessible to the other's gaze. And in its paranoia, the withdrawn inner self must constantly monitor its outer presentation of self through a perpetual unconscious self-observation, simultaneously enacting the outer persona and scanning that enactment, which is always at risk of being seen through because of the inherent contingency—or if you like uncontrollableness—of every actual encounter with the other. Think of the television newscaster's pseudo-familiarity and the panicky quickness with which he or she instantly corrects any slight slip of the tongue or misstatement, or the occasional completely incoherent "jokes" exchanged on these local news shows that the newscasters instantly "cover" with laughter as if the jokes made sense. These behaviors reveal—in both their artificial enacted quality and in the near-instantaneous corrections of any "role-mistakes"—the threat of humiliation posed by the surrounding others. And we are all newscaster-like to some degree, claiming to the other to "really" be the outer persona we appear to be while concealing, individually and together, the fragile inner self that both longs for and fears being seen.

I am saying that this is the general social climate that envelops us, the human race, across nationalities and across our cultural particularities. There is, of course, a much more hopeful and positive way of representing the situation that would emphasize the beauty and joy of being alive, the love and recognition that we have been able as individuals and as cultures to achieve, and the upward spiritual and political movement toward each other that we may be able to discern. But my aim in writing this article is to try to understand the dark side of our present social existence, and especially the paranoia in the face of the other and the terror of humiliation that still haunts our every interaction.

Faced with the painful contradiction between our desire to realize ourselves through the other in the I-Thou relation and the prohibition against doing so that appears to be the lesson of our conditioning, the withdrawn self is driven to imaginary solutions—that is, to solutions that are withdrawn from the actual, concrete terrain of embodied self-other interactions and are lived out in the withdrawn security of the mind. To the extent that the outward persona enacted for the other retains the characteristics of an artificial role (the newscaster, "Dad," the president's need to "look presidential," and so forth), the withdrawn self seeks the protection of anonymity, presenting a performance without actual ontological presence. To maintain this inaccessibility while still seeking to satisfy our longing for the completion of authentic social connection drives us to collude in creating imaginary communities "in our heads," in an inner existential space that is literally behind the bodily enactments of our personae. In other articles in *Tikkun* I have given many examples of these imaginary communities and the immense social power they acquire because of the essential longing for social connection that they address: Ronald Reagan's beatific invocation of "Morning in America"; the conservative appeals to "family values"; the sense of belonging and acceptance offered by the God and religious embrace of the Christian Right; the sense of connection to community elicited by inflated or hortatory patriotism and accompanying invocations of our bond with the "Founding Fathers."

These communities are imaginary in the sense that they are not enriched by the mutual presence of the I-Thou relation. Though they purport to constitute a "We," they do not manifest the presence to each other in concrete lived experience that characterizes the reciprocity of a real "We." Instead they reflect a disembodied shared allegiance to an image cathected "in the mind" and literally withdrawn back from the real relation to the other, an allegiance that is then incorporated into the artificiality of the outer persona through such signifiers as uniforms, pledges, narrative clichés (for example, the American history taught in civics classes to young teenagers), clubs, marching bands, and the like. Assisted by the passing on of intergenerational authority to those who coordinate the intergenerational transmission of these images, they provide us with fantasies of connection in the service of protecting us from the threat of humiliation posed by the real other. That is why belief in these images is directly or indirectly compulsory, not just in the normally coercive rituals of the pledge of allegiance and the Lord's Prayer (at least in their schoolroom versions), but in the covert prohibition against challenging the purported "reality" of the social façade, the "reality," say, of the claim that "we" are Americans living in a land of freedom, opportunity, and happiness. The cultural fascination with the post-1960s remake of the movie *Invasion of the Body Snatchers* (the Donald Sutherland version rather than the 1950s, anti-communist Peter Lawford version) resulted precisely from how well it conveyed this prohibition against revealing the truth of our alienation: the alien Pods seek to take over the world by replacing actual humans with identical fake replicas who in turn organize to ferret out those remaining humans who cannot conceal the signs of their actual humanity.

The Nazis were an imaginary community, a special intensification of the imaginary unity of "the German People." When I say "the German People" are imaginary, I am not denying that there are elements of actual relation and mutual recognition in the common language, culture, and history that really does connect them, that makes them feel German together. I am saying that this connection retains the spiritual impoverishment of the centuries of alienation we have yet to surpass. Whether we understand the origins of this alienation from the other in the material struggle for survival or as the consequence of sin and a fall from grace or as an expression of our evolutionary lack of spiritual development that made God-consciousness and the awareness that Love is the realization of Being only primitively available to us, nationalistic communities like "the German People" are not characterized by the mutual presence and recognition that imbues the I-Thou relation. Forged out of violence and war, pervaded by hierarchical images of status and divisions of class, race, and gender that contradict the capacity to fully experience the other as a "Thou" in a true relation of recognition, "the German People" with its "Fatherland" and its patriotic songs is a connected unity only as an image in the mind—in the existential reality of each present moment's social interspace, it remains corroded by the fear of each person in the face of each actual other, just as is true of "the American People" in this country. And this was the case also in post–World War I Germany.

Now we come to the crucial point. For insofar as communities are imaginary, they are unconsciously haunted by the very absence of connection which they have been constructed to deny. The threat of humiliation and non-recognition posed by the mere existence of the actual other toward whom we are at the same time inherently pulled by the desire for mutual recognition that constitutes us as reciprocal, social beings—this threat is what has led to the protective divisions in the self that I described earlier. And just as the artificial persona enacted toward the other must claim to be real in order to deny the other access to the longing of the withdrawn self within, so the imaginary community that purports to satisfy our socially inherent need for connectedness and recognition must be outwardly manifested as real in order to seal off the pain of our actual isolation and the desire for and fear of the other that accompany it. Yet the collusion that allows and even forces these false appearances of self and community to be taken as real cannot actually make them so. It only renders what is real socially invisible or what we call "unconscious," but it does not get rid of what is real—this longing to be seen and confirmed through relation with the actual other, the conditioned terror of disconfirmation and humiliation, and the volatility and passion of these conflicting impulses that constitute the energy field of real social life in its concrete existential dimension. And this reality haunts the collective allegiance to the imaginary communities that are intended to cover it up through the reciprocal collusion that denies it.

In present-day America, the emptiness of both mass culture and political life reveals the way that social alienation can at times achieve a relative stability. The general absence of authentic connection, of the presence to each other that characterizes the profound transparency of the I-Thou relation, the bland rotation of the outer-role systems, and the imaginary communities that purport to unite us which today are transmitted mainly by television ("we" all supposedly watched the final episode of *Seinfeld;*

according to "our" spokesperson, "we Americans" have more opportunity today than ever before; etc.)—all of these aspects of our contemporary culture sometimes seem so natural that their alienated character becomes almost invisible. Indeed, the very success with which social emptiness is managed today suggests that liberal late capitalism may aspire to solve the threat posed by a direct encounter with the other by trying to postpone it forever: by ironizing all seriousness, assimilating social existence itself to its televised representation, and disseminating legal drugs like Prozac that really do make meaninglessness feel better. That Francis Fukuyama could seriously suggest that the current period of moral void and spiritual and political disengagement is "The End of History" is an indication that this idea of infinite postponement is not so far-fetched.

But the situation in Germany in the 1920s and early 1930s was very different from our own. World War I had been a war of imaginary communities—nothing quite validates my description of the non-rational psychodynamics underlying social alienation more than the absurd irrationality of that war's origins and the utterly predictable catastrophic suffering that it would cause. Like the Vietnam War in which, as Tom Hayden has so eloquently put it, fathers sacrificed the lives of their real sons in order not to lose their connection to the image of America that they had gained in World War II, World War I revealed our capacity to disattend to easily foreseeable real consequences in order to preserve our allegiance to imaginary community. And as I have indicated, the reason for this is the real terror of the negation of our very social being, as yet so under-confirmed in history, that makes the dissociation from reality "worth it." In this context, the defeat of "the German People," coupled with the further humiliations of the reparations, the accelerating "worthlessness" of "the German currency," and the challenge to the very existence of a "German community" by Marxists intent on revealing it as epiphenomenal in relation to the underlying reality of the international class struggle, all of these forces threatened to disintegrate the imaginary recognition that each German experienced as "national pride."

When the world achieves the spiritual development that will, when it is achieved, permit a self-evident confidence in the confirmatory nature of the I-Thou relation, the type of recognition associated with pride and humiliation will be surpassed or significantly altered in its meaning. But in a world still addicted to imaginary communities as a defense against the threat posed by the actual other, the "belief" in the imaginary community uses the inflating character of pride as a means of keeping out of awareness the fear of humiliation that this "belief" is meant to deny. In the absence of a spiritual-political social movement that might have addressed the alienation that produced World War I and the mourning and healing needed to truly recover from it (and neither the League of Nations nor Marxism was capable of this kind of analysis and response), no social base existed that could soften the psychological effects of the Germans' loss of pride in their national identity. To desire in your being the recognition of the other and the blessed grace and completion of the I-Thou relation, and then to feel as a result of your conditioning that you are actually nobody in the face of a dominant other who will use the vulnerability of your desire to humiliate you—that is not a tolerable option, not even an option we can bear to become fully conscious of. And as a result, the degraded "German People" were drawn to a Nazi party capable of re-inspiring a sense of national pride powerful enough, at the imaginary level, to re-expel the threat of the other's non-recognition and humiliation from their conscious experience.

But while the grandiosity of Nazism was able to restore each under-recognized "little man's" sense of pride, worth, and self-recognition as "a German," as "one of the German people," the Nazi community remained an imaginary unity whose special character consisted in having been virulently infected by the humiliation that gave rise to it. Its violence, its megalomania, its preoccupation with purification, its desire to assert a world-dominance that would last forever—all of these elements of Nazi culture so clearly reveal a drivenness to get rid of some haunting inner demon—that sense of ontological inadequacy that is in fact a universal feature of social alienation but that had broken through into consciousness sufficiently to traumatize the Germans of the Weimar Republic. It had to be gotten rid of, this threat of humiliation; and yet—and here is the crucial point—it could not be gotten rid of because it was itself a constituent element of Nazi consciousness. Glassy-eyed, goose-stepping, and inflated into a prideful rage, the SS officers, like the young women feeling an erotic thrill as they watched the spectacle of the rally, were enacting themselves as if they were part of an upsurge of authentic affirmation and recognition. But they were deceiving themselves. The Nazis were an imaginary community, haunted by the same fear of humiliation and lack of true affirming reciprocity as other such communities, but the necessity of their grandiosity made the denial of their vulnerability to the threat of the actual other more urgent and more difficult to achieve.

Psychoanalysis has long recognized that one way to reconcile incompatible parts of the self is to engage in splitting and projection. In her book *For Your Own Good,* Alice Miller presents a thoughtful application of these concepts to the Nazi personality structure, but remains within the boundaries of conventional psychoanalysis. In the framework that I am presenting, we shall see that the Nazis did indeed engage in splitting and projection, but in order to deny the existence of the absence that haunted them—haunted their inflated outer personae and the imaginary nature of their grandiose unity as a master race. Let me repeat once again, because this is very important: to be absent in this way is to seek to be not present to the actual other, to withdraw one's innocent longing for the actual other's affirmation of one's authentic being and to seal off that longing behind the glassy eyes and rigid musculature of the external persona, so that in spite of the choreographed external unity of those enormous Nuremberg rallies, the core of each person's actual social presence remained pulled back into his or her head and removed from the inherent vulnerability of the truly embodied relation. And since this "outerness" of the Nazi movement was infected with the breakthrough of the humiliation that had given rise to it, it faced a perpetual threat that had to be warded off with great urgency.

This warding off of the threat of humiliation by the actual other took many forms, such as the disciplinary rigidification of the internal hierarchies of the Nazi party with its compulsory and decisive salutes and the internal use of the Gestapo, the SA, and the SS, all of which facilitated the maintenance of what might be called "disciplinary hegemony"—that is, the effective use of terror to monitor and secure the outer collusion of the German people as a whole in maintaining the appearance of unquestioned allegiance and "belief." These Germans were themselves actual others in the sense that I have been using the term—that is, each was an "existent," an inherently *relational* being with a consciousness capable of nihilating (in social combination, accidental or intentional) the false outer unity of the Nazi's pseudo-community. Warding off the threat of humiliation consisted first, therefore, of assuring—through real organization—the absolute allegiance among the Germans themselves to belief in the reality of the hallucination of their connection—the realness, for example, of Hitler's hallucinatory invocation of "the Blood" that incarnated Nazi German unity.

But the most important method of warding off the inner demon that so infected and threatened to dissolve this imaginary unity was to try to split off the threat of being revealed as false (an ever present threat emerging from the fear posed by the ever present pull towards authentic recognition that can arise only through the letting-go of our withdrawnness and the becoming-present-to-the-other in full relation) and to project this split-off threat onto other imaginary communities that were defined as the source of the threat to "the German People." To those of you who are familiar with the idea of splitting as a psychological defense, this may sound straightforward and even simple, but it actually involves a subtle transposition that is of great social importance. For in splitting off the internal demon and projecting its threat onto an external, demonized other, the Nazi transposes the haunting internal threat of humiliation of the fragile and withdrawn inner self (by its exposure, through the transparency of relation, to the actual other) into an *external* threat to the Nazi's "outer" imaginary community itself. This has the effect of not simply denying the inner absence that threatens the heart of Nazi identity, but rather of acknowledging the felt presence of the threat and then externalizing it and changing its object to fully remove it from the concrete domain of real social existence. In place of the ever present threat to the actual withdrawn self by the actual other that haunts and therefore divides the Nazi's being and that therefore can neither be acknowledged nor eliminated, the process of splitting off and projection allows the Nazi first to secure the undivided "reality" of the Nazi's outer imaginary community and second to make this imaginary community the threatened object in place of the vulnerable and frightened soul within. Through this ingenious, hallucinatory transposition, the Nazi can attempt to actively master a fear of humiliation which he must otherwise passively suffer and in relation to which he is otherwise helpless to affect: through it, he "unifies" himself, enables himself to actively acknowledge the threat that would otherwise have to be denied by expelling that threat from the self and projecting it in the form of a contemptible infection into the demonized other outside the self, and he gains the capacity to actively mobilize his energy, in the form of a truly "blind rage," against a threat that has now been transformed from a threat to the soul of exposure and authentic humiliation into a threat to the pseudo-integrity of the Nazi's outer persona and the imaginary community itself to which it belongs. Acknowledging the threat and transposing it in this way strengthens the Nazi's self-deception: it allows him or her to say, "We are perfect, real, and pure, and we will stamp out the 'them' who are external to us and impure and seek to infect us with an alien presence that is not in us."

As Bauman points out in his critique of Goldhagen, there were many groups who served as carriers of the Nazis' split-off projections, including those deemed mentally deficient, physically disabled, or sexually deviant, but the Jews were the primary demonized others. And certainly the selection of the Jews for this purpose has everything to do with the history of German anti-Semitism, which is to say with the history of the Jews having to absorb these same split-off projections in times of "normal" alienation, which did not produce a holocaust however much violence German Jews had to routinely endure. But one of the main points I wish to make here is that whatever the scope of the historical anti-Semitism that made the Jewish people the most likely object of Nazi demonization, within the distortions and conflicts of the Nazi mind the Jews were imaginary, as imaginary as the Nazi's master race of Germans themselves were. By this I mean that Nazism, as a catastrophic manifestation of alienated consciousness whose recurrence remains a possibility so long as the ubiquitous pain of social alienation and the longing for mutual recognition remain so poorly understood and so little responded to, produced a consciousness sufficiently cut off, through denial, from even the impoverished relational empathy that characterizes our experience of the actual other here in the real world, that the Jewish people became an "It" to them, to again use Buber's terminology.

ISRAEL IN CONFLICT

THE NEW HISTORIOGRAPHY

ISRAEL CONFRONTS ITS PAST

Benny Morris

ON JULY 11, 1948, the Yiftah Brigade's Third Battalion, as part of what was called Operation Dani, occupied the center of the Arab town of Lydda. There was no formal surrender, but the night passed quietly. Just before noon the following day, two or three armored cars belonging to the Arab Legion, the British-led and trained Transjordanian army, drove into town. A firefight ensued, and the scout cars withdrew. But a number of armed townspeople, perhaps believing that the shooting heralded a major Arab counterattack, began sniping from windows and rooftops at their Israeli occupiers. The Third Battalion—about four hundred nervous Israeli soldiers in the middle of an Arab town of tens of thousands—fiercely put down what various chroniclers subsequently called a "rebellion," by firing in the streets, into houses, and at the concentrations of POWs in the mosque courtyards. Israeli military records refer to "more than 250" Arabs killed in the town that afternoon. By contrast, Israeli casualties in both the firefight with the Arab Legion scout cars and the suppression of the sniping were between two and four dead (the records vary), and twelve wounded. Israeli historians called the affair a "rebellion" in order to justify the subsequent slaughter; Arab chroniclers, such as Aref al-Aref, did likewise in order to highlight Palestinian resolve and resistance in the face of Zionist encroachment.

Operation Dani took place roughly midway through the first Israeli-Arab war—the War of Independence, in official Israeli parlance. The Arab states' invasion on May 15 of the fledgling state had been halted weeks before; the newly organized and freshly equipped Israel Defense Forces (IDF) were on the offensive on all fronts—as was to remain true for the remainder of the war.

On July 12, before the shooting in Lydda had completely died down, Lt. Col. Yitzhak Rabin, officer in command of operations for Operation Dani, issued the following order: "1. The inhabitants of Lydda must be expelled quickly without attention to age. They should be directed towards Beit Nabala. Yiftah [Brigade HQ] must determine the method and inform [Operation] Dani HQ and Eighth Brigade HQ. 2. Implement immediately." A similar order was issued at the same time to the Kiryati Brigade concerning the inhabitants of the neighboring Arab town of Ramle.

On July 12 and July 13, the Yiftah and Kiryati brigades carried out their orders, expelling the fifty to sixty thousand inhabitants of the two towns, which lie about ten miles southeast of Tel Aviv. Throughout the war, the two towns had interdicted Jewish traffic on the main Tel Aviv–Jerusalem road, and the Yishuv's leaders regarded Lydda and Ramle as a perpetual threat to Tel Aviv itself. About noon on July 13, Operation Dani HQ informed IDF General Staff/Operations: "Lydda police fort has been captured. [The troops] are busy expelling the inhabitants [*oskim be'geirush ha'toshavim*]." Lydda's inhabitants were forced to walk eastward to the Arab Legion lines, and many of Ramle's inhabitants were ferried in trucks or buses. Clogging the roads (and the Legion's possible routes of advance westward), the tens of thousands of refugees marched, gradually shedding possessions along the way. Arab chroniclers, such as Sheikh Muhammad Nimr al-Khatib, claimed that hundreds of children died in the march, from dehydration and disease. One Israeli witness at the time described the spoor: The refugee column "to begin with [jettisoned] utensils and furniture and, in the end, bodies of men, women and children. . . ." Many of the refugees came to rest near Ramallah and set up tent encampments (which later became the refugee camps supported by the United Nations Relief and Works Agency [UNRWA], and the hotbeds of today's Palestinian rebellion which current Defense Minister Rabin is trying to suppress).

Israeli historians in the 1950s, 1960s, and 1970s were less than honest in their treatment of the Lydda-Ramle episode. The IDF's official *Toldot Milhemet Ha'komemiut* (History of the War of Independence), written by General Staff/History Branch and published in 1959, stated, "The Arabs [of Lydda], who had violated the terms of the surrender and feared [Israeli] retribution, were happy at the possibility given them of evacuating the town and proceeding eastwards, to Legion territory; Lydda emptied of its Arab inhabitants."

A decade later, the former head of the IDF History Branch, Lt. Col. Netanel Lorch, wrote in 1968 in *The Edge of the Sword,* the second revised edition of his history of the war, that "the residents, who had violated surrender terms and feared retribution, declared they would leave and asked [for] safe conduct to Arab Legion lines, which was granted."

A somewhat less deceitful, but also misleading, description of the events in Lydda and Ramle is provided by Lt. Col. Elhannan Orren, another former director of the IDF History Branch, in his *Ba'derekh El Ha'ir* (On the Road to the City), a highly detailed description of Operation Dani published by the IDF in 1976. Orren, like his predecessors, fails to state anywhere that what occurred was an expulsion, and one explicitly ordered from on high (originating, according to Ben-Gurion's first major biographer, Michael Bar-Zohar, from the prime minister himself). Orren also repeats a variant of the "inhabitants asked, the IDF graciously complied" story.

Yitzhak Rabin, ironically more frank than his chroniclers, inserted a passage into his autobiography, *Pinkas Sherut* (Service Notebook), which more or less admitted that what had occurred in Lydda and Ramle had been an expulsion. But the passage was excised by order of the Israeli government. (Subsequently, to everyone's embarrassment, Peretz Kidron, the English translator of *Pinkas Sherut,* sent the offending passage to the *New York Times,* where it was published on October 23, 1979.)

The treatment of the Lydda-Ramle affair by past Israeli historians is illustrative of what can be called, for want of a better term, the "old" or "official" history. That history has shaped the way Israelis and Diaspora Jews—or, at least, Diaspora Zionists—have seen and, in large measure, still see Israel's past; and it has also held sway over the way gentile Europeans and Americans (and their governments) see that past. This understanding of the past, in turn, has significantly influenced the attitudes of Diaspora Jews, as well as the attitude of European and American non-Jews, toward present-day Israel—which affects government policies concerning the Israeli-Arab conflict.

The essence of the old history is that Zionism was a beneficent and well-meaning progressive national movement; that Israel was born pure into an uncharitable, predatory world; that Zionist efforts at compromise and conciliation were rejected by the Arabs; and that Palestine's Arabs, and in their wake the surrounding Arab states, for reasons of innate selfishness, xenophobia, and downright cussedness, refused to accede to the burgeoning

Zionist presence and in 1947 to 1949 launched a war to extirpate the foreign plant. The Arabs, so goes the old history, were politically and militarily assisted in their efforts by the British, but they nonetheless lost the war. Poorly armed and outnumbered, the Jewish community in Palestine, called the Yishuv, fought valiantly, suppressed the Palestinian "gangs" (knufiyot in Israeli parlance), and repelled the five invading Arab armies. In the course of that war, says the old history—which at this point becomes indistinguishable from Israeli propaganda—Arab states and leaders, in order to blacken Israel's image and facilitate the invasion of Palestine, called upon/ordered Palestine's Arabs to quit their homes and the "Zionist areas"—to which they were expected to return once the Arab armies had proved victorious. Thus was triggered the Palestinian Arab exodus which led to the now forty-year-old Palestinian refugee problem.

The old history makes the further claim that in the latter stages of the 1948 war and in the years immediately thereafter Israel desperately sought to make peace with all or any of its neighbors, but the Arabs, obdurate and ungenerous, refused all overtures, remaining hell-bent on destroying Israel.

The old historians offered a simplistic and consciously pro-Israeli interpretation of the past, and they deliberately avoided mentioning anything that would reflect badly on Israel. People argued that since the conflict with the Arabs was still raging, and since it was a political as well as a military struggle, it necessarily involved propaganda, the goodwill (or ill will) of governments in the West, and the hearts and minds of Christians and Diaspora Jews. Blackening Israel's image, it was argued, would ultimately weaken Israel in its ongoing war for survival. In short, raisons d'état often took precedence over telling the truth.

The past few years have witnessed the emergence of a new generation of Israeli scholars and a "new" history. These historians, some of them living abroad, have looked and are looking afresh at the Israeli historical experience, and their conclusions, by and large, are at odds with those of the old historians.

Two factors are involved in the emergence of this new history—one relating to materials, the other to personae.

Thanks to Israel's Archives Law (passed in 1955, amended in 1964 and 1981), and particularly to the law's key "thirty-year rule," starting in the early 1980s a large number (hundreds of thousands, perhaps millions) of state papers were opened to researchers. Almost all the Foreign Ministry's papers from 1947 to 1956, as well as a large number of documents—correspondence, memoranda, minutes—from other ministries, including the prime minister's office (though excluding the Defense Ministry and the IDF), have been released. Similarly, large collections of private papers and political party papers from this period have been opened. Therefore, for the first time, historians have been able to write studies of the period on the basis of a large collection of contemporary source material. (The old history was written largely on the basis of interviews and memoirs, and, at best, it made use of select batches of documents, many of them censored, such as those from the IDF archive.)

The second factor is the nature of the new historians. Most of them were born around 1948 and have matured in a more open, doubting, and self-critical Israel than the pre–Lebanon War Israel in which the old historians grew up. The old historians had lived through 1948 as highly committed adult participants in the epic, glorious rebirth of the Jewish commonwealth. They were unable to separate their lives from this historical event, unable to regard impartially and objectively the facts and processes that they later wrote about. Indeed, they admit as much. The new historians, by contrast, are able to be more impartial.

Inevitably, the new historians focused their attention, at least initially, on 1948, because the documents were available and because that was the central, natal, revolutionary event in Israeli history. How one perceives 1948 bears heavily on how one perceives the whole Zionist/Israeli experience. If Israel, the haven of a much-persecuted people, was born pure and innocent, then it was worthy of the grace, material assistance, and political support showered upon it by the West over the past forty years—and worthy of more of the same in years to come. If, on the other hand, Israel was born tarnished, besmirched by original sin, then it was no more deserving of that grace and assistance than were its neighbors.

The past few months have seen the publication in the West of a handful of "new" histories including Avi Shlaim's *Collusion Across the Jordan* (Columbia University Press, 1988); Ilam Pappe's *Britain and the Arab-Israeli Conflict, 1948–51* (Macmillan/St. Anthony's, 1988); Simha Flapan's *The Birth of Israel* (Pantheon, 1987); and my own *The Birth of the Palestinian Refugee Problem, 1947–1949* (Cambridge University Press, 1988). Taken together, these works—along with a large number of articles that have appeared recently in academic journals such as *Studies in Zionism, Middle Eastern Studies,* and *The Middle East Journal*—significantly undermine, if not thoroughly demolish, a variety of assumptions that helped form the core of the old history.

Flapan's work is the least historical of these books. Indeed, it is not, strictly speaking, a "history" at all but rather a polemical work written from a Marxist perspective. In his introduction, Flapan—who passed away last year and who was the former director of the left-wing Mapam party's Arab department and editor of the monthly *New Outlook*—writes that his purpose is not to produce "a detailed historical study interesting only to historians and researchers," but rather to write "a book that will undermine the propaganda structures that have so long obstructed the growth of the peace forces in my country. . . ." Politics rather than historiography is the book's manifest objective.

Despite its explicitly polemical purpose, Flapan's book has the virtue of more or less accurately formulating some of the central fallacies—which he calls "myths"—that informed the old history. These were (1) that the Yishuv in 1947 joyously accepted partition and the truncated Jewish state prescribed by the UN General Assembly, and that the Palestinians and the surrounding Arab states unanimously rejected the partition and attacked the Yishuv with the aim of throwing the Jews into the sea; (2) that the war was waged between a relatively defenseless and weak (Jewish) David and a relatively strong (Arab) Goliath; (3) that the Palestinians fled their homes and villages either voluntarily or at the behest/order of the Arab leaders; and (4) that, at the war's end, Israel was interested in making peace, but the recalcitrant Arabs displayed no such interest, opting for a perpetual—if sporadic—war to the finish.

Because of poor research and analysis—including selective and erroneous use of documents—Flapan's demolition of these myths is far from convincing. But Shlaim, in *Collusion*, tackles some of the same myths—and far more persuasively. According to Shlaim, the original Zionist goal was the establishment of a Jewish state in the whole of Palestine. The acceptance of partition, in the mid-1930s as in 1947, was tactical, not a change in the Zionist dream. Ben-Gurion, says Shlaim, considered the partition lines of "secondary importance . . . because he intended to change them in any case; they were not the end but only the beginning." In acquiescing to partition schemes in the mid-1930s, Ben-Gurion wrote, "I am certain that we will be able to settle in all the other parts of the country, whether through agreement and mutual understanding with our Arab neighbors or in another way." To his wife, Ben-Gurion wrote, "Establish a Jewish state at once, even if it is not in the whole land. The rest will come in the course of time. It must come."

Come November 1947, the Yishuv entered the first stage of the war with a tacit understanding with Transjordan's king, Abdullah—"a falcon trapped in a canary's cage"—that his Arab Legion would take over the eastern part of Palestine (now called the West Bank), earmarked by the UN for Palestinian statehood, and that it would leave the Yishuv alone to set up the Jewish state in the other areas of the country. The Yishuv and the Hashemite kingdom of Transjordan, Shlaim persuasively argues, had conspired from 1946 to early 1947 to nip the UN Partition Resolution in the bud and to stymie the emergence of a Palestinian Arab state. From the start, while publicly enunciating support for the partition of the land between its Jewish and Arab communities, both Ben-Gurion and Abdullah aimed at frustrating the UN resolution and sharing among themselves the areas earmarked for Palestinian Arab statehood. It was to be partition—but between Israel and Transjordan. This "collusion" and "unholy alliance"—in Shlaim's loaded phrases—was sealed at the now-famous clandestine meeting between Golda Meyerson (Meir) and Abdullah at Naharayim on the Jordan River on November 17, 1947.

This Zionist-Hashemite nonaggression pact was sanctioned by Britain, adds Shlaim. Contrary to the old Zionist historiography—which was based largely on the (mistaken) feelings of Israel's leaders at that time—Britain's Foreign Secretary Ernest Bevin, "by February 1948," had clearly become "resigned to the inevitable emergence of a Jewish state" (while opposing the emergence of a Palestinian Arab state). Indeed, he warned Transjordan "to refrain from invading the areas allotted to the Jews."

Both Shlaim and Flapan make the point that the Palestinian Arabs, though led by Haj Amin al-Husayni, the conniving, extremist former mufti of Jerusalem, were far from unanimous in supporting the Husayni-led crusade against the Jews. Indeed, in the first months of the hostilities, according to Yishuv intelligence sources, the bulk of Palestine's Arabs merely wanted quiet, if only out of respect for the Jews' martial prowess. But gradually, in part due to Haganah overreactions, the conflict widened and eventually engulfed the two communities throughout the land. In April and May 1948, the Haganah gained the upper hand and the Palestinians lost the war, most of them going into exile.

What ensued, once Israel declared its independence on May 14, 1948, and the Arab states invaded on May 15, was "a general land grab," with everyone—Israel, Transjordan, Syria, Iraq, Lebanon, and Egypt—bent on preventing the birth of a Palestinian Arab state and carving out chunks of Palestine for themselves.

Contrary to the old history, Abdullah's invasion of eastern Palestine was clearly designated to conquer territory for his kingdom—at the expense of the Palestinian Arabs—rather than to destroy the Jewish state. Indeed, the Arab Legion—apart from one abortive incursion around Notre Dame in Jerusalem and the assault on the Etzion Bloc (a Jewish settlement zone inside the Arab state area)—stuck meticulously, throughout the war, to its nonaggressive stance vis-à-vis the Yishuv and the Jewish state's territory. Rather, it was the Haganah/IDF that repeatedly attacked the legion on territory earmarked for Arab sovereignty (Latrun, Lydda, Ramle).

Nevertheless, Shlaim, like Pappe in *Britain and the Arab-Israeli Conflict, 1948–51*, is never completely clear about Egypt, Syria, Iraq, and Lebanon's main purpose in invading Palestine: Was their primary aim to overrun the Yishuv and destroy the Jewish state, or was it merely to frustrate or curtail Abdullah's territorial ambitions and to acquire some territory for themselves?

Flapan argues firmly, but without evidence, that "the invasion . . . was not aimed at destroying the Jewish state." Shlaim and Pappe are more cautious. Shlaim writes that the Arab armies intended to bisect the Jewish state and, if possible, "occupy Haifa and Tel Aviv" or "crippl[e] the Jewish state." But, at the same time, he argues that they were driven into the invasion more by a desire to stymie Abdullah than by the wish to kill the Jews; and, partly for this reason, they did not properly plan the invasion, either militarily or politically, and their leaders were generally pessimistic about its outcome. Pappe points out that Egypt initially did not seem determined to participate in the invasion, and all the Arab states failed to commit the full weight of their military power to the enterprise—which indicates perhaps that they took the declared aim of driving the Jews into the sea less than seriously. In any event, Transjordan frustrated the other Arabs' intentions throughout and rendered their military preparations and planning ineffective.

One of the most tenacious myths relating to 1948 is the myth of "David and Goliath"—that the Arabs were overwhelmingly stronger militarily than the Yishuv. The simple truth—as conveyed by Flapan, Shlaim, Pappe, and myself—is that the stronger side won. The map showing a minuscule Israel and a giant surrounding sea of Arab states did not and, indeed, for the time being still do not accurately reflect the military balance of power. The pre-1948 Yishuv had organized itself for statehood and war; the Palestinian Arabs, who outnumbered the Jews two to one, had not. And in war, command and control are everything, or almost everything. During the first half of the war (December 1947–May 14, 1948), the Yishuv was better armed and had more trained manpower than the Palestinians, whose forces were beefed up by several thousand "volunteers" from the surrounding Arab states. This superior organization, command, and control meant that at almost every decisive point in the battle the Haganah managed to field more and better-equipped formations than did the Palestinians. When the Yishuv put matters to the test, in the Haganah offensives of April and early May 1948, the decision was never in doubt; the Arab redoubts fell, in domino fashion, like ripe plums—the Jerusalem Corridor, Tiberias, Haifa, Eastern Galilee, Safad. When one adds to this the Yishuv's superiority in morale and motivation—it was a bare three years after the Holocaust, and the Haganah troopers knew that it was do-or-die—the Palestinians never had a chance.

The old history is no more illuminating when it comes to the second stage of the war—the conventional battles of May 15, 1948–January 1949. Jewish organization, command, and control remained superior to those of the uncoordinated armies of Egypt, Syria, Iraq, and Lebanon; and throughout the Yishuv also, the IDF had an edge in numbers. In mid-May 1948, for example, the Haganah fielded thirty-five thousand armed troops while the Arab invaders fielded twenty-five to thirty thousand troops. By the time of Operation Dani in July, the IDF has sixty-five thousand men under arms, and by December it had eighty to ninety thousand—outnumbering its combined Arab foes at every stage of the battle. The Haganah/IDF also enjoyed the immensely important advantage, throughout the conventional war, of short lines of communication, while the Iraqis and Egyptians had to send supplies and reinforcements over hundreds of kilometers of desert before they reached the front lines.

Two caveats must be entered. First, Transjordan's Arab Legion was probably the best army in the war. But it never numbered much more than five thousand troops, and it had no tanks or aircraft. Second, in terms of equipment, during the crucial three weeks between the pan-Arab invasion of Palestine on May 15 and the start of the First Truce on June 11, the Arab armies had an edge in weaponry over the Haganah/IDF. The Haganah was much weaker in terms of aircraft, and had no artillery (only heavy mortars) and very few tanks or tracked vehicles. For those three weeks, as the Haganah's officer in command of operations, Yigal Yadin, told the politicians, it was "fifty-fifty." But before May 15 and from the First Truce onward, the Yishuv's military formations were superior both in terms of manpower and in terms of weaponry.

Apart from the birth of the State of Israel, the major political outcome of the 1948 war was the creation of the Palestinian refugee problem. How the problem came about has been the subject of heated controversy between Israeli and Arab propagandists for the past four decades. The controversy is as much about the nature of Zionism as it is about what exactly happened in 1948. If the Arab contention is true—that the Yishuv had always intended "transfer" and that in 1948 it systematically and forcibly expelled the Arab population from the areas that became the Jewish state—then Israel is a robber state that, like young Jacob, has won the sympathy and support of its elders in the West by trickery and connivance, and the Palestinians are more or less innocent victims. If, on the other hand, the Israeli propaganda line is accepted—that the Palestinians fled "voluntarily" or at the behest of their own and other Arab leaders—then

Israel is free of original sin. As I have set out in great detail in *The Birth of the Palestinian Refugee Problem, 1947–1949,* the truth lies somewhere in between. While from the mid-1930s most of the Yishuv's leaders, including Ben-Gurion, wanted to establish a Jewish state without an Arab minority, or with as small an Arab minority as possible, and supported a "transfer solution" to this minority problem, the Yishuv did not enter the 1948 war with a master plan for expelling the Arabs, nor did its political and military leaders ever adopt such a master plan. There were Haganah/IDF expulsions of Arab communities, some of them with Haganah/IDF General Staff and/or cabinet-level sanction—such as at Miska and Ad-Dumeira in April 1948; in Zarnuqa, Al-Qubeiba, and Huj in May; in Lydda and Ramle in July; and along the Lebanese border (Bir'im, Iqrit, Tarbikha, Suruh, Al-Mansura, and Nabi Rubin) in early November. But there was no grand or blanket policy of expulsions.

On the other hand, at no point during the war did Arab leaders issue a blanket call for Palestinians to leave their homes and villages and wander into exile. Nor was there an Arab radio or press campaign urging or ordering the Palestinians to flee. Indeed, I have found no trace of any such broadcasts—and throughout the war the Arab radio stations and other press were monitored by the Israeli intelligence services and Foreign Ministry, and by Western diplomatic stations and agencies (such as the BBC). No contemporary reference to or citation from such a broadcast, let alone from a series of such broadcasts, has ever surfaced.

Indeed, in early May 1948 when, according to Israeli propaganda and some of the old histories, such a campaign of broadcasts should have been at its height, in preparation for the pan-Arab invasion, Arab radio stations and leaders (Radio Ramallah, King Abdullah, and Arab Liberation Army commander Qawuqji) all issued broadcasts calling upon the Palestinians to stay put and, if already in exile, to return to their homes in Palestine. References to these broadcasts exist in Haganah, Mapam, and British records.

Occasionally, local Arab commanders and/or politicians ordered the evacuation of women and children from war zones. Less frequently, as in Haifa on April 22, 1948, local Arab leaders advised and instructed their communities to leave rather than stay in a potential or actual war zone or "treacherously" remain under Jewish rule. But there were no Arab blanket orders or campaigns to leave.

Rather, in order to understand the exodus of the 600,000 to 760,000 Arabs from the areas that became the post-1948 Jewish state, one must look to a variety of related processes and causes. What happened in Haifa is illustrative of the complexity of the exodus (though it too does not convey the full complexity of what transpired in the various regions of Palestine at the time).

The exodus from Haifa (which initially had an Arab population of seventy thousand), as from the other main Arab Palestinian centers, Jaffa and Jerusalem, began in December 1947 with the start of sporadic hostilities between the various Jewish and Arab neighborhoods. The exodus slowly gained momentum during the following months as the British Mandate administration moved toward dissolution and final withdrawal. The first to go were the rich and the educated—the middle classes with second homes on the Beirut beachfront, in Nablus or Amman, or those who had either relatives abroad with large homes or enough money to stay in hotels for long periods. The Palestinians' political and economic leadership disappeared. By mid-May 1948, only one member of the Arab Higher Committee, the Palestinians' shadow government, was still in the country.

The flight of the professionals, the civil servants, the traders, and the businessmen had a harsh impact on the Haifa Arab masses, who already were demoralized by the continual sniping and bomb attacks, by the feeling that the Jews were stronger, and by the sense that their own ragtag militia would fail when the test came (as, indeed, it did). The Arabs felt terribly isolated and insecure—Arab Haifa was far from other major Arab population centers and was easily cut off by Jewish settlements along the approach roads. Businesses and workshops closed, policemen shed their uniforms and left their posts, Arab workers could no longer commute to jobs in Jewish areas, and agricultural produce was interdicted in ambushes on the approach roads to the city. Unemployment and prices soared. Thousands of people left.

Then came the Haganah attack of April 21 to April 22 on the Arab districts. Several companies of Carmeli Brigade troops, under cover of constant mortar fire, drove down the Carmel mountain slopes into the Arab downtown areas. Arab militia resistance collapsed. Thousands of Arabs fled from the outlying Arab neighborhoods (such as Wadi Rushmiya and Hailssa) into the British-controlled port area, piled into boats, and fled northward to Acre. The leaders who remained sued for a cease-fire. Under British mediation, the Haganah agreed, offering what the British regarded as generous terms. But then, when faced with Moslem pressure, the Arab leaders, most of them Christian Arabs, got cold feet; a cease-fire meant surrender and implied agreement to live under Jewish rule. They would be open to charges of collaboration and treachery. So, to the astonishment of the British officers and the Jewish military and political leaders gathered on the afternoon of April 22 at the Haifa town hall, the Arab delegation announced that its community would evacuate the city.

The Jewish mayor, Shabtai Levy, and the British commander, Maj. Gen. Hugh Stockwell, pleaded with the Arabs to reconsider. The Haganah representative, Mordechai Makleff, declined to voice an opinion. But the Arabs were unmoved, and the mass exodus, which had begun under the impact of the Haganah mortars and ground assault, moved into top gear, with the British supplying boats and armored car escorts to the departing Arab convoys. From April 22 to May 1, almost all the Arab population departed. The rough treatment—temporary evictions, house-to-house searches, detentions, the occasional beating—meted out to the remaining population during those days by the Haganah and the IZL (Irgun Zvai Leumi) troops who occupied the downtown areas led many of the undecided also to opt for evacuation. By early May, the city's Arab population had dwindled to three or four thousand.

The bulk of the Palestinian refugees—some 250,000 to 300,000—went into exile during those weeks between April and mid-June 1948, with the major precipitant being Jewish (Haganah/IZL) military attack or fears of such attack. In most cases, the Jewish commanders, who wanted to occupy empty villages (occupying populated villages meant leaving behind a garrison, which the units could not afford to do), were hardly ever confronted with deciding whether or not to expel an overrun community: Most villages and towns simply emptied at the first whiff of grapeshot.

In conformity with the Tokhnit Dalet (Plan D), the Haganah's master plan, formulated in March 1948, for securing the Jewish state areas in preparation for the expected declaration of statehood and the prospective Arab invasion, the Haganah cleared various areas completely of Arab villages—in the Jerusalem corridor, around Kibbutz Mishmar Ha'emek, and along the coast road. But in most cases, expulsion orders were not necessary; the inhabitants had already fled, out of fear or as a result of Jewish attack. In several areas, Israeli commanders successfully used psychological warfare ploys ("Here's some friendly advice. You better get out now, before the Jews come and rape your daughters") to obtain Arab evacuation.

The prewar basic structural weaknesses of Palestinian society led to the dissolution of that society when the test of battle came. Lack of administrative structures, as well as weak leaders, poor or nonexistent military organization beyond the single-village level, and faulty or nonexistent taxation mechanisms, all caused the main towns to fall apart in April and May 1948. The fall of the towns and the exodus from them, in turn, brought a sense of fear and despondency to the rural hinterlands. Traditionally, the villages, though economically autarchic, had looked to the towns for political leadership and guidance. The evacuation of the middle classes and the leaders, as well as the fall of the towns, provided the Palestinians in the hinterlands with an example to emulate. Safad's fall and evacuation on May 10 and May 11, for example, triggered an immediate evacuation of the surrounding Arab villages; so, earlier, did the fall of Haifa and the IZL assault on Jaffa.

Seen from the Jewish side, the spectacle of mass Arab evacuation certainly triggered appetites for more of the same: Everyone, at every level of military and political decision-making, understood that a Jewish state without a large Arab minority would be stronger and more viable both militarily and politically. Therefore, the tendency of local military commanders to "nudge" Palestinians into flight increased as the war went on. Jewish atrocities—far more widespread than the old historians have indicated (there were massacres of Arabs at Ad Dawayima, Eilaboun, Jish, Safsaf, Hule, Saliha, and Sasa besides Deir Yassin and Lydda)—and the drive to avenge past Arab wrongs also contributed significantly to the exodus.

The last major fallacy tackled incidentally or directly by the new historians concerns an Israel that in 1948 to 1949 was bent on making peace with its neighbors, and an Arab world that monolithically rejected all such peace efforts. The evidence that Israel's leaders were not desperate to make peace and were unwilling to make the large concessions necessary to give peace a chance is overwhelming. In Tel Aviv, there was a sense of triumph and drunkenness that accompanied victory—a feeling that the Arabs would "soon" or "eventually" sue for peace, that there was no need to rush things or make concessions, that ultimately military victory and dominance would translate into diplomatic-political success.

As Ben-Gurion told an American journalist in mid-July 1949: "I am prepared to get up in the middle of the night in order to sign a peace agreement—but I am not in a hurry and I can wait ten years. We are under no pressure whatsoever." Or, as Ben-Gurion records Abba Eban's telling him: "[Eban] sees no need to run after peace. The armistice is sufficient for us; if we run after peace, the Arabs will demand a price of us—borders [i.e., in terms of territory] or refugees [i.e., repatriation] or both. Let us wait a few years."

As Pappe puts it in Britain: ". . . Abdullah's eagerness [to make peace] was not reciprocated by the Israelis. The priorities of the state of Israel had changed during 1949. The armistice agreements brought relative calm to the borders, and peace was no longer the first priority. The government was preoccupied with absorbing new immigrants and overcoming economic difficulties."

Israel's lack of emphasis on achieving peace was manifested most clearly in the protracted (1949–51) secret negotiations with Abdullah. Israeli Foreign Minister Moshe Sharett described his meeting with Transjordan's king at the palace in Shuneh on May 5, 1949, in the following way: "Transjordan said—we are ready for peace immediately. We said—certainly, we too want peace but one shouldn't rush, one should walk." Israel and Jordan signed an armistice agreement, after much arm-twisting by Israel, which British and American diplomats compared to Hitler's treatment of the Czechs in 1938 to 1939. (As Abdullah put it, quoting an old Turkish saying: "If you meet a bear when crossing a rotten bridge, call her 'dear Auntie.'") But the two sides never signed a peace treaty or a nonbelligerence agreement—something that was proposed at one point by Abdullah.

Shlaim—who in *Collusion* expands the description of the secret Israeli-Jordanian negotiations first provided in Dan Schueftan's *Ha'Optziya Ha'-Yardenit* (The Jordanian Option), published in Hebrew in Israel in 1986—more or less lays the blame for the failed negotiations squarely on Israel's shoulders. A more generous, less anti-Israeli interpretation of the evidence would blame the Israelis and the Jordanians equally.

Israel refused to offer major concessions in terms of refugee repatriation or territory (Abdullah was particularly keen on getting back Lydda and Ramle) and was for too long unwilling to offer Jordan a sovereign corridor through its territory to the sea at Gaza. Throughout, Israel was prodded if not guided by the "blatant expansionism" of some of Ben-Gurion's aides, such as Moshe Dayan. As Yehoshafat Harkabi, one of Dayan's military colleagues, put it (according to Shlaim): "The existential mission of the State of Israel led us to be demanding and acquisitive, and mindful of the value of every square metre of land." In any case, Ben-Gurion refused to meet Abdullah, and the Israeli leaders often spoke of Abdullah with undeserved contempt.

Shlaim writes that "two principal factors were responsible for the failure of the postwar negotiations: Israel's strength and Abdullah's weakness." Nevertheless, Shlaim seems to attribute too much weight to the first and too little to the second. Shlaim does not sufficiently acknowledge the importance of the "Palestinization" of Jordan following the Hashemite annexation of the West Bank, which quickly resulted in a curtailment of Abdullah's autonomy and his freedom of political movement both within Jordan and in the Arab world in general. The twin pressures exercised by the Arab world outside and by his successive cabinets inside the kingdom successfully impeded Abdullah's ability to make a separate peace with Israel. He almost did so a number of times, but he always held back at the last moment and refused to take the plunge. It is possible, Shlaim argues, that more generous concessions by Tel Aviv at certain critical points in the negotiations would have given Abdullah greater motivation to pursue peace as well as the ammunition he needed to silence his antipeace critics, but the truth of such a claim is uncertain. What is clear is that Abdullah, though showing remarkable courage throughout, simply felt unable in those last years to go against the unanimous or near-unanimous wishes of his ministers and against the unanimous antipeace stand of the surrounding Arab world.

What happened with Abdullah occurred in miniature and more briefly with Egypt and with Syria. In September to October 1948, Egypt's King Farouk, knowing that the war was lost, secretly sent a senior court official to Paris to sound out Israel on the possibility of a peace based on Israeli cession of parts of the Negev and the Gaza Strip to Egypt. Sharett and the senior staff at the Foreign Ministry favored continued negotiations, but Ben-Gurion—bent on a further round of hostilities to drive the Egyptian army out of the Negev—flatly rejected the overture. Shlaim summarizes: "[Ben-Gurion] may have been right in thinking that nothing of substance would come out of these talks. But he surely owed his cabinet colleagues at least a report on what had taken place so that they could review their decision to go [again] to war against Egypt on the basis of all the relevant information." New Egyptian peace overtures in November, after Israel's Operation Yoav, again came to naught.

As for Syria, in May 1949, its new ruler, Husni Za'im, made major peace proposals which included recognition of Israel as well as Syrian readiness to absorb hundreds of thousands of Palestinian refugees. Za'im wanted Israel to concede a sliver of territory along the Jordan River. He asked to meet with Ben-Gurion or Sharett. Again, Ben-Gurion rejected the proposal, writing on May 12: "I am quite prepared to meet Colonel Za'im in order to promote peace . . . but I see no purpose in any such meeting as long as the representatives of Syria in the armistice negotiations do not declare in an unequivocal manner that their forces are prepared to withdraw to their prewar territory [i.e., withdraw from the small Syrian-occupied Mishmar Ha'yarden salient, west of the Jordan]."

Continued feelers by Za'im resulted again in Israeli refusal. As Sharett put it on May 25: "It is clear that we . . . won't agree that any bit of the Land of Israel be transferred to Syria, because this is a question of control over the water sources [i.e., of the Jordan River]." Shabtai Rosenne, the legal adviser at the Foreign Ministry, put it simply: "I feel that the need for an agreement between Israel and Syria pressed more heavily on the Syrians." Therefore, why rush toward peace? A few weeks later Za'im was overthrown and executed, and the Syrian peace initiative died with him. Whether the overture was serious or merely tactical—to obtain Western sympathy and funds, for example—is unclear. What is certain is that Israel failed to pursue it.

What was true of Israel's one-to-one contacts with each of the Arab states was true also of its negotiations with the Arabs under UN auspices at Lausanne in the spring and summer of 1949. There, too, Israel was ungenerous (though, needless to say, the Arabs were equally obdurate). For months, UN officials and the U.S. pressed Israel to make what they felt might be the redemptive gesture: to proclaim its willingness to take back several hundred thousand refugees. As the months dragged on and Israel remained inflexible, the Arabs became just as obstinate. When, at least, Israel offered to take back "one hundred thousand" which, in reality, as Sharett explained to his colleagues, was only sixty-five thousand (Sharett told his colleagues in Mapai that some thirty-five thousand refugees had already returned to Israel illegally or were about to return as part of the family reunification scheme, and these refugees would be deducted from the one hundred thousand), it was a case of too little too late. And Israel's more realistic offer—to take the Gaza Strip with its resident and refugee populations—was never seriously entertained by Egypt. Lausanne was probably the last chance for a comprehensive Israeli-Arab peace.

In *Pirkei Avot* it is written: "Rabbi Shimon Ben Gamliel was wont to say: On three things the world rests: On justice, on truth and on peace" (1:18). And he would quote Zechariah: ". . . execute the judgment of truth and peace in your gates" (8:16). Telling the truth thus seems to be an injunction anchored in Jewish tradition, and the scriptures apparently link truth to peace in some indeterminate manner.

The new history is one of the signs of a maturing Israel (though, no doubt, there are those who say it is a symptom of decay and degeneration). What is now being written about Israel's past seems to offer us a more balanced and a more "truthful" view of that country's history than what has been offered hitherto. It may also in some obscure way serve the purposes of peace and reconciliation between the warring tribes of that land.

LAND FOR WHAT?

Daniel Pipes

THE ELECTION OF ARIEL SHARON allows us to look back with amazement at the last eight years. The Israeli government pursued a course without parallel in the annals of diplomacy.

The best known of its negotiations were with Yassir Arafat and the Palestinians, but these were paralleled by no less important discussions with the Syrians and Lebanese. In all tracks, the Jewish state pursued a similar approach, which might be paraphrased as follows: "We will be reasonable and will give you what you can legitimately demand; in turn, we expect you to have a change of heart, ending your campaign to destroy Israel and instead accepting the permanence of a sovereign Jewish state in the Middle East." In brief, the Israelis offered land for peace, as the U.S. government had long pressed them to do.

This policy prompted Israel to take a series of steps which struck some observers as bold and others as fool-hardy: to the Palestinians it offered a state, complete with Jerusalem as its capital and sovereignty over the Temple Mount. To the Syrians, it offered full control over the Golan Heights. To Lebanon, it not only offered but actually carried out a complete and unilateral withdrawal of Israeli forces from the southern part of that country in May 2000. These concessions won Israel in return precisely nothing. Reaching out a hand of friendship won not Arab acceptance but ever-increasing demands for more Israeli concessions. Palestinians and Syrians disdained successive Israeli offers, always demanding more. Lebanese took everything Israel did and made more demands.

Worse, the jaw-dropping array of Israeli concessions actually increased Arab and Muslim hostility. When the Oslo process, as that episode of diplomacy is called, began in 1993, Israel was feared and respected by its enemies, who were beginning to recognize Israel as a fact of life and reluctantly giving up their efforts to destroy it. But those efforts revived as Arabs watched Israel forsake its security and its religious sanctities, overlook the breaking of solemn promises, and make empty threats. The impression was of an Israel desperate to extricate itself from further conflict.

What Israelis saw as far-sighted magnanimity came across as weakness and demoralization. Combined with other sources of Arab confidence—especially demographic growth and resurgent faith—this led to a surge in anti-Zionist ambitions and rekindled the hopes of destroying the "Zionist entity." Steps intended to calm the Palestinians instead heightened their ambitions, their fury, and their violence. For all its good will and soul-searching, Israel now faces a higher threat of all-out war than at any time in decades. No doubt that is why Sharon was elected by so wide a margin. Land-for-peace contained a plethora of errors, but the two most fundamental were economic. One overestimated Israeli power, the other misunderstood Arab aspirations.

First, the Oslo process assumed that Israel, by virtue of its economic boom and formidable arsenal, is so strong that it can unilaterally choose to close down its century-old conflict with the Arabs. Israel's GDP is nearly $100 billion a year and the Palestinians' is about $3 billion; Israel's per-capita income of $16,000 is slightly higher than Spain's, while the Syrian per-capita income of about $800 compares to that of the Republic of Congo. The Israel Defense Forces deploy the finest aircraft, tanks, and other materiel that money can buy; the Palestinian police force has rudimentary weapons.

This materiel strength, it turns out, does not permit Israel to impose its will on the Arabs. In part, it cannot do this because the Arabs initiated the conflict and have continued it; only they, not the Israelis, can end it. The key decisions of war and peace have always been made in Cairo, Damascus, and Baghdad, not in Jerusalem and Tel Aviv.

However formidable Israel's strength is in planes and tanks, its enemies are developing military strategies that either go lower (to civil unrest and terrorism, as in the recent Palestinian violence against Israel) or higher (to weapons of mass destruction, as in the Iraqi threat).

Finally, a high income or a mighty arsenal are not as important as will and morale; software counts more than hardware. In this respect, Israelis do not impress their opponents. In the words of philosopher Yoram Hazony, Israelis are "an exhausted people, confused and without direction."

Loud announcements for all to hear that Israelis are sick of their conflict with the Arabs—how they loath reserve military duty that extends
into middle age for men, the high military spending, the deaths of soldiers,
and the nagging fear of terrorism—do not inspire fear. How can an "exhausted people" hope to impose its will on enemies?

Thus is Israel's hope to coerce its enemies illusory.

A second assumption behind the Oslo diplomacy was that enhanced
economic opportunity would shift Arab attention from war to more constructive pursuits. The logic makes intuitive sense: satisfy reasonable claims
so the Palestinians, Syrians, and Lebanese can look beyond anti-Zionism
to improve their standard of living. If they only had a nice apartment and
a late-model car, the thinking went, their ardor for destroying Israel would
diminish. There is little evidence for this expectation. As shown by the
Arab readiness to accept economic hardship in the pursuit of political aims,
politics usually trumps economics. The Syrian government has for decades
accepted economic paralysis as the price of staying in power.

More dramatic is Palestinian refusal to give up the "right of return." To
fend off Palestinian claims to territory and buildings abandoned by their
ancestors in Israel over fifty years ago, the idea was sometimes bruited of
buying them off, in return for giving up of a distant and seemingly im-
practical aspiration. No deal. A reporter in Baqaa, a Palestinian camp in
Jordan, recently found no one willing to take cash in return for forgoing
claims to Palestine. As one middle-aged woman put it: "We will not sell
our [ancestral] land for all the money in the world. We are Palestinians
and we'll remain Palestinians. We don't want compensation, we want our
homeland." The owner of a pharmacy concurred, adding, "Even if Arafat
agreed to compensation, we as Palestinians can't agree to it."

Israelis had devised an elegant push-pull theory of diplomacy: between
Israeli strength and Arab hopes for a better future, they figured the Arabs
would find themselves compelled to shut down the long anti-Zionist campaign. Both assumptions, however sensible sounding, were dead wrong.

In this, the Oslo process belonged to a tradition of failed diplomacy that
relies on granting an opponent some of what he wants in the hope that this
will render him less hostile. It did not work for Neville Chamberlain with
Hitler; nor for Richard Nixon with Brezhnev. The Israelis offered far more
than either of these and ended up with even less.

OCCUPATION AND ANTISEMITISM

Jerome Slater

ALMOST ALL JEWS OF MY GENERATION, coming of age in America in the 1930s and 1940s, personally experienced antisemitism, thought of themselves as passionate Zionists, and rejoiced at the establishment of the State of Israel and its 1948 and 1967 victories over its Arab enemies. Indeed, following three years as an antisubmarine warfare destroyer officer in the U.S. Navy in the late 1950s, I volunteered my services to the Israeli Navy, should the need arise.

I say all this as a partial explanation for the depth of disillusion and outrage that I and so many other Jews feel over what we regard as the Israeli betrayal of the humanism and liberal values of the Jewish tradition, especially in its relationship with the Palestinians. Sadly, most Israelis and many American Jews feel no such disillusion, partially because they remain ignorant—or rather, in many cases, they willfully *choose* to remain ignorant—of the real Israeli-Palestinian story, and partially because their focus on historical antisemitism and Jewish impotence is so deep-rooted that they are simply impervious to new realities.

Thus, one of the abiding themes in contemporary Zionist discourse is a portrayal of the Jews as having been powerless and therefore vulnerable to periodic outbursts of murderous antisemitism. An interesting example of this account has recently been developed by Harvard Jewish Studies Professor Ruth Wisse, who makes a powerful case that the historic vulnerability of the Jewish people and the catastrophes this vulnerability have repeatedly engendered are the consequence of three factors: the ideological antisemitism of the masses, the high visibility and achievements of small Jewish minorities scattered in many different countries throughout the diaspora, and the essential powerlessness of the Jews, whose position and very lives were entirely dependent on the protection of governments whose power or pro-Jewish policies could change at any moment.

The real point of Wisse's historical argument is to provide the foundation for her assessment of the Arab-Israeli conflict from 1948 until today, and to support her conclusion that Israeli concessions to the "Arabs"—by which she mainly means the Palestinians—would be taken as signs of weaknesses and therefore an invitation to disaster.

Wisse's account of the Arab-Israeli conflict ignores all the findings of the Israeli new history and simply repeats the now-discredited standard mythology. In 1947 Israel accepted the UN compromise plan, the partition of Palestine. But "the Arabs" turned it down, causing the 1948 war. Their defeat in this war did not lead them to the conclusion that they had to accept the new reality of an independent Jewish state, for they were convinced they would reconquer Palestine in time. Indeed, she writes, the subsequent Israeli record of "visible achievement" combined with "a demonstrated ideological disinclination to aggress" made the Jews an even more inviting target.

In the view that Wisse represents so clearly, then, the root cause of Israel's predicament is its powerlessness, along with Arab hatred that (by obvious implication) has had nothing to do with actual Israeli behavior but can only be explained by an a priori antisemitism.

Even Palestinian nationalism is explained by Wisse in this manner. Instead of accepting that the goal of Palestinian nationalism, like all other nationalist movements—including, of course, the Zionist movement—has been to create an independent state of their own, Wisse asserts that "the Palestinians are the first people whose nationalism consists *primarily* of opposition to the Jews." Similarly, she insists: "It is clear from the political behavior of the Arab countries that the desire to secure a Palestinian homeland has been merely the excuse, not the reason for anti-Zionism, a sentiment which grows arguably stronger as Israeli concessions reconfirm the image of the accommodating Jew." The position of Israel today is therefore no different from Jews in the diaspora: "a no-fail target."

The conclusion, of course, follows: Israel must make no concessions to the Arabs, who would only redouble their efforts to destroy Israel. Since peace is a mere "fantasy," Israel must be prepared to indefinitely fight war after war, pending some future (but evidently unlikely) profound shift in Arab attitudes.

What is most troubling about this argument is not that a relatively obscure professor holds it but precisely that it accurately represents a worldview that has become part of the popular lore of the Jewish people, making
it very difficult for us to make rational assessments of our situation in the
early 21st century, especially on how to best achieve security for Israel,
the Jewish people, and indeed the world as a whole.

To begin with, the Wisse or popular view of the course of the Arab-
Israeli conflict is not merely at variance with the demonstrable facts, it
turns them completely inside-out, simply ignoring—whether out of ignorance, ideological blindness, or simple disingenuousness—more than twenty
years of meticulous Israeli historical and political scholarship as well as
investigative journalism.

True, many scholars today acknowledge that there are antisemitic references in some classic Islamic texts—just as there are anti-Muslim references in some of the most revered Jewish thinkers of the past 1,300 years.
Moreover, both because early Zionism became aligned with British colo-
nialism in the Mideast and because some Jews who lived in Arab lands
sought to ally themselves with European imperialism, Arab anticolonial-
ism in the early 20th century included an element of antisemitism.

Even so, in Palestine itself the Jewish and Arab communities lived in
relatively peaceful coexistence until fears of a huge onslaught of European
Jewish immigration led many Palestinians to believe that Western colo-
nialism was going to solve Europe's "Jewish problem" at the expense of
the Palestinians. It was this Palestinian fear of losing their political rights,
land, and society to a European Jewish influx that led to the conflict between the Yishuv and the Arab peoples of Palestine.

The Arab-Israeli Conflict, 1947–1949

The demythologized history of the Arab-Israeli conflict challenges the
standard version in a number of ways. To begin with, Ben-Gurion and
other leading Zionists did not truly accept the UN partition in any meaningful sense. On the contrary, the historical evidence is incontrovertible
that Ben-Gurion agreed to the UN plan as a necessary tactical step that
would later be reversed: "when we become a strong power after the establishment of the state." Later, Ben-Gurion told the Zionist congress, "we
will abolish partition and spread throughout all of Palestine."[1]

And that is exactly what happened. Far from having "a disinclination
to aggress," Israel under Ben-Gurion, Begin, Dayan and others sought to
expand to the limits of Biblical Palestine, which in their conception included all of Jerusalem, the West Bank, the Gaza strip, substantial parts

of Jordan, southern Lebanon, the Golan Heights and other parts of southern Syria, and Egypt's Sinai peninsula. Typically, Ben-Gurion made no bones about it: "Before the founding of the state our main interest was self-defense. But now the issue at hand is conquest, not self-defense. As for setting the borders—it's an open-ended matter."[2]

As for the attitude of the Palestinians toward the Israelis, it would be helpful to keep in mind some incontrovertible historical facts. To begin with, the Arabs of Palestine were the overwhelming majority for recent centuries, and had been promised by the British that they would gain political sovereignty over it after World War I. To be sure, the Jews had a claim on Palestine as well, a claim that certainly became more powerful after the Holocaust irrefutably demonstrated the need for a Jewish state, for which by the 1930s there was no alternative to Palestine. Even so, it is not hard to understand Palestinian anger at the loss of their political rights, without the necessity of introducing unreasoning, a priori antisemitism as the explanation.

Secondly, even before the Arab invasion in the spring of 1948, and continuing well after Israel won the war, some 600,000–700,000 Palestinians were deliberately driven out of their country, their homes, and their villages, in what prominent Israeli and American Jewish historians (e.g., Meron Benvenisti and Ian Lustick) are beginning to acknowledge was nothing less than "ethnic cleansing." Emotionally loaded as that term is, it is justified by the Israeli psychological warfare, economic pressures, artillery bombardments, political assassinations, terrorist attacks, and even massacres that forced the Palestinians to flee.

To be sure, the Israelis had their reasons. From early in the Jewish influx into Palestine after 1917, Zionist leaders realized that it would be hard to build a secure Jewish state with a large, resentful Arab minority—which one day, because of the higher Arab birth rate, might even become a majority. Therefore, they began discussing various ways in which the Palestinians could be "transferred" (the preferred Zionist euphemism) out of the country—including, if necessary, by force.

To the general demographic and security problem was added the desire to find space, homes, and productive land for the post-Holocaust Jewish immigrants. These were indeed serious problems. Even so, it does not follow that the utterly ruthless methods by which the transfer mentality was implemented in the Palestinian expulsion in 1947–1949 were justified. And still less does it make it difficult to understand why the Palestinians might hate the Israelis.

It is true that in the aftermath of the 1948 war, hundreds of thousands of Jewish citizens either fled or were driven out of such Arab countries as

Tunisia, Morocco, Algeria, Iraq, and Iran, and some regard this as establishing a refugee symmetry that, in effect, cancels out Palestinian refugee claims against Israel. While it is easy to understand the emotional force behind this argument, especially by those Israeli Jews or their descendants who experienced Arab antisemitism, it is hard to accept the current implications. The symmetry is largely a false one, because the Palestinian Arabs were not responsible for the actions of the Arab states, and there is no justice in making them pay for it.

The standard mythology of the Arab-Israeli conflict also oversimplifies the motivations, policies, and actions of the Arab states in 1948, in asserting that there was an overwhelming, unprovoked Arab aggression which could only have been motivated by fanatical antisemitism, and which was intended to destroy Israel, an outcome that was averted only because of the David-vs.-Goliath Israeli defeat of the invaders.

To begin with, the Arab intervention in Palestine was far too ill-coordinated and small to destroy Israel—the Israelis both outmanned and soon outgunned the combined total of the Arab armies, which was only about 13,000 men. Secondly, it cannot be excluded that the intervention was also at least in part a reaction to the Jewish massacres and expulsions of the Palestinians, as well as the Israeli seizure of territory outside the UN-designated boundaries. Even if it were true that the autocratic Arab states of Egypt, Syria, and Jordan cared nothing about the fate of the Palestinians, they could not completely ignore the emotional response of the Arab masses to the 1947–48 events in Palestine.

None of this is to deny that at the time and for many years afterward the Israelis and, for that matter, the Jewish diaspora around the world had plenty of reason to fear that they were being attacked by powerful countries fanatically determined on their destruction. In the immediate aftermath of the Holocaust, how could they have felt differently? Even so, more than fifty years after the event, serious historians cannot avoid the responsibility of correcting the historical record that is now much clearer—or, at least, much more complex—than it appeared to be in 1948.

The Arab-Israeli Conflict, 1967–Present

In June 1967, Egypt and Syria again seemingly threatened Israel's existence when Egypt violated the 1957 agreement under which Israel had returned the Sinai peninsula to Egypt (captured by Israel in the 1956 war), in return for its demilitarization and the stationing of UN peacekeeping forces there. When Nasser forced the removal of the UN forces, moved his own armies toward the Israeli borders, and filled the airwaves with threatening rhetoric about solving the problem of Israel once and for all, the Israeli public feared for its existence and the government decided on a preemptive strike against both Israel and Syria.

It is now known that neither the U.S. government nor the Israeli military command shared the Israeli public's fears, for they did not expect Egypt or Syria to attack, and they expected Israel to win if there was an attack. Even so, there remains a good case that the Israeli preemptive strike against Egypt, though not against the Golan Heights, was justified. However, if the preemptive war was justified, the subsequent expansion of Israel and the hardening of its terms for peace was not.

After Israel captured the Golan Heights, the Gaza strip, Jerusalem, and the West Bank in 1967, it established an occupation that is still in existence. While there is a reasonable argument that the Israeli expansion from the 1947 UN-established boundaries to its post-1948 boundaries was a response to genuine security needs, that cannot be said about the continued occupation of the post-1967 territories. On the contrary, the West Bank and East Jerusalem are security liabilities; the primary motivation for their seizure was ideological, as the terms "Judea and Samaria" make evident.

Immediately following the war, another 100,000 or so Palestinians were expelled, either from Jerusalem into the West Bank or out of the West Bank into Lebanon, Syria and Jordan, and the process of "creating facts on the ground" began: the tenfold expansion of the boundaries of "Jerusalem"; the building of Jewish neighborhoods in Arab East Jerusalem; the use of economic and administrative pressures to force out the Palestinians in Jerusalem; the building of Jewish settlements, some of them by the most fanatical elements in Israeli society, throughout Gaza and the West Bank, the openly declared purpose of which was to prevent the Palestinians from ever establishing an independent state in those areas; the seizure of the water aquifers of the West Bank and the use of that water to serve Jewish rather than Palestinian needs; the use of various means of economic pressures and collective punishment to suppress Palestinian resistance; the ongoing demolitions of Palestinian homes, destruction of orchards, and land confiscation, either to make way for Israeli roads and settlements, or simply as punishment; and the violent suppression of the first and second Palestinian Intifadas or anticolonial revolutions, including political assassinations and undercover death squads to liquidate the activists.

Might all this have something to do with Palestinian antisemitism? To acknowledge this reality, of course, does not mean that one should not react against some of the crude antisemitic stereotypes and insults that continue to appear in Palestinian textbooks and newspapers. That said, one must also take note of a recent major Israeli study that found that antisemitism in Palestinian textbooks is actually *declining*—perhaps even in contrast to anti-Arab racism that often appears in some Israeli newspapers, synagogues, schools, and public discourse.

In the end, of course, a true Israeli-Palestinian reconciliation and political settlement will require the removal of both Palestinian and Jewish racism, whatever their causes.

But it was not racism, but the displacement of the Palestinian people in 1948, that led to the creation of the PLO. In the early years after its formation, the PLO was clearly maximalist, insisting on the complete "liberation" of all of Palestine, which it sought to achieve by guerrilla warfare and outright terrorism. However, by the late 1960s this rejectionist position began gradually giving way to a willingness to consider a two-state diplomatic solution with Israel. Nothing came of it, because Israel ignored the many indications of an emerging Palestinian pragmatism, refusing even to talk with the PLO, let alone compromise with it.

Nonetheless, the PLO's position continued to evolve, accelerated in part by the defeat of military fantasies that had led it to imagine that it could launch a liberation struggle from Lebanon. But although defeated in Lebanon and relegated to a relatively powerless position in Tunis in the mid-1980s, it still articulated the desire for homeland and national self-determination that persisted among a large number of Palestinians. In 1988 it finally officially proposed a detailed two-state solution. Under the terms of the PLO commitment, a Palestinian state in the West Bank and Gaza, with East Jerusalem as its capital, would agree to be largely demilitarized, would accept the stationing of international peacekeeping forces along its borders with Israel, would end terrorism and all forms of attack on Israel from its territory, would enter into some kind of confederal arrangement with Jordan while refraining from alliances with Arab rejectionist states, and in all probability would agree to a settlement of the refugee problem on the basis of a token return to Israel, combined with large-scale international economic compensation of the refugees and their resettlement in the new Palestinian state and in other countries.

Under American pressure, [Israeli Prime Minister] Shamir agreed to U.S.-mediated talks with the Palestinians at Madrid in 1991, but no progress was made; as Shamir later cheerfully admitted, "I would have conducted negotiations for ten years, and in the meantime we would have added half a million souls in Judea and Samaria."

The first meaningful agreement between Israel and the PLO was the Oslo Accords of 1993, the terms of which were the mutual recognition of

Israel and the PLO and a five-year transitional period under which Israel would gradually withdraw its troops and administrative structure from the major Palestinian population centers. At the end of the transitional period, there would be a permanent settlement. In turn, Arafat promised to end anti-Israeli violence in the territories and suppress all forms of terrorism, even agreeing to direct cooperation with Israeli security forces.

Although the Oslo accords did not quite specify that a permanent settlement must include the establishment of an independent Palestinian state, there was no doubt that this was the universal expectation of the Palestinians, the United States, the international community, and indeed of the Israeli government and public opinion. The more serious flaw of Oslo was that it postponed until the final status negotiations all the other difficult issues: the borders of the Palestinian state, the Jerusalem issue, the disposition of the Israeli settlements, and the refugee issue.

Arafat was severely criticized by many Palestinians for these gaping loopholes in the Oslo agreements, and in retrospect the critics were right. Yet, because there was no balance of power between Israel and the PLO, the Israelis held all the cards. It is hard to see what practical options Arafat had at the time, other than to hope that the Israeli position on these issues would soften, so long as he kept the peace in the areas he controlled.

What perhaps could not be foreseen was the extent to which the Rabin, Peres, and—of course—Netanyahu governments remained committed to a hard-line position that, in effect, would have prevented any truly viable independent Palestinian state from being created.

In the next few years, Rabin and Peres violated both the spirit and the letter of the Oslo agreements. In October 1995 Rabin announced before the Knesset his detailed plans for a permanent settlement: there would be no return to the pre-1967 borders; a united Jerusalem, including settlements in East Jerusalem and suburbs, would remain under exclusive Israeli sovereignty; most of the settlements in the West Bank and Gaza would stay in place under Israeli sovereignty; a wide-ranging series of Israeli-only new roads would be built throughout the territories, to ensure free access to and military control over the settlements; Israel would retain settlements and military bases in the Jordan River valley, deep inside Palestinian territory; and the Palestinians would receive an "entity" that would be the "home to most of the Palestinian residents living in the Gaza Strip and the West Bank. . . . We would like this to be less than a state."

Over the next five years, Israel implemented Rabin's conception of peace with the Palestinians, the result of which would have been that even if Israel had finally agreed to a Palestinian "state," the Palestinians would have ended up with a series of isolated enclaves on less than 50% of the West

Bank and Gaza, cut off from each other and surrounded by Israeli settlers and military bases, and with little or no control of their water resources.

From Rabin to the present, Jewish settlement throughout the West Bank and in an ever-expanding "Jerusalem" has continued, accompanied by massive roadbuilding, often requiring the confiscation and destruction of Palestinian homes and orchards. Even the letter of the Oslo accords has been disregarded by all Israeli governments since 1993: the scheduled series of Israeli withdrawals from the West Bank was repeatedly delayed and has still not been completed; many Palestinian prisoners that Israel had committed to release remain in jail; the promised Palestinian air field in Gaza has been delayed; detailed provisions requiring free Palestinian passageway between Gaza and the West Bank, as well as free access of people, vehicles and goods within the territories, have often been interrupted by Israeli closures that caused great personal and economic hardship; Palestinians living outside Jerusalem are often prevented from attending services at the Muslim mosques on the Temple Mount; and tax collections and money from the sale of Palestinian goods that was to have been transferred by Israel to the Palestinian authority have been frequently held up.

Yet, until the Al-Aqsa Intifada in late 2000, with the exceptions of brief periods following the Goldstein massacres in Hebron and the 1996 Peres-authorized Israeli assassination of a Palestinian activist accused of terrorism, the Palestinians complied with their obligation to end violence and terrorism, and the Palestinian security forces under Arafat worked hand in hand with Israeli security forces, often in joint patrols, to identify and jail extremists and suspected terrorists, some of them from lists drawn up by the Israelis.

Barak and the Peace Process

By the time Barak took office in 1999, not only had Israel's actions (rather than those of the Palestinians) subverted the Oslo process, but they had also gravely undermined Arafat's position among the Palestinians, who were now in worse shape—politically, economically, and psychologically—then they had been when the agreements were signed in 1993.

Barak's performance in office was so strange that it does not seem an exaggeration to term it schizoid. On the one hand, it is true that at Camp David he went considerably further than any other Israeli prime minister in making concessions toward the Palestinians. On the other hand, not only did his proposals still fall considerably short of what was necessary to make peace, in both his rhetoric and actions he continuously subverted his own peace plan.

The general perception of the Camp David summit negotiations in late 2000 is that Barak made an unprecedented offer to the Palestinians, far more generous than anything the Israelis had ever been prepared to concede, only to be met by a shocking if not perverse rejection by Arafat, who was not only unwilling to compromise but rewarded Barak by ordering a violent uprising at just the moment when the chances for peace had never been greater.

There is just enough plausibility in this narrative to have initially persuaded even the Israeli peace camp that they had naively misunderstood the real intentions of the Palestinian leadership, and that Israel really did lack "a partner for peace." But this disillusion with the Palestinians quickly gave way to a more sober reassessment among serious Israeli analysts, the great majority of whom now are far more critical of the Barak proposals and have a much greater empathic understanding of the plight of Arafat and the Palestinians.

The main lines of Barak's unwritten proposals at Camp David were that Israel would agree to a demilitarized Palestinian state in Gaza and about 90% of the West Bank (later increased to about 92–94%), with sovereignty over (and its capital in) those parts of East Jerusalem that still were Palestinian. The Jewish neighborhoods in East Jerusalem would remain under Israeli sovereignty, as would most of the Old City of Jerusalem, especially what the Jews call the Temple Mount, the Arabs Haram al-Sharif. Israel would annex 8–10% of the West Bank along the old 1967 border, within which 80% of the settlers were located; the fate of the remaining 20%, most of whom were the most hardcore ideological Jewish fundamentalists, located in the West Bank and Gaza heartland, was left unclear: whether they would be withdrawn, whether they would be left in place to decide on their own whether they wished to return to Israel or become Palestinian citizens, or whether they would be only nominally under Palestinian sovereignty while continuing under Israeli military protection.

In exchange for the Israeli annexations, the Palestinians would receive some Israeli land in the Negev desert adjacent to the Gaza Strip—though this land, aside from being barren, would be only about 10–15% of the size of the Israeli-annexed areas. In addition, Israel would retain troops, early warning stations, and military bases in the Jordan River Valley and mountain passes, perhaps as part of an international peacekeeping force, for a transitional period of about twelve years.

There were no detailed proposals on how the West Bank water sources would be controlled, other than an Israeli proposal to work with the Palestinians in developing desalinization plants and other sources of new water. However, the very silence of the Israeli proposals, together with the fact that the proposed Israeli annexations included most of the West Bank water aquifers—which was precisely why the settlements had been put there in the first place—made it obvious that Israel would continue its control over most of the West Bank water.

Finally, while Israel might agree to the return of about 10,000 Palestinian refugees to Israel under a "family reunification" plan, there would be no general Palestinian right of return, and Israel would not even acknowledge that it bore any political or moral responsibility for the expulsions of 1948 and 1967.

Thus, while it is true that Barak went further than any previous Israeli leader, he didn't go nearly far enough. In the end, there would have been a non-viable, impoverished Palestinian state, with Israel in control of most of Jerusalem and its suburbs, with Gaza separated from the West Bank and the West Bank itself divided into at least three different enclaves separated from each other by Israeli-controlled settlements, military bases, and roads, with the Israeli army continuing indefinitely to occupy the Jordan River Valley, and with Israel refusing to even acknowledge that it bore any responsibility for the refugee problem, let alone allowing more than a token number of refugees to return to Israel.

It was the perception not only of the Palestinians but of the rest of the world that Oslo essentially was an agreement under which the Palestinians officially abandoned any claim to all of Palestine and recognized Israel and its right to be a Jewish state which gave special privileges to its Jewish inhabitants, in return for the creation of an independent Palestinian state in the West Bank and Gaza, with the most minimal border changes, and its capital in Palestinian-controlled East Jerusalem.

But the subsequent negotiations turned out not to be over the pace of these changes, but whether they would ever be truly implemented—and this was nearly as true under three Labor governments as it was under Netanyahu. When the Palestinians finally exploded with rage last fall, Arafat had few options. In the abstract, perhaps he might have chosen the course of nonviolent resistance, following the examples of Gandhi, Martin Luther King, and Mandela. On the other hand, even if he had been so inclined personally, it is doubtful that he had the power or authority to impose such a demanding strategy on his own public, and there is also plenty of reason to doubt that it would have moved the Israelis to concessions they were clearly unwilling to make: a return of Israel to the pre–June 4, 1967, lines (with some minor and equitable territorial trades that would allow the incorporation of some Israeli settlements into Israel); the complete Israeli military withdrawal from all the occupied territories; the dismantling of the remaining settlements, including the Jewish neighborhoods in East Jerusalem; the turning over of most or all of the West Bank water aquifers to the Palestinians; Palestinian sovereignty over their mosques on the Temple Mount; a fair and equitable partition of Jerusalem; and at least some kind of fair solution to the refugee problem.

Since there was no chance at all that Barak or the Israeli public would agree to such terms, a strategy of nonviolence would have allowed the Israelis to continue "creating facts": expanding the settlements, continuing the land confiscations and roadbuilding, solidifying Jewish control over East Jerusalem, continuing the economic punishment of the Palestinian people, and so on.

The use of violence, even in a just cause, is bound to be highly problematic, both for the obvious moral reasons and also on practical grounds. That is the case for the present Palestinian revolution, not least because it has produced Sharon. Yet, it is an issue over which reasonable people can and do disagree, and there is no gainsaying the dilemma: after all, if it had not been for the first Palestinian uprising, the Intifada of the late 1980s, Israel would have refused even to meet with the Palestinians, let alone make any concessions to them.

Conclusion

Palestinian outrage or even hatred of the Israelis is not a consequence of a generalized, a priori "antisemitism," but of the Zionist dispossession of the Palestinians and over fifty years of Israeli injustice, repression, and violence. Furthermore, it has not been Israeli "powerlessness" that has been the problem, but precisely the opposite. Blinded by their ideology and mythology, the Israelis have not been significantly constrained in their treatment of the Palestinians by considerations of justice or morality. In such situations, constraints will exist only when dictated by self-interest, meaning the presence of countervailing power: precisely what has been missing in the conflict between the Palestinian David and the Israeli Goliath.

Even under the questionable assumption that the Palestinian uprising today is the result of Arafat's strategy rather than simply an uncontrollable explosion from below, the goal clearly is to restore some kind of balance of power as well as to convince the Israelis that they cannot simply impose their will on the Palestinians without paying an unacceptable cost to their own self-interests.

Perhaps the *Palestinian* strategy, if there is one, will eventually work, perhaps not. Sharon may set back the cause of peace irretrievably, but it is just as likely that eventually the Israelis will indeed decide that their own peace and security requires concessions to the Palestinians beyond any they have made so far.

In any case, whether or not one agrees with Palestinian tactics, their turn to revolution and armed struggle cannot be explained by antisemitism but by over half a century of Israeli repression. Still less can it be attributed to Israeli powerlessness, for the problem today is the absence of countervailing power to constrain Israel. Ruth Wisse and the Israelis would do well to remember Lord Acton's brilliant aphorism: Power tends to corrupt, and absolute power tends to corrupt absolutely.

NOTES

1. Quoted in Benny Morris, *Birth of the Palestinian Refugee Problem* (New York: Cambridge University Press, 1987), p. 24.

2. From the 1949 Israeli archives, quoted by Tom Segev, *The First Israelis,* Arlen Neal Weinstein, English language editor, (New York: Henry Holt, 1998), p. 6.

A NOVELIST'S OPTIMISM

RECLAIMING THE JEWISH TRADITION

Aharon Appelfeld

I CAME TO ISRAEL AFTER THE HOLOCAUST. I was in a concentration camp (Trannistria) and then, after, I hid in the woods. I was fourteen years old. I came as an orphan with no language, no parents, no education, nothing. Israel became my home. And this was the experience of a hundred thousand children who came to Israel. We would have been criminals in Europe—in Israel we became human beings. This was something Israel gave us, and we will never forget it. It is something very deep and important to me.

I have been living in Israel for fifty-one years, and most of my writing is about Europe. I am deeply affiliated with the Jews in Europe, and with Diaspora Jews. I am a Jew and feel myself to be Jewish. I'm an Israeli Jew but first a Jew.

One of the tragedies of Israel is that the secular Zionists misunderstood the depths of Jewishness. When I came to Israel, the illusion was that we were going to "create the new Jew." But how can you change a nation, its characters, its mentality? The tragedy was that ideological secular Israelis wanted to change the character of a nation and that is impossible to do. Moreover, what was so bad about being Jewish? Why did we need to change? There was a general conception among secular Zionists that the Jew was too weak, too spiritual, and that our real task should be to be more like other nations. The Zionists said we had walked willingly to the slaughter; but we had been slaughtered not because of our deficiencies, but because we were surrounded by barbarians. If Jews had really been weak, they would never have survived for two thousand years in this kind of European circumstance.

Jews in the Diaspora were, generally speaking, very courageous people, because they lived under conditions of threat and neither converted nor ran away. So there was no fundamental need to transform who we were as a people. In fact, who we were as a people was something to be proud of. We were a spiritual nation, and we should be a spiritual nation, and spirit should be at the center of our lives, and classical Judaism should be at the center of our lives. Can you imagine if French people, or even Germans, were to say we don't want to be French or German anymore? This form of Zionism was a kind of self-hatred. It came from the Haskallah (Jewish Enlightenment), but was accepted because of self-hatred. This self-hatred was a product of our oppression, a way in which we slowly began to accept the concepts of our oppressor.

Today, many secular Israelis understand that this was a mistake. Many people have turned to religion, and some to a nationalist religion, because the secular life in Israel that was so rich in the beginning became empty. Now Israeli culture is struggling about what we are going to be, what kind of Jews we are going to be; how we are going to absorb and reclaim our long cultural heritage. On the one side, we have liberal secularists who are mostly anti-religious, and on the other side we have a religious community that is slowly becoming anti-liberal and anti-state.

The long Jewish tradition in Israel and the Diaspora is very dear to me—both the religious and secular traditions are very dear to me. I believe that the Conservative movement can make a serious contribution to Israel, adding back into Israel the original spirit of B'nai Akiba, with its combination of Torah and *derech eretz* (common decency and sensitivity to others).

Actually, I am optimistic. I have a feeling that something new and good will emerge in Israel to heal our present situation. I know my friends will find me naïve. But I went through Hell and I remain an optimist. I feel that in Israel there is a thirst for Jewish spirituality, a real spirituality that would provide a Jewish meaning to people's lives. From that will emerge a Jew who doesn't hate his heritage, doesn't hate himself, and who will be good to his community and his surroundings. Israel could then become a Jewish state. I don't mean a halachic state; I mean a state that reflects the cultural, religious, and historical wisdom during the past two hundred years since the French revolution. Mendelsohn is part of our experience, Freud, Wittgenstein, Herzl, Marx—all these are a part of our experience that must be reintegrated into our life. We cannot become halachic Jews again, but we should not become assimilated into the dominant values of the West either.

FROM BOOKING PASSAGE

Sidra DeKoven Ezrahi

"Our Homeland, the Text"

("The road sucks us in and thus disappears. . . . Ink shrinks
space down to the letter. You will print the earth in its split atten-
tion. You will print the sky in its diffuse impossibility. Rectangles
of grass or sand, or blue or clouds. The rays of the sun are pen-
holders which night gorges with ink."—Reb Adal)

Edmond Jabès, Le Retour au Livre

Edmond Jabès is one of the modern architects and exemplars of text-centeredness as an exilic priority: "Gradually I realized that the Jew's real place is the book. In the book he questions himself, in the book he has his freedom, which has been forbidden him everywhere. . . . Moses, in the act of breaking the tablets, gave the word a human origin."[1]

But after 1948, the book has once again to compete with the soil as center of gravity. Those who continue to dwell in the book when an earthly home has become available to the Jews cannot, according to this reading, partake of its materiality: their wandering consists in keeping their distance from the Land, in remaining loyal to the ever-deferred promise.

George Steiner carries this argument to its logical extreme in his polemic with the "territorial imperative"; he has become the most contentious postwar exponent of exile as both the necessary condition of and the catalyst for that particular Jewish prerogative of being, "unhoused" in the world and "at home in the word." Arguing for "our homeland, the text," Steiner writes:

> Heine's phrase is exactly right: "das aufgeschriebene Vaterland." The "land of his fathers," the *patrimoine,* is the script. In its doomed immanence, in its attempt to immobilize the text in a substantive, architectural space, the Davidic and Solomonic Temple may have been an erratum, a misreading of the transcendent mobility of the text. . . . The deeper truth of unhousedness, of an at-homeness in the word, . . . are the legacy of the Prophets and of the keepers of the text. . . . When the text *is* the homeland, even when it is rooted only in the exact remembrance and seeking of a handful of wanderers, nomads of the word, it cannot be extinguished.[2]

Steiner does not limit the Jewish "homeland" to canonic Jewish texts or to texts housed in Jewish languages. "Each seeking out of a moral, philosophic, positive verity, each text rightly established and expounded is an *aliyah,* a homecoming of Judaism to itself and to its keeping of the books," he says. Invoking the highly charged language of '*aliyah* to the Torah while blocking its modern Zionist connotations, Steiner is polemically affirming the primacy of rites of reading over rites of pilgrimage and settlement on holy land. He regards Mandelstam, Kafka, and Celan as latter-day prophets and any place where there is a library as an "'Israel' of truth-seeking."[3]

The literacy of the exile becomes, by these lights, a kind of semiotic privilege through which the library as sacred center and reading as an act of devotion and deciphering can be extended infinitely. It is not only specific books, and not only books, that are read, but the world itself. The metaphor of nature as a book and of wandering as the way to "read" it is at least as old as the Latin Middle Ages; from Paracelsus, for whom the "whole earth is a book or a library in which the pages are turned with our feet, which must be used 'pilgrimly,'" it reappears in every age with its emphasis and premise of legibility slightly different.[4] In many border crossings, the exile claims to comprehend the book of nature as well as the social contract with a different intelligence. Learning to read the inscriptions of nature, rather than of the self into nature, to "spell the landscape" as an intelligible text,[5] would then be a *deciphering but not a proprietary or political act.* The travelers on the road, like the fingers on the page, trace in their meanderings the imprints of a universally accessible universe.

When the journey across space is a pilgrimage to a holy site, however, then the sentence constructed or construed is more likely to resonate with that *other* book, the Good Book whose inscriptions of natural phenomena are infused with specific, culturally tendentious meanings.[6] The religious imagination reconciles Scriptures with the Book of Nature, while creating in the very idea of the book room for a third—*human*—form of imagining, of authorship, and of authority.[7]

Granted, in its Jewish versions that license implies the diminished or derivative status of local landscapes as well as the diminished status of human authors. The generalization that postbiblical Jews knew more about the flora and fauna of Palestine than about their immediate diasporic environs, that the world in Yiddish literature was "almost devoid of trees" and the "skies practically empty of birds," belongs to the hyperbolic language of the maskilic (Enlightenment) and the Zionist polemic with Jewish culture-in-exile.[8] But while the vernacular worlds are not quite as denatured as such polemicists would have it, the Jewish calendar and classical vocabulary do reflect the relative weight ascribed over time to Palestine as the "real" place, the only place where topography and climate *matter.*

The assignment of status to the Holy Land as center of the earth's blessing and the Bible as its map does not, however, limit God's dwelling to a specific shrine. The Jews living within the broad confines of a postrabbinic monotheism were in "God's country" anywhere. One could even argue that monotheism evolved into a strategy for making the world one's home; the God whose glory fills the earth is simply not to be confined. As *HA*-makom, God is not only *THE* place, but place itself. A rabbinic midrash on "Jacob's pillow" relates to the rock under Jacob's head at Bethel (Gen. 28) as metonymy for the entire Land of Israel—arguably a proprietary, Palestine-centered reading. But Rabbi Shimeon refines this by suggesting that God folded the rock like a notebook or ledger (*pinkas*) and put it under Jacob's head.[9] This reductive image (Eretz Yisrael as text) is striking as a sign of the rabbinic project of creating a viable, portable Jewish civilization in exile through its signifying practices.

In his discussion of Jewish aesthetics, Kalman Bland explores the plastic dimensions of the sacred text through its late medieval sources, a tradition in which "Scripture formally recapitulates sacred, architectural space," in which the Hebrew Bible's tripartite division is "isomorphic" with the Temple itself.[10] In traditions culminating in the Kabbala, time and space become conflated so that the sanctity of place is projected not only onto texts but also onto the rhythm of weekly ritual: The Sabbath becomes a sacred center, analogous to Jerusalem and the Garden of Eden, and the synagogue a miniature temple (*mikdash m'at*), allowing for a regular re-creation of cosmos out of chaos. Time carved out of the quotidian and sanctified as sacred space provides a nonmaterial as well as an ahistorical accommodation or provisional resolution to exile.[11]

So the parameters of the religious Jewish imagination as it developed over the centuries became emancipated from dependence on sovereignty conceived within any geographically specific boundaries. In fact, the position of the Jew as citizen of the cosmopolis, articulated most provocatively in recent times by Steiner and Jabès, becomes a curiosity only when measured against very ancient or very new forms of sedentary life. The idea of *galut* or *golus* as a viable condition in an unredeemed world made it possible over many centuries to establish social and cultural connections that were nonterritorial and nonproprietary. The terms of group survival, the principles of exclusion and inclusion, would be renegotiated at every crisis point in the early development of Jewish collective existence, and the status of major variables—territory and ritual space, genealogy, and faith—would vary as the historical conditions changed.[12] The centrality of "the Book" entails a wide culture of substitution for or imitation of the territorial dimension; in its devotional procedure and performative substitute for Temple rites, it created the rationale and the instruments for a mobile civilization—incorporating, spiritualizing, temporarily superseding, but never entirely effacing the memory and the promise of "Yerushalayim shel mata," of terrestrial Jerusalem as linchpin of the *axis mundi*.

And yet in late-twentieth-century constructions of Jewish memory and imagination, the elevation of textuality or even of temporality as a diasporic privilege based on the traditional Jewish valuation of the book and the calendar tends to camouflage a major shift in the value of means relative to ends, the value of the now-time and this-place relative to the End-of-Time and Ultimacy-of-Place. By turning necessity into a virtue, as it were, latter-day Diasporism challenges the very premise of provisionality as the key to Jewish theodicy and destabilizes the mimetic imagination as a non-absolute marker of place. Steiner's metaphoric Talmud is a text signifying the *vacancy of place* (not the *vacated place*). From a modern point of view, this appears compatible with the character of a religious culture that, in its portable ritual spaces, designates holiness as a systemic (i.e., referentially arbitrary) category:[13] a culture that delineates diaspora in its most fundamental function as the place of replica and imitation—as *imaginative* space. But presented as a kind of textual essentialism, unmoored from

specific sources of authority and codes of faith, Jewish textuality is reduced to a set of gestures or postures, and the Jew becomes simply a
generic social or moral critic, a "reader" of culture. A barricade of books
and poststructuralist claims to life "in the text" may be a good hedge
against the territorialization and fetishization of the Jewish word, but they
often invoke a language that signifies the vacancy of content and displays
the cultural valorization of signifiers without the specific and stable, if distant, referents that licensed cultural mobility.

With the (re)territorialization of the Jewish imagination in the twentieth
century, a radical shift takes place in the relative position of ends and means,
of original and mimetic space, of holy and profane, of ownership and ten-
ancy. If exile is narrative, then to historicize the end of the narrative is to
invite a form of epic closure that threatens the storytelling enterprise itself—
an enterprise that remained alive, like Scheherazade, by suspending endings. Conversely, to claim an absolute place for the exilic imagination is to
privilege *the story* as the *thing itself;* the map for the territory, language without referent;[14] and to regard "nomadic writing" as the inherently Jewish
vocation. The danger of turning scrolls into sacraments by which to conse-
crate the soil is matched by the danger of dissociation, of dissolution, that
has afflicted generations of emancipated Jewish Quixotes.

The relative value of places to the Place as both territorial and divine
locus maintained a tension and an ambiguity throughout a long history of
Jewish journeys, and it is that ambiguity and the new forms it has generated, especially over the last century, that will shape the chapters of this
book. If Land was transfigured into texts-in-exile, then we are examining
how in one context it has begun to come back and "reanimate" the texts—
as if the words were so many custodians or shelters that allowed the elements of a world in ruins to be preserved until such time as it could be
reclaimed—and how, in another context, it retains its status as sacred center, unpossessable, elusive, and generative of an infinity of possible worlds.

Jewish Geography

Jews constructed not only memory temples and Sabbaths out of the ruins
of their material existence but also stories out of the relics of hearths that
were abandoned along the way and were, by definition, remote from the
sacred center. Rahel carried her *teraphim,* her household gods, from place
to place, even when admonished that holiness could not be confined in local
icons and lowercase homelands. But the safest and most enduring hiding
places for the lares and penates of deserted homes were the stories that
contained and superseded them.

In the modern Yiddish and Hebrew fiction that began to appear in the late nineteenth century, the changing status of lowercase and uppercase homelands helped to launch a new constellation of imaginary and actual worlds—encompassing both a fictional universe that more freely experiments with the laws of narrative conventions and an ancient Jewish territory subjecting its returnees to the laws of gravity. The prospect of a resettled Jewish homeland, as it took on political dimensions, also regenerated a notion of original space to which the text culture could return. In the implicit dialectic that ensued between Hebrew and the other Jewish languages, this return, a secularized reflection of the religious vision of reunification with sacred space, would eventually embolden the diasporic imagination of writers from S. Y. Abramovitsh and Sholem Aleichem to Philip Roth to pursue fictional alternatives, mimetic counterparts to the very idea of original, unduplicable space.

By the early twentieth century, the shtetl had become the specific locus of Eastern European Jewish life and imagination; its viability was a function of its presumed ubiquity. The small-town, small-minded Jews in S. Y. Abramovitsh's Yiddish and Hebrew prose compose a static picture animated by the lively narrational skills of Mendele the Bookpeddler, whose mobility is his passport to the future. His Kabtzielites, remote descendants of the Babylonian and Roman exiles, forced by a great "conflagration" to leave their shtetl, hang their rags on a willow or two.[15] No lyres, no songs of Jerusalem, and just enough memory for self-debasement: yet in those very tatters and fragments of royal clothes and royal texts lie the domesticated dimensions of a modern replay of exile and desire.

Sholem Aleichem, in his later Yiddish prose, decontextualizes Kasrilevke, his invented town in the Russian pale of settlement; now weightless like a figure on a Chagall canvas, Kasrilevke reappears on the train, in London, and finally in America. Traveling by train, by ship, by foot, Motl the cantor's son lands with both feet on American soil; only the death of the author would eventually arrest his progress. Over the course of our century, the diasporist cultural paradigm reshuffles old forms and shifts its locus westward. America emerges as a different kind of homeland, as a continent that houses the wayward imagination and the liberal invention of counterlives. America is the site of Sholem Aleichem's most forward-looking, self-created character and the licensing bureau for Philip Roth's most zany diasporist plots.

Most of the Jews of Eastern Europe were, however, headed for another destination. As in so many accounts of the Jewish experience in the twentieth century, the blank page that separates the two sections of this book signifies the black hole that may or may not be considered a "location" on the Jewish map. Is Auschwitz a Jewish place? Is there a symbolic vocabulary that belongs there? German Jewish poet Paul Celan wrote "Todesfuge" [Deathsfugue] just after he was released from labor camps in Transnistria and probably before the war had ended. In that poem, which was to become the site of both the most reverential and the most incriminatory readings, the Jews are commanded to "shovel a grave in the air there you won't lie too cramped." His compatriot from Bukovina, Dan Pagis, who survived the war to become one of Israel's foremost scholars and poets, writes in the "posthumous" first person: "Against my will/I was continued by this cloud" ("Footprints").[16] Are Celan's "grave in the air" and Pagis's "cloud" the most authentic postwar signifiers of the awful portability of Jewish geography? The struggle between the centripetal and centrifugal forces is also a struggle between materialization and demate-rialization in twentieth-century reconfigurations of Jewish culture in the wake of Jewish history.

The simultaneous effacement of homelands in Europe and creation of a central Homeland in Palestine forms the primary metanarrative of mod-ern Jewish culture; its most powerful counternarratives represent "home" as overdetermined by the ideology and enactment of a collective repatri-ation in Israel while at the very same time, for the majority of Jews of Eu-ropean extraction, even an *imagined* return to native grounds is preempted by devastation. In modern Hebrew literature, this paradox is expressed most powerfully by Dan Pagis in his forgetful poetry and his remember-ing prose and by Aharon Appelfeld in his displaced fictions.

In their very status as "nonoriginal" ground of reference, Jewish spaces outside of the Land of Israel were always emblematic of a very particular, elastic state of mind. But after the physical destruction of Jewish Europe, can such places be contained even within the vast open borders of post-war poetry? Why do *we go* to such places in search of palpable traces of the past? Should we read what Pierre Nora might call "lex lieux de mé-moire juive" not as new memory palaces but as *reliquaries,* constructed outside of the Holy Land by a modern imagination increasingly intoxi-cated by the sanctification of *place?* Founded belatedly on nostalgia and on incomplete mourning, the diasporic imagination will eventually gen-erate a postwar Europe without walls as a site of pilgrimage—literary at first and then literal, a substitution for Jerusalem as the ruined shrine.[17] I. B. Singer will reinvent Jewish Eastern Europe and Paul Celan will pre-side as high priest of the scattered relics of Jewish Central Europe.

While it is still too early to draw any conclusions regarding the relative impact on the imagination of the destruction of Jewish spaces in the an-cient Holy Land and in modern Europe, a pattern does begin to suggest itself: what was destroyed becomes over time an authentic original that can be represented but not recaptured; it becomes accessible to the pilgrim/tourist only as an unredeemed ruin, subject to a nonproprietary gaze. Hence the Holocaust may have turned the European exile from a place in which Home is imagined to a "real" home that can only be recalled from somewhere else and reconstructed from its shards; retrospectively, that is, the destruction seems to have territorialized exile as a lost home.

What is the fate of specific Jewish languages that inhered in specific places outside the sacred center? Do Yiddish and the other "secret" languages of the Jews, like their secret places, persist as primary points of reference and reverence, long after—or because—they have been effaced?[18] Is there a subtle exchange, over the years, between Yiddish and Hebrew as the locus of mystery and ruin, if not of authenticity? And the Hebrew that has been lost in Europe and found in Zion—how does it resonate through the echo chambers of the one and the crowded marketplaces of the other? As two German-speaking compatriots from Romania, Paul Celan comes to Hebrew (and to Zion) as pilgrim, Dan Pagis as immigrant. For Pagis, Hebrew is the material of a new social grammar, and his poetry is located in the interplay of its deep and its surface structures. For Celan, Hebrew appears as the only authentic, and still undeciphered, ur-language of the Jew—as both marker of a vanished civilization and utopian pledge to some idea of a deferred future. In his totemic images Hebrew words survive as incantatory fragments of a liturgical, scriptural lexicon.

The return to the Land, perceived simultaneously (by different interpretive communities) as the *beginning* and the *end* of history, has the potential to undermine the power of its own metaphors and to demonstrate the dangers of literalization. Pagis's poetry exemplifies a radical skepticism directed at the heart of the utopian/messianic enterprise; through a series of defamiliarizations, it calls attention to the implications of the encounter between Jewish modes of imagining homecoming as part of the narrative of exile and that homecoming as actualized in history. Emanating from the chaotic matter of his destroyed world and suspended just above the newly created cosmos that would absorb them, these poetic fragments enact the tensions between the myth of perfection and the messy actualities of any homecoming in real time.

Whether the cultural phenomenon we are examining is utopian or messianic in its political or religious manifestitations,[19] whether it is an apocalyptic modernism that takes refuge in the autonomy of the imagination[20] or a theodicy that culminates in a place and time perceived as *athalta dege'ula,* the opening bars in the symphony of redemption, what struggles to emerge—even (especially?) in a civilization that had for so long managed successfully to resist its own "sense of an ending"—is an aesthetics of total perfection, of the perfection of totality. Utopian desire is the very fire of fiction; utopia "realized" threatens to consume the fictive by subsuming all alternative worlds.[21] Banishing the poets from the new republic is an act that the architects and guardians of Hebrew culture would not have countenanced; but even as only a logical, hypothetical extension of the utopian project, such exclusion signals the dangers of any all-encompassing cultural vision.

Utopias take up a lot of room. The correspondence—or distance—between what Israeli anthropologists Zai Gurevitch and Gideon Aran call *makom katan* and *makom gadol*, place and Place[22]—between physical locatedness or nativism as a natural human state (and a "normal" Jewish state) and "Eretz" as the idea of sacred, redemptive territory—is a measure of the struggle between quotidian and utopian negotiations with place in modern Israel: and this struggle assumes a wide spectrum of cultural expressions. Different literary strategies replace the deferred, *u-topian* imagination of place with the topos of an actual, physical presence. The appeal of the visual, the original, and the palpable as opposed to the verbal and the mimetic reconnects the modern Jewish imagination with deep, archaic forms of relating to divinity.

The question at the center of this book is how the reacquisition of the spatial dimension has affected the Jewish literary imagination in the twentieth century; more specifically, it asks whether (particular) space as the manifestation of holiness replaces the text that has served as its surrogate.

Probably the purest representation of "return" and repossession in contemporary Hebrew literature—the one that comes closest to a perfect fit between places "Large" and "small"—can be found in the writings of S. Y. Agnon, whose prose incorporates most of the layers of Hebrew memory. His novella *In the Heart of the Seas* (1934) is our only exemplum of a modern triumphal epic; in this slim but fully articulated narrative of return we can see how the enactment of both journey and arrival gives a different resonance to the biblical verses that, having served as place markers for thousands of years, are now reinscribed as landmarks. While much of Agnon's fiction comes as close as any modern Hebrew text to opening a stable passage between cosmic planes, a yearning for place that is so much greater than arrival could possibly satisfy makes any nonironic encounter with the shrine a studied act of piety saturated with pathos. Gravitational forces have to work overtime in order to keep ingathered a people so used to wandering and to investing every way station with temporary holiness and provisional value; confining the deity to the geopolitical borders of a modern state becomes then an urgent task, fraught with consequence. (Will the Green Line, redrawn, keep Him in—or set Him free?)[23] Divinity in postrabbinic Judaism was not localized, and current attempts to localize it inevitably involve a move toward interdicted forms of idol worship. A modern replay of the conflict between priestly and prophetic orientations moves between localized and mobile concepts of the godhead. Efforts to rescue Diasporism are also efforts to preserve the God-in-Exile as the truest form of monotheism.

For Jews during the centuries of their exile, pilgrimage to the Land of Israel was not confined to any single structure or ruin; the soil itself had the properties of holiness that had once inhered in specific edifices. But if for the Jewish pilgrim the sacred territory was always a place to visit and then to leave, a different kind of coming and going would have to evolve in order to secure life in the place where divinity had been localized in habitations of earth and stone only in its earliest monotheistic phases. The unselfconscious paganism that begins to reinform Jewish culture in Israel ensues in a tension between myth and fiction, between the stable, unchanging "real" and the forces that refuse to be held down. The Wailing Wall—for ages a pilgrimage site, ground zero, the very *axis mundi*—not only is the final resting place of all the writing, of all the petitions deposited in its cracks, but also becomes a kind of bulwark against any threat (or promise) of flight: "the last stop of history . . . a blank wall with no open-sesames or hidden crypts . . . the ultimate dam, built to hold back the Jews in their restless proclivity to return to their past. 'Halt!' it says. 'No Passage Allowed Beyond This Point.' "[24] Where, then, is the restless Jewish spirit to go?

As modern Hebrew literature attempted to "spatialize" or stabilize the Jewish imagination while the Arab-Israeli conflict confined that space to a claustrophobic, hermetic sphere,[25] time could be rescued only in the interstices where the unquenched desire of the not-yet-arrived continually invaded sacred space to make room for narrative. In his most pious or nostalgic stories, Agnon represents the possibility of a close fit between Place and place; his nightmarish tales represent the misfits. Yehuda Amichai provides the most elastic poetic representations of the *im*perfect fit between the spaces—the very seas on which the Temple Mount can set sail from what is otherwise the most landlocked city in the world.[26] Amichai's verses hover over the chapters of this book as an ongoing commentary on the sentences that preceded him. He reengraves the psalm of exile, Psalm 137, back into the native landscape through ironic reversals and the intrusion of private, even unspoken, sentences into the formulas of collective memory:

If I forget thee, Jerusalem,
Then let my right be forgotten.
Let my right be forgotten, and my left remember.
Let my left remember, and your right close
And your mouth open near the gate.

I shall remember Jerusalem
And forget the forest—my love will remember,
Will open her hair, will close my window,
Will forget my right,
Will forget my left[.][27]

The poet-in-Jerusalem rescues the human beloved, the woman *in* Jerusalem, from the suffocating grasp of the metaphoric woman who *is* Jerusalem. The literalizing occasion allows this poet to ground, but also to undermine and to personalize, biblical texts—to inscribe on the private body what has been inscribed on the landscape in ways that do not denature either.

The whimsy of a poetry that can play wantonly in its own backyard can also be a response to the dangers of reconnecting a long-preserved memory with its source—memory that, looping back on its own epic beginnings, would stubbornly refuse the blessings of a forgetting that is always also a forgiving.[28] The second half of the psalm that began the journey, the half that is rarely quoted, reveals the potentially vindictive horrors of total recall:

Remember, O Lord, against the Edomites
The day of Jerusalem's fall
How they cried, "Strip her, strip her
To her very foundations."
Fair Babylon, you predator,
A blessing on him
Who repays you in kind
What you have afflicted on us.
A blessing on him who seizes your babies
And dashes them against the rocks.

This is memory with a vengeance, against which the imagination wages a desperate battle. The danger of total recall matches the seduction of ultimate arrival. It gives rise to what I call the "denaturing" of Jerusalem in such texts as Uri Zvi Greenberg's poem "Bizkhut em u-vena viyirushalayim" [For the Sake of a Mother and Her Son and Jerusalem], written during the Israeli War of Independence. Appropriating biblical imagery and medieval poetic cadences such as those we will encounter in the verses of Yehuda Halevi, Greenberg realizes the sacramental potential in the literalizing and grounding of metaphor. The keening mother yields up her private grief to the consecrating soil, "knowing" that her son is no longer in his grave, that his "small body" has been utterly incorporated into the place of sacrifice. Personified as mother earth, as lover, and as "wife," absorbing into the soil the sacrificed body of the young soldier, Jerusalem takes on a kind of mystical materiality that supersedes and therefore denies its status as poetic symbol.[29]

Beneath the apparently benign surfaces of an idea of total homecoming lie the impulse to literalize, the pledge to vengeance, and the death wish inevitably associated with arrival. Israel's first real-estate transaction in ancient Canaan was the purchase of the burial cave of Machpelah. As Arnold Eisen has argued, "one can live in the land, 'sojourn' there . . . without possessing it. To die in it, however, one needs a . . . holding. So when Sarah dies, Abraham must negotiate the purchase of a grave property."[30] Throughout the Jewish literature that spans our century, the shore of the Mediterranean is also life's final shore.[31] Exile and narrative, the time or *durée* of life itself, can yield only to homecoming, closure, and the place of (the place that is) death.

Once cursed with eternal life, the Wandering Jew could celebrate an end to wandering by trading his immortality for a simple grave. But it is the simple grave that is hardest to gain in a society intoxicated by the idea of staying put for eternity. As ancient burial sites are turned up almost daily by tractors with other agendas, Israel appears as one vast cemetery for the ancient dead whose unearthed skeletons provide bones of contention among archaeologists, ultra-orthodox burial societies, and the still quick who want only to compete for some of the *real estate*.

The ancient graves and the ancient caves are believed to carry the "answer" to the riddles of this people's beginning and destination. The dry bones and scrolls are the secret rememberers; they make the act of arrival an act of return and the act of discovery an act of recovery. But *recovery* and *return* both territorialize the Jewish imagination through closure. Their ultimate expression—death and the "necrophoria"[32] that has always been a part of the imagination of arrival, of the ultimate reunion and consummation with the beloved—has possessed the Hebrew imagination from its earliest manifestations in medieval love poems to Jerusalem to its most recent forms of grave worship in the Holy Land.

Where return and recovery are the prevailing political and aesthetic gestures and the biblical text both a code of memory and a travel guide, the Arab becomes the romantic embodiment of the self through a paradox of identification. In literary and visual representations that run through the early decades of this century, the Arab, as Bedouin, is at the same time the native, autochthonous man in an organic, preindustrialized connection to the land *and* the aboriginal Semite, the ancestral Jew moving naturally in his surroundings next to the predatory and mechanized locutions of the Jewish pioneer.[33] The Arab woman appears as more than reincarnation of the exotic and dangerous female other; she is the primordial Rebecca, still drawing water from the well after all these years. Like the Dead Sea Scrolls, they surface as relics of an authentic past, of the lost self. But the Arab who is thus claimed as ancestral self is in danger of becoming invisible as *other*— not by being overlooked but by being so totally incorporated.

Leah Goldberg's "Songs of Zion" (1955) lament what could be benignly defined as a deficit of attention:

> Sing us from the Songs of Zion!
> How shall we sing a song of Zion in the land of Zion
> if we have not begun to listen?[34]

Back in the land of Zion, the first act should be to put one's ear to the ground. To the chorus of this land's "other population"—its ancient dead—come the voices of Palestine's other, *live* population. Asserting their claims as narrating subjects with stakes in geopolitical as well as sacred space in Palestine, the Arab voices that have begun to be heard resonate with the silenced voices of Jewish exile.

The pledge to memory, to vengeance, and to the autism that insulates them should not, then, outlast the longing or the journey; as a compass to help the community of the faithful navigate through the uncharted paths of exile, memory has performed its office. Even the dead, who have finally received proper burial, can stay safe in the ground where graves belong; their remembering dust can relieve the poet of the memory that, like Joseph's mummified bones carried through the forty years in the desert, is the burden—and the story—of exile.[35] Back "home," a different kind of transference can be restored between objects and memory, between things and language, between material and spirit—and between different rememberers. The celebratory can replace the mnemonic. Amichai in Jerusalem can, finally, begin to *forget:*

> Let the memorial hill remember instead of me,
> that's what it's here for.
> . . . .
> Let the beasts of the field and the birds of the heavens eat and
> remember.
> Let all of them remember so that I can rest.[36]

The ultimate challenge to the Israeli writer is how to keep images from becoming icons, archaeology from becoming eschatology, "arrival" from becoming the terminus of a vengeful excess of memory, the eros of an unconsummated journey from being extinguished in the killing fields of exclusive visions—how to *reopen* the narrative so that narrative itself can continue and one can hear the suppressed, the silenced, the restless and unpatriated voices.

And If When You Arrive You Find Her Poor . . .

> The city plays hide-and-
> seek among her names:
> Yerushalayim, El-Quds, Shalem, Jeru, Yeru, all
> the whole
> whispering her first, Jebusite name: Y'vus,
> Y'vus, Y'vus, in the dark. She weeps
> with longing: Ilia Capitolinia, Ilia, Ilia.
> She comes to any man who calls her
> at night, alone. But we know
> who comes to whom.
>
> *Yehuda Amichai, "Jerusalem 1967"*

The poet in Jerusalem who manages to write a poem of longing has outwitted death. As long as there is desire, the stones glitter with enchantment; arrival necessarily brings disenchantment. The secret of the Jews in the years of their exile was in having the memory and the promise of home *and* the freedom of the road, in cherishing a home without having to defend it or even keep its roads free of potholes. Turning toward Jerusalem in prayer from whatever spot one inhabited, the Jew was reminded that the sacred center was somewhere *else;* it was *the not-here.* On the level of the theodicy of exile and the ever-deferred return, the places outside of the Land of Israel were provisional, never invested with the ultimate status of real, original space.

Jerusalem, for her part, is preserved in the imagination over the centuries of Israel's wandering as a *hurva* awaiting redemption, a shrine suspended in its ruin.[37] Nothing significant can happen elsewhere, but nothing significant will happen *there* until the Jews return to complete the redemption. Even if it tarries a bit, the real drama will unfold only in Jerusalem.

And the only official municipal designation for the city until that drama begins is as a vast graveyard and a dusty shrine. The only death that really
counts will take place in—or be translated to—Jerusalem. For centuries the
Jews of Samarkand, Uzbekistan, in preparing to meet their Maker, would
buy one grave site in the local cemetery and another plot in Jerusalem. It
was, by all reports, a valid legal transaction, with a bill of purchase placed
in the hands of the deceased and buried with him or her; thus on the day
of redemption, when there will no doubt be a grand traffic jam in the sub-
terranean passages to Jerusalem as all the bodies are rolling toward the site
of the resurrection, the dearly departed Samarkandians will already have
reserved places.[38] In terms of narrative as diasporic privilege and Zion as
its deferred end, it is the best way to preserve *both plots.*

Where death and resurrection are the ultimate ratifiers of place, distance becomes insignificant. As long as the vision remains unrealized, it
creates an infinitely elastic umbilical cord to link the dispersed tribe of the
faithful to the matrix of their faith. Reconnection with the material world,
reacquisition of the territorial dimension, reduces the elasticity and releases toxins into the erotic forces. The poet who heads back to Jerusalem,
to her vineyards and gardens, to her alleyways and gates, recovers the real,
material world from under the allegorical weight of her imagery. But here,
in the *ultimate* resting place from which there can be no more departures,
and in its most sensuous poetry, lurks the danger of death and (that is) literalization: the landscape that becomes so palpable in Yehuda Halevi's last
poems seems about to lose its symbolic, poetic status. Images of death are
as abundant in this poetry as images of consummated love: *thanatos* as
significant other and devourer of *eros.* Jerusalem as a ruin welcomes the
poet into her rubble and lures him to his death. For all the travelers we
have followed, beginning with Yehuda Halevi, the final port of disem-
barkation is the place of death. Distance is diminished to the point where
it is nearly eradicated by an ecstatic, mystic vision of arrival. So the danger of arrival is also the challenge to the symbolic universe, the materialization of desire, the move from symbol to sacrament.

The tension between "Eretz" as the idea of sacred, redemptive territory
and native soil as the natural human realm, between "large" and "small"
space, has escalated into tribal warfare in our own time. In the poetic imagination the boundaries of the city expand easily to include all of Zion and
then just as easily contract to the dimensions of the Old City. "May the
day come when Jerusalem extends as far as Damascus, and in every direction," says the 104-year-old Tehila to the narrator in S. Y. Agnon's story
by that name. "But the eye that has seen all Jerusalem enclosed within her
walls cannot accustom itself to viewing what is built beyond the walls as

the City itself. It is true that all the Land of Israel is holy and, I need hardly say, the surroundings of Jerusalem: yet the holiness that is within the walls of the City surpasses all else."[39] When this poetic image *denies its status as poetry,* it makes such claims on the political imagination that the "final status" of Jerusalem becomes nonnegotiable. The Jerusalem of the mind can extend as far as Damascus. The most landlocked city in the world, Jerusalem-of-the-mind can abut rivers and even oceans, the Jordan as well as the Sambatyon. Earthly Jerusalem must be divided into distinct boroughs and many intersections. It is only when the symbolic and the material dimensions are *severed* that dreamscapes can be preserved alongside well-groomed landscapes.

The psalm that inaugurates the poetics of exile concludes with a pledge to vengeance, demonstrating that the other side of the apocalyptic death wish is the apocalyptic vision of revenge. The links between the remembering community's amazing capacity for total recall and its undying vow to even the score are the consequence of the obliteration of distance, as the act of return entails picking up the old stories and finishing them, leaving no forgotten enmities, no loose ends. Words that were hypothetical in exile become consequential when they are repatriated. Put just one letter back into the canon and you have a ballistic device.[40]

The insistence that endings must reconnect with beginnings—that what has traveled through space as a symbol, when finally (re)grounded in sacred soil, stakes an incontrovertible, inalienable, and *total* claim—reveals the seduction of an *aesthetics of the whole.* The whole holy land. Undivided Jerusalem. The aesthetics and politics of wholeness are built on sacrifice and exclusivity, on a messianic perfection of the form that can be fully realized only in death. The eternity of Jerusalem is privileged over the ephemeral lives of its inhabitants, fulfillment over deferral, original and indivisible space over all forms of partiality, imitation, fragmentation, or duplication. Death celebrated as glorious, as sacrificial or heroic, preserves the image of the integrity of the body, unsullied by the ravages of the battlefield. It is the postromantic imagination that has come to the recognition that death is rarely beautiful.[41]

NOTES

1. Edmond Jabès, "This Is the Desert: Nothing Strikes Root Here," interview by Bracha Ettinger Lichtenberg, in *Routes of Wandering: Nomadism, Voyages, and Transitions in Contemporary Israeli Art,* ed. Sarit Shapira, exhibition catalogue, bilingual edition (Jerusalem: Israel Museum, 1991), pp. 247, 248, 250.

2. George Steiner, "Our Homeland, the Text," *Salmagundi*, no. 66 (winter-spring 1985): 5, 24–25. References to modern Judaism as a text culture can be seen in Yiddish literary circles much earlier in this century. See, for example, Ba'al-Makhshoves [Israel Isidor Elyshev], who wrote in 1918 that "the literature of oppressed peoples has always been their own territory, where they feel entirely at home. . . . We Jews have been able to survive history because of this exterritoriality. . . . The term 'People of the Book,' with which history has crowned us, clearly contains the notion that our earth, our very home, has always been literature." Ba'al-Makhshoves, "Tsvey shprakhen: Eyn eyorsiker literature," tr. as "One Literature in Two Languages," in *What Is Jewish Literature?* ed. Hana Wirth-Nesher (Philadelphia: Jewish Publication Society, 1994), p. 75. In France, the growing influence of Emmanuel Levinas and, through Levinas, of Franz Rosenzweig, adds to the impact of Jabès and Steiner in redefining a late-twentieth-century "text-centered" polemic with Jewish statehood. See Harold Bloom, *Agon: Towards Theory of Revisionism* (New York: Oxford University Press, 1982); see also Robert Gibbs, *Correlations in Rosenzweig and Levinas* (Princeton: Princeton University Press, 1992), p. 137; and Jill Robbins, *Prodigal Son/Elder Brother: Interpretation and Alterity in Augustine, Petrarch, Kafka, and Levinas* (Chicago: University of Chicago Press, 1991).

3. Steiner, "Our Homeland, the Text," p. 19. For a discussion of Jewish intellectuals and postmodernism, see Norman Finkelstein, *The Ritual of New Creation: Jewish Tradition and Contemporary Literature* (Albany: State University of New York Press, 1992); relying heavily on Harold Bloom and Gershom Sholem, Finkelstein defines the "modern ritual of new creation" as comprising "the matter of 'wandering meaning'. . . [and] the matter of loss and exile" (p. 3). See also his discussion of the utopian/messianic element in George Steiner's thought and of the role of art as the arena of the struggle between the real and the ideal (pp. 97–116).

4. Paracelsus is quoted in E. R. Curtius, *European Literature and the Latin Middle Ages*, tr. Willard R. Trask (New York: Pantheon Books, 1953), p. 322. For a general discussion of "the book of nature" and "the book as symbol" generally, see chap. 16.

5. Vladimir Nabokov, *The Real Life of Sebastian Knight* (London: Weidenfeld and Nicolson, 1960), p. 150.

6. "Because he travels there by way of Venice, Athens or Constantinople, Chateaubriand approaches the 'term' Jerusalem (signifying 'term' as a sign and 'terminus') in a certain way," writes Michel Butor.

"One stopping-place produces the effect of a parenthesis or a digression, while another is, on the contrary, an essential stage of an argument." The correlative of travel as writing is "writing as travel": "The terms Rome, Athens, Jerusalem are arranged in a particular order by the sentence which is my journey, and they can be varied at the instruction of my travelling-writing." Butor, "Travel and Writing," *Mosaic* 8, nos. 1–2 (fall 1974): 15.

7. Jesse Gellrich finds the poetic language of such medieval writers as Dante and Chaucer to be a kind of "fictional signifying" that both endorses and

expands the boundaries and destabilizes the fixity of meaning inscribed in both the "Book of God's Work (nature)" and its "speculum," the "book of His Word (the Bible)." *The Idea of the Book in the Middle Ages* (Ithaca: Cornell University Press, 1985), p. 18.

8. Maurice Samuel, *The World of Sholem Aleichem* (1943; reprint, New York: Schocken Books, 1965), pp. 194–95. See, among others, the Hebrew writing of Y. H. Brenner and H. N. Bialik; and see in chapter 2 my discussion of Abramovitsh's *Travels of Benjamin the Third* for a satiric, maskilic representation of the effect of "text-centeredness" on the Jewish powers of observation. See also Jonathan Z. Smith, *Map Is Not Territory: Studies in the History of Religions* (Leiden: E. J. Brill, 1978), pp. 104–28.

9. Genesis Rabbah 49:4. In commenting on this passage, Israeli anthropologists Zali Gurevitch and Gideon Aran note the astounding correlation or identification between the Land of Israel and the text. "'Al ha-makom" [On Place], *Alpayim* 4 (1991): 16. For the abridged English version of this essay, see note 22 below.

10. Bland cites a fifteenth-century Hebrew grammarian who wrote that "because this sacred Book is equal in its properties to the Temple, it was originally divided into three sections just as was the arrangement of the Temple." Kalman Bland, "Medieval Jewish Aesthetics: Maimonides, Body, and Scripture in Profiat Duran," *Journal of the History of Ideas* 54, no. 4 (October 1993): 549. See also Bland, *The Artless Jew: Medieval and Modern Affirmations and Denials of the Visual* (Princeton: Princeton University Press, 2000).

11. The vision of confluence of the temporal and the divine Sabbath was homologized to the return to Zion and an end to exile. Elliot K. Ginsburg, *The Sabbath in the Classical Kabbalah* (Albany: State University of New York Press, 1989), pp. 85–92; see also Schweid, *Land of Israel*, pp. 79–90.

12. For intrabiblical prooftexts of the changing relations of territory, blood, and faith, see 1 Samuel 26:19; 1 Kings 20:28; Ruth 1:16; Ezra 9; Esther 3:8. For a succinct but thorough discussion of the classical biblical and postbiblical sources on territoriality, see W. D. Davies, *The Territorial Dimension of Judaism* (Berkeley: University of California Press, 1982). For a discussion of the violence entailed in group identity formation, see Regina M. Schwartz, *The Curse of Cain: The Violent Legacy of Monotheism* (Chicago: University of Chicago Press, 1997).

13. See, for instance, Jonathan Z. Smith's claim that the Temple in Jerusalem was itself a "self-referential system" that in an arbitrary way signified, quite simply, *difference,* and that, like the "phonemes in Roman Jakobson's linguistic theories[,]. . . [formed] . . . a system 'composed of elements which are signifiers and yet, at the same time, signify nothing.'" The priestly documents recorded in the Bible "already reduced the rituals of the Temple from performances to systems—primarily by mapping modes of emplacement . . . [and] these maps allow a prescission from place. They could be thought about in abstract topographies; they could be transported to another place; they could be extended to other sorts of social space." Smith's reading of

the temple described in Ezekiel 40–48, a temple envisioned from the perspective of the Babylonian exile, together with the very different renderings in the Mishnah, is of a "systemic" rather than a primarily "historical" phenomenon; therefore it can be replicated. *To Take Place: Toward Theory in Ritual* (Chicago: University of Chicago Press, 1987), pp. 73, 108–9.

14. "Simulation is no longer that of a territory, a referential being or a substance," writes Jean Baudrillard. "It is the generation by models of a real without origin or reality: a hyperreal. The territory no longer precedes the map, nor survives it. Henceforth, it is the map that precedes the territory[;] . . . it is the map that engenders the territory." *Simulations*, tr. Paul Foss, Paul Patton, and Philip Beitchman (New York: Semiotext(e), 1983), p. 2.

15. " 'Al 'aravim be-tokha talu ha-kabtzielim tarmilehem u-smartutehem vayishtatakhu lahem shatoah 'al pnei ha-adamah." S. Y. Abramovitsh, "Haaisrafim," in *Kol kitvei Mendele mokher sfarim* [The Complete Works of Mendele Mokher Sfarim] (Tel Aviv: Dvir, 1958), pp. 444–45.

16. Paul Celan, "Todesfuge," tr. John Felstiner, in Felstiner, *Paul Celan: Jew* (New Haven: Yale University Press, 1995), p. 31; Dan Pagis, " 'Akevot" [Footprints], from *Gilgul*, in *Points of Departure*, tr. Stephen Mitchell (Philadelphia: Jewish Publication Society, 1981), p. 29.

17. Parallels with the literary and then the literal pilgrimages of Jews from Arab countries to their countries of origin, especially to North Africa, as the walls of enmity between Israel and its Arab neighbors crumble and these Jews challenge the Ashkenazi hegemony over Israeli culture and reconstruction of the past, are drawn by Amiel Alcalay, *After Jews and Arabs: Remaking Levantine Culture* (Minneapolis: University of Minnesota Press, 1993).

18. Primo Levi, who "remembered" Auschwitz and narrated his own salvaged humanity through his native Italian, claims in later stories that the "lager jargon" was in fact Yiddish, which should be granted a "privileged position in the reconstruction of memory." This claim is only surprising, argues Sander L. Gilman, because Levi didn't really know Yiddish. Gilman, "To Quote Primo Levi: 'Redest Keyn Jiddisch, bist nit kejn jid' [If you don't speak Yiddish, you're not a Jew]," *Prooftexts* 9, no. 2 (May 1989): 143. See especially Levi's 1982 novel, *If Not Now, When?*

19. See Gershom Scholem, *The Messianic Idea in Judaism* (New York: Schocken Books, 1971) and later discussions by Jacob Talmon, Moshe Idel, and others who further advanced the debate on the continuities and discontinuities between messianism and Zionism. See also *Jews and Messianism in the Modern Era: Metaphor and Meaning*, ed. Jonathan Frankel, *Studies in Contemporary Jewry* 7 (New York: Oxford University Press, 1991); and Rahel Elboim-Dror, *Ha-mahar shel ha-etmol* [Yesterday's Tomorrow] (2 vols. [Jerusalem: Yad Ben-Zvi, 1993]) for a study of the major texts and influences of Zionist utopianism.

20. Frank Kermode and Michael Hamburger, among others, have identified the apocalyptic undercurrents in modernist forms and sensibility that are the legacy of romanticism; writers such as D. H. Lawrence, W. B. Yeats, T. S. Eliot, R. M. Rilke, and even Wallace Stevens share what Kermode defines

as "the conviction that [they] exist at the end of an epoch, in a time of transition, on a ridge of history from which the contours of the whole are visible. That vision [encompasses] . . . the design of history . . . the outcome of the great narrative plot." Kermode, "Apocalypse and the Modern," in *Visions of Apocalypse: End or Rebirth?* ed. Saul Friedlander, Gerald Holton, Leo Marx, and Eugene Skolnikoff (New York: Holmes and Meier, 1985), p. 94. This position is more fully explored in Kermode, *The Sense of an Ending: Studies in the Theory of Fiction* (New York: Oxford University Press, 1967). See also Michael Hamburger, "Absolute Poetry and Absolute Politics," in *The Truth of Poetry: Tensions in Modern Poetry from Baudelaire to the 1960s* (London: Methuen, 1982), pp. 81–109.

21. Ernst Bloch remains one of the most powerful exponents of the utopian function of art as a theory of desire and "anticipatory illumination" that does not detach landscapes from "wish-landscapes." *The Utopian Function of Art and Literature: Selected Essays*, tr. Jack Zipes and Frank Mecklenburg (Cambridge, Mass.: MIT Press, 1988), p. ⁿ55. See also Theodor Adorno, *Minima Moralia: Reflections from Damaged Life*, tr. E.F.N. Jephcott (London: New Left Books, 1974), pp. 247 ff. The binary structures that evolve in response to an absence of utopian fulfillment can yield to the more organic, postmodern thrust of the not-yet-realized, generating an infinitude of fictive possibilities.

22. Zali Gurevitch and Gideon Aran, "The Land of Israel: Myth and Phenomenon," in *Reshaping the Past: Jewish History and the Historians*, ed. Jonathan Frankel, Studies in Contemporary Jewry 10 (New York: Oxford University Press, 1994), pp. 195–96. This is an abridged version of their essay "Al ha-makom." For an elaboration of this idea, with special attention to the sense of place gleaned by modern Zionist pioneers from the ancient biblical story of Israel, see Zali Gurevitch, "The Double Site of Israel," in *Grasping Land: Space and Place in Contemporary Israeli Discourse and Experience*, ed. Eyal Ben-Ari and Yoram Bilu (Albany: State University of New York Press, 1997), pp. 203–16.

23. Conversely, the sacralization of territory can result in attempts to expand sacred space so that space and Place will correspond; religious Jewish settlers' ongoing staking of claims to the West Bank can be understood in this light.

24. A. B. Yehoshua, *Mr. Mani*, tr. Hillel Halkin (San Diego: Harcourt Brace, 1992), p. 256.

25. In one of the earliest analyses of responses to claustrophobia in Israeli literature, Robert Alter argues that there was an essential difference between the "imaginative horizons" in fiction and in poetry, especially among those Hebrew writers who came of age in the 1950s and 1960s; the poets more naturally manage to overcome the "geographical limits that define the imagined world of the literary work" while the fiction becomes more often than not a representation of "claustrophobic collective existence, . . . a nervous shuttling between home and horizon." Alter, "A Problem of Horizons," in *Contemporary Israeli Literature*, ed. Elliot Anderson (Philadelphia: Jewish Publication Society, 1977), pp. 329, 332.

26. "Jerusalem is a port city on the shore of eternity./The Temple Mount is a huge ship, a magnificent/luxury liner." Yehuda Amichai, "Yerushalayim 'ir namal 'al sfat ha-netzah" [Jerusalem Is a Port City on the Shore of Eternity], in *Songs of Jerusalem*, bilingual edition (Jerusalem: Schocken, 187), p. 79.

27. Yehuda Amichai, "If I Forget Thee, Jerusalem," in ibid., p. 13.

28. See Ernst Renan's often-quoted lecture, "Qu'est-ce qu'une nation?" (delivered at the Sorbonne on March 11, 1882), in which he argued that "forgetting . . . is a crucial factor in the creation of a nation." He referred to different forms of forgetting: the effacement of individual origins in the forging of a nation as well as the effacement of "deeds of violence which took place at the origin of all political formations." Renan, "What Is a Nation?" tr. Martin Thom, in *Nation and Narration*, ed. Homi K. Bhabha (London: Routledge, 1990), p. 11.

29. Uri Zvi Greenberg, "Bizkhut em u-vena viyirushalayim" [For the Sake of a Mother and Her Son and Jerusalem], in *Kol Ketavav* [Collected Work] (Jerusalem: Mossad Bialik, 1994), vol. 7, pp. 57–59.

30. Arnold M. Eisen, *Galut: Modern Jewish Reflection on Homelessness and Homecoming* (Bloomington: Indiana University Press, 1986), p. 10.

31. See, for example, Y. H. Brenner in "'Atzabim" [Nerves], in which the "hof" which is the shore of the Land of Israel is also the *final* shore (see note 33 below); Ya'acov Fichman, "Tzlalim 'al sadot" [Shadows over the Fields]—and Dan Miron on Fichman in his *Bodedim be-mo'adam: le-diyukana shel ha-republika ha-sifratit ha-'ivrit be-tehilat ha-mea ha-'esrim* [When Loners Come Together: A Portrait of Hebrew Literature at the Turn of the Twentieth Century] (Tel Aviv: Am Oved, 1987), pp. 545–48. On the "Charon complex" as a theme in modern Israeli art, see Sarit Shapira, "Vehicles," in Shapira, *Routes of Wandering*, p. 197. One could argue, though, that it is the figure on that other shore, Jacob at the Jabbok ford (Gen. 32), that mimics Charon and his ferry; see Silvie-Anne Goldberg, *Crossing the Jabbok: Illness and Death in Ashkenazi Judaism in Sixteenth- through Nineteenth-Century Prague*, tr. Carol Cosman (Berkeley: University of California Press, 1996), esp. pp. 87–88. The biblical equivalent of the modern site of return, the pioneer's landing in Jaffa Port, would be the crossing of the Jordan River.

32. "The necrophore is a coleopter beetle that buries carrion, cadavers of moles and mice, on which it lays its eggs." *Le Petit Robert*, quoted in Henri Raczymow, *Writing the Book of Esther*, tr. Dori Katz (London: Holmes and Meier, 1995), p. 93.

> "Modern psychoanalytic theory teaches us that fictions of closure are linked to the death drive," writes Regina M. Schwartz, "that, as the end of desire, fulfillment is tantamount to death. Desire itself, however, perpetual desire, ensures textuality—in our parlance, scripturality. The Bible complicates this picture for it gives us at once desire (the promised land is, after all, promised) and nostalgia. . . . [In the Hebrew Bible] there are many dyings and risings rather than a single resurrection." Schwartz, "Joseph's Bones and the Resurrection of the Text: Remembering in the Bible," *PMLA* 103, no. 2 (March 1988): 122.

Freud's connections between psychoanalysis and archaeology, between the mother's body/mother earth/motherland as original home and transcendental homelessness as the state of civilized humanity, developed in *Totem and Taboo* and *Civilization and Its Discontents*, as well as the connections he draws between the fufillment of desire and death, have not yet been fully explored in the context of Zionist images of return and the fulfillment (= denial) of desire. On Freud's sense of "homelessness" and fascination with archaeology and the "primitive," see Marianna Torgovnik, *Gone Primitive: Savage Intellects, Modern Lives* (Chicago: University of Chicago Press, 1990), pp. 194–209.

33.   I may have been living all that time with the hope . . . of finding a foothold . . . in our picturesque ancestral corner of Asia, in which Bedouin, the great-grandchildren of Abraham the Hebrew, pitch their tents to this day and bring to the well real camels as once did his bondsman Eliezer . . . and in which . . . third- and fourth-generation children of Polish Jewish money-lenders are learning to follow the plow. . . . So that I thought . . . "Let me cross over and see that goodly land, its fair mountains and the Lebanon."
      "Well, what do you think now? Did you find your foothold?"

      Y. H. Brenner, "Nerves"['Arzabim], tr. Hillel Halkin, in *Eight Great Hebrew Short Novels*, ed. Alan Lelchuk and Gershon Shaked (New York: New American Library, 1983), p. 36.

34.   shiru lanu mi-shirei tzion!
      eikh nashir shir tzion 'al admat tzion
      ve-'od lo hithalnu lishmo'a?

                  Leah Goldberg, "Mi-shirei Tzion," in *Shirim* [Poems]
                  (Tel Aviv: Sifriat po'alim, 1986), vol. 2, p. 219.

35.   "Rearticulating the bones" by assigning absolute and redemptive value, the value of total recall, would thus be a defiance of Jewish hermeneutics understood as a lack of completion. See Schwartz, "Joseph's Bones and the Resurrection of the Text."
      The unburied dead of the Holocaust, like the unmarked grave of Moses, maintain the tension and critique of the well-articulated narrative in modern Israel. See Don Handelman and Lea Shamgar-Handelman's fascinating comparison between the memorials to the dead in Israel's wars and to the dead of the Shoah; they argue that because the dead of Europe *and their world* are so absent in the landscape of Israel, the memorials to them must be elaborately realized, unlike the simple and uniform cemeteries and memorials to the dead of Israel's wars. "Each type visualizes some relationship of the dead to the land, such that their absence on its surface signifies their presence within its earth . . . [contributing differentially] to the molding of landscapes of collective memory." On the one hand, in a kind of "synthetic holism," the bodies of the soldiers are perceived as "belonging" to the land, while the "land is felt to acquire contours that resonate with

the bodies buried within it." On the other hand, the absence of both the "authentic body of sacrifice and of the place of sacrifice, that typifies Holocaust memorialism in Israel," depends on "metaphorization"—figuration or "copies," in the Baudrillardian sense—of that life above ground, stressing their "discontinuous relationship to the surrounding landscapes." Handelman and Shamgar-Handelman, "The Presence of Absence: The Memorialism of National Death in Israel," in Ben-Ari and Bilu, *Grasping Land*, pp. 89, 90, 101, 114–15.

36. Yehuda Amichai, from "Songs of Zion the Beautiful," in *Songs of Jerusalem*, p. 109.

37. *Hurva*, or ruin, is cognate with the designation for the destruction of the Temple of Solomon (*hurban*); it is also the Yiddish word (*hurbn*) for the Holocaust, and enters in its Arabic form into the Israeli dialogue on the expulsion and occupation of the Arabs: "*Hirbet* Hiz'ah" is the title of a 1949 story by S. Yizhar.

38. Pinkhes Kohn, "Oysterlishe minhogim fun yidn in Samarkand" [Outlandish Practices of the Jews of Samarkand], *Der Moment*, no. 144 (June 22, 1928): 6. I am grateful to Vera Solomon for this reference. For analogous practices elsewhere in Europe, see Sylvie-Anne Goldberg, *Crossing the Jabbok: Illness and Death in Ashkenazi Judaism in Sixteenth- through Nineteenth-Century Prague*, tr. Carol Cosman (Berkeley: University of California Press, 1996).

39. S. Y. Agnon, "Tehila," tr. Walter Lever, in *Firstfruits: A Harvest of 25 Years of Israeli Writing*, ed. James A. Michener (Philadelphia: Jewish Publication Society, 1973), p. 39.

40. No matter where we start our investigation—with the Jebusites, the Hebrews, the Romans, the Saracens, the Crusaders—one group's claim comes at the expense of every other's. Jerusalem remembers them all and in her own way contains them all. It is we who insist on exclusive rights, erasing the graffiti of our predecessors in order to cover the walls with our own name and our own story. The most dramatic recent signs of that mutual effacement are the graffiti-covered walls of the Intifada.

41. See Aharon Ezrahi, *Rubber Bullets: Power and Conscience in Modern Israel* (New York: Farrar, Straus, and Giroux, 1997).

   The tension between these two aesthetics is nowhere more dramatically enacted than at the scene of a suicide bombing in Israel. The cameras that focus on body parts strewn all over the streets and on the blood in the intersections are not only engaged in reportage; they allow for an aesthetics of fragmentation, of horror. At the same time, however, members of the Jewish Burial Society in bright yellow vests are collecting body parts that must be buried with the mutilated corpses in order to ensure the aesthetics of the whole that is associated with the sacrificial representation of death and the resurrection of the body.

POEMS

Yehuda Amichai

From In My Life, On My Life

12

I, may I rest in peace—I, who am still living, say,
May I have peace in the rest of my life.
I want peace right now while I'm still alive.
I don't want to wait like that pious man who wished for one leg
of the golden chair of Paradise. I want a four-legged chair
right here, a plain wooden chair. I want the rest of my peace now.
I have lived out my life in wars of every kind: battles without
and within, close combat, face-to-face, the faces always
my own, my lover-face, my enemy-face.
Wars with the old weapons—sticks and stones, blunt axe, words,
dull ripping knife, love and hate,
and wars with newfangled weapons—machine gun, missile,
words, land mines exploding, love and hate.
I don't want to fulfill my parents' prophecy that life is war.
I want peace with all my body and all my soul.
Rest me in peace.

From Jerusalem, Jerusalem, Why Jerusalem?

7

In Jerusalem, everything is a symbol. Even two lovers there
become a symbol like the lion, the golden dome, the gates of
    the city.
Sometimes they make love on too soft a symbolism
and sometimes the symbols are hard as a rock, sharp as nails.
That's why they make love on a mattress of six hundred thirteen
    springs,
like the number of precepts, the commandments of Shalt and
    Shalt Not,
oh yes, do that, darling, no, not that—all for love
and its pleasures. They speak with bells in their voices
and with the wailing call of the muezzin, and at their bedside,
    empty shoes
as at the entrance of a mosque. And on the doorpost of their house
    it says,
"Ye shall love each other with all your hearts and with all your
    souls."

19

I always have to go in the opposite direction to whatever
is passing and past. That's how I know I live in Jerusalem:
I go against the tide of pilgrims parading in the Old City,
brush by them, rub up against them, feel the weave of their
    clothes,
breathe in their smell, hear their walk and their song
as they fly past my cheeks like beautiful clouds.
Sometimes I get tangled in a funeral procession
and emerge at the other end, heading toward the good life.
And sometimes I'm held captive by the joy-parades and I raise
    my arm
like a swimmer against the stream, or as if to say: Go in peace,
go, go away, and I head for the other side, toward
my griefs and my peace. I go against the longings the prayers
to feel their warm breath on my face,
the buzz and rustle of the stuff of longing and the prayer.
This could be the start of a new religion,
like striking a match to make fire, like the friction
that sparks electricity.

The Jewish Time Bomb

On my desk is a stone with "Amen" carved on it, one survivor
     fragment
of the thousands upon thousands of bits of broken tombstones
in Jewish graveyards. I know all these broken pieces
now fill the great Jewish time bomb
along with the other fragments and shrapnel, broken Tablets
     of the Law
broken altars broken crosses rusty crucifixion nails
broken houseware and holyware and broken bones
eyeglasses shoes prostheses false teeth
empty cans of lethal poison. All these broken pieces
fill the Jewish time bomb until the end of days.
And though I know about all this, and about the end of days,
the stone on my desk gives me peace.
It is the touchstone no one touches, more philosophical
than any philosopher's stone, broken stone from a broken tomb
more whole than any wholeness,
a stone of witness to what has always been
and what will always be, a stone of amen and love.
Amen, amen, and may it come to pass.

HOVERING AT A LOW ALTITUDE

Dahlia Ravikovitch

I am not here.
I am on those craggy eastern hills
streaked with ice,
where grass doesn't grow
and a wide shadow lies over the slope.
A shepherd girl appears
from an invisible tent,
leading a herd of black goats to pasture.
She won't live out the day,
that girl.

I am not here.
From the deep mountain gorge
a red globe floats up,
not yet a sun.
A patch of frost, reddish, inflamed,
flickers inside the gorge.

The girl gets up early to go to the pasture.
She doesn't walk with neck outstretched
and wanton glances.
She doesn't ask, Whence cometh my help.
I am not here.

I've been in the mountains many days now.
The light will not burn me, the frost
won't touch me.
Why be astonished now?
I've seen worse things in my life.

I gather my skirt and hover
very close to the ground.
What is she thinking, that girl?

Wild to look at, unwashed.
For a moment she crouches down,
her cheeks flushed,
frostbite on the back of her hands.
She seems distracted, but no,
she's alert.

She still has a few hours left.
But that's not what I'm thinking about.
My thoughts cushion me gently, comfortably.
I've found a very simple method,
not with my feet on the ground, and not flying—
hovering
at a low altitude.

Then at noon,
many hours after sunrise,
that man goes up the mountain.
He looks innocent enough.

The girl is right there,
no one else around.
And if she runs for cover, or cries out—
there's no place to hide in the mountains.

I am not here.
I'm above those jagged mountain ranges
in the farthest reaches of the east.
No need to elaborate.
With one strong push I can hover and whirl around
with the speed of the wind.

I can get away and say to myself:
I haven't seen a thing.
And the girl, her palate is dry as a potsherd,
her eyes bulge,
when that hand closes over her hair, grasping it
without a shred of pity.

THE PLEASURE OF
JEWISH CULTURE

MAKING JUDAISM COOL

Jonathan Schorsch

I SIT LISTENING TO THE NEWEST and skankiest dub beat, bass thumping, high reverb shimmering, cool horns sliding around the syncopation, the chorus droning:

> Slaughter, slaughter, they want to slaughter 'em
> Slaughter, slaughter, watch out murderer.

The "em" is slurred enough to be "us." The singer drawls in deep Jamaican accents, the words strobe-lighted by the heavy reverb:

> I want to tell you sometin about my granfader,
> my granfader was a concentration camp survivor
> taken from his home in the Second World War
> separated from his family by the Nazis mister
> and herded like an animal into a cattle car.

Is this some Rasta philosemite? No, only a recent CD by a collection of New York's hottest Jewish musicians. Doing the Holocaust as Jamaican dub, it struck me, marked the quintessence of a near decade of making Judaism cool.

Already in the mid-1990s, when living in Jerusalem, I noticed that the ultra-religious radio stations played all sorts of updated songs that were little more than covers of tunes from cool genres—usually from Africa or its diaspora—with words from the Bible or the like. The last decade has also witnessed the rise of the heavy metal Hasidic rock of Yossi Piamenta, the Jewish rap of Blood of Abraham, Rebbe Soul, the New Orleans Klezmer All-Stars, and the whole Lower East Side avant-garde Jewish music scene: the Klezmatics, John Zorn, the Radical Jewish Culture/Tzadik label, etc. A Reggae Passover disc came out a few years back, while an announcement for a Reggae Chanukah disc popped up recently in my email. Even the stodgy Israeli Duo Re'emim did a hip-hop/D.J.-mix cover of the traditional Ashkenazic Rosh Hashanah melodies.

This borrowing approach has a long history in music, Jewish and otherwise, and especially so in Ladino and Hasidic music, many of whose tunes originated in secular, non-Jewish contexts (for instance, as drinking songs). The Hasidim sought to elevate the fallen sparks hidden within the melodies by attaching them to words that called forth the holiest qualities. In the twentieth century, popular Jewish music also went in search of the newest fashion, in search of making the old new and the global local, like the tangos played by Polish Jewish orchestras in the 1920s, or the American "klezmer" musicians in the first part of this century who invented "authentic" old-world Jewish music by updating it with thoroughly American instruments and styles.

Today, post–baby boomers, alive to ethnicity and the rise of religiosity since the 1980s, have come to appreciate the arts of their own ethnic culture. The movement of *ba'alei teshuvah* (those who have made *teshuvah*, "returned" to Jewish observance) has shifted the demographics of the institutional Orthodox world such that the yeshivah-bochers can groove quite easily to the secular, cool, ethnic *riddims* of their sinful youths.

Indeed, such grooves typify the general trend of making Judaism cool. Just think of Madonna and Roseanne studying Kabbalah, radical Jewish culture (Tatooed Jew, etc.), Carlebach followers and fans, the hip currency of Sephardi and Mizrahi music, the style of Chabad missionizing (not to mention the popularity of the Chabad telethon), a Jewish lounge club in New York named Makor (Source). It's not just that Judaism and things Jewish are "in," though that is part of it. No, we are being told that things Jewish—traditionally very uncool—are actually cool. Some Jews are even acting as if it's cool to be Jewish. An Upper West Side paper reported that Friday nights at shul are as popular now as discos! People are converting to Judaism right and left; in some synagogues on the West Coast, converts to Judaism make up 30 percent or more of the congregation. Indeed, if one looks closely one sees that Jewish cool signifies a kind of amusing and perverse but much needed *tikkun,* or repair, for Judaism and our culture at large.

Still, isn't there something a little wrong here? Cool marks ironic distance, detachment, and anti-establishmentarianism, an overemphasis on style. "Mama, I wanna make rhythm, don't wanna make music," crooned Cab Calloway in 1937 New York, as he slid into a mock ethnic voice and scenario (a boy playing rhapsodies on a violin), before exploding into a crescendo of scat ("noise," according to the contemporary mainstream understanding of music and taste). "Pop" music, television, and Hollywood host, if not breed, irony and sarcasm as a *weltanschauung*. Meanwhile, observant Judaism for the most part entails utter seriousness, without much room for humor, sarcasm, or irony, especially in the ultra-Orthodox world. There would seem to be some tension, to say the least, between hip-hop and *tehillim* (psalms), no? Doesn't some inherent semiotics of heavy metal preclude it from serving the seriously sacred?

According to the Jerusalem-based paper *Kol Ha-Ir* some years ago, many ultra-Orthodox rabbis of Me'ah She'arim thought so and came out against the rock-and-roll religious music that had become popular enough to keep open a large, allegedly disruptive music store on one of their neighborhood's main streets. It makes sense that many of the late-night religious D.J.s in Israel broadcast while obviously stoned. Though supposedly radically different in content, the fit between the pre- and post-teshuvah lifestyles appears stylistically continuous. The newly religious traded in their black leather for the stylistics of black suits and fedoras; mohawks for the myriad of specific pe'ot styles, each representing a different Hasidic group. The ornate, patterned, textured chintz vests of the Hasidic rebbes—the fabric origin of the derogatory adjective "chintzy"—now signified for them the height of cool. (Remember the haute-fashion ripoff of Hasidic garb from a few years back?) No surprise that the rebbes worried that the seepage of the pre-teshuvah life into the ba'al-teshuvah life would threaten to undermine the entire point of the transformation.

A close look at two recent releases provides a fascinating glimpse into the paradoxes of cool Judaism. Trumpet player Steven Bernstein's disc, *Diaspora Soul* (1999), on John Zorn's Tzadik label features a small postmodern Latin jazz ensemble belting out versions of "Ani Ma'amin," "Manishtanah," "Rock of Ages," "Roumania, Roumania," and others. The playing is both straight and ironic, funky and funny; Bernstein blows a mean trumpet. In a revealing chain of associations, Bernstein describes the sound he sought:

> Not just the rhythms, but the phrasing and air flow of the R&B players are a continuation of the [New Orleans] marching style. . . . This led me to thinking not just about a New Orleans sound, but rather the

Gulf Coast sound, encompassing Texas and Cuba—and the last part of the Gulf Coast was Miami. And who retired to Miami? The most popular Cuban export of the '50s was the cha-cha. . . . Who loves a cha-cha more than the Jews? And the final piece of the grail—the hora bass pattern—one, two-and, and-four-and—is the first half of the clave, the heart of Afro-Cuban music.

Bernstein's music is clearly a loving tribute. Note, however, that Jews here are only the recipients, the listeners to the great ethnic musics, not their creators.

The tension between the disparate elements in Bernstein's music parallels the tension in the problematic of ethnic identity itself at play in the production of this music and the manufacture of this disc. The Cuban percussions, languid dance-groove bass, vibe-like electric piano, or swelling organ underpin the Jewish melodies which make up the horn themes. These melodies, however, are more icing than cake; Bernstein's soloing, for instance, only occasionally takes up allusions to Jewish music.

Bernstein has (purposefully? ironically?) re-created the overall feeling of exactly those Fifties and Sixties Jewish groups (Mickey Katz, the Barry Sisters) who incorporated "exotic" elements. He makes fun of (and pays respect to) them just as these groups had fun with (and made fun of) the "exotic" musics they were borrowing and even the Jewish music they were simultaneously transforming, down to the cheapo arrangements, "tacky" production values, often uninspired lounge-music tracks—amusing and almost desperate efforts to make cheesy songs cool. Is this the music that Jews who love cha-cha produced? The playing is great and the concept often works; Bernstein has forged a unified sound and it constitutes convincing Jewish music. But the effect cannot be listened to unironically. Perhaps all this has to do with Bernstein's comment about being asked to do a "Jewish" album:

> How does a Jewish musician who has spent his entire life studying "other" musical cultures make a "Jewish" record? How does one make a "Jewish" record, when by nature, all of one's music is already "Jewish"?

Another new release, on the Knitting Factory label, provides one answer to Bernstein's question. *Keter* (1999), the first disc from Zohar, an ensemble made up of eclectic pianist Uri Caine, singer/hazzan Aaron Bensoussan, and other adept players of cutting-edge music scenes in the States and Israel, presents a seamless D.J. mix of Mizrahi and Sephardi trance music over extended renditions of standards such as "Eli Eli," "Avraham Avinu," and many more. The Arabic improvisational singing, Ladino ballads, deep syncopated percussions, throbbing bass lines, avant-garde jazz piano, samples, and tape manipulation all come and go in the overarching mix, constituting equal, interchangeable elements from the databank of world music sounds. Yet this music does not sound ironic. The titles, intensity, and ecstasy all aim to produce a Jewish answer to Nusrat Fateh Ali Khan, Yoruba street percussions, or techno: Jewish music is the primal thang, the oldest and most up-to-date, connected to the grooves of the universe.

The disc's unintended irony resides in the degree to which the music's features come from "other" musical cultures. This shouldn't surprise: the Zohar and Kabbalah itself represent utterly miscegenated texts, a seamless mix of Hellenistic, Arabic, Christian, and Jewish elements. Another unintended irony is that normalizing Jewish music, making it just one among all other ethnic grooves/styles, is done at the cost of accepting the marketing of multiculturalism, the manufacture of cultures. In some ways the music on *Keter* is what I imagine the just-opened Jewish "club" Makor in New York must be like—I've only heard from a sister-in-law who was there herself—with its three stories of Jewish happenings, a bar and strictly kosher food, hip world music imported via the mavens from the Lower East Side, mosh pit above, *shiurim* below, a mind-body *yosher* (balance) that would do the Maharal proud.

Convivencia, man! Judaism for the new millennium! But what does it really mean when lyrics yearning for the speedy rebuilding of the Temple float over the beautiful explosions of Afro-Cuban drumming, a drumming (with its own lyrics, by the way) whose rhythms, like those of Haiti, Brazil, and elsewhere, derive from worship devoted to deities/heroes of Yoruba or Fon or Nago origin, and energize the Afro-Cuban religion known as Santeria? The ironies here abound. Does using this beat imply that the artists condone the Santeria practice—so controversial in parts of the United States—of animal sacrifice? They should, since they sign for the revival of the Temple-based cult of animal sacrifice in Judaism. Do they really want the speedy rebuilding of the Temple and return of the sacrificial system? (Do we, when we sing this song at wedding parties?) One can certainly dance to it, but I wonder. . . .

The cool Jewish trip could only be American. On one side, the roots of Jewish cool lie in New Age terminology and attitude: positivity and openness to the non-modern, to the non-rational. But New Age was never cool. It is a pretend religion for people with pretend traditions. The homogenized, boundaryless music of New Age well reflects its sanitized, denatured, fake solution to personal and world problems. New Age is goofy, yet self-serious, with *no* sense of irony. On the other side, Jewish cool derives from cool aesthetes, from the beat poets to their progeny of the Sixties. These were self-serious, adolescent rebels with a cause, goofy only unintentionally. But their extreme anti-establishment cool left no escape from alienation and anomie.

One brand of Jewish cool that seems to escape this existential angst is the ecstatic neo-Hasidic style developed by the late Shlomo Carlebach. That Carlebach style is a variety of cool can readily be seen from its staunch hippie anti-fashion hierarchy, its rainbow-people politics, and its ease with way-long ecstatic praying and dancing, a product of its followers' affection for way-long guitar and drum solos. Carlebach style owes much to the optimistic, cheerful searching of New Age religiosity, but it derives as well from working-class rebellion and from a hippie back-to-the-land spirit, with roots in serious personal and political *tikkun:* Bob Dylan, the Grateful Dead, Gil Scott-Heron. It's more a whole-person Jungian-balance, caring-people kind of trip. (This might be particularly true for Jewish boys and men, whose self-involved energies adulating cool can thus be channeled into community-oriented, world-healing activities. A great deal of overlap binds Jewish renewal with the men's movement.) Carlebach followers favor a Sephardi/kabbalistic/neo-Hasidic *nusach* for prayer, a rebellion against the insipid Protestant harmonies of American Conservative and Reform synagogues and homes. Carlebach followers are very sincere. A Carlebachy approach maintains interest in the ritual efficacy of particular traditions, all of them, and is never mocking.

Yet even Carlebach style is not free from the ironies of sincerity. The very passion of Carlebach followers can lead to sometimes amusing, sometimes unsettling results. Their search for an "authentic" Judaism has led many to embrace some less-than-savory aspects of Judaism because of their seeming "authenticity." A friend of mine, for example, an inveterate hippie carpenter, pot-smoker and all, is building a piece of the ritual furniture needed for the third Temple planned by some extreme nationalist and ultra-Orthodox groups. Friends of friends apparently hold the "contract" for making the harps to be used therein by the Levitical choirs.

Likewise, I am dismayed to hear that in Israel Rabbi Carlebach's songs and image have now been usurped by right-wing settlers. I have been told that yeshivah-bochers belted out Shlomo *niggunim* (melodies) at a recent rally against dismantling West Bank settlements. I am not surprised by this: anyone can claim pieces of discourse, and Carlebach himself had a strain of nationalism. But it's one thing to market "authentic" ancient-style weddings or biblical clothing, and quite another to make mysticism into militarism by other means. Jewish passion doesn't always lead to ugly nationalism. Without any irony, however, without some critical, skeptical attitude, Carlebachy cool readily becomes too serious, a tool for the Right, and thus no longer cool at all. Can Jewish cool be ironic and serious all at once? Can it survive if it's not?

A recently released anthology of previously untranslated stories of the Ba'al Shem Tov contains a tale in which the wonder rabbi cures a Jew who was passing as a hedonistic Polish noble of his "negativity and insidious addictions." The tale explains to some degree the relationship between cool and Judaism, at least in ba'al teshuvah circles. In his healing speech, addressed both to and not to the disguised Jew, the Besht says:

> Anybody who really wants to progress on the spiritual path must look into his very own soul and see clearly what is stopping him from getting close to God. In my experience there are two traits that obstruct one from truly proceeding on the path. The first one is irrational anger, and the other is sarcasm.

In this Hasidic view, sarcasm, a form of irony, simply must be eliminated. It is easy to understand why. Irony and especially sarcasm imply disdain, haughtiness, mockery, negation, and they act as corrosive agents. Spiritual Judaism, even of the cool variety inspired by pseudo-Kabbalah, entails a voluntary move away from irony. There is to be no more camp for Madonna, who made her name camping and vamping Catholicism. Now, I am told in all seriousness, Roseanne gives *shiurim* at the Kabbalah Learning Center. Even cool Jewish culture that is openly ironic seems to be so these days only affectionately (I'm thinking of the San Francisco Bay area group Charming Hostess' covers of Eastern European and klezmer tunes, or even of Israeli comedian Gil Kopetch).

It all makes sense. People are desperate to escape the postmodern condition, which is fundamentally marked by an ironic stance toward the world. Neo-Hasidim's vision of traditional Judaism's no-nonsense approach to the world offers Jewish kids who grew up in the most assimilated, up-to-date, worldly spheres a means of maintaining the stylistics of cool while escaping cool's alienation and disinterest. A world in which nothing matters or can be done is replaced by one in which every action makes a difference and saves worlds.

Cool Judaism has enabled young Jews to express ethnic pride in themselves and in Judaism, now that they've discovered that the "true" Judaism repressed by their bourgeois parents is ethnic, oppressed and Other. Such "ethnicity" has allowed young Jews to express sincerity in acceptable cool fashion (reggae, hip hop, cutting-edge klezmer) since, unlike whites, oppressed Others are permitted to be sincere, oppositional, searching, and positive while fighting for cultural survival. And it has allowed Jews who have discovered the transcendent in "other" cultures to be open enough to themselves and others about their finding the transcendent "at home."

Through the stylistics of cool Judaism, the rebellion manufactured and harnessed for marketing the rebel youth culture is channeled into a rebellion against the very things producing these styles and attracting young people to them in the first place: the secular culture industry, bourgeois living, individualism, emotional deadness. Hopefully. One cannot forget the extent to which even seemingly authentic efforts of cultural resistance, "the relics of counterculture," as Thomas Frank writes, "reek of affectation and phoniness, the leisure-dreams of white suburban children." All too often cool Judaism harnesses transgression for the sake of mere posture, even for profits. It remains to be seen whether cool Judaism is just another style to consume or whether it helps lead to an authentic and lasting personal rebellion against materialism, against abused worldly power, against the destructive cult of the individual and the ego, the source of the need to be cool.

Judaism will survive cool. Cool might just survive Judaism. After all else is said, these two new CDs make fantastic music for simchas! The question of whether they can survive together, however, depends in each case on the fundamental formula contained in Pierre Bourdieu's theory of the "habitus," as articulated by Duke Ellington: it ain't what you do but the way that you do it. Passion and the search for "authenticity" cannot become substitutes for thinking, for the eternal effort to juggle the necessary opposites of God and human, devotion and critique, self-confidence and humility. Planning for the third Temple is not merely a larger equivalent of the drumming circles of men's groups. The dangers of soul without mind continue to be very real. This said, however, the potential power of cool Jewish culture remains strong. If cool Judaism helps young people avoid the Orwellian carelessness, ignorance, and idiocy induced by the culture industry, it makes a damn good noble lie.

OLD MAN

C. K. Williams

Special: Big Tits, says the advertisement for a soft-core magazine
    on our neighborhood newsstand,
but forget her breasts—a lush, fresh-lipped blonde, skin glowing
    gold, sprawls there, resplendent,
Sixty nearly, yet these hardly tangible, hardly better than harlots
    can still stir me.

Maybe coming of age in the American sensual darkness, never
    seeing an unsmudged nipple,
an uncensored vagina, has left me forever infected with an
    unquenchable lust of the eye:
always that erotic murmur—I'm hardly myself if I'm not in a state
    of incipient desire.

God knows, though, there are worse twists your obsessions can
    take: last year, in Israel,
a young ultra-Orthodox rabbi, guiding some teen-aged girls
    through the shrine of the *Shoah,*
forbade them to look in one room because there were images in it
    he said were licentious.

The display was a photo: men and women, stripped naked, some
    trying to cover their genitals,

others too frightened to bother, lined up in snow waiting to be
    shot and thrown in a ditch.
The girls to my horror averted their gaze: what carnal mistrust had
    their teacher taught them?

Even that, though . . . Another confession: once, in a book on
    pre-war Poland, a studio-portrait,
an absolute angel, with tormented, tormenting eyes, I kept finding
    myself at her page;
that she died in the camps made her, I didn't dare wonder why,
    more present, more precious.

"Died in the camps": that, too, people, or Jews anyway, kept from
    their children back then,
but it was like sex, you didn't have to be told. Sex and death: how
    close they can seem.
So constantly conscious now of death moving towards me,
    sometimes I think I confound them.

My wife's loveliness almost consumes me, my passion for her goes
    beyond reasonable bounds;
when we make love, her holding me, everywhere all around me,
    I'm there and not there,
my mind teems, jumbles of faces, voices, impressions: I live my life
    over as though I were drowning.

. . . Then I am drowning, in despair, at having to leave her, this,
    everything, all: unbearable, awful . . .
Still, to be able to die with no special contrition, not having been
    slaughtered or enslaved,
and now having to know history's next mad rage or regression—
    it might be a relief.

No, again no, I don't mean that for a moment, what I mean is the
    world holds me so tightly,
the good and the bad, my own follies and weakness, that even this
    counterfeit Venus,
with her sham heat and her bosom probably plumped with gel, so
    moves me my breath catches.

Vamp, siren, seductress, how much more she reveals in her glare of
    ink than she knows;

how she incarnates our desperate human need for regard, our
    passion to live in beauty,
to be beauty, to be cherished, by glances if by no more,
    of something like love, or love.

POEMS

Yona Wallach

When You Come to Sleep with Me, Come Like My Father

When you come to sleep with me
come like my father
come in darkness

speak in his voice
so I won't know
I'll crawl on all fours
and I'll speak about what I don't have
and you'll scold me:
"my substance"
separate from me
at the gate
say goodbye
a thousand times
with all the yearnings
there are
until God says:
"enough"
and I'll let go
I won't sleep
not with God

not with my father
I'll want to sleep with you
but you say no
together with my father
suddenly you'll be revealed
as the one in charge of
the restraints
my father will be an angel
officer of hosts
and the two of you will try to make of me
something
I'll feel
like nothing
and I'll do everything
you tell me to do.
On the one hand you'll be God
and I'll wait for afterwards
and you won't be the authority
and I'm just down and out
trying to be polite
I'll divide you in two
and also myself
part soul
part body
and you'll appear like two
and I
like two seals
one wounded
dragging a fin
or two women
one always limping
and you one face
and the other hardly seen

Hebrew

English has all the possibilities for gender
every I—in actuality
is every possibility of sex
and every you feminine is you masculine
and every I is sexless
and there's no difference between you feminine and you masculine
and all things are so—not a man not a woman
you don't have to think before relating to sex
Hebrew is a sex maniac
Hebrew discriminates for bad or good
is generous gives privileges
with an account longer than the Exile
in the plural they have the right of way
with great subtlety and secrecy
in the singular chances are equal
who says all hope is lost
Hebrew is a sex maniac
wants to know who's speaking
almost a vision almost a picture
what's forbidden in the whole Torah
at least to see the sex
Hebrew peeks through the keyhole
like me at your mother and you
when you both were bathing then in the shack
your mother had large buttocks
but I never stopped thinking
the days passed like vanishing ink
you feminine remained a thin and soapy girl
afterwards you both sealed all the holes
sealed all the cracks
Hebrew peeks at you feminine singular from the keyhole
the language sees you naked
my father didn't permit me to look
he turned his back when he pissed
I never really had a good look at him
he always hid the sex
the way the plural hides a woman
like a crowd is male in conjugations
like *word* is male and female

there's nothing like those sweet things
Hebrew is a woman bathing
Hebrew is a clean Bathsheba
Hebrew is a carving that doesn't cut out
she has small dimples and birthmarks
as she grows up she gets prettier
her judgment is sometimes prehistoric
such a neurosis is for the best
tell me in the masculine tell me in the feminine
every childish I is an unfertilized egg
it's possible to pass over sex
it's possible to give up sex
who will tell the sex of a chick?
the man who nature creates
before he's implanted with his identifying verb.
Memory is masculine
creating sexes
propagation is imperative
since she is life
Hebrew is a sex maniac (feminine)
and whatever shrill feminists complain about
seeking stimulation outside language
with intonation that interprets things
signs only of the masculine and feminine in a sentence
will offer strange sexual relationships
on every female a sign, on every male a different sign
when every verb and conjugation is assigned
what the man does to the woman
what he gets in return
what power she exerts over him
and what sign is given to the object
and to an abstract noun and articles
we'll get a rather natural game
a psychological occurrence like a young forest
a game of the common powers of nature
from which all the details are derived,
common signs for all events
that can possibly happen at one time or another
look what body the language has what dimensions
I will love her now with a free tongue

ESTHER AND YOCHANAN

Nomi Eve

My father writes:
Rabbi Yochanan Schine, a student of the famous Chatam Sofer, was engaged to Esther Sophie Goldner Herschell, the granddaughter of the chief rabbi of the British Empire. Esther and Yochanan were my great-great-grandparents. They immigrated to Palestine and married in 1837 in Jerusalem.

I write:
Esther was pious but in a peripheral way. She knew the *mitzvot,* she knew to make the Sabbath holy, but she felt that there was no real harm in putting her own creative interpretation on the old rules because certainly creativity was an essential and blessed quality of Man and it would be a sin not to use it.

At first she did not like Jerusalem; she was from a long line of people who lacked sense of direction. The stony city, with all of its obscurant walls, twists and turns, seemed to her a nasty place without any recognizable plan.

Three months and two days after the young couple arrived, she ventured out alone for the first time. Quickly lost, but not frightened, Esther decided she would just wander. She knew that if she wanted to she could ask someone to show her the way back to their house, which was a half-grand, half-decrepit habitation on Rav Pinchas Street. It was located across from the Peace of Israel Synagogue in the center of town.

And then Esther smelled the bread. She turned a corner, walked a few more steps. Soon she was standing outside an arched open door watching a bare-armed baker slide a tray of dough into a furnace. Esther stood and stared. The steam and sweat and dough and bare baker skin created in the room an atmosphere magnetic, carnally alluring. The baker was a young man, no more than twenty. Esther, married less than four months, was nineteen.

Although she was not ordinarily a believer in astrology, and had absolutely no idea how sailors used the night sky to tell them where to go, she felt certain that crucial stars had descended into that tiny baker room to make for her a perfect navigational tool. In short, she was inspired, and knew for once in her life exactly in which direction she was supposed to go.

The baker stood before her—a destination slim and brown. He was lithe and beautiful in a coltish, boyish way. Only a bit taller than she. Esther immediately took in his huge almondy eyes, and his hair—thick dark brown hair—gathered in a low braid at the back. He seemed to her like something carved out of precious wood; miniature, masculine, and muscular all at once.

The bakery was only two rooms. One with a low, wooden baking table rutted and eternally floury from years of use, and the other with a brick furnace that had been hewn, by the baker's grandfather, out of the limestone wall. It was behind what would later be the public pavilion but was then a rubbly clump of lower-class homes bordering the more prosperous center of town. When the baker saw the young woman with the full skirt, cinched at the waist, when he saw the big brown eyes of the woman, when he saw her white skin, full lips, and attractive face, he invited her in. He gave her a fresh roll and asked her, in nervous, clumsy Yiddish (which, like a mule, kicked and brayed itself off of his tongue; he was embarrassed at his language's lack of manners) if she would like some sweet mint tea. This was the start of her nine-year love affair with the baker and her lifelong passionate entanglement with Jerusalem, the city whose twists, turns, bakers, and twin arcane whispers of piety and perversity ultimately spoke straight to her heart.

Esther would make love with her husband at night "through her front door" and then, in the daytime, she carried out an affair with the baker, a third-generation Palestinian Jew. Their sexual game was ruled by the fact that the baker would only enter into her "rear door." Both euphemism (which in the entire nine years they never breached) and position (which in the entire nine years they never varied except slightly in angle) suited them. Titillating not only the tenderest parts of their anatomies, but also the deeply humorous sense of sex that they found they shared.

She came once a week, on Tuesdays, in the late afternoon when her husband would be busy participating in his civic meetings and the rest of the town, in classic Mediterranean style, would be indoors either scheming, studying, or sleeping. The baker, whose hands Esther always thought were strangely thin-fingered and uncalloused for a baker, would lock the door to the back of the shop. And as he walked over to her, she would be laying a clean cloth down on the baking table. She loved lifting a finger to his lips, putting her fingers in his mouth and then tracing the graceful outline of his face, from mouth to nose, eyes and into ears.

Always, when they were both ready, she would turn away from him and lean her body over the table. He pulled up her skirts, pulled down her undergarments and his own pants. Then he licked the fingers on his right hand and slowly, passionately, opened her up. Soon he slid right into her. She loved the feel of his body angling its way upward. She loved the feel of her heavy breasts hard pressing into the wooden table. He gripped her hips and thrust himself deep.

They kissed and panted and hungered at and for each other's skin— more, not less, fervently as the years went by. Theirs, they agreed, was an ancient elemental passion that must have existed, like sand, earth, and sky, long before either of them had been born. And despite the intense physicality of their togethering, both Esther and the baker always felt insubstantial, flimsy, oh so light in the presence of this passion. But this was not a bad feeling. When they made love, it was as if they were wrapping their bodies not only around each other but also, and more essentially, around something else that had before been naked. It was, they agreed, as if the passion were the real creature, and they, though temporarily deprived of the normal trappings of personhood, were lucky to have been chosen as its favorite clothes. They dressed the passion in carnal finery, and the passion wore them with secret frequency.

My great-great-grandmother, Esther Sophie Goldner Schine, granddaughter of the chief rabbi of the British Empire, thought her husband's coming in through her front door and her lover's coming in through her back door was the perfect arrangement for a Jewish woman. The notion of separate facilities fit nicely into the ready framework of *kashrut*. Milk here, meat there, and as long as there was proper distance between things, everything stayed quietly kosher.

My father writes:
Yochanan came from a part of East Prussia called Sheinlanka, which means "pretty terraces." Today it is part of Poland, not far from the town of Posnan. He came to Palestine under the following circumstances:

In 1836, the chief rabbi of the British Empire, Rabbi Shlomo Berliner Herschell, sent out a messenger to search for a *shidach* for his granddaughter, Esther. A *shidach* is the Yiddish word for a marriage match. The marriage was to be found by the condition that the young couple marry and reside in Jerusalem. This was before the existence of Zionism. Most Jews still believed that Israel should not and could not be established until the Messiah came to Zion. Rabbi Herschell disagreed with prevailing thought. He was among a group of radical European Orthodox Jews who believed that moving to Palestine was not in opposition to the messianic ideal.

The messenger traveled for almost an entire year. Finally, he arrived at the city of Pressburg, at the house of study of the famous Prussian rabbi, the Chatam Sofer. Yochanan had long been a student there. Like the chief rabbi, the Chatam Sofer also disagreed with prevailing thought—that is, he believed in Israel as a realistic homeland, not just a spiritual one. In response to the rabbi's messenger, the Chatam Sofer promptly sent his prized student, Yochanan. Yochanan and Esther met in London and became engaged almost immediately.

I write:
On the third Tuesday of Cheshvan, four months after they arrived in Jerusalem, Yochanan finished early with his civic meeting and decided to make for home. He was just about to walk past the Glory of Israel Synagogue when he saw Esther step out of the front door of their house and turn to walk the other way. It was late fall, and chilly. She was wearing her long maroon coat and the wide-brimmed black hat that tipped down over her right eye and made her vision, she always explained, "a bit drunk feeling, you know, only half there and wobbly, but not too bad. I find my way after all." Yochanan loved his wife's way of speaking. Her sentences were curvy and full of original character.

Yochanan called out to Esther but he was too far for her to hear and so he walked on and meant to call again, but then he found himself walking quietly, stealthily after his wife around a corner, and again, another corner, and then down the street and into an alley. He stopped at the mouth of the alley and watched his wife walk through the bakery's back door. Her maroon coat wafted behind her for several seconds and then too, disappeared into the warm realm of dough and yeast.

Pulling back and into a doorway on which was graffitied the word *sky* in sloppy Aramaic, he looked up at the real sky, which was darkening with the foredream of a storm. He watched as the baker poked his head out and then shut the front door of his shop. Hidden, but only ten feet away, Yochanan didn't say a word. Then he walked to the closed bakery door and put his ear to the old wood of it. Soon he could hear his wife groaning. He stepped away from the door and looked up and down the street. No one was in the alley, nor walking toward it. He walked back and listened some more.

He became aroused almost immediately, and soon was picturing the baker holding Esther's naked breasts, petting them gently and then lifting up the nipples to his mouth. First one and then the other. And the baker's hand. Yochanan imagined the baker's left hand reaching in between Esther's legs, which she pressed together tightly. Soon, in his mind, they were pressing their naked bodies together and moving, back and forth, toward and away, with the tempestuous ease of a storm just brewing. The storm outside began to blow. Yochanan huddled into his coat, raised his collar, and ducked deeper into the doorway. Shutting his eyes, he leaned into the images as if they were the real door, open and welcoming, while the wooden one, closed and cold against his body, kept him out of all this. Now he heard the baker groaning. Esther let out a small, passionate yelp. And as the two lovers inside reached satiety, the one outside reached down and touched himself, pressed there, pressed and pulled himself to solitary, intense pleasure. Only then did he leave.

Yochanan put his hands over his hat and ran through the rain. His feet swish-swished into puddles already forming in the narrow, stony streets. As he ran, he heard himself reciting an angry litany like an opposite prayer.

> *The baker has a face of moldy clay.*
> *The baker has hands of heavy stinking wood.*
> *The baker is a deformed gentile in disguise.*
> *The baker is an eater of clams.*
> *A descendant of Amalek.*
> *The devil of devils.*
> *The baker is . . . the baker is . . . the baker is shtupping my wife!*

The rain hit him harder now, pelting from every angle and also straight up from the ground. He felt slowed by it, slowed and assaulted, as if each raindrop were a separate obstacle. Reaching home, he went inside, took off his great coat and hat, and set them upon the fine wooden rack that they had brought with them from London. Shaking out his beard and hair, he ran his fingers through them. Then he held his hands up to his mouth and breathed into his open palms. The warm air hovered there, but only for a second, and soon his skin was cold again. He breathed again, felt warm for several seconds and then cold again, warm and then cold. Cold. He dropped his hands down to his sides, thrust them into his pockets, and sighed deeply. But then everything changed. His mood rocked and swayed, and Yochanan felt a smile flutter to his lips.

Laughing out loud, he turned and looked at his image in the gilt hall mirror. My, how shaggy! Wet! How disheveled! But happy! Happy! He found himself possessed of an excited and yet cautious confusion.

He had taken great pleasure outside the baker's door and yet there were so many sins and so much shame growing on the fields where this kind of pleasure bloomed. Where was his anger? He could not feel it now. Where was his litany, his sour prayer? Yochanan loved his wife and trusted her too. Strangely, he still trusted her. The image of Esther in the baker's arms was an excruciatingly beautiful flower. Vicarious, criminal, devastating, and yet thrilling. He ached with every petal, leaf, and fresh-cut stem of it.

Once again, he imagined the baker's dark hands thrusting upward into Esther's body, her mouth half open, lips wet. Yochanan imagined and imagined, and grew once again aroused while standing alone in the antechamber still dripping from the rain. But he didn't touch himself this time. He was in his own house and the walls were lined with holy books. Yochanan could not bring such odd illicit flowers home with him. Rubbing his hands together, he put them once more through his beard. As if he could comb out the confusion. A servant walked into the antechamber.

"Oh, sir, I didn't hear you . . . come in, sit by the fire, take off your wet clothes and eat some fresh rolls just come from the baker. Esther, the lady, your wife, she has just brought them in through the kitchen courtyard door."

THE TWENTY-SEVENTH MAN

Nathan Englander

THE ORDERS WERE GIVEN from Stalin's country house at Kuntsevo. He relayed them to the agent in charge with no greater emotion than for the killing of kulaks or clergy or the outspoken wives of very dear friends. The accused were to be apprehended the same day, arrive at the prison gates at the same moment, and—with a gasp and simultaneous final breath—be sent off to their damnation in a single rattling burst of gunfire.

It was not an issue of hatred, only one of allegiance. For Stalin knew there could be loyalty to only one nation. What he did not know so well were the authors' names on his list. When presented to him the next morning he signed the warrant anyway, though there were now twenty-seven, and yesterday there had been twenty-six.

No matter, except maybe to the twenty-seventh.

The orders left little room for variation, and none for tardiness. They were to be carried out in secrecy and—the only point that was reiterated—simultaneously. But how were the agents to get the men from Moscow and Gorky, Smolensk and Penza, Shuya and Podolsk, to the prison near the village of X at the very same time?

The agent in charge felt his strength was in leadership and gave up the role of strategist to the inside of his hat. He cut the list into strips and sprinkled them into the freshly blocked crown, mixing carefully so as not to disturb its shape. Most of these writers were in Moscow. The handful who were in their native villages, taking the water somewhere, or locked in a cabin trying to finish that seminal work would surely receive a stiff cuffing when a pair of agents, aggravated by the trek, stepped through the door.

After the lottery, those agents who had drawn a name warranting a long journey accepted the good-natured insults and mockery of friends. Most would have it easy, nothing more to worry about than hurrying some old rebel to a car, or getting their shirts wrinkled in a heel-dragging, hair-pulling rural scene that could be as messy as necessary in front of a pack of superstitious peasants.

Then there were those who had it hard. Such as the two agents assigned to Vasily Korinsky, who, seeing no way out, was prepared to exit his bedroom quietly but whose wife, Paulina, struck the shorter of the two officers with an Oriental-style brass vase. There was a scuffle, Paulina was subdued, the short officer taken out unconscious, and a precious hour lost on their estimated time.

There was the pair assigned to Moishe Bretzky, a true lover of vodka and its country of origin. One would not have pegged him as one of history's most sensitive Yiddish poets. He was huge, slovenly, and smelly as a horse. Once a year, during the Ten Days of Penitence, he would take notice of his sinful ways and sober up for Yom Kippur. After the fast, he would grab pen and pad and write furiously for weeks in his sister's ventless kitchen—the shroud of atonement still draped over his splitting head. The finished work was toasted with a brimming shot of vodka. Then Bretzky's thirst would begin to rage and off he would go for another year. His sister's husband would have put an end to this annual practice if it weren't for the rubles he received for the sweat-curled pages Bretzky abandoned.

It took the whole of the night for the two agents to locate Bretzky. They tracked him down in one of the whorehouses that did not exist, and if they did, government agents surely did not frequent them. Nonetheless, having escaped notice, they slipped into the room. Bretzky was passed out on his stomach with a smiling trollop pinned under each arm. The time-consuming process of freeing the whores, getting Bretzky upright, and moving him into the hallway reduced the younger man to tears.

The senior agent left his partner in charge of the body while he went to chat with the senior woman of the house. Introducing himself numerous times, as if they had never met, he explained his predicament and enlisted the help of a dozen women.

Twelve of the house's strongest companions—in an array of pink and red robes, froufrou slippers, and painted toenails—carried the giant bear to the waiting car amid a roar of giggles. It was a sight Bretzky would have enjoyed tremendously had he been conscious.

The least troubling of the troublesome abductions was that of Y. Zunser, oldest of the group and a target of the first serious verbal attacks on the cosmopolitans back in '49. In the February 19 edition of *Literaturnaya Gazeta* he had been criticized as an obsolete author, accused of being anti-Soviet, and chided for using a pen name to hide his Jewish roots. In that same edition they printed his real name, Melman, stripping him of the privacy he had so enjoyed.

Three years later they came for him. The two agents were not enthusiastic about the task. They had shared a Jewish literature instructor in high school, whom they admired despite his ethnicity and who even coerced them into writing a poem or two. Both were rather decent fellows, and capturing an eighty-one-year-old man did not exactly jibe with their vision of bravely serving the party. They were simply following instructions. But somewhere amid their justifications lay a deep fear of punishment.

It was not yet dawn and Zunser was already dressed, sitting with a cup of tea. The agents begged him to stand up on his own, one of them trying the name Zunser and the other pleading with Melman. He refused.

"I will neither resist nor help. The responsibility must rest fully upon your conscience."

"We have orders," they said.

"I did not say you were without orders. I said that you have to bear responsibility."

The first tried lifting him by his arms, but Zunser was too delicate for the maneuver. Then one grabbed his ankles while the other clasped his chest. Zunser's head lolled back. The agents were afraid of killing him, an option they had been warned against. They put him on the floor and the larger of the two scooped him up, cradling the old man like a child.

Zunser begged a moment's pause as they passed a portrait of his deceased wife. He fancied the picture had a new moroseness to it, as if the sepia-toned eyes might well up and shed a tear. He spoke aloud. "No matter, Katya. Life ended for me on the day of your death; everything since has been but nostalgia." The agent shifted the weight of the romantic in his arms and headed out the door.

The solitary complicated abduction that took place out of Moscow was the one that should have been the easiest of the twenty-seven. It was the simple task of removing Pinchas Pelovits from the inn on the road that ran to X and the prison beyond.

Pinchas Pelovits had constructed his own world with a compassionate God and a diverse group of worshipers. In it, he tested these people with moral dilemmas and tragedies—testing them sometimes more with joy and good fortune. He recorded the trials and events of this world in his notebooks in the form of stories and novels, essays, poems, songs, anthems, tales, jokes, and extensive histories that led up to the era in which he dwelled.

His parents never knew what label to give their son, who wrote all day but did not publish, who laughed and cried over his novels but was gratingly logical in his contact with the everyday world. What they did know was that Pinchas wasn't going to take over the inn.

When they became too old to run the business, the only viable option was to sell out at a ridiculously low price—provided the new owners would leave the boy his room and feed him when he was hungry. Even when the business became the property of the state, Pinchas, in the dreamer's room, was left in peace: *Why bother, he's harmless, sort of a good-luck charm for the inn, no one even knows he's here, maybe he's writing a history of the place, and we'll all be made famous.* He wasn't. But who knows, maybe he would have, had his name—mumbled on the lips of travelers—not found its way onto Stalin's list.

The two agents assigned Pinchas arrived at the inn driving a beat-up droshky and posing as the sons of now poor landowners, a touch they thought might tickle their superiors. One carried a Luger (a trinket he brought home from the war), and the other kept a billy club stashed in his boot. They found the narrow hallway with Pinchas's room and knocked lightly on his door. "Not hungry" was the response. The agent with the Luger gave the door a hip check; it didn't budge. "Try the handle," said the voice. The agent did, swinging it open.

"You're coming with us," said the one with the club in his boot.

"Absolutely not," Pinchas stated matter-of-factly. The agent wondered if his "You're coming with us" had sounded as bold.

"Put the book down on the pile, put your shoes on, and let's go." The agent with the Luger spoke slowly. "You're under arrest for anti-Soviet activity."

Pinchas was baffled by the charge. He meditated for a moment and came to the conclusion that there was only one moral outrage he'd been involved in, though it seemed to him a bit excessive to be incarcerated for it.

"Well, you can have them, but they're not really mine. They were in a copy of a Zunser book that a guest forgot and I didn't know where to return them. Regardless, I studied them thoroughly. You may take me away." He proceeded to hand the agents five postcards. Three were intricate pen-and-ink drawings of a geisha in various positions with her legs spread wide. The other two were identical photographs of a sturdy Russian maiden in front of a painted tropical background wearing a hula skirt and making a vain attempt to cover her breasts. Pinchas began stacking his notebooks while the agents divvied the cards. He was sad that he had not resisted temptation. He would miss taking his walks and also the desk upon whose mottled surface he had written.

"May I bring my desk?"

The agent with the Luger was getting fidgety. "You won't be needing anything, just put on your shoes."

"I'd much prefer my books to shoes," Pinchas said. "In the summer I sometimes take walks without shoes but never without a novel. If you would have a seat while I organize my notes—" and Pinchas fell to the floor, struck in the head with the pistol grip. He was carried from the inn rolled in a blanket, his feet poking forth, bare.

Pinchas awoke, his head throbbing from the blow and the exceedingly tight blindfold. This was aggravated by the sound of ice cracking under the droshky wheels, as happens along the river route west of X. "The bridge is out on this road," he told them. "You'd best cut through the old Bunakov place. Everybody does it in winter."

The billy club was drawn from the agent's boot, and Pinchas was struck on the head once again. The idea of arriving only to have their prisoner blurt out the name of the secret prison was mortifying. In an attempt to confound him, they turned off on a clearly unused road. There are reasons that unused roads are not used. It wasn't half a kilometer before they had broken a wheel and it was off to a nearby pig farm on foot. The agent with the gun commandeered a donkey-drawn cart, leaving a furious pig farmer cursing and kicking the side of his barn.

The trio were all a bit relieved upon arrival: Pinchas because he started to get the idea that this business had to do with something more than his minor infraction, and the agents because three other cars had shown up only minutes before they had—all inexcusably late.

By the time the latecomers had been delivered, the initial terror of the other twenty-three had subsided. The situation was tense and grave, but also unique. An eminent selection of Europe's surviving Yiddish literary community was being held within the confines of an oversized closet. Had they known they were going to die, it might have been different. Since they didn't, I. J. Manger wasn't about to let Mani Zaretsky see him cry for rachmones. He didn't have time to anyway. Pyotr Kolyazin, the famed atheist, had already dragged him into a heated discussion about the ramifications of using God's will to drastically alter the outcome of previously "logical" plots. Manger took this to be an attack on his work and asked Kolyazin if he labeled everything he didn't understand "illogical." There was also the present situation to discuss, as well as old rivalries, new poems, disputed reviews, journals that just aren't the same, up-and-coming editors, and, of course, the gossip, for hadn't they heard that Lev had used his latest manuscript for kindling?

When the noise got too great, a guard opened the peephole in the door to find that a symposium had broken loose. As a result, by the time numbers twenty-four through twenty-seven arrived, the others had already been separated into smaller cells.

Each cell was meant to house four prisoners and contained three rotting mats to sleep on. In a corner was a bucket. There were crude holes in the wood-plank walls, and it was hard to tell if the captors had punched them as a form of ventilation or if the previous prisoners had painstakingly scratched them through to confirm the existence of a world outside.

The four latecomers had lain down immediately, Pinchas on the floor. He was dazed and shivering, stifling his moans so the others might rest. His companions did not even think of sleep: Vasily Korinsky because of worry about what might be the outcome for his wife; Y. Zunser because he was trying to adapt to the change (the only alteration he had planned for in his daily routine was death, and that in his sleep); Bretzky because he hadn't really awakened.

Excepting Pinchas, none had an inkling of how long they'd traveled, whether from morning until night or into the next day. Pinchas tried to use his journey as an anchor, but in the dark he soon lost his notion of time gone by. He listened for the others' breathing, making sure they were alive.

The light bulb hanging from a frayed wire in the ceiling went on. This was a relief; not only an end to the darkness but a separation, a seam in the seeming endlessness.

They stared unblinking into the dim glow of the bulb and worried about its abandoning them. All except Bretzky, whose huge form already ached for a vodka and who dared not crack an eye.

Zunser was the first to speak. "With morning there is hope."

"For what?" asked Korinsky out of the side of his mouth. His eye was pressed up against a hole in the back wall.

"A way out," Zunser said. He watched the bulb, wondering how much electricity there was in the wire, how he would reach it, and how many of them it would serve.

Korinsky misunderstood the statement to be an optimistic one. "Feh on your way out and feh on your morning. It's pitch dark outside. Either it's night or we're in a place with no sun. I'm freezing to death."

The others were a bit shocked when Bretzky spoke: "Past the fact that you are not one of the whores I paid for and this is not the bed we fell into, I'm uncertain. Whatever the situation, I shall endure it, but without your whining about being cold in front of an old man in shirtsleeves and this skinny one with no shoes." His powers of observation were already returning and Yom Kippur still months away.

"I'm fine," said Pinchas. "I'd much rather have a book than shoes."

They all knitted their brows and studied the man; even Bretzky propped himself up on an elbow.

Zunser laughed, and then the other three started in. Yes, it would be much better to have a book. Whose book? Surely not the pamphlet by that fool Horiansky—this being a well-publicized and recent failure. They laughed some more. Korinsky stopped, worrying that one of the other men in the room might be Horiansky. Horiansky, thankfully, was on the other end of the hall and was spared that final degradation before his death.

No one said another word until the light bulb went off again, and then they remained silent because it was supposed to be night. However, it was not. Korinsky could see light seeping through the holes and chinks in the boards. He would tell them so when the bulb came back on, if it did.

Pinchas could have laughed indefinitely, or at least until the time of his execution. His mind was not trained, never taught any restraint or punished for its reckless abandon. He had written because it was all that interested him, aside from his walks, and the pictures at which he had peeked. Not since childhood had he skipped a day of writing.

Composing without pen and paper, he decided on something short, something he could hone, add a little bit to every day until his release.

Zunser felt the coldness of the floor seeping into his bones, turning them brittle. It was time anyway. He had lived a long life, enjoyed recognition for something he loved doing. All the others who had reached his level of fame had gone to the ovens or were in America. How much more meaningless was success with the competition gone? Why write at all when your readers have been turned to ash? Never outlive your language. Zunser rolled onto his side.

Bretzky sweated the alcohol of his blood. He tried to convince himself that it was a vision of drink, a clearer vision because he was getting older, but a hallucination nonetheless. How many times had he turned, after hearing his name called, to find no one? He fumbled for a breast, a soft pink cheek, a swatch of satin, and fell asleep.

Before closing his eyes only to find more darkness, Pinchas recited the first paragraph a final time:

The morning that Mendel Muskatev awoke to find his desk was gone, his room was gone, and the sun was gone, he assumed he had died. This worried him, so he said the prayer for the dead, keeping himself in mind. Then he wondered if one was allowed to do such a thing, and worried instead that the first thing he had done upon being dead was sin.

When the light came on, Korinsky stirred noticeably, as if to break the ice, as if they were bound by the dictates of civilized society. "You know it isn't morning, it's about nine o'clock or ten, midnight at the latest."

Pinchas was reciting his paragraph quietly, playing with the words, making changes, wishing he had a piece of slate.

Korinsky waited for an answer, staring at the other three. It was hard to believe they were writers. He figured he too must be disheveled, but at least there was some style left in him. These others, a drunk, an incontinent old curmudgeon, and an idiot, could not be of his caliber. Even the deficient Horiansky would be appreciated now. "I said, it's not morning. They're trying to fool us, mess up our internal clocks."

"Then go back to sleep and leave us to be fooled." Bretzky had already warned this sot yesterday. He didn't need murder added to his list of trumped-up charges.

"You shouldn't be so snide with me. I'm only trying to see if we can maintain a little dignity while they're holding us here."

Zunser had set himself up against a wall. He had folded his mat and used it like a chair, cushioning himself from the splinters. "You say 'holding' as if this is temporary and in the next stage we will find ourselves someplace more to our liking."

Korinsky looked at Zunser, surveying him boldly. He did not like being goaded, especially by some old coot who had no idea to whom he was talking.

"Comrade," he addressed Zunser in a most acerbic tone, "I am quite sure my incarceration is due to bureaucratic confusion of some sort. I've no idea what you wrote that landed you here, but I have an impeccable record. I was a principal member of the Anti-Fascist Committee, and my ode, *Stalin of Silver, Stalin of Gold*, happens to be a national favorite."

"'We spilled our blood in revolution, only to choke on Stalin's pollution.'" Bretzky quoted a bastardization of Korinsky's ballad.

"How dare you mock me!"

"I've not had the pleasure of hearing the original," Zunser said, "but I must say the mockery is quite entertaining."

"'Our hearts cheered as one for revolution, now we bask in the glory of great Stalin's solution.'" All three heads turned to Pinchas, Korinsky's the quickest.

"Perfect." Korinsky sneered at the other two men. "I must say it is nice to be in the presence of at least one fan."

Among the many social interactions Pinchas had never before been involved in, this was one. He did not know when adulation was being requested.

"Oh, I'm no fan, sir. You're a master of the Yiddish language, but the core of all your work is flawed by a heavy-handed party message that has nothing to do with the people about whom you write." This with an eloquence which to Korinsky sounded like the fool was condescending.

"The characters are only vehicles, fictions!" He was shouting at Pinchas. Then he caught himself shouting at an idiot, while the other two men convulsed with laughter.

"They are very real," said Pinchas before returning to his rocking and mumbling.

"What are you two fops making fun of? At least I have a body of work that is read."

Bretzky was angry again. "Speak to me as you like. If it begins to bother me too much, I'll pinch your head off from your neck." He made a pinching motion with his massive fingers. "But I must warn you against speaking to your elders with disrespect. Furthermore, I have a most cloudy feeling that the face on the old man also belongs to the legendary Zunser, whose accomplishments far exceed those of any of the writers, Yiddish or otherwise, alive in Russia today."

"Zunser?" said Korinsky.

"Y. Zunser!" screamed Pinchas. He could not imagine being confined with such a singular mind. Pinchas had never even considered that Zunser was an actual person. My God, he had seen the great seer pee into a bucket. "Zunser," he said to the man. He stood and banged his fist against the door, screaming "Zunser" over and over again, like it was a password his keepers would understand and know the game was finished.

A guard came down the hall and beat Pinchas to the floor. He left them a bowl of water and a few crusts of black bread. The three ate quickly. Bretzky held up the casualty while Zunser poured some water into his mouth, made him swallow.

"The man is crazy, he is going to get us all killed." Korinsky sat with his eye against a knothole, peering into the darkness of their day.

"Maybe us, but who would dare to kill the poet laureate of the Communist empire?" Bretzky's tone was biting, though his outward appearance did not reflect it. He cradled Pinchas's limp form while Zunser mopped the boy's brow with his sleeve.

"This is no time for joking. I was going to arrange for a meeting with the warden, but that lunatic's screaming fouled it up. Swooning like a young girl. Has he never before met a man he admired?" Korinsky hooked a finger through one of the larger holes, as if he were trying to feel the texture of the darkness outside. "Who knows when that guard will return?"

"I would not rush to get out," said Zunser. "I can assure you there is only one way to exit."

"Your talk gets us nowhere." Korinsky stood and leaned a shoulder against a cold board.

"And what has gotten you somewhere?" said Zunser. "Your love ballads to the regime? There are no hoofbeats to be heard in the distance. Stalin doesn't spur his horse, racing to your rescue."

"He doesn't know. He wouldn't let them do this to me."

"Maybe not to you, but to the Jew that has your name and lives in your house and lies next to your wife, yes." Zunser massaged a stiffening knee.

"It's not my life. It's my culture, my language. No more."

"Only your language?" Zunser waved him away. "Who are we without Yiddish?"

"The four sons of the Passover seder, at best." Korinsky sounded bitter.

"This is more than tradition, Korinsky. It's blood." Bretzky spat into the pail. "I used to drink with Kapler, shot for shot."

"And?" Korinsky kept his eye to a hole but listened closely.

"And have you seen a movie directed by Kapler lately? He made a friendship with the exalted comrade's daughter. Now he is in a labor camp—if he's alive. Stalin did not take too well to Jewish hands on his daughter's pure white skin."

"You two wizards can turn a Stalin to a Hitler."

Bretzky reached over and gave Korinsky a pat on the leg. "We don't need the Nazis, my friend."

"Feh, you're a paranoid, like all drunks."

Zunser shook his head. He was tiring of the Communist and worried about the boy. "He's got a fever. And he's lucky if there isn't a crack in that head." The old man took off his shoes and put his socks on Pinchas.

"Let me," said Bretzky.

"No," Zunser said. "You give him the shoes, mine won't fit him." Pinchas's feet slipped easily into Bretzky's scuffed and cracking shoes.

"Here, take it." Korinsky gave them his mat. "Believe me, it's not for the mitzvah. I just couldn't stand to spend another second trapped with your righteous stares."

"The eyes you feel are not ours," said Zunser.

Korinsky glowered at his wall.

Pinchas Pelovits was not unconscious; he had only lost his way. He heard the conversations, but paid them little heed. The weight of his body lay on him like a corpse. He worked on his story, saying it aloud to himself, hoping the others would hear and follow it and bring him back.

> Mendel figured he'd best consult the local rabbi, who might be able to direct him in such matters. It was Mendel's first time visiting the rabbi in his study—not having previously concerned himself with the nuances of worship. Mendel was much surprised to find that the rabbi's study was of the exact dimensions of his missing room. In fact, it appeared that the tractate the man was poring over rested on the missing desk.

The bulb glowed. And with light came relief. What if they had been left in the darkness? They hated the bulb for its control, such a flimsy thing.

They had left a little water for the morning. Again, Bretzky held Pinchas while Zunser tipped the bowl against the boy's lips. Korinsky watched, wanting to tell them to be careful not to spill, to make sure they saved some for him.

Pinchas sputtered, then said, "Fine, that's fine." He spoke loudly for someone in such apparent ill health. Zunser passed the bowl to Korinsky before taking his own sip.

"Very good to have you with us," said Zunser, trying to catch the boy's eyes with his own. "I wanted to ask you, why is my presence so unsettling? We are all writers here, if I understand the situation correctly."

Zunser used Bretzky to belabor the point. "Come on, tell the boy who you are."

"Moishe Bretzky. They call me The Glutton in the gossip columns."

Zunser smiled at the boy. "You see. A big name. A legend for his poetry, as much for his antics. Now, tell us. Who are you?"

"Pinchas Pelovits."

None had heard the name. Zunser's curiosity was piqued. Bretzky didn't care either way. Korinsky was only further pained at having to put up with a madman who wasn't even famous.

"I am the one who doesn't belong here," Pinchas said. "Though if I could, I'd take the place of any of you."

"But you are not here in place of us, you are here as one of us. Do you write?"

"Oh, yes, that's all I do. That's all I've ever done, except for reading and my walks."

"If it makes any difference, we welcome you as an equal." Zunser surveyed the cubicle. "I'd much rather be saying this to you in my home."

"Are you sure I'm here for being a writer?" Pinchas looked at the three men.

"Not just for being a writer, my friend." Bretzky clapped him lightly on the back. "You are here as a subversive writer. An enemy of the state! Quite a feat for an unknown."

The door opened and all four were dragged from the cell and taken by a guard to private interrogation chambers—Bretzky escorted by three guards of his own. There they were beaten, degraded, made to confess to numerous crimes, and to sign confessions that they had knowingly distributed Zionist propaganda aimed at toppling the Soviet government.

Zunser and Pinchas had been in adjoining chambers and heard each other's screams. Bretzky and Korinsky also shared a common wall, though there was silence after each blow. Korinsky's sense of repute was so strong that he stifled his screaming. Bretzky did not call out. Instead he cried and cried. His abusers mocked him for it, jeering at the overgrown baby. His tears did not fall from the pain, however. They came out of the sober realization of man's cruelty and the picture of the suffering being dealt to his peers, especially Zunser.

Afterward, they were given a fair amount of water, a hunk of bread, and some cold potato-and-radish soup. They were returned to the same cell in the darkness. Zunser and Pinchas needed to be carried.

Pinchas had focused on his story, his screams sounding as if they were coming from afar. With every stripe he received, he added a phrase, the impact reaching his mind like the dull rap of a windowpane settling in its sash:

> "Rabbi, have you noticed we are without a sun today?" Mendel asked by way of an introduction.
>
> "My shutters are closed against the noise."
>
> "Did no one else mention it at morning prayers?"
>
> "No one else arrived," said the rabbi, continuing to study.
>
> "Well, don't you think that strange?"
>
> "I had. I had until you told me about this sun. Now I understand— no sensible man would get up to greet a dawn that never came."

They were all awake when the bulb went on. Zunser was making peace with himself, preparing for certain death. The fingers of his left hand were twisted and split. Only his thumb had a nail.

Pinchas had a question for Zunser. "All your work treats fate as if it were a mosquito to be shooed away. All your characters struggle for survival and yet you play the victim. You had to have known they would come."

"You have a point," Zunser said, "a fair question. And I answer it with another: Why should I always be the one to survive? I watched Europe's Jews go up the chimneys. I buried a wife and a child. I do believe one can elude the fates. But why assume the goal is to live?" Zunser slid the mangled hand onto his stomach. "How many more tragedies do I want to survive? Let someone take witness of mine."

Bretzky disagreed. "We've lost our universe, this is true. Still, a man can't condemn himself to death for the sin of living. We can't cower in the shadows of the camps forever."

"I would give anything to escape," said Korinsky.

Zunser turned his gaze toward the bulb. "That is the single rule I have maintained in every story I ever wrote. The desperate are never given the choice."

"Then," asked Pinchas, and to him there was no one else but his mentor in the room, "you don't believe there is any reason I was brought here to be with you? It isn't part of anything larger, some cosmic balance, a great joke of the heavens?"

"I think that somewhere a clerk made a mistake."

"That," Pinchas said, "I cannot bear."

All the talking had strained Zunser and he coughed up a bit of blood. Pinchas attempted to help Zunser but couldn't stand up. Bretzky and Korinsky started to their feet. "Sit, sit," Zunser said. They did, but watched him closely as he tried to clear his lungs.

Pinchas Pelovits spent the rest of that day on the last lines of his story. When the light went out, he had already finished.

They hadn't been in darkness long when they were awakened by the noise and the gleam from the bulb. Korinsky immediately put his eye to the wall.

"They are lining up everyone outside. There are machine guns. It is morning, and everyone is blinking as if they were newly born."

Pinchas interrupted. "I have something I would like to recite. It's a story I wrote while we've been staying here."

"Go ahead," said Zunser.

"Let's hear it," said Bretzky.

Korinsky pulled the hair from his head. "What difference can it make now?"

"For whom?" asked Pinchas, and then proceeded to recite his little tale:

> The morning that Mendel Muskatev awoke to find his desk was gone, his room was gone, and the sun was gone, he assumed he had died. This worried him, so he said the prayer for the dead, keeping himself

in mind. Then he wondered if one was allowed to do such a thing, and worried instead that the first thing he had done upon being dead was sin.

Mendel figured he'd best consult the local rabbi, who might be able to direct him in such matters. It was Mendel's first time visiting the rabbi in his study—not having previously concerned himself with the nuances of worship. Mendel was much surprised to find that the rabbi's study was of the exact dimensions of his missing room. In fact, it appeared that the tractate the man was poring over rested on the missing desk.

"Rabbi, have you noticed we are without a sun today?" Mendel asked by way of an introduction.

"My shutters are closed against the noise."

"Did no one else mention it at morning prayers?"

"No one else arrived," said the rabbi, continuing to study.

"Well, don't you think that strange?"

"I had. I had until you told me about this sun. Now I understand—no sensible man would get up to greet a dawn that never came."

"This is all very startling, Rabbi. But I think we—at some point in the night—have died."

The rabbi stood up, grinning. "And here I am with an eternity's worth of Talmud to study."

Mendel took in the volumes lining the walls.

"I've a desk and a chair, and a shtender in the corner should I want to stand," said the rabbi. "Yes, it would seem I'm in heaven." He patted Mendel on the shoulder. "I must thank you for rushing over to tell me." The rabbi shook Mendel's hand and nodded good-naturedly, already searching for his place in the text. "Did you come for some other reason?"

"I did," said Mendel, trying to find a space between the books where once there was a door. "I wanted to know"—and here his voice began to quiver—"which one of us is to say the prayer?"

Bretzky stood. "Bravo," he said, clapping his hands. "It's like a shooting star. A tale to be extinguished along with the teller." He stepped forward to meet the agent in charge at the door. "No, the meaning, it was not lost on me."

Korinsky pulled his knees into his chest, hugged them. "No," he admitted, "it was not lost."

Pinchas did not blush or bow his head. He stared at Zunser, wondered what the noble Zunser was thinking, as they were driven from the cell.

Outside all the others were being assembled. There were Horiansky and Lubovitch, Lev and Soltzky. All those great voices with the greatest stories of their lives to tell, and forced to take them to the grave. Pinchas, having increased his readership threefold, had a smile on his face.

Pinchas Pelovits was the twenty-seventh, or the fourteenth from either end, if you wanted to count his place in line. Bretzky supported Pinchas by holding up his right side, for his equilibrium had not returned. Zunser supported him on the left, but was in bad shape himself.

"Did you like it?" Pinchas asked.

"Very much," Zunser said. "You're a talented boy."

Pinchas smiled again, then fell, his head landing on the stockingless calves of Zunser. One of his borrowed shoes flew forward, though his feet slid backward in the dirt. Bretzky fell atop the other two. He was shot five or six times, but being such a big man and such a strong man, he lived long enough to recognize the crack of the guns and know that he was dead.

AGAINST LOGIC

Rebecca Goldstein

ONCE UPON A TIME, I resolved to live a rational life. This was a long time ago and I was very young, having quite recently emerged from the allegedly enchanted age of early childhood. I exited a skeptic.

Among other things, my plan for rationality called for hyper-vigilance in the matter of my beliefs. I would examine each one for blemishes, much as, say, my mother examined her chickens, which in those days she used to have to kosher herself—gutting, then salting and soaking them. Whenever my mother opened a chicken and found something questionable—a perforated lung, a spotted liver—she would proceed with caution, seeking rabbinical guidance as to whether the chicken was acceptable. As it was with my mother and her chickens, so it would be with me and my beliefs. I would examine each one for the taints of wishful thinking and faulty logic. Never would I allow the accidental features of my particular situation—the fact that I happened to have been born, for instance, into an Orthodox Jewish family—influence me in the solemn business of my beliefs.

And so it was that I became an analytic philosopher. If my story ended there, it would make sense. But against logic, I also became a writer of fiction. My hopeless passion for fiction had seemed to me, in the days when I hung exclusively with philosophers, a rather shameful little aberration. Plato had planned to rid his utopia of the epic poets, who were the novelists of his day. Fiction writers are enchanters, those who spread their dreams abroad; and Plato—whom I still revere—thoroughly disapproved of enchantment.

Even more implausibly, my stories often are—often enough, at least, for me to be asked to contribute to this forum—Jewish. This, to me, is odd. For though I have reconciled myself, philosophically, to my love for fiction, I still chafe at allowing "the accidents of precedents" (as one of my own characters once put it) to determine the borders of my points of view. And so, unlike others whom I sometimes find myself grouped with as representatives of the re-awakening in Jewish American letters, I don't write exclusively on Jewish themes or about Jewish characters. My collection of short stories, *Strange Attractors,* contained nine pieces, five of which were, to some degree, Jewish, and this ratio has provided me with a precise mathematical answer (for me, still the best kind of answer) to the question of whether I am a Jewish writer. I am five-ninths a Jewish writer.

But even this fraction of Jewish is far more than I would ever have anticipated being back in the days when I was determined to let my mind be free from origins. Cynthia Ozick once said that her goal is to dream Jewish dreams. My own early goal could not have been more different. I wanted (like Descartes) to know and not dream, to know that I did not dream. And I wanted, too (like Spinoza), to leave my Jewishness firmly behind.

My desire to emulate, specifically, Spinoza was not unrelated to my experiences as, specifically, a girl. The long arm of patriarchy, well-muscled in Orthodoxy, had joined forces with the complicated dynamics of family life, to wreak its damage on my wee little psyche. I had hit on reason as my salvation, and yet my mind, as girl's mind, was not to be taken as seriously as a boy's. The very course of its instruction was different, insidiously non-Talmudic in a culture in which the *gemorah-kopfs* rule.

Yet here I am, five-ninths a Jewish writer, and that is five-ninths more than I can rationally explain. I am dreaming, and at least five-ninths of the time, I am dreaming Jewish dreams. Deep down in the regions of psyche where fiction is born, regions supremely indifferent to criteria of rationality, being Jewish seems to matter to me quite a lot; and in this way my own small and personal story might be offered up as a metaphor for the very re-awakening in Jewish American letters which is the topic of this forum. For here we all of us are, after several generations that have tried their damnedest to shrug off the accidents of our shared precedents; here we all are, having sufficiently assimilated the culture at large to be able to inhabit, should we so choose, the inner worlds of characters to whom Jewishness is nothingness; here we all are, against logic, dreaming Jewish dreams.

Sanford Pinsker recently found cause, like me, to comment on the goal of Jewish dreaming that Cynthia Ozick once appropriated to herself, calling it "an honorable effort" but asserting that it was one that "a writer like I. B. Singer never had to undertake. Every dream he had was, by definition, a *Jewish* dream. . . ." None of us writing today can be a Jewish writer in the same sense that I. B. Singer was. We are all of us perfectly capable of dreaming non-Jewish dreams, so perfectly capable that what calls out for explanation is that we can—*still can*—dream Jewish dreams, that we want to. At this particular, perhaps transient, stage in Jewish history, it takes a distinctly anomalous desire to become a Jewish dreamer, as it takes, as well, a sustained effort. For it is a very real problem to be able to discover *how* to do it, this Jewish-dreaming thing, in terms that make contemporary sense. We obviously cannot express the Jewish difference by testifying, as other generations of Jewish writers have so eloquently testified, to the yearning to be let in to the *other's* dream: to go to the good schools, live in the fine neighborhoods, mix with and marry the goldenly Christian girls and boys. Yearning flows in some other direction.

I have found, like several others linked in this suggested revival of Jewish American letters, that my Jewish dreams, at least sometimes, take me backward in time, into a past in which the texture of Jewishness was more richly felt. Perhaps it can be argued that some gathered strands from that textured past must always find their way into the Jewish dreams we weave, that to experience the world Jewishly is to experience it historically. The effort to imaginatively inhabit the past does not mean writing the sorts of stories that writers in the past would have written. To me, for example, it is of much interest to try to imagine what it must have been like to have been a gifted woman living back in some hidden-away little place in, say, Eastern Europe. This doesn't mean, of course, that the writers of that time—having lived, as they did, without the benefits of contemporary feminism—would have found such a woman fascinating material. Obviously (extrapolating from us), there must have been a great number of such wildly brilliant women, and (again extrapolating) I imagine that many of them must have been just as wildly neurotic. Since writing about such a girl in my last book, *Mazel*, I have heard from various people who have confirmed my imagination. One professor of Jewish Studies, who originally came from Poland, startled me by coming up to me after a talk and saying, "I knew your Fraydel. She lived in my village. She died as you said." So here is an aspect of the real past that has found its way into my dreams only because of my contemporary sensibility, which finds the plight of women of genius worthy of imagination.

But whichever way we choose to dream Jewishly these days, for us, it is a choice among many. And knowing, as we do, so many ways of being, other than being Jewish, it is only by desire, by anomalous and not very practical desire, that we delimit our imaginations so that they occupy this particular region in the spread of possibilities that are open to them. And what explains this desire? I can only say that for me this pull back into particularity has the unmistakable feel of love. It is a love far too complicated to yield me joy (only pages), but it is love. And love, luckily or not, makes a habit of silencing logic.

THE HEALING POWER
OF JEWISH STORIES

Tsvi Blanchard

LET ME TELL YOU HALF A STORY. This is a story that starts when the Jews are at the Red Sea, with the Egyptian army at their back and the sea in front of them. The sea splits. The Jews go through, and what emerges is an enormously powerful praise poem called *"Shirat Ha-Yam*: A Song of the Sea." Later, the rabbis tell the following *midrashic* story about that occasion. It says, "The Angels sought to give forth in song," celebrating their victory. When God heard the angels he turned to them and said, "Quiet. My handiwork is drowning in the sea, and you want to sing a song of praise?"

Now, it's half a story because at the very same time that God is quieting the angels down below, the Jewish people are indeed singing that song; while the angels are quieted from singing, the Jewish people are praising God for their miraculous redemption at the Red Sea. So how come the angels don't get to sing and people do?

I first understood this story many years ago thanks to Rabbi Chaim Tsvi Hollander, who in an offhand comment explained its meaning in the most clear way. He said angels, you see, are the kind of beings that only do one thing, and they do it 100 percent. Whatever their task is, they're 100 percent focused and that's it, whereas human beings are just a little bit more complex. People can entertain at least two and sometimes three or four contradictory and conflicting views and feelings all at once. So for God to allow the angels to recite *"Shirat Ha-Yam,"* to sing his praises while people were drowning, would be to allow unconditional celebration at a time when people were dying. On the other hand, the Jews could at one and the same time rejoice that they were saved and redeemed and also suffer that it cost the lives of those Egyptians. That's why on the Passover *seder*, when we recite the ten plagues, we dip ten times into the cup of wine and take out a drop to say that our joy can never be complete if the price of human redemption is the death of others.

Now the reason I'm interested in that half a story is the fact that human beings are complex, and we keep things that are at odds with each other all floating around within the same human being—we are not angels! This is the center of how stories and rituals are able to heal people. For when we are wounded, parts of ourselves are at odds with other parts of ourselves. Something that belongs in this corner is not connected to something that belongs in another corner. When you are wounded, when you get hurt, when you get separated, you find that the wholeness of yourself is for a moment fragmented and shattered.

And if you start with the notion that human wholeness is our ultimate goal, then it is symbols and stories that enable us to take the various parts of ourselves, and of our society and of our history and of our people and of the wider consciousness of the entire human race, and access, get a hold of them, bring them together, and make them present in ways that find a harmony together, find a wholeness together. And when that process is complete for a moment, there is a kind of healing that takes place.

If you figure that the Jewish people could tell the story of enslavement in Egypt in such a way that, with all the bitterness of that event, it still turns out that 94 percent of the Jewish people run to a *seder* every year to retell that story and to gobble down that bitter herb, and then say, "Wow, that was great!"—then you have to figure that stories create symbolic contexts that make even the most bitter enslavements and pains tolerable. Only a story that can make slavery in Egypt into a symbol for redemption. To accomplish that, we have to go back to Abraham, talk about a promise and a prediction of that enslavement, and tell about Moses and Mount Sinai, and then, when we've told the whole story, all of a sudden it doesn't feel like the same pain that it was before.

Some stories tell about wounds and about pain that cannot be cured, that can only be endured. Here's a story from my family. My father-in-law was one of the most successful pediatricians in the New York area. This is a story that's still told about him in the hospital and in the family.

My father-in-law was a pediatric anesthesiologist working with a boy who had continually recurring cancer. The treatments were very painful, but, in this boy's case, my father-in-law could usually alleviate that pain.

THE COMPLEX FATE OF THE
JEWISH AMERICAN WRITER

Morris Dickstein

AS EARLY AS THE 1960s, influential critics argued that American Jewish writing no longer existed as a distinct and distinguished body of work: younger Jews were so assimilated, so remote from traditional Jewish life, that only nostalgia kept it going. Ted Solotaroff wrote some exasperated pieces about younger writers whose work already seemed to him derivative—thin, tiresome, voguish, strained, or sentimental. Irving Howe and Robert Alter launched similar complaints. I once heard the Israeli writer Aharon Appelfeld tell a New York audience that Jewish writing was grounded in the Yiddish culture and way of life that had flourished in Eastern Europe, something that died with I. B. Singer in New York and S.Y. Agnon in Israel. Gazing down benignly at an audience that included his good friend Philip Roth and the novelist E. L. Doctorow, he said that while there were certainly writers who happened to be Jews, there really were no more Jewish writers.

Other critics have been equally firm in anchoring American Jewish writing to the immigrant experience, a point brought home by Irving Howe in a famous attack on Philip Roth in *Commentary* in 1972. Howe saw Roth, whose first book he had warmly acclaimed, as a writer with "a thin personal culture," the kind of writer who "comes at the end of a tradition which can no longer nourish his imagination" or one who simply has "chosen to tear himself away from that tradition." Certainly there was very little sense of history, Jewish or otherwise, in Roth's finely crafted early fiction. Yet in the light of his humor, his characters, his subjects, and above all his later development, Roth hardly stood outside the Jewish tradition; instead he had a family quarrel with the Jewish world that profoundly affected everything he wrote. Yet Howe's charge struck home. A good deal of Roth's subsequent writing can be seen as a rejoinder to Howe's attack, which so rankled him that a decade later he wrote a furious novel, *The Anatomy Lesson,* lampooning Howe as a hypocrite, a pompous moralist, and even, in a remarkable twist, a fast-talking pornographer.

What was the substance of the Jewish literary tradition that Howe and Roth, two of its most gifted figures, could come to such angry blows over it? My subject here is how Jewish writing has changed and even grown, how it survived even the best-informed predictions of its demise. The conflict between Roth and Howe was partly temperamental, but some of it was generational. Howe was the product of the Yiddish-speaking ghetto, of socialism and the Depression; Roth came of age in postwar America, a world he would alternately satirize and recall with nostalgia. There is a streak of the moralist, the puritan, in Howe's criticism, while Roth took pride, especially when he wrote *Portnoy's Complaint,* in playing the immoralist, or at least in treating Jewish moral inhibitions as an ordeal, a source of conflict. For Howe, as for writers of his generation like Bernard Malamud, this moral burden was the essence of our humanity; for Roth it led to neurosis, anger, and dark, painful comedy.

It comes as a surprise to realize that the major current of Jewish writing in America dates only from the second world war. Irving Howe once compared the Jewish and the Southern literary schools with a provocative comment: "In both instances," he said, "a subculture finds its voice and its passion at exactly the moment it approaches disintegration." But in what sense was Jewish life in America approaching disintegration in the first two decades after the war, when the best Jewish writers emerged? What was dying, quite simply, was the vibrant immigrant culture evoked by Howe in *World of Our Fathers.* After the war Jews became freer, richer, more influential. As they moved up the economic ladder, professions like academic life opened up to them that had always been off limits. Thanks largely to the vague sense of shame induced by the Holocaust, social anti-Semitism in America became virtually a thing of the past. Surely the great literary flowering owed much to the way Jews in America had finally arrived, although the writers were often critical of what their middle-class brethren did with their freedom.

In any ethnic subculture, it's almost never the immigrant generation that writes the books. The immigrants don't have the language; their lives are focused on survival, on gaining a foothold in the new world and ensuring an education for their children. That education not only makes literature possible; it ignites a conflict of values that makes it urgent and inevitable. The scattering of excellent novels by individual writers before the war belongs less to a major literary movement than to the process by which the children of immigrants claimed their own identity. In powerful works of the twenties and thirties like Anzia Yezier-ska's *Bread Givers,* Mike Gold's *Jews Without Money,* and Henry Roth's *Call It Sleep,* the writers pay tribute to the struggles of their parents yet declare their independence from what they see as their narrow and limited world. These works could be classed with Sherwood Anderson's *Winesburg, Ohio* and Sinclair Lewis's *Main Street* as part of what Carl Van Doren called the "revolt from the village," the rebellion against local mores and patriarchal authority in the name of a freer, more universal humanity.

Ironically, the parochial world these writers rejected was the only authentic material they had. Their painful memories of small-mindedness and poverty, parental intolerance and religious coercion, fueled their imagination as nothing else could. In these works the driving impulse of the sensitive, autobiographical protagonist—Sara Smolinsky in *Bread Givers,* little Mike Gold in *Jews Without Money,* the impetuous Ralph Berger, hungry for life, in Clifford Odets's play *Awake and Sing!,* even young David Schearl in *Call It Sleep*—is to get away from the ghetto, with its physical deprivation, its materialism and lack of privacy, its desperately limited horizons, but also to get away from the suffocating embrace of the Jewish family—the loving but overly emotional mother, the domineering but ineffectual father, and the inescapable crowd of siblings, aunts, uncles, cousins, and neighbors, all completely entwined in each others' lives. These works were a blow for freedom, a highly ambivalent chronicle of emancipation, and often, sadly, they were the only books these writers could write. Their autonomy was hard-won but incomplete; this new identity liberated them personally but did little to fire their imagination.

Henry Roth once told me that only when he began to depart from the facts of his life did his novel begin to take on a life of its own; it then proceeded almost to write itself. In *Beyond Despair,* Aharon Appelfeld made the same point to explain his preference for fiction over autobiography. It gave him the freedom he needed to reshape his own recollections, especially the wartime experiences that bordered on the incredible. "To write things as they happened means to enslave oneself to memory, which is only a minor element in the creative process." The early Jewish-American novelists were not so lucky. They were stuck not only with what they remembered but with a naturalistic technique that could not do full justice to their experience. Their escape from their origins, never fully achieved, became a mixed blessing; they found themselves caught between memory and imagination, ghetto sociology and personal need. Mere rebellion and recollection, it seemed, could not nurture a full career. Their literary development was stymied. Only the postwar writers managed to break through this sterile pattern.

Saul Bellow, Bernard Malamud, Delmore Schwartz, Paul Goodman, and their Yiddish cousin, I. B. Singer, were the first Jewish writers in America to sustain major careers, not as immigrant writers but in the mainstream of American letters. As modernism replaced naturalism as the dominant literary mode, as fresh influences like psychoanalysis and existentialism exploded the sociological approach of many prewar writers, a new generation found powerful new vehicles for dealing with their experience. Straightforward realism was never an option for Jewish writers in America; it belonged to those who knew their society from within, who had a bird's-eye view, an easy grasp of its manners and values. As newcomers dealing with complex questions of identity, Jews instead became specialists in alienation who gravitated toward outrageous or poetic forms of humor, metaphor, and parable—styles they helped establish in American writing after the war.

The key to the new writers was not only their exposure to the great modernists—Kafka, Mann, Henry James—but their purchase on Jews not simply as autobiographical figures in a social drama of rebellion and acculturation but as parables of the human condition. Though Saul Bellow admired the power of an authentic naturalist like Theodore Dreiser, though Flaubert helped forge his aesthetic conscience, his first two novels, *Dangling Man* and *The Victim*, were more influenced by Dostoevsky and Kafka than by any writers in the realist tradition. Bellow and his friends were the children of the Holocaust rather than the ghetto. They did not write about the recent events in Europe—they hadn't directly experienced them—but those horrors cast their shadow on every page of their work, including the many pages of desperate comedy.

The atrocities of the Holocaust, the psychology of Freud, and the dark vision of certain modern masters encouraged Jewish writers to find some universal significance in their own experience. Kafka was the prophet, not of totalitarianism—that was too facile—but of a world cut loose from will and meaning, the world as they experienced it in the 1940s. Saul Bellow's engagement with the themes of modernist culture can be traced from novel to novel, but even a writer as private as Malamud was able to combine the stylized speech rhythms of the ghetto with a form adapted from Hawthorne and Kafka to turn parochial Jewish tales into chilling fables of modern life. This was the brief period when the Jew became the modern Everyman, everyone's favorite victim, schlemiel, and secular saint. Yet there was also an innovation in language, a nervous mixture of the literary and the colloquial, of art talk and street talk, that was almost poetic in its effects. Bellow himself brought the buoyant, syncopated rhythms of the vernacular into his prose. As he put it in his eulogy of Malamud after his death in 1986: Well, we were here, first-generation Americans, our language was English and a language is a spiritual mansion from which no one can evict us. Malamud in his novels and stories discovered a sort of communicative genius in the impoverished, harsh jargon of immigrant New York. He was a myth maker, a fabulist, a writer of exquisite parables.

We can find these effects almost anywhere we turn in Malamud's stories, from animal fables like "The Jewbird" and "Talking Horse" to wrenching tales like "Take Pity," which he put at the head of his last collection of stories. It includes the following bit of dialogue, supposedly between a census taker, Davidov, and a recalcitrant citizen named Rosen:

> "How did he die?"
> "On this I am not an expert," Rosen replied. "You know better than me."
> "How did he die?" Davidov spoke impatiently. "Say in one word."
> "From what he died?—he died, that's all."
> "Answer, please, this question."
> "Broke in him something. That's how."
> "Broke what?"
> "Broke what breaks."

Eventually we discover that the man answering the questions in this Kafkaesque exchange is himself dead, and his reckoning with the "census taker" takes place in some bare, shabby room of heaven or hell, though it feels like a forlorn pocket of the ghetto. (Malamud himself later described it as "an institutional place in limbo.") Rosen, an ex-coffee salesman, has killed himself in a last-ditch effort to impose his charity, pity, or love on the fiercely independent widow of the man who died. Rosen takes pity on her, but she will not *take* his pity. Even after he turns on the gas and leaves her everything, she appears at the window, adrift in space, alive or dead, imploring or berating him in a final gesture of defiance.

Like all of Malamud's best work, this is a story of few words but resonant meanings. Anticipating Samuel Beckett, Malamud strips down the sociology of the ghetto into a spare, post-apocalyptic landscape of essential, even primitive emotions, finding eerie comedy on the far side of horror. After her husband's death, as the business disintegrated, the woman and her children came close to starving, but the story is less about poverty than about the perverseness of the human will. Again and again Rosen tries to help the widow, but she adamantly refuses to be helped. Both are stubborn unto death, and the story explores the fine line between goodness and aggression, generosity and control, independence and self-sacrifice. Rosen will get the proud woman to take his help, whether she wants to or not, but neither can truly pity the other; their unshakable self-will isolates and destroys them. And the interrogator, standing in for both author and reader, makes no effort to judge between them. The story leaves us with a sense of the sheer human mystery.

The raw power of Malamud's stories is based on a simple principle—that every moral impulse has its Nietzschean dark side, its streak of lust or the will to power, just as every self has its anti-self, a double or shadow that exposes its vulnerabilities and limitations. This dialectic of self and other is at the heart of Malamud's stories and novels. The 'self' in his stories is often a stand-in for the writer, the artist as assimilated Jew—someone fairly young but never youthful, well educated but not especially successful, Jewish but nervously assimilated, full of choked-up feeling. Repeatedly, this figure is brought up short by his encounter with some ghetto trickster, a wonder-working rabbi, an ethnic con man who represents the suppressed, tribal part of his own tightly controlled personality.

Malamud's work is full of examples of such symbolic figures, half real, half legendary, including the ghetto rat, Susskind, a stateless refugee in Rome in "The Last Mohican," who steals the hero's manuscript on Giotto, and Salzman, the marriage broker in "The Magic Barrel," whose ultimate gift to a young rabbinical student is his own fallen daughter. These old world characters point to the ambiguous, even disreputable qualities that the young hero has bleached out of his own identity. They are slightly magical figures who come and go with almost supernatural ease. At different times they stand for ethnic Jewishness, carnality, wild emotion, even a sense of magic and the irrational. Or else they are figures from another culture—the Italian helper in *The Assistant,* the black writer in *The Tenants*—who test the limits of the protagonist's humanity and sometimes put him on a tentative path toward redemption and self-recognition.

There's a later treatment of this theme in a story called "The Silver Crown." The main character is a high school teacher called Gans (or "goose"), and the figure who puts him to the test is a rather dubious wonder rabbi named Lifschitz. For an odd sum of money, this Lifschitz promises to cure Gans's ailing father by fashioning a silver crown. We never discover whether Rabbi Lifschitz is a holy man, a con man, or both. But when the skeptical Gans eventually loses faith, curses his father and demands his money back, the old man quickly expires. This could be a coincidence—Malamud loves ambiguity—but he leads us to suspect that the son, who seemed so desperate to save his father, actually does him in. His suspicions about the rabbi and the money signified an unconscious ambivalence, even a hostility toward the father, that he couldn't directly express. Seemingly sensible and cautious, he's only the stunted husk of a man, going from filial piety to symbolic parricide in just a few lines. Malamud took this story from one of the newspapers, but he shaped it into something entirely his own, a test of the moral limitations of our assimilated selves, our rational and secular humanity, which has killed off some essential part of who we are.

Malamud's own piety toward the past is not much in evidence in the next generation. Coming of age in the late 1950s and early sixties, writers like Philip Roth belonged to a new group of rebellious sons and daughters, even parricidal sons like Malamud's Albert Gans. This was the black humor generation, rebelling not against the constraints of the ghetto—they were too young to have known any real ghetto, but against the mental ghetto of Jewish morality and the Jewish family. If Anzia Yezierska or Clifford Odets inveighed against the actual power of the Jewish father or mother, Roth and his contemporaries, who grew up with every apparent freedom, were doing battle with the internal censor, the mother or father in the head. (Much later Roth would build *The Human Stain* around a character who jettisons his whole family, including his doting mother, to grasp a new identity for himself.)

The work of these writers proved deliberately provocative, hugely entertaining, always flirting with bad taste, and often very funny, but with an edge of pain and giddiness that borders on hysteria. As Portnoy gradually discovers that he's living inside a Jewish joke, the novel's comic spirits turn self-lacerating. Like Roth, writers such as Stanley Elkin, Bruce Jay Friedman, Joseph Heller, Jerome Charyn, and Mark Mirsky practice an art of incongruity, deploying a wild mockery in place of the old moral gravity. Howe's charge against Roth—that he writes out of a "thin personal culture"—could be leveled against them as well, but it would be more accurate to say they looked to a different culture, satirical, performative, intensely oral. They identified less with modernists like Kafka and Dostoevsky than with provocateurs like Céline, Nathanael West, and Lenny Bruce. They looked less to literature than to stand-up comedy, the oral tradition of the Jewish jokes that Freud collected, the tirade of insults that ventilated aggression, the vaudeville *shtick* that brought Jews to the forefront of American entertainment.

The usual targets of their derision, besides Jewish mothers and Jewish husbands, were the new suburban Jews who had made it after the war, the vulgar, wealthy Patimkins in *Goodbye, Columbus,* who live in a posh

Newark suburb, play tennis and send their daughter to Radcliffe, and—this got me when I first read it—have a separate refrigerator for fruit in their finished basement. (Actually, it was their *old* fridge they were thrifty enough to save, the way they've held onto remnants of their old Newark personality.) As a foil to the Patimkins of Short Hills, Roth gives us the inner-city blacks of Newark, where the Jews used to live. We get glimpses of black workmen ordered around by the Patimkins' callow son, and especially of a young boy who runs into trouble simply because he wants to read a book on Gauguin in the local public library. At the heart of the book then, for all its irreverence, is a sentimental idea of the virtue of poverty and the simple life, something the upwardly mobile Jews have left behind but the black boy still seeks in Gauguin's noble vision of Tahiti.

Goodbye, Columbus was published in 1959, at the outset of a decade in which outrage and irreverence would become the accepted cultural norms. Even Saul Bellow would take a spin with black humor in *Herzog* (1964), as Bernard Malamud would do, unconvincingly, in *Pictures of Fidelman* in 1969. Here these stern moralists dipped into sexual comedy as never before, the comedy of adultery in Bellow, of sexual hunger and humiliation in Malamud. But they were soon outflanked by their literary son, Philip Roth, who would make epic comedy out of Jewish dietary laws, rabbinical pomposity, furtive masturbation, plaintive longing for *shikses,* and above all the family romance in *Portnoy's Complaint.* With its deliberately coarse comic stereotypes, especially of the histrionic Jewish mother, the long-suffering father, and their son, the young Jewish prince, this was the work that elicited Irving Howe's attack, the book that turned the vulgar spritz of stand-up comedy into literature.

The oedipal pattern in *Portnoy* belongs to a larger history: Roth and other black humorists were rebelling not only against their own parents but against their literary parents, the moralists of the previous generation, who were still around and did not take kindly to it. Bellow responded to the carnival aspect of the 1960s by taking on the voice of the censorious Jewish sage in *Mr. Sammler's Planet,* arraigning middle-aged adulterers along with women, blacks, and young people in one sweeping image of moral decay—of "sexual niggerhood," as he put it in one indelible phrase. The date was 1970, the bitter end of that tumultuous decade; Bellow's and Howe's responses were extreme but typical of the overheated rhetoric of the generation gap and the culture wars. Bellow's outrage perhaps was tinged with the envy that so many middle-aged Americans, not simply Jews, felt toward the new sexual freedoms of the young.

Bernard Malamud responded just as pointedly in a 1968 story called "An Exorcism," but it is scarcely known because he never reprinted it in his own lifetime. More than any other text, this story brings to a head the Oedipal tensions among Jewish writers, shedding light on some key differences. It is closely related to a story of generational conflict Malamud wrote the same year, "My Son the Murderer," about a bitter stand-off between an anxious, intrusive father and his 22-year-old son, who is angry at everyone, unhinged by images from Vietnam, and grimly awaiting his own draft notice. (Malamud had a son just the same age.) The central figure in "An Exorcism" is an austere older writer—like Malamud himself, but far less successful—a lonely man rigorously devoted to his craft, a kind of saint and hero of art. An aspiring writer, a young sixties type, attaches himself to the older man at writers' conferences—virtually the only places he ventures out. The older man, Fogel, is grudging and taciturn, but gradually his defenses drop, for he feels "grateful to the youth for lifting him, almost against his will, out of his solitude." Having won his confidence, the boy betrays him; he publishes a story based on an embarrassing sexual episode in the life of the older man. Fogel first confronts, then forgives him. But when the student, as a provocative stunt, seduces three women in a single night, the writer feels a wave of nausea and violently exorcises him from his life.

Not given to wielding fiction as cultural polemic, Malamud clearly felt uneasy with the naked anger of this story, which indicts not simply one unscrupulous young man but a whole generation for its freewheeling life and confessional style. In the eyes of an exacting craftsman who fears that *his* kind of art is no longer valued, these facile new writers simply don't invent enough. (Fogel accuses the young man of doing outrageous things simply to write about them, of being little more than "a walking tape recorder" of his "personal experiences.") When Fogel tells his surrogate son that "Imagination is not necessarily Id," Malamud could even be referring to Portnoy's recent line about "putting the Id back in Yid." Roth would give his own version of his spiritual apprenticeship to Malamud and Bellow ten years later in *The Ghost Writer.* In any case, "An Exorcism" remained unknown while *Portnoy's Complaint* became the ultimate piece of second-generation black humor, a hilarious whine against the neurotic effects of prolonged exposure to Jewish morality and the Jewish family.

Portnoy's complaint was an Oedipal complaint, but even at the time, long before he published *Patrimony,* his powerful 1991 memoir of the death of his father, it was clear how deeply attached Roth was to the parents he mocked and mythologized—the eternally constipated father, the effusively overbearing mother who loved and forgave him as no other woman could, loved him even for his transgressions. All through the 1970s Roth kept rewriting the novel in increasingly strident works like *The Breast,* a misconceived fantasy; *My Life as a Man*, a misogynist account of his first marriage; and *The Professor of Desire*. Roth seemed unable to escape the facts of his life but also seemed desperate to offend. He attacked critics for taking his work as autobiographical yet repeatedly fell back on exaggerated versions of the known facts. In *My Life as a Man* he even played on the relationship between fact and invention by giving us what claimed to be the 'real' story behind some fictional versions. But of course he felt free to make up this story as well.

None of these almost military maneuvers against critics and readers, which Roth also carried on in essays and interviews, quite prepared us for his next book, *The Ghost Writer*, which launched the next stage of Jewish-American writing, the one we are still in today. Let's call it the return, or the homecoming. If the second stage was debunking and satiric, even parricidal, the third stage began with Roth's filial homage to the two writers with whom his name had always been linked. Malamud appears in the book as E. I. Lonoff, very much the ascetic devotee of craft we meet in Malamud's own late work. Bellow (with a touch of Mailer) figures as the prolific, much-married, world-shaking Felix Abravanel, a man who, as it turns out, "was clearly not in the market for a twenty-three-year-old son." Roth himself appears as the young Nathan Zuckerman, a dead ringer for the author at that age. Zuckerman has just published his first, controversial stories, as Roth himself had done, and his own father is angry at him for washing the family linen in public. ("Well, Nathan, you certainly didn't leave anything out, did you?") His father has gotten the elders of the Jewish community on his case, in the person of one Judge Leopold Wapter, who sends him a questionnaire (!) that concludes: "Can you honestly say there is anything in your short story that would not warm the heart of a Julius Streicher or a Joseph Goebbels?"

Judge Wapter stands for all the professional Jews and rabbinical critics who had been upset by Roth's early stories—stories which, after all, had surely been written to ruffle people's feathers, even to offend. With very broad satirical strokes, the older Roth is now caricaturing his enemies, nursing old grievances, parading his victimization as wounded virtue. Roth demands from his readers what only his parents had given him: unconditional love. He wants to transgress and wants to be forgiven, wants to be outrageous yet also to be accepted, to be wickedly clever and be adored for it. When his women or his critics fail to give this to him, he lashes out at them. This rehearsal of old grievances is the tired and familiar part of *The Ghost Writer*, but the book included much that, in retrospect, was daringly fresh:

First, there is a surprising and resonant literariness that matches the book's evocative tone and warm filial theme. Roth's angry iconoclasm, his need to offend and outrage, has for now been set aside. *The Ghost Writer* deals with Nathan Zuckerman's literary beginnings, and Roth's virtuoso portraits of the older writers are perfectly in tune with the literary allusions that form the backdrop of the story—references to Isaac Babel, the great Soviet-Jewish writer murdered by Stalin; to Henry James's story *The Middle Years,* which also deals with a young acolyte's relation to an older writer; and most importantly, to the diary of Anne Frank. She is the figure behind Amy Bellette, the young woman in Roth's story who may actually *be* Anne Frank, and who may be having an affair with Lonoff.

Second, for all the *shtick* and satire in Roth's earlier fiction, this is his most Jewish book, not only for Roth's tribute to earlier Jewish writers but in his tender retelling of Anne Frank's story. Both the literariness and the Jewishness had always been latent in Roth's work, just barely masked by its satiric edge, its willed vulgarity. Roth's literary bent had been evident in his essays on contemporary fiction, his brilliant story about Kafka, the interviews he had published about each of his novels, and especially the invaluable series he was editing for Penguin, "Writers from the Other Europe," which launched the Western careers of little known Polish and Czech writers such as Milan Kundera. No critic, to my knowledge, has yet tried to gauge the effect of this large editorial enterprise on Roth's later fiction. As his own work bogged down in *Portnoy* imitations and paranoia, this project took Roth frequently to Eastern Europe where he made a wealth of literary contacts. Thus Roth found himself editing morally serious and formally innovative work that, despite its congenial absurdism, cut sharply against the grain of what he himself was writing. This material exposed Roth to both the Holocaust and Soviet totalitarianism, and ultimately gave his work a historical dimension, and especially a Jewish dimension, it had previously lacked. These books brought him back to his distant European roots. The angry young man, the prodigal son, was gradually coming home.

In *The Ghost Writer* Roth still nurses his old quarrel with the Jewish community, just as he would pursue his vendetta against Irving Howe in *The Anatomy Lesson.* He eulogizes Lonoff as "the Jew who got away," the Jew of the heart, or art—the non-institutional Jew—and portrays Anne Frank as a secular detached Jew like himself. In a bizarre moment, Zuckerman even imagines himself *marrying* Anne Frank, perhaps the ultimate rejoinder to his Jewish critics, to all the Judge Wapters of the world. But apart from this defensiveness, there's a strain of reverence toward art in the book, toward the Jewish historical experience, even toward the Jewish family, which creates something really new in Roth. Instead of rebelling against the father, he wants to be anointed by him: he's come "to submit myself for candidacy as nothing less than E. I. Lonoff's spiritual son."

Adopted by Lonoff, married to Anne Frank, he will no longer be vulnerable to the Howes and Wapters who criticize his writing for not being Jewish or tasteful enough.

In retrospect we can see how so much of value in Roth's later work—the wider political horizons in *The Counter-life* and *Operation Shylock,* the unexpected play with metafiction and magic realism in both those books, with their ingenious variations on what is made up and what is 'real,' and finally, his loving tribute to his late father in *Patrimony* and to the figure of the Good Father in *American Pastoral*—can be shown to have originated in *The Ghost Writer.* Moreover, they are strikingly typical of what I call the third phase of American Jewish writing, when the Jewishness that once seemed to be disappearing returned with a vengeance. In this phase the inevitability of assimilation gives way to the work of memory.

There's nothing so surprising about this pattern. The great historian of immigration, Marcus Lee Hansen, long ago enunciated the influential three-generation thesis that came to be known as Hansen's Law: "What the son wishes to forget the grandson wishes to remember." Sociologists have shown that this actually begins in the later years of the second generation. In *Patrimony* Roth presents his aged father as in some ways a pain in the neck but also as the keeper of the past, the storyteller, the Great Rememberer. Driving around Newark with his son, the former insurance agent, like a real census taker, recalls every occupant of every building. "You mustn't forget anything—that's the inscription on his coat of arms," his son writes. "To be alive, to him, is to be made of memory."

The father's motto is also part of the artistic credo of the son. Roth's protagonists are always astonished to meet old friends who cannot recall every single minute of their mutual childhood. This is why the narcissistic side of Roth, obsessed with self-scrutiny, cannot let go of any of his old grievances. Every object in his life—the old typewriter he got for his bar mitzvah, for example, which his first wife pawned—carries some heavy baggage of personal history. It leads him to idealize his youth in *Portnoy,* to see the postwar years as a Golden Age in *American Pastoral.* It enables him to remember his past with a hallucinatory intensity. Yet by the mid-eighties Roth also developed a wider historical purview, a sense of all that life that was lived before him, or far away from him—in Eastern Europe, where he sets "The Prague Orgy," in England or Israel, where some of the best parts of *The Counterlife, Deception,* and *Operation Shylock* take place. This is a more cosmopolitan Roth, reaching outside himself for almost the first time, in dialogue with Zionism, acutely sensitive to anti-Semitism, finding new life in the Jewish identity he had once mocked and scorned.

Much of *The Counterlife* still belongs to the old self-involved Roth of the Zuckerman saga—the fears of impotence, the scabrous comedy, the Wagnerian family uproar—but the sections set in England and Israel are something else. Until the early 1980s, there was as little trace of the Jewish state in American fiction as there was of the old European diaspora in Israeli writing. American writers by and large were not Zionists, and Israeli writers were not nostalgic for the shtetl or the Pale. With its insistence on nationhood as the solution to the Jewish problem, Israel was perhaps too tribal, too insular to capture the attention of assimilated writers, however much it preoccupied ordinary American Jews. Israel was the place where Portnoy couldn't get an erection—surely the least memorable part of that larger-than-life novel.

But more than a decade later, when Zuckerman's brother Henry becomes a *baal t'shuva,* a penitent, and Zuckerman looks him up among the zealots of the West Bank, Roth's work crosses that of Amos Oz and David Grossman, novelists who had written so well about the tensions dividing Israeli society. Like them, Roth finds great talkers who can articulate sharp ideological differences, which also reflect his own inner conflicts. He begins to relish the sheer play of ideas, the emotional bite of Jewish argument. *The Counterlife* inaugurates a dialogic phase of Roth's writing that gets played out in *Deception,* an experimental novel which is all dialogue, *The Facts,* where Nathan Zuckerman appears at the end to offer a rebuttal to Roth's memoir, and *Operation Shylock,* which returns to the Israeli setting of *The Counterlife.* In this new fiction of ideas, Roth's work acquires a real historical dimension, which would also lead to an acclaimed but uneven trilogy about postwar America beginning with *American Pastoral.*

Zuckerman in Israel, like Zuckerman recounting other people's stories in the American books, is also Roth escaping from the self-absorption of his earlier work. In England, cast among the not-so-genteel anti-Semites, Zuckerman develops an extraordinary pride, aggressiveness, and sensitivity about being Jewish. With their layers within layers, both *The Counterlife* and *Operation Shylock* are Roth's most Jewish books, even as Zuckerman defends himself (and Jewish life in the Diaspora) against the imperious claims of orthodoxy and Zionism. They mark his return to the fold, as well as his most formally complex fiction, pointing not only to the confusions between art and life but to the multiple layers of Roth's identity.

By giving so much attention to Roth, I run the risk of making it seem like it's only *his* development that is at stake, not larger changes in American Jewish writing. But every facet of Roth's later work has its parallel in other writers who have emerged in the last twenty years: the more explicit and informed Jewishness, the wider historical framework, the play with metafiction or magic realism, and the more intense literariness. In line with the wave of identity politics in America, there has been a persistent search for roots among younger Jewish writers, as there has been for older writers from assimilated backgrounds such as Leslie Epstein, Anne Roiphe, and Alan Isler. If we add to the themes listed above a concern with gender and sexual preference and a fascination with strict religious observance, we would have a complete inventory of issues that have attracted the younger generation, including Steve Stern, Allegra Goodman, Lev Raphael, Thane Rosenbaum, Melvin Jules Bukiet, Pearl Abraham, Rebecca Goldstein, Aryeh Lev Stollman, Nathan Englander, Myla Goldberg, Tova Mirvis, and Ehud Havaze-let. They have written about subjects as varied as the old and new Jews of Memphis, the lives of young Jews in Oxford and Hawaii, the orthodox communities of New York and Israel, the attractions of Jewish mysticism, the problems of gay Jewish identity, the surreal experiences of the walking wounded—Holocaust survivors and their children—and the old world of the shtetl and of Europe after the war. Some of their writing, arduously researched, smells of the library. They work best in short novels like Stollman's hypnotic *The Far Euphrates* or in collections of overlapping stories like Goodman's *The Family Markowitz,* composed of scenes and vignettes that allude nostalgically to the old-style family chronicle. The larger synthesis so far eludes them.

The interests of these emerging writers were foreshadowed not only by the shifting stance of Philip Roth but by the themes explored by another older writer, Cynthia Ozick. Like Roth she spent many years indentured to the 1950s gospel of art according to Henry James, and only later discovered her own vein of Jewish storytelling typical of what I've called the third stage. To put it bluntly, Ozick's work is far more Jewish than that of her main predecessors, richer with cultural information, proudly nationalistic, even sentimentally orthodox. Some of her stories and essays, such as her angry piece in *The New Yorker* on Anne Frank's diary (reprinted in *Quarrel & Quandary*), launched stinging attacks on secular Jews. Yet she began as a feminist and became the most articulate woman in a largely patriarchal line that rarely produced strong writing by women apart from such isolated figures as Emma Lazarus, Mary Antin, Anzia Yezierska, Grace Paley, or Tillie Olsen. This is something else that has changed dramatically since 1970.

Bellow and Malamud had Jewishness in their bones, but what they actually knew about Judaism could have been written on a single page. They knew the ghetto neighborhoods, the character types, the speech patterns, and what they took in at the kitchen table. They were born into Yiddish-speaking homes. Their Judaism was instinctive, domestic, introspective.

But their determination to navigate the literary mainstream prevented them from getting too caught up with specifically Jewish subjects. They refused to be consigned to any literary ghetto. "I conceived of myself as a cosmopolitan man enjoying his freedom," said Malamud. Ozick, on the other hand, like I. B. Singer or Steve Stern, was fascinated by the whole magical side of Judaism—the popular lore and legend, the Dybbuks and Golems of Jewish mystical tradition. For Singer this was part of his experience of growing up in Poland, the curious son of a learned rabbi, entranced by hidden and forbidden byways of the Jewish tradition. For Ozick and Stern it sometimes becomes a bookish, vicarious Judaism based on reading and research. But this very bookishness—a certain remoteness from life—becomes a key theme in their work.

Until recently a fear haunted Jewish American writing: that the subject was exhausted, that we live in inferior times, that giants once walked the earth, and said everything that had to be said; the rest is commentary. From her first important story, "Envy, or Yiddish in America" in 1969, to her keynote story, "Usurpation: Other People's Stories" in the mid 1970s, to *The Messiah of Stockholm* and *The Puttermesser Papers,* Ozick repeatedly writes stories about writers, or stories about other people's stories. This is a latecomer's literature, almost a textbook example of the postmodern profusion of texts upon texts or of Harold Bloom's famous theory of the anxiety of influence, which emphasizes the Oedipal relations between writers and their precursors. We risk becoming footnotes to our forebears.

Like *The Ghost Writer,* Ozick's "Envy"—the very title is revealing—is most memorable for its portraits of two older writers, one a lethal caricature of I. B. Singer—widely translated, fabulously successful, yet cruel, egotistical, and rejected by most other Yiddish writers—the other loosely based on the great poet Jacob Glatstein, celebrated among fellow Yiddishists yet never properly translated into English. (Ozick herself later did some translations of his work.) But the key figure is a young woman, perhaps based on Ozick herself, whom the poet seizes upon as his life-line into English, the potential savior of all of Yiddish culture.

This poet is envious of the Singer character but even more contemptuous of American Jewish writers for their ignorance: "*Jewish* novelists! Savages!" he says bitterly. "Their Yiddish! One word here, one word there. *Shikseh* on one page, *putz* on the other, and that's the whole vocabulary." Like Roth's novella, this is a kind of ghost story; the characters embody a dead culture trying to come alive. But it's also a vampire tale, since the young woman eventually rejects them as blood-suckers trying to live at her expense. Fascinated by the high drama of an expiring Yiddish culture, she decides she cannot allow it to take over her own life. Cynthia Ozick is thought of as some kind of pious traditionalist but this, her best story, written with ferocious energy and style, is a work that radiates hostility from first to last, reminding the reader of those sharp polemical turns she often takes in her essays.

In Ozick's story "Usurpation," the spirit of envy takes over the protagonist herself. It begins with a young author at the 92nd Street Y listening to a reading by a famous older writer. After two or three sentences, her ears begin to burn, for she feels he's telling a story that truly belongs to her, that she was born to write. As it happens, the writer and the story can easily be identified, since Ozick retells it. It's "The Silver Crown," Malamud's story about the wonder rabbi, which is precisely about the conflict of generations that is virtually the signature of this third or latecomer's generation. It's also a story of the kind of Jewish mystery and magic so dear to Ozick that she feels sharp regret at not having written it herself. Malamud had been there first but Ozick, like Steve Stern, makes her literary belatedness the theme of her story.

It's no accident that Ozick's stories overlap with her eloquent literary essays, or that metafiction and postmodernism here make a surprising entry into Jewish writing. Postmodernism, as I understand it, conveys the sense that all texts are provisional, that we live in a world already crowded with familiar texts and images, that originality is a Romantic illusion and techniques like collage, pastiche, and pseudo-commentary are better than realism for conveying our sense of belatedness and repletion. At the heart of Ozick's fine story "Puttemesser Paired" (in *The Puttermesser Papers*) are some brilliantly told episodes from the life of George Eliot, which the heroine partly reenacts, just as Ozick weaves a lost novel by the murdered Polish writer Bruno Schulz into *The Messiah of Stockholm*. As in the work of Jorge Luis Borges, this is writing about writing, situated vicariously on the fine line between commentary and invention.

It's not often that literary history so closely mirrors social history, but the conflict of literary generations I've described here is part of a larger pattern. It's no news that America has experienced a revival of ethnicity, or that the world has been rocked by waves of resurgent nationalism. With their longstanding commitment to the universalism of the Enlightenment, to which they owed their emancipation, Jews have been ambivalent about participating in this process. Thanks to the near-disappearance of anti-Semitism, Jewish life in America has become far more assimilated, but younger Jewish writers have both taken advantage of this and sharply criticized it. They have turned to Israel, to feminism, to the Holocaust, to earlier Jewish history, and to their own varied spiritual itineraries, ranging from neo-Orthodoxy and mysticism to Eastern religion, as a way redefining their relation to both Jewish tradition and contemporary culture. If they have lost the old connection to Europe, to Yiddish, or to immigrant life, they have begun to substitute their own distinctive Jewish and American experiences. They are not simply living on the inherited capital of past literary generations. The new writing so far may lack the power of a Malamud, a Bellow, or a Grace Paley but it is certainly not enervated by the bland, assimilated aspects of Jewish life. Jewish writers have quarreled with each other and with themselves but these have been family quarrels, not holy wars. Whatever tension this creates, it certainly gives no sign that they are about to give up the ghost, especially now that the ghost, the past, has taken on new flesh and blood.

BELLOW AT 85, ROTH AT 67

Norman Podhoretz

I AM NOT THE ONLY CRITIC to have been reminded in recent months that once during the 1950s, when novelists of Jewish origin had suddenly moved to center stage in this country, Saul Bellow—referring to a well-known men's-clothing manufacturer of the time—characteristically cracked that he, Bernard Malamud, and Philip Roth had become the Hart, Schaffner & Marx of American literature. With the death of Malamud in 1986, only Bellow, who has just turned eighty-five, and Roth, sixty-seven, are left among us, and both have just produced new novels.

Roth's, entitled *The Human Stain,*[1] is his third in as many years, which is a remarkable feat for a serious writer at any stage of his career; and the continued vitality Bellow demonstrates in *Ravelstein*[2] at so advanced an age is equally remarkable. What is perhaps an even more impressive sign of vitality is that, in addition to a new novel, Bellow recently fathered a new baby. When asked by an old friend how he did it, the much-married Bellow's answer was just as characteristic as his Hart-Schaffner-&-Marx crack: "I've had a lot of practice." Well, he has also had a lot of practice writing—and it shows. As for Roth, though nearly eighteen years younger, he too has had a lot of practice writing (having, in fact, turned out more books than Bellow), and it shows as well.

But it is not merely the coincidence of publication dates that justifies discussing these two writers and their latest works together. For a start, there are certain curious similarities between the two novels. I hasten to add that these similarities do not extend to the all-important issue of style. No sentient or experienced reader could possibly mistake *Ravelstein* for a book by Roth, or by anyone else, for that matter: the word "inimitable," so promiscuously thrown about by reviewers, applies perfectly to Bellow's unique fusion of the high-literary and the demotic, with a spicy dash of the locutions and rhythms of Yiddish mixed in. Nor would *The Human Stain* sound to anyone with ears to hear like the writing of Bellow. If Roth's prose does not bear quite so identifiable a signature as Bellow's, it is still his and his alone.

Style aside, there remain interesting resemblances between *Ravelstein* and *The Human Stain*. The most obvious and striking is that both novels use almost exactly the same narrative device. Thus, it is at the behest of a late friend that Chick, the narrator of *Ravelstein,* has produced this book about the title character. Bellow makes so little effort to distance himself from Chick that it becomes impossible to regard the narrator as comparable to, say, Nick Carraway in F. Scott Fitzgerald's *The Great Gatsby* or the figure of Marlow in a number of Joseph Conrad's stories and novels. Besides being, like Bellow, a Jewish writer in Chicago, Chick speaks in Bellow's voice and gives vent to Bellow's views and opinions; he also undergoes experiences that Bellow himself has undergone and that are hardly altered in the rendering. Practically the only such alteration he makes is to present himself not as the Nobel-prize-winning novelist he is but as a humble "midlist biographer."

In *The Human Stain,* the narrator—for the eighth time in Roth's novels—is Nathan Zuckerman, whom Roth has dubbed not so much his alter ego as his "alter brain." How much distance exists here, or in previous novels, between Roth and Zuckerman is difficult to determine. In the postmodernist spirit of mystification to which Roth has an unfortunate tendency to succumb now and then, he wants to keep us in the dark as to how fully he is to be identified with Zuckerman. But as the years pass and the novels pile up, it becomes harder and harder for someone like myself, who has been following Roth's work from the very beginning and has read just about every word he has ever published, to distinguish between the author and even most of his other protagonists or narrators (going all the way back to Neil Klugman of *Goodbye, Columbus* and Alexander Portnoy of *Portnoy's Complaint*), let alone to Nathan Zuckerman. Indeed, it is even hard to tell how much distance there is between the author and a character actually named Philip Roth in *Operation Shylock.*

This close identification between Roth and Zuckerman (to stick with him) does not necessarily include the details of Roth's life to the degree that it does with Bellow in *Ravelstein*. I happen to know that Bellow, like Chick in *Ravelstein,* nearly died from eating a poisoned fish in the Caribbean, whereas I do not know (and have never tried to find out) whether Philip Roth has, like Zuckerman, suffered from prostate cancer and then been left impotent and incontinent by surgery.

I also happen to know that every character in *Ravelstein,* including Ravelstein himself, is based on a real person, though "based" is too weak a word to describe what are actually portraits of persons who are fictionalized only to the point of appearing under made-up names. I do not, however, know any such thing about *The Human Stain.* Though I suspect that it helps itself freely to the experience of Roth and people he has met or heard about, I would bet that much more of this book is the product of invention than *Ravelstein* is. It has repeatedly been proposed, for instance, that the model for the hero of *The Human Stain* was the critic Anatole Broyard, but even if that is true, Broyard had so different a biography from the one Roth gives to his hero that the character can be accepted as a genuinely fictional creation.

In due course I will go into the question of why all this is worth bringing up, but for the moment I want to dwell a bit more on the parallels between these two books by writers as different as Bellow and Roth. If Chick has produced *Ravelstein* because the late Abe Ravelstein himself—a college professor—asked him to write his biography, so too, the genesis of *The Human Stain* lies in a request by Nathan Zuckerman's late friend Coleman Silk—also a college professor—to do a book about certain horrific things that had happened to him but which he himself had been unable to get down properly on paper.

As Hamlet lies dying, he tells his friend Horatio not to follow him immediately into the grave:

> O good Horatio, what a wounded name
> (Things standing thus unknown) shall live behind me!
> If thou didst ever hold me in thy heart,
> Absent thee from felicity awhile,
> And in this harsh world draw thy breath in pain,
> To tell my story.

Bellow and Roth, each in his own way, play Horatio in their latest works to departed friends. In doing so, they both inevitably find themselves dwelling much on mortality. This is a theme that has preoccupied Roth almost obsessively since the two novels—*An American Pastoral* and *I*

Married a Communist—that immediately preceded *The Human Stain* and that he somewhat mysteriously regards as the first two volumes of a trilogy of which his new book is the completion. (I say "mysteriously" because I cannot detect much that brings the three novels together.)

For his part, Bellow, whose nature contains very little, if any, morbidity, has (if memory serves) never before focused quite so sharply on death as he does in *Ravelstein*. Obviously, he has written about it often, but—so it seems to me—the idea of mortality hovers more heavily over this book than it does over any of his others.

Another theme that is central both to *Ravelstein* and *The Human Stain* is sex. It was, of course, largely (though by no means entirely) because of the explicit scenes of sexual activity in *Portnoy's Complaint* that Roth first achieved great fame and notoriety; and it has become increasingly evident that age has not withered his interest in the subject nor custom staled the infinite variety of erotic delights he feels compelled to explore in his writings.

After (to speak very relatively indeed) giving sex a bit of a rest in *An American Pastoral* and *I Married a Communist,* Roth has returned to it with a vengeance in *The Human Stain.* At the center of this novel is a torrid affair between a seventy-one-year-old man, helped along by Viagra, and a woman in her thirties symbolically named Faunia. This creature (one of the most implausible characters Roth has ever given us) has sexual appetites that are almost, if not quite, on a par with those of Drenka, the heroine of *Sabbath's Theater.* Drenka excited so much lust in the men on whom she bestowed her favors that, after her death, they took to masturbating over her grave (thereby showing that Roth, having in *Portnoy's Complaint* been perhaps the first serious American novelist to write openly about masturbation, could go even himself one better).

Just as an affair between an old man and a young woman is at the heart of *The Human Stain,* so *Ravelstein* has as one of its main threads the story of a marriage between an old man (Bellow posing as Chick) and a young woman. True, this thread does not wind itself in *Ravelstein* through descriptions of sexual activity (and in general, where sex is concerned, Bellow has been a reticent prude as compared with Roth). But to both writers, the preoccupation with death is tempered by their continuing interest in sex.

Sex is not conceived either by Roth or Bellow as an escape from death. On the contrary: in *The Human Stain,* if his affair with Faunia revives Coleman Silk from a long bout of despair, it also eventually leads to his death; and if Chick is snatched from the grave by his young wife's (nonsexual but loving) diligence, the homosexual Ravelstein is sent to his grave by AIDS. J. Bottum of the *Weekly Standard* has discerned in these contrasting fates of Chick and Ravelstein a statement about the essential difference between heterosexuality and homosexuality. It is an intriguing interpretation, but not one that entirely convinces. For the upshot—admittedly encrusted with many complications—is that to Bellow, as to Roth, sex signifies life, not death.

Finally, *Ravelstein* and *The Human Stain* provide new variations on a theme that runs through almost all the works of Bellow and Roth alike: the drive of so many Americans to cut loose from the genetic and social moorings of birth and to create themselves anew in images of their own devising. With Roth's characters, this drive has usually assumed the form of an effort to escape from Jewishness and the constrictions that he—and they—have associated with it.

In Bellow, who has always had more positive and affectionate feelings toward Jewishness than Roth, what needs to be fled is the imposition of the conventional wisdoms that happen to be around at any given time. This is what connects one of his earliest heroes, Augie March, who was determined to "go at things" his own way, to his latest, Ravelstein, who (admittedly in this respect more Roth- than Bellow-like) loathes his Midwestern Jewish family and forges a new self through the Great Books stemming from Athens and Jerusalem (if more the former than the latter) with which he falls in love at the University of Chicago.

There is also a line between, say, Alexander Portnoy and Coleman Silk, but it is given a highly ironic twist by Roth. In this instance, the character fleeing his origins, who we are at first told is a Jew (but, as a professor of classics, more a product of Athens than Jerusalem—in *this* respect being more Ravelstein- than Portnoy-like), turns out to be a light-skinned black who has successfully been passing as a Jew.[3]

Obviously, Silk's decision to renounce his racial and ethnic heritage is taken, and rightly so, as a gross betrayal by his family, and especially by his brother. The attitude of Roth (or am I supposed to say Nathan Zuckerman?) is more ambivalent: to him, there is something heroic about Silk, but he does not dismiss the charge of betrayal out of hand. The two are inexorably intertwined. As Roth told Charles McGrath, the editor of the *New York Times Book Review,* in a rare interview: "Self-transformation. Self-invention. The alternative destiny. Repudiating the past. Powerful stuff."

It struck me as strange, however, that Roth makes so little of the fact that Silk should have decided to pass as a Jew rather than as a white Gentile. Given the evolution of Roth's own attitudes toward Jewishness—from the outright disaffection expressed in the youthful *Goodbye, Columbus* and *Portnoy's Complaint* to a growing sympathy and identification in some of his later works—I would have expected him to do more than he does with the changes in American society which have persuaded Silk that pretending to be Jewish has in some quarters become a greater advantage than passing as a WASP. But when McGrath suggests that this is "a book . . . about issues of race and of Judaism and where the two intersect," Roth quickly disagrees, declaring that there was "nothing about Judaism in this book," and going on to explain why Silk chooses to take on a Jewish identity:

> As a means of deception, as a social disguise, as a pretext for his appearance. He doesn't want to be a Jew for anything like the reasons that Frank Alpine, say, in Malamud's novel *The Assistant* wants to be a Jew. Coleman's choice has nothing to do with the ethical, spiritual, theological, or historical aspects of Judaism. . . . It's a cunning choice that successfully furnishes him with a disguise in the flight from his own "we." The choice is strictly utilitarian.

All this is true, but one reason I would have expected Roth to explore the implications of it in the novel itself is that, in the same interview, he stresses the importance of historical and political events in his "trilogy." If I could find nothing that binds these three novels together, to their author they are of a piece because the lives of their characters are interpenetrated by the "historical moments in postwar America that have had the greatest impact on my generation." The three moments he mentions are McCarthyism, Vietnam, and the impeachment of Bill Clinton. Yet surely the change for the better in the fortunes and status of Jews and blacks in American has a better claim to a place on that list than the impeachment of Clinton; and while Roth does go on to include race as another of the great developments of the era, he ignores the Jewish issue almost entirely.

It is at this juncture that I wish to delve into the question of why such factors are worth considering. In order to answer that question, I have to begin by affirming my belief in the principle of the autonomy of art, according to which works of art should be judged primarily on their aesthetic merits and extraliterary considerations should either be kept out of such judgments or brought in only under two conditions. One is when they impinge on the quality of the work in question—as when the imperatives of propaganda have clearly overridden the dictates of aesthetics (any piece of "socialist realism" will do for an example). The other is when it becomes useful in understanding a work to evoke the broader context out of which it has emerged. Yet even then, I would insist that aesthetic considerations come first.

This does not mean that moral or political factors are *entirely* ruled out in the framing of critical judgments. It does mean, however, that anyone who cares about literature is obligated to acknowledge the expressive and evocative powers of—to reach into the political sewers for an especially egregious instance—a novel like Louis-Ferdinand Céline's *Journey to the End of the Night*—before going on to condemn it on moral and political grounds. And the converse also applies. That is, the aesthetic weaknesses of a work of art ought not to be overlooked or denied just because it happens to embody moral or political sentiments of which the reader approves.[4]

Philip Roth, while perhaps an even more devout believer in the autonomy of art than I am, has always run into problems with these principles. He is a novelist whose talent is immense and many-sided. His ear and his mimetic skills are of the highest order. He can with equal success be hilarious and vulgar at one moment, almost theologically solemn and even priggish at another, and as lyrical as a first-rate poet at yet another. Topping it all off, he is capable of producing, to borrow a word he himself has used in praising another writer, "gorgeous" prose when the mood is upon him (as it has more and more been in his later years). Reading him, I invariably end up feeling that there is no weapon in the literary arsenal he cannot fire with perfect accuracy—or, to use a somewhat more appropriate metaphor, no instrument in the literary orchestra he cannot play like a virtuoso.

This has been true of him from the word go. When his first book, the collection of stories entitled *Goodbye, Columbus,* appeared in 1959, it was Saul Bellow himself, reviewing it in these pages, who said, "*Goodbye, Columbus* is a first book, but it is not the book of a beginner. Unlike those of us who came howling into the world, blind and bare, Mr. Roth appears with nails, hair, and teeth, speaking coherently. At twenty-six he is skillful, witty, and energetic, and performs like a virtuoso."[5]

More than 40 years and 22 books later, Roth has not only retained those powers with which he came into the world but developed and refined and added to them. Despite a few lapses and stumbles as he went along (*When She Was Good, The Breast,* and *The Great American Novel,* to name a few), and unlike so many other of his contemporaries who fell by the wayside—either drying up altogether or failing to fulfill their early promise—he has stayed the course, proving himself to be not only a serious writer but an *homme sérieux:* a serious man who demands and deserves to be taken with the utmost seriousness.

To do so, however, requires more than a recognition of his gifts and the admirable tenacity with which he has nourished and exercised and deepened them. It also demands following him into what Lionel Trilling famously called the "dark and bloody crossroads" where literature and politics (and, I would add, morality) meet. For despite Roth's strong commitment to the autonomy of art, he has never been able to keep himself from straying into those crossroads, jumping around in them with abandon when feeling antic or genuflecting on his knees when infected by a bout of (almost always liberal) piety.

In the political sphere, I am not referring here mainly to a book like *Our Gang*, the crude and cliché-ridden satire he wrote about Nixon during Watergate. Nor, in the moral realm, do I have in mind the fun he made of American Jews early in his career in *Goodbye, Columbus* and *Portnoy's Complaint* that got him into so much trouble with the Jewish community. More to the point is the "thematic trilogy" consisting of his last three novels.

The first, *American Pastoral,* is in my opinion the best thing Roth has ever written, and only its structural flaws prevent me from unequivocally pronouncing it a great novel. I was very disappointed by *I Married a Communist,* and my hope that he would soon recover his form has been dashed by *The Human Stain.*[6]

Yet I cannot help asking myself how much the politics of these novels has influenced my critical judgment of them. Did I admire *An American Pastoral* so much because I was delighted by the surprising attack Roth launches there on the radicalism of the '60s and its liberal apologists, and his even more unexpected defense of the middle-class values that were under such ferocious assault by that radicalism (and by his own younger self)? Was I disheartened by *I Married a Communist* because, instead of following up on what I, and not I alone, admired so much about *An American Pastoral*—the intellectually and spiritually heroic feat it performed in reconsidering the negative attitude toward this country Roth had always shared with most of the literary community—he returned to the same old stale attitudes in dealing with McCarthyism? And was the dashing of my prediction that this might turn out to be just a temporary regression—possibly even caused by an irresistible urge on Roth's part to reassure his perplexed and worried faithful admirers that he had not sold out to the neoconservative enemy—responsible for my disappointment in *The Human Stain?*

In all honesty, I cannot dismiss the possibility that such considerations played some part in my differing judgments of these three novels. But only, I must immediately protest, a small one. I claim entitlement to this qualification on the ground that I felt let down by *The Human Stain* even though it centers on what is, to me, a highly congenial and satisfying account of the plague of political correctness in the universities.

Coleman Silk is victimized twice over by political correctness. First his academic career is ruined when he uses the word "spooks" (meaning ghosts) to describe two students who never show up in class. Though he does not even know they are black, he is accused of racism, and when he refuses to dignify this preposterous accusation with an apology, none of his friends or colleagues springs to his defense.[7] Then, as if being ruined by a false charge of racism were not enough, Silk (by now a widower) is excoriated for sexual harassment when he enters into an affair with a female janitor at the college. This additional blow lands on him even though he has by then resigned, thereby becoming immune from the charge that he is using his power to coerce sexual favors from a subordinate in the workplace.

By ridiculing the prevailing tyrannies of political correctness on the issues of both race and sex, Roth shows that McCarthyism—which he surveyed with an unqualifiedly orthodox liberal eye in *I Married a Communist*—has now migrated to the Left; and in this, so far as I am concerned, he is on the side of the angels. Unfortunately, he winds up in less exalted company through his stated ambition to deal with "the historical moments that have had the greatest impact on [his] generation." The way he pursues this ambition in *The Human Stain* is to connect both Vietnam and the impeachment of Bill Clinton with the trouble Coleman Silk gets into as a result of the tyranny of political correctness in matters of sex.

Despite being kept mostly implicit, this link still requires quite a stretch. But it does help explain why Roth should have made the peculiar choice of the impeachment as a moment of historical impact comparable to that of McCarthyism and Vietnam. Here again, as in *I Married a Communist*, he gives full play to the side of himself that has remained stuck in and intransigently uncritical of the liberal attitudes with which he grew up.

As *The Human Stain* tells it, Clinton (like Silk) was guilty in his alliance with Monica Lewinsky of nothing more than being a normal guy marked, as all of us are, by "the human stain" (something like original sin?). Not a word, not a syllable, in the passages devoted by Roth to the Clinton scandals so much as hints that the President (*unlike* Silk) committed and suborned perjury, and that this was the legal basis on which the attempt was made to remove him from office. Just the opposite: "What was being enacted on the public stage," Roth informs McGrath in their *New York Times Book Review* interview, "seemed to have the concentrated power of a great work of literature. The work I'm thinking of is *The Scarlet Letter*." I rub my eyes in disbelief. Can Philip Roth actually imagine that at its "moral core," today's America, "this huge and unknowable country," is no different from the America of 17th-century Salem?

Such a statement would be breathtaking coming from anyone living at a time and in a place where sex in every shape and form is easily available, advocated, and even celebrated in every public forum and medium of entertainment, and where the only scarlet letters are pasted on those who offer so much as a smidgen of resistance to this tidal wave of eroto-mania. But issuing from the mouth of a man who has achieved fame, honor, and riches with books that would have served as the kindling for burning him alive in the world described by Hawthorne, the comparison between the America of today and the America of *The Scarlet Letter* is very nearly demented.

As for Vietnam, it comes in through Lester Farley, the ex-husband of Silk's girlfriend. Farley is a crazed veteran of that war who eventually contrives to kill both his former wife and her present lover, and who, as even Lorrie Moore, one of Roth's liberal admirers, has said in the *New York Times Book Review,* is constructed "from every available cliché of the Vietnam vet." Has Roth forgotten what he revealed about these very clichés in *An American Pastoral*? Or is he once more offering reassurance to those who worried after reading that book that he might be converting to neo-conservatism?

If so, he has only partly succeeded. The same Lorrie Moore who, to her credit as a critic, spotted the character of Lester Farley as a literary weakness, immediately made up for this deviation from her own party line by complaining that *The Human Stain* "indulges in the sort of tirade against political correctness that is far drearier and more intellectually constricted than political correctness itself." But in my opinion what Roth "indulges" in here is not a "tirade": it is, rather, the determination to tell a truth that goes against the grain of his own liberal impulses, and this is to *his* credit.

I suppose the conclusion to be drawn is that in responding to a novel that raises contentious political (and/or moral) issues, it is virtually impossible to ignore—and, worse yet, to blind oneself to—those issues in reaching a critical judgment. To repeat: the aesthetic qualities of the work at hand ought to be the critic's primary concern. But when the novelist insists on leaping into "the bloody crossroads," it is the right and even the duty of the alert reader to follow after and to join in.

If Roth's last few novels bring into sharp focus the troublesome problems surrounding the concept of the autonomy of art, Bellow's *Ravelstein* does much the same thing with the possibly even more irksome problem of the relation between novels and the realities on which they often draw. As all the interested world knows, the character of Abe Ravelstein is based on the late Allan Bloom, who was Bellow's dear friend. What is less well-known is that it was at Bellow's urging that Bloom wrote *The Closing of the American Mind*. To everyone's amazement, that book became a huge best-seller in 1987, making a previously penurious and relatively obscure professor at the University of Chicago both rich and famous.

But the hero is not the only portrait in *Ravelstein* of a real-life model. As with himself playing narrator, Bellow takes so little trouble to disguise the characters who appear here that they are all easily recognizable as this or that person. Calling *Ravelstein* a roman à clef therefore verges on understatement. Except for the names of the characters, nothing in it seems to be fictional; nothing seems to be invented. The "plot" consists entirely of incidents surrounding Bellow's friendship with Bloom or that occurred until it ended with Bloom's death. There is the breakup of Bellow's fourth unhappy marriage and the contracting of his presently happy one to a student of Bloom's; there are the spending sprees on which Bloom goes, frequently accompanied by Bellow, after his book becomes a great best-seller; there is Bloom's illness and death; and there is the near-death of Bellow himself after eating a poisoned fish in the Caribbean.

What we have here, in short, is all clef and no roman: not a novel but a memoir.

Taking the opposite tack, Cynthia Ozick, in a long review in the *New Republic,* advises us to "throw away the clef." Her argument is that "When it comes to novels, the author's life is nobody's business. A novel, even when it is autobiographical, is not an autobiography." Nor is a novel a biography: "Ravelstein is not Bloom." And she concludes, "What is a novel? A persuasion toward dramatic interiority. A word-hoard that permits its inventor to stand undefined, unprescribed, liberated from direction or coercion. Freedom makes sovereignty; it is only when the writer is unfettered by external expectations that clarity of character . . . can be imagined into being."

Ozick's brief in support of her position about the novel in general, and of *Ravelstein*'s right to be considered one, is dazzling and written with her usual brilliant flair. But it flows from two assumptions that are less than self-evident or axiomatic. One is that "the literary novel (call it the artist's novel)" is superior in kind to such other literary forms as biography and memoir. Bellow would undoubtedly agree with Ozick, which is almost certainly one of the reasons he decided to offer this book about Allan Bloom as a novel rather than as a straightforward memoir. (Other reasons may involve a different and lower order of "freedom" from the one celebrated by Ozick: that is, the freedom to give the business to certain people—an ex-wife and an ex-friend or two—without the complications involved in using their real names.)

In her review of *Ravelstein,* however, Ozick comes close to ignoring the bold and brave warning she once sounded against violating the second of the Ten Commandments by turning art into an idol to be worshipped. Here she reminds me of the great British critic F. R. Leavis. It was Leavis who taught that the quasireligious attitude toward poetry in the Victorian age was a significant factor in the decline of that form, whereas the lesser regard in which the novel was held had the opposite effect. Yet Leavis himself later went on to speak of the novelists he admired in tones that were reminiscent of the very transports of exaltation for which he had faulted the Victorians.

In any event, with all due respect to Ozick's veneration of the novel, it is no insult or denigration of *Ravelstein* to read it as a memoir. I would go even further by contending that a proper appreciation of Saul Bellow is impossible without recognizing that he is not now or ever has been a natural novelist. A wonderful writer, yes: probably the best American writer in any genre of the past half-century. But not a born novelist.

The born novelist is defined, for better or worse, by the power to express whatever it is he understands of the world and of life through the telling of stories about people who are made to seem real. Bellow, by contrast, is always telling us what he knows—which is much more than practically any of the born novelists who have marched across the literary stage beside him—through his own voice as informed by his own deep and vast intellect. Hence his stories are not gripping narratives, and his characters rarely, if ever, achieve the separation from their creators of authentic fictional creations. "Every major character in a Bellow novel is, in some way, Bellow," as D. T. Max succinctly puts it in his *New York Times Magazine* article.

What I am trying to get at might be clarified by looking at "How Many Children Had Lady Macbeth?" a once-notorious essay by L. C. Knights. This British scholar-critic raised the question after noticing that, while Lady Macbeth speaks of having "given suck," there is no indication in *Macbeth* of the size of her family. But it was a silly question. Lady Macbeth is not a real person; she is a creature of Shakespeare's imagination,[8] and since he neglects to provide this information in his play, there is no way to unearth it. Nevertheless, silly and unanswerable as the question might have been, it testified vividly to Shakespeare's success in, as it were, liberating Lady Macbeth from his own head and spinning her off into the illusion of an independent existence of her own.

Rarely, if ever, does anything comparable happen to Bellow's characters. Even those who least resemble him (Tommy Wilhelm of *Seize the Day*, Henderson of *Henderson the Rain King*, Mr. Sammler of *Mr. Sammler's Planet*, among others) soon turn into mouthpieces or counters for his own ideas. To exaggerate only slightly, Bellow's books are monologues—almost always of surpassing brilliance and great fascination—forced into novelistic form.

I am not suggesting any deliberate deception on Bellow's part. I am saying, rather, that his native talent (like that of certain other contemporary writers, James Baldwin for one and Bellow's childhood pal Isaac Rosenfeld for another) got deflected into the wrong channel by the special prestige of the novel as the supreme form of literary art in our time, comparable to what poetry was to the Victorians. This is why, on the few occasions when Bellow has managed to liberate himself from the compulsion to dress up as novels the fruits of his own endlessly fascinating mind and magnificent literary gift, he has been able to bring characters more vividly to life than any who appear in those novels. What is more, these characters are neither mouthpieces for Bellow nor reflections of him.

To Jerusalem and Back—his memoir of a stay in Israel—was one such occasion, and *Ravelstein* (though not presented as a memoir the way *To Jerusalem and Back* was) is, I believe, another. Cynthia Ozick has a point when she asks: "Why should we care for . . . those ephemeral figures that fictional characters are 'based on'? The originals vanish; their simulacra, powerful marvels, endure." But the Allan Bloom depicted as Ravelstein might better be compared with the portrait of, say, Richard Savage by Samuel Johnson. Savage, an otherwise forgotten 18th-century poet, has endured because he was evoked so vividly and poignantly by Dr. Johnson's memoir; and so, I speculate, will be the happy fate of Bloom-Ravelstein. My only regret is that Bellow did not see fit to drop the pretense that he was writing a novel and simply given us much the same book in the form of a memoir called *Bloom*.

Having had a number of encounters with Allan Bloom, I can testify that Bellow captures him with such marvelous accuracy that Ravelstein might actually be, so to speak, the fully realized fictional creation Cynthia Ozick wishes to see in him. Admittedly, my testimony may be impeached by the fact that I was only acquainted with Bloom casually. Many who were much closer to him have heatedly denied that he is adequately depicted in *Ravelstein,* and some have even accused Bellow of betraying Bloom in his book, and in two different senses.

The first is to have "outed" him as homosexual. The friends of Bloom who denounce this as a betrayal rightly assert that Bloom himself was careful never to make a public point of his homosexuality, and certainly never wanted anything to do with the politicization of his own sexual proclivities as represented by the gay-rights movement. The alleged betrayal here, then, is to have revealed something Bloom wished to keep hidden.

In this perspective, all the worse does the betrayal become when one considers that with his assault on contemporary culture and the degradation of the universities in *The Closing of the American Mind,* Bloom emerged as one of the most influential conservative intellectuals in the world. Never mind that he eschewed the term "conservative" not only for himself but for the entire school of thought deriving from his master and teacher, the philosopher Leo Strauss. Despite his protestations, virtually everyone else (with good reason, I would say) thought of him as a conservative. Consequently, in the context of the "culture war" in which Bloom's book has played so large a part—a war that has featured the contention over homosexuality as one of its central fronts—Bellow stands accused of providing aid and comfort to his supposedly beloved friend's liberal enemies. Again, never mind that Bloom himself never made an issue of homosexuality one way or the other in his many reflections on eros. By outing him, Bellow has—so the charge goes—made the entire conservative side in the culture war look hypocritical.

To this my response is that Allan Bloom's homosexuality was no great secret, and that Bellow neither intends nor does harm to him or to his reputation in talking so easily about it. Writing in the *New Republic* as a gay-rights activist who is at the same time a self-declared conservative, Andrew Sullivan hopes that "One day, there will be a conservatism civilized enough to deserve [Bloom]." But the only way Sullivan the gay-rights activist can stake a claim to Bloom is to interpret the latter's silence on homosexuality as a loud affirmation: "Bloom was gay, and he died of AIDS. The salience of these facts is strengthened, not weakened, by Bloom's public silence about them."[9] Yet silence, whether public or private, was not the always exuberantly garrulous Allan Bloom's notion of how to express an idea or make a point.

The second sense in which Bellow has been accused of betraying Bloom is—according to some of his other friends—to have shown him not as the great soul he is repeatedly called in the book (and that, they maintain, he indeed was in life) but as a vulgar materialist. Having become rich through his best-selling book, he seems to care about nothing but spending his money on expensive clothes, meals, and suites in luxurious hotels. The most passionate expression of this complaint I have come upon has been voiced by one of Bloom's students, Kenneth R. Weinstein, in the *Weekly Standard:*

> Rather than serving up Bloom's thought, Bellow expounds upon the man's colorful habits, including his taste for luxury goods. . . . But without a clear understanding that Bloom's acquisition of Lalique crystal or Lanvin jackets was a lighthearted reflection of his love for beauty itself—the form of beauty, in Plato's sense—he comes off in *Ravelstein* as merely a high-end consumer, an American fop on the Faubourg St. Honoré.

Weinstein's rather solemn explanation of Bloom's taste for luxury could have used a little lightheartedness itself (in truth, Bloom loved luxury for its own sake—and why not?), but otherwise it is fair enough: Bellow does give only a small taste of Bloom's intellectual passions. If *Ravelstein* were really a self-contained novel, this omission would be a serious fault. But not so when we read the book as the memoir of a friendship that takes Bloom's philosophical concerns for granted and (sometimes even explicitly) refers us to his written work for light on him as a thinker instead of attempting to summarize his ideas. (In his "Life of Richard Savage," if I remember rightly, Dr. Johnson does not quote much of Savage's poetry.)

Besides, this criticism of *Ravelstein* for leaving out "Bloom's thought" fails to grasp *Bellow's* conception of what it means to be, or to have, a great soul. Cynthia Ozick quotes a remark from *The Adventures of Augie March* that captures the essence of Bellow's take on the matter: "He had rich blood. His father peddled apples." This remark is one of my own favorites, too, though my gloss on it differs from hers. Extrapolating from it, I would say that for Saul Bellow, the richness of Allan Bloom's blood (and mind) was thickened by his entanglement with what some dismiss as the grosser things of this world. There is also in Bellow's eyes a kind of greatness—as spiritual as it is material—in the extremity of Bloom's extravagance, no less than in his insatiable appetite for gossip, especially about the doings in high places, in his presumptuous meddling with the lives of his students, in his delight in dirty jokes (which he exchanges on his deathbed with one of his close friends), and so on and so on into the lower depths and the higher reaches of life as it is lived from day to day.

Betrayal? If we are to speak of it at all in discussing the two latest works by Saul Bellow and Philip Roth, the word would better be applied to how Roth's *The Human Stain* has reneged on the tantalizing hopes held out by *An American Pastoral* than to how Bellow treats Allan Bloom in *Ravelstein*. That this infinitely loving portrait should be considered a betrayal is to me nothing short of amazing.

Bellow has always been especially good with closing lines. I will cite only two. *Augie March* ends with: "Columbus too thought he was a flop, probably, when they sent him back in chains. Which didn't prove there was no America." And *Mr. Sammler's Planet*, like *Ravelstein*, concludes in a meditation on the death of a friend: "[This man] was aware that he must meet, . . . and he did meet, the terms of his contract. The terms which, in his inmost heart, each man knows. As I know mine. As all know. For that is the truth of it—that we all know, God, that we know, that we know, we know, we know."

Tough acts to follow, but Bellow pulls it off in the last line of *Ravelstein:* "You don't easily give up a creature like Ravelstein to death."

Not easily, and thanks to this memoir decked out in the false finery of a novel, maybe not at all. By which I mean that, good as his books are, if Allan Bloom lives on, it will not be through his own writings—though I would not be surprised if *Ravelstein* were to drive readers to seek them out in the future—but in the delightful and wondrous person of Ravelstein and through the love that enabled Saul Bellow to bring his friend back to life more truly than so many of his more pious disciples and comrades-in-arms want to think.

NOTES

1. Houghton Mifflin, 361 pp., $26.00.

2. Viking, 233 pp., $24.95.

3. The main character in Ralph Ellison's posthumous novel *Juneteenth* is also a black passing as white. Conceivably Roth, a great admirer of Ellison, was more inspired by this literary precedent than he was by the life of Anatole Broyard.

4. I am restricting myself here to literature, and more specifically the novel, but the same rule applies to the other arts as well. It has long been recognized that the novel, implicated as it almost always is in the world around it, is an aesthetically "messier" form than lyric poetry or music or painting, which are more capable of remaining fixed within the boundaries of their own formal qualities. For better or worse, then, it is harder for the novel (and this goes for theatrical works as well) than for the other arts to remain sealed off from political and moral issues. Or at least it used to be in the days before painters and sculptors became even more political than writers.

5. On the other hand, as D. T. Max recounts in a recent article in the *New York Times Magazine,* Bellow later grew less enthusiastic: "If you crossed him, he didn't forget. After Philip Roth caricatured him in his novel *The Ghost Writer* as Felix Abravanel, a nattily dressed superstar writer who lived 'in the egosphere,' Bellow got back at him on the Dick Cavett show in 1981: 'What hath Roth got?' he said."

6. I voiced this hope in an article entitled "The Adventures of Philip Roth," written shortly after the appearance of *I Married a Communist* and published in the October 1998 issue of COMMENTARY.

7. Roth, while fully aware of the irony involved in the fact that Silk, unbeknown to everyone else, is himself black, seems oddly blind to the additional irony that, from another angle, passing for white does convict Silk of racism. I would have thought that Roth—one of whose favorite authors is Franz Kafka—would pursue this fascinating twist. But he never does. Then again, why should he be expected to do so here when he has never been

able to understand that the repudiation of Jewishness by Jews can be taken as a form of anti-Semitism?

8. To forestall the obvious objection, I should note that the characters in *Macbeth* were historical personages. In writing a play about them, however, Shakespeare not only relied on his imagination but (lest he be accused of calling into question the legitimacy of Britain's ruling dynasty) misrepresented Macbeth as a usurper when it was actually the other way around.

9. The question of AIDS brings up a subsidiary aspect of this particular allegation of betrayal on Bellow's part, which is not that he reveals a hidden truth about Bloom but that he spreads a lie. Bloom did not, say his other friends, die of AIDS as Ravelstein does; and Bellow has now admitted that he was not sure about this but merely assumed it.

JEWISH WRITING AND THE SPIRITUAL JOURNEY

A SPECULATIVE ESSAY

Rodger Kamenetz

I RECENTLY TAUGHT a writer's workshop at a Jewish retreat center called Elat Chayyim in upstate New York. I was intrigued with the idea of teaching in a context where people were on retreat, praying each morning, doing yoga and Jewish meditation as well, and singing thanks after every meal. Most of the people who come there feel they are on a spiritual journey and I believe they are—well, partly I believe all of us are, but some of us just haven't realized it yet. People who say I'm not a spiritual person are pretty incomprehensible to me. It's a bit like saying, I don't have a soul, or I was born without a conscience, or, my life is meaningless. There are moments when we feel all of these things, but can we be so wholeheartedly sure that those moments stand for all of our truth? I much doubt it. If we doubt everything, shouldn't we also doubt our doubt, at least once in a while?

Anyway, I wanted to teach this course in writing personal autobiography and decided on the theme of the spiritual journey, in part because I view the book of Genesis—in Hebrew the book of "beginning"—as being about all kinds of individual spiritual journeys. There's Abram receiving the mysterious call "lekh lekhah"—take yourself out—abandon your home and father's house and go where I tell you. Imagine, he actually listened. There's Sarah chuckling and joking with an angel. There's their grandson Jacob wrestling with an angel and perhaps also his conscience; there's Jacob's dream-vision of angels moving down a ladder; there's also Hagar's encounter by the well of living seeing, and her unique name of God that arises from her own experience, "Atah El Roi," or "You God see me." (That's a name worth meditating on.) In fact, each of these heroes and heroines, Jewish or non-Jewish, male or female, seems to go on a journey, and encounter new and fresh names of God, "El Shaddai" the guarding one, and "pachad Yitzhak," the fear of Isaac. This is another way of saying, each of these spiritual ancestors finds through a unique journey a personal and fresh language for encounters with the unaccountable. So as a lover of fresh language, I love these terse stories and read them as the deepest non-fiction—not only did they happen, but as the kabbalists tell us, they are happening in our own lives, if we would but make the felt connection.

But how are they happening and how can we make the connection deeper and stronger? Here the practice of writing non-fiction becomes a spiritual practice as well.

For whatever reason I've always considered myself a Jewish writer, rather than just a writer. My very first book of poetry, *The Missing Jew*, was pretty blunt about that. At least three of my books have the word "Jew" or "Jewish" in the title or subtitle.

It is difficult to say, of course, what a Jewish writer or a Jewish poet is. I know one when I see one, or read one. My friend Steve Stern, the fiction writer, is another one, and he once suggested that one simply plug in a JEW-O-METER—like the old applause-o-meter on the *Queen for a Day* show—and see how Jewish a writer really is. I know if you plugged the electrodes in to Steve, the needle would be buried—while there are other writers, nominally Jewish, who would barely move it a flicker. Identifying writers as Jewish because of birth or religion, though, is something I'd object to—it has very little to do with how I would define Jewish writing, which must be an inner quality to the writing—or nothing at all.

Jewish writing can also be writing about Jews or Judaism—real Jewish writing is both, Jewish inside and out—and it takes place everywhere, not just Manhattan or Brooklyn. But I would like to suggest that there's something particularly Jewish about the genre of non-fiction, especially the personal essay.

I began my life's work as a Jewish poet, a hopeless category. There are large classes of readers who hate the word "poetry" and others will never, on principle, open a book that's "Jewish"—combining the two is an audience eradicator.

I'm not complaining. I'm lucky. I wrote *The Missing Jew* and snagged a rare university teaching job. Perhaps the hiring committee at Louisiana State took "missing Jew" literally and decided to toss me in the bayous of Baton Rouge like Brer Rabbit in the briar patch.

As a Jewish writer, I benefited immensely from the geographical isolation, living in a town where the Jewish population, at approximately one in a thousand, reflected precisely the proportion on the planet. I could never take being a Jew for granted. I think I understood better why Bernard Malamud, for instance, spent so much of his writing career teaching in a small town in Oregon. Writing about Jews and Jewish texts and Judaism in a place where you are a rare bird can be a great help. I could never write about Jews living in Brooklyn or Manhattan: too much input from the surrounding environment would crowd out my quiet inner voices. The Russian revolutionary poet Mayakovsky talks about this: if you want to write a sonnet about pineapples in the tropics, there's no use living in Hawaii—far better to be in Siberia with the ink freezing in your pen— then you will have true desire for your subject. In the same way, in a town where corned beef was a rare commodity, I spent my first three years in Baton Rouge reconstructing the Jewish Baltimore of my childhood, and even more immense, my Jewish mother—an inner reality undisturbed by even a vibration from the outer world of crawfish, Mardi Gras, and zydeco.

I was also in those years learning how to write prose non-fiction, the un-cola of literary categories, as Buddhism is the un-cola of religions. Just as Buddhists are non-theists and speak about reality as an open space— so non-fiction, beautifully ill defined, encompasses a vast landscape of possibilities, and subsumes within it exquisite descriptive writing, poetic riffs, story telling, and idea mongering. I also happen to think non-fiction is a quintessentially Jewish form of writing. First because the personal essay, or *essai,* was in fact invented by the 16th century author Michel de Montaigne, who was Jewish on his mother's side. Is it any wonder that this master created an entirely new form of writing, intensely personal and rooted in the facts of his life, while capable of the fullest range of meaning and association?

But there's another reason non-fiction is Jewish. It's because we are the people of the book—and our book, the Torah, considered as literary genre, happens to be a work of non-fiction.

Sure, some poets might want to claim the Torah for poetry, citing the Psalms and the Book of Job. Some fiction writers would argue it's pure narrative. But I have on my side not only all non-fiction writers, but the ranks of the faithful, who have always read the Torah as though it were fact and truth.

I moved from poetry to non-fiction out of necessity when I wrote a personal account of my mother's death, and her life, and mine within hers. I felt profoundly that my writing existed to bear witness. In my case, bearing witness required an allegiance to the facts and poetry.

I was inspired in this task by a great Jewish writer, Primo Levi, especially his autobiography, *The Periodic Table.* Levi was a chemist and might never have become a writer were it not that he'd endured the immense suffering we call Auschwitz. Ever after, he was sworn by his life to be a certain kind of writer—in his case, a witness. So he brought to his non-fiction writing the precision of the trained scientist and the eye and ear of a poet; the strange blend of faculties created an unforgettably powerful writing, immensely moving and deeply restrained—and above all, true.

Primo Levi lived through the worst of the Holocaust; he witnessed its effects on himself and others. Because the truth he bore witness to was so immensely important not just personally but for all the world, he took the task of writing very seriously. The precision of his writing was a kind of guarantee, a seal of truth. So one finds in his work a tremendous humility. I don't mean necessarily that he was personally humble, but rather that he knew that his writing was more important than he was. Writers often forget that.

One of my questions for the writing students at Elat Chayyim was, Who writes? I meant it very much as a meditation. Who writes? Does "I" write? The grammar of the act can be misleading. I write poetry. I write non-fiction. The grammar suggests that some well defined being, an "I" usually identified with the ego, performed an act with complete conscious control. The truth is much more complex and immensely more interesting. True, I write, but only if the writing lets me. It's much more of a collaborative relationship with language and also with soul. (For the so-called non-spiritual person, I'd define soul as all the experiences of life I carry with me in deep memory.) Because listening to language and listening to the soul are so vital, I've come to think that at one level writing is, basically, listening.

Writing is also a kind of wrestling. One translation of Israel, the new name granted to Jacob after his encounter with an angel, is "one who wrestles with El," one who struggles with God. It's said in midrash that the angel had the face of Jacob's enemy brother, Esau, so the wrestle was in part with the darker forces of the self. Robert Duncan, an American visionary poet deeply influenced by his reading of the Zohar, added another twist: he imagined the poet as Jacob wrestling with the angel syntax.

Anyone who has struggled with an unruly sentence, the stubborn resistance of words that refuse to obey, will find Duncan's image powerful. So the wrestling with language is one kind of spiritual encounter that every writer faces word by word, sentence by sentence.

But there's also a level of soul wrestling involved. There's the effort to be true to experience, to bear true witness and not false witness to one's vision and shame one's soul.

This is particularly true in writing non-fiction, where there is a constant struggle between the truth as one remembers it and the truth as it actually was. Friedrich Nietzsche put the struggle nicely: Pride and Memory had an argument. Memory said, It was this way. Pride said, It couldn't be. And Pride won.

Throwing the match to pride is a kind of fake wrestling move that might win temporary applause from an audience that does not want to be disturbed by the truth, but in the long term faking cheapens the game. It's an issue that's particularly important when I am a witness not only to my own life story, as in simple autobiography, but also to experiences that belong to history. A very important example is the Holocaust, a difficult truth the Jewish people are trying to record and remember, at the same moment others are actively seeking to deny and erase. In such a context, in the past year we've all been troubled by the story of author Binjamin Wilkomirski, who wrote an extraordinary work of fiction, *Fragments,* recounting his shattering experiences as a young child in Auschwitz. Unfortunately, the book was published as a memoir. The exposure of Wilkomirski's deceptions and self-deceptions led to a scandal. Rightly so, because we readers ask of non-fiction that it tell the truth—or at the least that it express the author's struggle to tell the truth.

Wilkomirski may well have deluded himself before he deluded others. His story may be an extreme version of the eternal wrestling between Pride and Memory, with a pathological twist. But every writer who tries to bear witness to the truth—which I think at core is what non-fiction is about—must enter the ring and wrestle with language and with soul.

That is why I asked my students "who writes?" I wonder if there's a paradox between the necessary egotism of the writer and the ability to be open to a true spiritual encounter. When I read the story of *lekh lekhah,* I wonder what the openness was to inner voices that allowed Avram to respond and act. If he had been ego bound, he might have dismissed those voices as utter nonsense. A person whose mind is always made up, who "knows what he thinks," could never be open to transformation. Nor could such a person be much of a writer.

Likewise, when I read the story of Hagar's vision at the well, I see that a person who is rejected, humiliated, utterly humbled may be granted a vision denied to a person who is secure in her ego. In short: if having an ego gets in the way of true spiritual encounter, and yet having an ego is necessary to be a writer, as it seems to be in our marketplace society, can one be both a writer and open to spiritual experience at the same time?

Being a writer is a tough racket. Out of the thousands of people who write, very few make a living from it alone. Most people feel that writers must have immense egos to survive and I think that's true. It may be more so for the Jewish writer. Whatever we might say about Moses as humble, very few Jewish leaders or role models have adopted his style. Jews admire a person with chutzpah, even though chutzpah at an extreme is hardly a spiritual value. The poet who is personally humble is likely to be trampled by lesser talents who have the enormous yearning just to be known. I have dealt with poets all my life and Charles Reznikoff stands out in my mind as one of the few genuinely humble personalities. He was the most important Jewish American poet of the twentieth century and if his name seems entirely unfamiliar, that only illustrates my point: Mr. Reznikoff did not have the personality to push his work on the public. And his work itself, profoundly quiet, modest and observant in the best sense, was not likely to call attention to itself either.

One summer I studied in Jerusalem with a teacher named Colette Albouker-Muscat. I always called her Madame. Her students visited her in the cool of Jerusalem mornings, and she taught us how to dream while we were awake, and how to heal ourselves and others through our dreams. We spoke in French, which she enjoyed, because she was born in Algeria and descended from a noble Jewish family. She claimed lineage to the royal advisors of Charlemagne, those Jews who were made nobility at the beginning of Europe's history—and even more royally, from a family, like King Solomon, descended from King David himself.

Madame had a student who wished to write a memoir. One morning, in her Jerusalem apartment, she told this student she had to choose between the spiritual life or the life of a writer because a writer at bottom needs to have a sturdy ego and that is precisely what the person on a spiritual path would have to do without.

The student cried. Madame pulled out her handkerchief clinically and handed it over—she was quite used to producing such effects on her students, which she called *donnant les petits chocs*, giving little shocks.

The question struggles within me though I'm hardly far along enough to think I have no ego, the question struggles, at least abstractly and sometimes more concretely in my life. Was Madame correct?

One thinks immediately of the greatest spiritual teachers of all time—Socrates, the Buddha, Jesus—they never wrote a word. Or in the Jewish scheme of things, of the great ARI, Rabbi Isaac Luria, that master of the abstruse and complex, beautiful kabbalah of Safed, who raised up many students, but who himself could not write, complaining that the moment he set pen to page, so many ideas rushed to the tip at once he could scarcely write a sentence for all the confusion.

He said, "I can hardly open my mouth to speak without feeling as though the sea had burst its dams and overflowed. How then shall I express what my soul has received, and how can I put it down in a book?"

So yes, it can be that there are certain great oral masters like the Baal Shem Tov, who are always inspired in the moment of encounter, inspired by immediate contact with a student's need for wisdom. Such masters could no more write down in advance what they have to teach than they could later recollect that wisdom in tranquility. And this may be the deepest purest wisdom—the wisdom that cannot be written down but can only be told, face to face.

THE ONE HUNDRED BEST
CONTEMPORARY JEWISH BOOKS

Michael Lerner

WHY ONLY A HUNDRED? There could easily be a thousand!

I asked dozens of Jewish writers, thinkers, rabbis, academics, and community leaders to make recommendations and a smaller group of them to help me narrow down the list. By the end of the process I still had two hundred books that deserved to be noted and room to list only half of them.

I decided to limit my list to books that are available in English and have been written since 1985. That helped winnow the list somewhat, but it pained me to not be able to cite some books that have had tremendous influence in the current period but were published before 1985. I am thinking particularly of the work of my teacher Abraham Joshua Heschel, Emmanuel Levinas, and Martin Buber; the poetry of Don Pagis and Denise Levertov; the best fiction of Cynthia Ozick, Tillie Olsen, Chaim Grade, Chaim Potok, and Bernard Malamud; the writing of Irving Howe; the early and probably more significant works of Elie Wiesel; and the influential works that appeared in the "Jewish Catalogue"(s) or in the writing of the most important Jewish feminists, collected by Susannah Heschel in 1983.

In saying "best" books, I actually mean "most significant" books. By significant, I mean books that have a profound message or are written in ways that are overwhelmingly beautiful and compelling or have had a profound impact on public Jewish discourse or have influenced the most creative people in their take on reality or are likely to have that impact.

Some people suggested that I list my own *Jewish Renewal: A Path to Healing and Transformation* (HarperCollins, 1995) or my dialogue with Cornel West, *Blacks and Jews: Let the Healing Begin* (Putnam, 1995). I appreciated their enthusiasm, but I demurred. In fact, if anything I've sinned against anyone close to me by bending over backward to avoid playing favorites. I've listened to others, and included books that I don't like (and some that I really can't stand) but have played an important role in contemporary Jewish discourse.

What's the point of this kind of list? Well, its primary value is as a way to cut through hundreds of hours of research and focus on the books that are central to contemporary Jewish literacy. I can safely say that if you read the books listed here, you'll be amply prepared to participate in contemporary discussions in the Jewish world. But I do apologize to the many, many authors whose works are equally deserving to be on this list.

1. Rachel Adler, *Engendering Judaism*
2. S. Y. Agnon, *Only Yesterday*
3. Rebecca Alpert, *Like Bread on the Seder Plate*
4. Robert Alter, *Canon and Creativity*
5. Yehuda Amichai, *Open Closed Open*
6. Judith S. Antonelli, *In The Image of God*
7. Aharon Appelfeld, *The Conversion*
8. Yehuda Bauer, *Rethinking the Holocaust*
9. Saul Bellow, *Ravelstein*
10. Meron Benvenisti, *Sacred Landscape: The Buried History of the Holy Land Since 1948*
11. Ellen Bernstein, *Ecology and the Jewish Spirit*
12. David Biale, *Power and Powerlessness in Jewish History*
13. Harold Bloom, *The Book of J*
14. Daniel Boyarin, *Carnal Israel*
15. Melvin Jules Bukiet, *Stories of an Imagined Childhood*
16. Jules Chametzky and others (eds.), *The Norton Anthology of Jewish American Literature*
17. Steven M. Cohen and Arnold M. Eisen, *The Jew Within: Self, Family, and Community in America*
18. David Cooper, *God Is a Verb*
19. Anita Diamant, *The Red Tent*
20. Elliot N. Dorff and Louis E. Newman (eds.), *Contemporary Jewish Ethics and Morality*

21. Evan Eisenberg, *The Ecology of Eden*
22. Yaffa Eliach, *There Once Was a World*
23. Sidra DeKoven Ezrahi, *Booking Passage*
24. Marcia Falk, *The Book of Blessings*
25. Michael Fishbane, *The Exegetical Imagination*
26. Eva Fogelman, *Conscience and Courage: Rescuers of Jews During the Holocaust*
27. Ellen Frankel, *The Five Books of Miriam*
28. Saul Friedlander, *Nazi Germany and the Jews*
29. Tikva Frymer-Kensky, *In the Wake of the Goddesses*
30. Neil Gilman, *Sacred Fragments: Recovering Theology for the Modern Jew*
31. Sander L. Gilman, *Jewish Self-Hatred*
32. Allan Ginsberg, *Selected Poems, 1947–1995*
33. Daniel Jonah Goldhagen, *Hitler's Willing Executioners*
34. Elyse Goldstein (ed.), *The Women's Torah Commentary*
35. Rebecca Goldstein, *Mazel: A Novel*
36. Allegra Goodman, *Paradise Park*
37. Roger S. Gottlieb, *A Spirituality of Resistance*
38. Arthur Green, *Seek My Face, Speak My Name*
39. Irving Greenberg, *The Jewish Way: Living the Holidays*
40. David Grossman, *See Under Love*
41. Moshe Halbertal, *The People of the Book*
42. David Hartman, *Israelis and the Jewish Tradition*
43. Geoffrey Hartman, *The Longest Shadow*
44. Judith Hauptman, *Rereading the Rabbis*
45. Susannah Heschel (ed.), *Moral Grandeur and Spiritual Audacity: Writings of Abraham Joshua Heschel*
46. Lawrence Hoffman, *My People's Prayer Book: Traditional Prayers, Modern Commentaries*
47. Paula Hyman and Deborah Dash Moore, *Women in America*
48. Rodger Kamenetz, *Jew in the Lotus*
49. Aryeh Kaplan, *Innerspace*
50. Judith A. Kates and Gail Twersky Reimer (eds.), *Reading Ruth*

51. Alfred Kazin, *God and the American Writers*

52. Irena Klepfisz and Melanie Kaye-Kantrowitz (eds.), *The Tribe of Dina: A Jewish Women's Anthology*

53. David Kraemer, *Reading the Rabbis*

54. Chana Kronfeld, *On the Margins of Modernism*

55. Lawrence Kushner, *God Was in This Place and I, i Did Not Know*

56. Tony Kushner, *Angels in America*

57. Lawrence Langer, *Art from the Ashes*

58. Emmanuel Levinas, *Nine Talmudic Readings*

59. Deborah E. Lipstadt, *Denying the Holocaust*

60. Bernard Malamud, *The Complete Stories of Bernard Malamud*

61. Daniel Matt, *The Essential Kabbalah*

62. Diane Matza (ed.), *Sephardic American Voices*

63. Benny Morris, *Righteous Victims*

64. Jacob Neusner, *Recovering Judaism*

65. Peter Novick, *The Holocaust in American Life*

66. Carol Ochs, *Our Lives as Torah*

67. Debra Orenstein, *Lifecycles: Jewish Women on Life Passages and Personal Milestones*

68. Amos Oz, *In the Land of Israel*

69. Grace Paley, *Collected Stories*

70. Marge Piercy, *The Art of Blessing the Day*

71. Peter Pitzele, *Our Fathers' Well*

72. Judith Plaskow, *Standing Again at Sinai*

73. Letty Cottin Pogrebin, *Deborah, Golda, and Me*

74. Marcia Prager, *The Path of Blessing*

75. Riv-Ellen Prell, *Fighting to Become Americans*

76. Adrienne Rich, *Selected Poems, 1950–1995*

77. Thane Rosenbaum, *Elijah Visible*

78. Philip Roth, *The Counterlife*

79. Steven J. Rubin (ed.), *A Century of American Jewish Poetry*

80. Zalman M. Schachter-Shalomi, *Paradigm Shift*

81. Nosson Scherman (ed.), *The Stone Edition of the Chumash*

82. Howard Schwartz (ed.), *Gabriel's Palace: Stories from the Jewish Mystical Tradition*

83. Tom Segev, *The Seventh Million*

84. Rami M. Shapiro, *Minyan*

85. Laurence J. Silberstein and Robert L. Cohn (eds.), *The Other in Jewish Thought and History*

86. Isaac Bashevis Singer, *Shadows on the Hudson*

87. Art Spiegelman, *MAUS: A Survivor's Tale*

88. Ilan Stavans (ed.), *The Oxford Book of Jewish Stories*

89. Adin Steinsaltz (ed.), *The Steinsaltz Edition of the Talmud*

90. Aryeh Lev Stollman, *The Far Euphrates*

91. Joseph Telushkin, *The Book of Jewish Values*

92. Ellen M. Umansky and Dianne Ashton, *Four Centuries of Jewish Women's Spirituality*

93. Michael Walzer and others (eds.), *The Jewish Political Tradition*

94. Arthur Waskow, *Down-to-Earth Judaism*

95. Susan Weidman Schneider, *Jewish and Female: Choices and Changes in Our Lives Today*

96. Elie Wiesel, *Memoirs*

97. Leon Wieseltier, *Kaddish*

98. A. B. Yehoshua, *Mister Mani*

99. Richard Zimler, *The Last Kabbalist of Lisbon*

100. Avivah Gottlieb Zornburg, *Genesis: The Beginning of Desire*

THE EDITOR

Michael Lerner is editor of *Tikkun: A Bimonthly Jewish Critique of Politics, Culture and Society,* rabbi of Beyt Tikkun synagogue in San Francisco, holder of two separate Ph.D.'s in philosophy and clinical psychology, and described by *Utne Reader* as "one of America's 100 most outstanding visionaries." *Conservative Judaism* magazine described his book *Jewish Renewal: A Path to Healing and Transformation* as "stunning, miraculous and faith-renewing . . . sensitive, complex and deeply insightful." His book co-authored with Harvard University professor Cornel West, *Blacks and Jews: Let the Healing Begin,* helped precipitate Black-Jewish dialogues. And his most recent book, *Spirit Matters: Global Healing and the Wisdom of the Soul,* won a PEN Award and was selected as one of "the most significant books of 2000" by the *Los Angeles Times.*

Jim Wallis, editor of *Sojourners* magazine, has written that "Michael Lerner is one of America's most important spiritual teachers, a contemporary prophet whose insightful and visionary thinking has already had a profound impact on American culture and thought," and Rabbi Michael Paley, director of Outreach for the New York UJA/Federation wrote that "Michael Lerner is America's preeminent liberal Jewish intellectual."

THE CONTRIBUTORS

RACHEL ADLER, one of the mothers of Jewish feminist theology, teaches at the University of Southern California and Hebrew Union College and is author of *Engendering Judaism: An Inclusive Theology and Ethics.*

YEHUDA AMICHAI was one of Israel's most respected poets. His poetry has been translated into more than twenty-eight languages. Amichai also published a novel, short stories, and a number of plays, and was awarded the prestigious Israel Prize.

AHARON APPELFELD, after escaping a Nazi concentration camp, moved to Israel and authored twelve novels including *Badenheim 1939, The Iron Tracks, Unto the Soul, The Retreat,* and *The Age of Wonders.*

ZYGMUNT BAUMAN is emeritus professor of sociology at the University of Leeds and the University of Warsaw and the author of *Modernity and the Holocaust, Postmodernity and Its Discontents, The Individualized Society, Liquid Modernity,* and *Globalization: The Human Consequences.*

DAVID BIALE holds the Emanuel Ringelblum Chair of Jewish History at the University of California, Davis, and is the author of *Gershom Scholem: Kabbalah and Counter-History, Eros and the Jews,* and *Power and Powerlessness in Jewish History.*

TSVI BLANCHARD is an Orthodox rabbi and teaches at CLAL, the Center for Leadership and Learning.

DANIEL BOYARIN is Taubman professor of talmudic culture at the University of California, Berkeley, and author of several books, including *Carnal Israel: Reading Sex in Talmudic Culture,* and *A Radical Jew: Paul and the Politics of Identity.*

ANITA DIAMANT is a prize-winning journalist whose work has appeared in the *Boston Globe Magazine* and *Parenting* magazine. She is the author of several books about contemporary Jewish practice, including *The New Jewish Wedding* and *Choosing a Jewish Life: A Guidebook for People Converting to Judaism.*

MORRIS DICKSTEIN teaches English at the City University of New York Graduate Center. He is a senior fellow of the Center for the Humanities, which he founded in 1993. His books include *Gates of Eden, Double Agent,* and a new study of postwar American fiction, *Leopards in the Temple.*

NATHAN ENGLANDER was raised in New York and now lives in Jerusalem. He graduated from the Iowa Writers' Workshop and recently received the Pushcart Prize. His stories have appeared in *Story* magazine and *The New Yorker,* and he is the author of *For the Relief of Unbearable Urges.*

NOMI EVE lives in Cambridge, Massachusetts. *The Family Orchard* is her first novel.

SIDRA DEKOVEN EZRAHI is senior lecturer at the Hebrew University of Jerusalem and author of *By Words Alone: The Holocaust in Literature* and *Booking Passage: Exile and Homecoming in the Modern Jewish Imagination.*

NANCY FLAM is a rabbi and creator of the first Jewish Healing Center in the United States.

PETER GABEL is president and professor of law at New College of California and associate editor of *Tikkun.* He was a founder of the Critical Legal Studies movement and is the author of *The Bank Teller and Other Essays on the Politics of Meaning.*

MORDECAI GAFNI is an Orthodox rabbi in Jerusalem and author of *Soul Prints: Your Path to Fulfillment.*

REBECCA GOLDSTEIN is the author of *The Mind-Body Problem* and *Properties of Light: A Novel of Love, Betrayal, and Quantum Physics.*

ARTHUR GREEN is Philip W. Lown Professor of Jewish Thought at Brandeis University and a fellow of the Institute of Advanced Studies at the Hebrew University. His latest book, *These Are the Words: A Vocabulary of Jewish Spiritual Life,* is being published by Jewish Lights Books.

STEVE GREENBERG is an Orthodox Rabbi who teaches at CLAL, the Center for Leadership and Learning.

MARTIN JAY, chair of the department of history at University of California, Berkeley, is author of *Cultural Semantics: Keywords of Our Time.*

RODGER KAMENETZ is the author of *The Jew in the Lotus, The Missing Jew,* and *Stalking Elijah,* which won the National Jewish Book Award for Jewish Thought. His latest publication is *Terra Infirma: A Memoir of My Mother's Life in Mine.*

IRENA KLEPFISZ is the author of "A Few Words in the Mother Tongue" (poetry) and "Dreams of an Insomniac" (essays). She teaches Jewish Women's Studies at Barnard College.

KENNETH KOCH teaches poetry at Columbia University.

JOSEPH I. LIEBERMAN, United States Senator from Connecticut, was the Democratic candidate in 2000 for the office of Vice President of the United States.

JONATHAN MARK is associate editor of the *Jewish Week* in New York. He was twice named writer of the year by the New York State Press Association.

BENNY MORRIS is the most prominent of Israel's "New Historians" and teaches at Ben Gurion University in Beer Sheva. He is the author of *Righteous Victims: A History of the Zionist-Arab Conflict, 1881–1999.*

JACQUELINE OSHEROW is the author of four books of poetry, most recently, *Dead Men's Praise* (Grove, 1999); she's been awarded fellowships by the Guggenheim Foundation, the National Endowment for the Arts, the Ingrain Merrily Foundation, and the Wittier Bynner Prize from the American Academy and Institute of Arts and Letters.

ILANA PARDES is associate professor of comparative literature at Hebrew University and author of *The Countertraditions in the Bible: A Feminist Approach* and *The Biography of Ancient Israel*.

MARGE PIERCY is the author of *To Be of Use; Stone, Paper, Knife; The Art of Blessing the Day; Gone to Soldiers; Vida, Going Down Fast; Dance the Eagle to Sleep; Small Changes; Woman on the Edge of Time*; and many more.

ROBERT PINSKY served as poet laureate of the United States from 1997 to 2000. He teaches in the graduate creative writing program at Boston University and is poetry editor of the weekly Internet magazine *Slate*.

DANIEL PIPES is director of the Middle East Forum, editor of the *Middle East Quarterly,* and a columnist for *The Jerusalem Post*. His website, containing many of his writings, is www.DanielPipes.org.

NORMAN PODHORETZ is America's most prominent neo-conservative Jewish intellectual and former editor of *Commentary* magazine.

SARAH POLSTER was the founder and publishing director of the Jossey-Bass Religion-in-Practice series, and the prime mover and house editor for this book. She died on July 4, 2001, as this book was nearing publication. She has left her family, colleagues, and friends a lasting legacy of intelligence, clear vision, compassion, and inspirational leadership in her work and in her life.

DENNIS PRAGER is a nationally syndicated radio talk show host based on KRLA Radio in Los Angeles. He has written four books, two of which are on Judaism. He lectures around the world, and hundreds of his lectures are available on tape—including his commentary on thus-far three books of the Torah verse by verse. For information, his website is www.dennisprager.com.

DAHLIA RAVIKOVITCH is one of Israel's most prominent poets and has received many literary prizes. She studied at Hebrew University in Jerusalem and has worked as a teacher and journalist. In addition to her poetry, she has written fiction and books for children.

RACHEL NAOMI REMEN, M.D., is cofounder and medical director of the Commonweal Cancer Help Program in Bolinas, California; a founding fellow of the Fetzer Institute; professor of family and community medicine at the University of California at San Francisco Medical School; and author of *Kitchen Table Wisdom* and *My Grandfather's Blessings.*

ADRIENNE RICH'S most recent books of poetry are *Dark Fields of the Republic (Poems 1991–1995)* and *Midnight Salvage (Poems 1995–1998).* A new selection of her essays, *Arts of the Possible: Essays and Conversations,* and a new volume of poems *Fox (Poems 1998–2000)* will be published in 2001. She has recently been the recipient of the Dorothea Tanning Prize and of the Lannan Foundation Lifetime Achievement Award. She lives in California.

JONATHAN ROSEN created the Arts & Letters section of the *Forward,* which he edited for ten years. He is the author of the novel *Eve's Apple* and of *The Talmud and the Internet: A Journey Between Worlds.*

THANE ROSENBAUM is literary editor of *Tikkun* and author of *Elijah Visible* and *Second Hand Smoke.*

PHILIP ROTH won the National Book Critics Circle Award for *The Counterlife;* the National Book Award for *Goodbye, Columbus;* the National Book Critics Circle Award for *Patrimony*; and has published many other acclaimed novels including *Portnoy's Complaint.*

WILLIAM SAFIRE received a Pulitzer Prize for his twice-weekly political column in the *New York Times.* He has written twenty-four books, including *Safire's New Political Dictionary, Lend Me Your Ears,* and *Freedom,* a bestselling historical novel about Lincoln and the Emancipation Proclamation.

SUSAN SCHNUR is a rabbi, Editor-at-Large of *Lilith* magazine, and has written a weekly column for the *New York Times.*

JONATHAN SCHORSCH is Jewish book editor for *Tikkun* magazine and has coathored books and articles on socially responsible investing and Judaism and ecology.

RUTH KNAFO SETTON is the author of *The Road to Fez.* In January 2001, she joined the faculty of the Berman Center for Jewish Studies as writer-in-residence. She was born in Safi, Morocco.

ZALMAN M. SCHACHTER-SHALOMI received ordination from Chabad Hasidim (the Lubavitcher movement) and is the spiritual founder and guide of the Jewish Renewal movement. He is professor of religious studies at Naropa University; professor emeritus, Temple University; founder of ALEPH, Alliance for Jewish Renewal; and Yesod. His writings include *Paradigm Shift* and *From Age-ing to Sage-ing*

ALAN SHAPIRO received the 2001 Kingsley Tufts Award for his collection, *The Dead, Alive and Busy.* His new book, *Song and Dance,* will be published by Houghton Mifflin in February 2002.

RAMI SHAPIRO is a rabbi, director of the Sh'ma Center for Jewish Meditation in Miami, Florida, and author of *Minyan, Wisdom of the Jewish Sages: A Modern Reading of Pirke Avot* and *The Way of Solomon.*

JEROME SLATER is a university research professor at SUNY Buffalo.

JOSEPH TELUSHKIN is a rabbi and author of *Jewish Literacy* and *The Book of Jewish Values.*

YONA WALLACH is one of the great poets of Israel where she is revered as a mystical and provocative figure. Her poems have appeared in the *American Poetry Review,* the *Harvard Review,* and *Tikkun* and are collected in *Wild Light,* translated by Linda Zisquit.

ARTHUR WASKOW, one of the founders of the Jewish Renewal movement, is director of the Shalom Center and author of *Godwrestling, Down-to-Earth Judaism,* and *Seasons of Our Joy.*

C. K. WILLIAMS won the Pulitzer Prize for *Repair: Poems* in 2000. His other books include *The Vigil, The Cup,* and his memoir, *Misgivings: My Mother, My Father, Myself.*

NAOMI WOLF is author of *The Beauty Myth* and *Promiscuities.*

DAVID WOLPE is the rabbi of Sinai Temple in Los Angeles. He is an author, most recently of the best-seller *Making Loss Matter: Creating Meaning in Difficult Times.*

431

Reclaiming the Spirit in Judaism

ZALMAN M. SCHACHTER-SHALOMI "Toward an Emerging Credo" by Rabbi Zalman M. Schachter-Shalomi. Used by permission of Rabbi Zalman M. Schachter-Shalomi.

DAVID WOLPE "Eternity Utters a Day," David Wolpe's article on Shabbat, is reprinted from *Olam* magazine, Winter 2000/5761, with the permission of the author.

ARTHUR GREEN "A Kabbalah for the Environmental Age" by Arthur Green. Reprinted from *Tikkun: A Bimonthly Jewish Critique of Politics, Culture and Society*, Vol. 14, No. 5. Used by permission.

DENNIS PRAGER "Is God in Trees?" was written for this volume and appears with the author's permission.

ARTHUR WASKOW "The Emergence of Eco-Judaism," by Arthur Waskow. Previous version: *CCAR Journal*, Winter 2001. Copyright © 2000 by Arthur Waskow. Reprinted by permission.

NANCY FLAM "A Theology of Illness and Healing" from "Reflections Toward a Theology of Illness and Healing" by Rabbi Nancy Flam. Reprinted from *Sh'ma: A Journal of Jewish Responsibility*, May 27, 1994. Used by permission of Rabbi Nancy Flam.

RAMI SHAPIRO "Death and What's Next" by Rabbi Rami Shapiro. Reprinted from *Tikkun: A Bimonthly Jewish Critique of Politics, Culture and Society*, Vol. 13, No. 4. Used by permission.

MORDECHAI GAFNI "Eros and the Ninth of Av" by Mordechai Gafni. Reprinted from *Tikkun: A Bimonthly Jewish Critique of Politics, Culture and Society*, Vol. 14, No. 4. P. 9. Used by permission.

JOSEPH TELUSHKIN From *The Book of Jewish Values* by Rabbi Joseph Telushkin. Copyright © 2000 by Rabbi Joseph Telushkin. Used by permission of Bell Tower, a division of Random House, Inc.

JACQUELINE OSHEROW "Yom Kippur Sonnet" and "Science Psalm" from *Dead Man's Praise* by Jackie Osherow. Copyright © 1999 by Jackie Osherow. Used by permission of Grove Atlantic, Inc.

Rereading Sacred Texts of Our Tradition

RACHEL ADLER From "And Peace and Justice Shall Kiss" in *Engendering Judaism: An Inclusive Theology and Ethics* by Rachel Adler. Copyright © 1998 by Rachel Adler. Used by permission of The Jewish Publication Society.

Living in the Shadows of the Holocaust